The Prohibition of Collective Expulsion

International Refugee Law Series

VOLUME 24

The titles published in this series are listed at *brill.com/irls*

The Prohibition of Collective Expulsion

Protecting against Arbitrary Expulsion in Human Rights Treaty Law

By

Lena Riemer

BRILL | NIJHOFF

LEIDEN | BOSTON

Library of Congress Cataloging-in-Publication Data

Names: Riemer, Lena, author.
Title: The prohibition of collective expulsion : protecting against arbitrary expulsion in human rights treaty law / by Lena Riemer.
Description: Leiden ; Boston : Brill Academic Publishers, Inc., 2025. | Series: Irls, 22133836 ; 24 | Includes bibliographical references and index.
Identifiers: LCCN 2025024553 | ISBN 9789004535060 (hardback) | ISBN 9789004535077 (pdf)
Subjects: LCSH: Deportation. | Emigration and immigration law. | Human rights. | International law and human rights. | Treaties.
Classification: LCC K3277 .R54 2025 | DDC 342.08/2--DC23/ENG/20250523
LC record available at https://lccn.loc.gov/2025024553

Typeface for the Latin, Greek, and Cyrillic scripts: "Brill". See and download: brill.com/brill-typeface.

ISSN 2213-3836
ISBN 978-90-04-53506-0 (hardback)
ISBN 978-90-04-53507-7 (e-book)
DOI 10.1163/9789004535077

This book is printed on acid-free paper and produced in a sustainable manner.

For Selda and Edgar
In the hope that they grow up in a more just and equitable world

Contents

Preface

I enjoy reading the preface of monographs because they offer a unique window into the author's writing process, challenges, perspectives, and values. They reveal what truly matters to the author, both in their scholarship and beyond. In this sense, my preface is no exception.

First, I want to share a word about the perspective this book takes. While I am an academic working on migration law and policy, my understanding of the subject has been deeply shaped by over a decade of volunteering and advocating for asylum seekers and migrants. In this area I have worked in Berlin, Cape Town, a detention camp in Texas, and at the US-Mexico border in Tijuana. These experiences, coupled with my core values and convictions, profoundly influence how I view migration and asylum law and practice.

Law and policies are human-made, and in migration contexts, their impact can be devastating for those seeking protection. I have witnessed this far too often. This is why I feel so strongly about defending core guarantees, such as the prohibition of collective expulsion, as hopefully becomes clear in this book.

This book is dedicated to all those who, due to circumstances beyond their control, have been forced to flee. I often reflect on the individuals I met in migration detention or at the border, many of whom were consumed by fear for their lives and those of their families. I think about the many families I met in oftentimes horrific situations, but who, so many times impressed and inspired me, and I hope fervently that all of them have found safety. It is a matter of historical chance whether we live in safety, and we often fail to recognize how fragile that safety truly is.

I also want to use this preface to express my gratitude to those who supported me in writing my doctoral thesis, upon which this book is based. Without their encouragement and assistance, this book would not exist, and my life would be immeasurably less joyful.

First and foremost, I must express my deepest gratitude to my *Doktorvater*, Helmut Aust. I intentionally use the German term *Doktorvater* rather than supervisor because it far better captures the profound role he has played in my academic journey. Without his encouragement and belief in me, I would never have dared to envision myself writing a Ph.D., let alone pursuing an academic career. His unwavering support was the catalyst for what has now become my professional path.

Helmut Aust not only inspired me to undertake this journey but also suggested the very topic of my doctoral research. As a mentor and role model, both academically and personally, he has set a standard that I aspire to emulate. His generosity, wisdom, and kindness have shaped me profoundly, and I hope to offer my future students the same guidance and encouragement he extended to me. I am deeply and forever grateful for his ongoing feedback, support, and mentorship, which extended far beyond the completion of my thesis.

Next, I want to express my heartfelt gratitude to my family for their unwavering love and support. I am especially thankful to the women who raised me and continue to be my pillars of strength, even when I am once again thousands of miles away. My mother Angelika Riemer, my grandmother Sieglinde Ruhland, my godmother Sandra Gehring, and my sister Rike Hitzinger have been constants in my life, offering encouragement and grounding me in their care and wisdom. I am also deeply grateful to my father Günter Riemer and his wife Stefanie Riemer, to my brothers Lukas Lehmann, Leo Riemer, Tom Riemer, and Mats Riemer, as well as to my brother-in-law Benjamin Hitzinger. Each of them, individually and collectively, has profoundly shaped who I am and the beliefs I hold dear. Their influence has been invaluable, and I carry their love and support with me in all that I do.

Equally important, I want to express my gratitude to my closest friends, many of whom have accompanied me for decades. Thank you to Pia Jürgens de Saucedo, Anna Rudolph and Julius Rudolph, Enis Arkat, Sabrina Klein and Roland Klein, Natalie Reglinski, Camille Van Peteghem, Taís Penteado, and Anna Vesaluoma. My life would be unimaginably dull without them. With their companionship, I have traveled the world, enjoyed nature, laughed and cried and spent countless hours sharing meaningful conversations over coffee and cake. Their unwavering support and friendship mean the world to me. In this context, I want to highlight my gratitude to Sebastian Thess. Without his support and encouragement, I would never have completed my Ph.D. He believed in me more than I believed in myself throughout this process. Countless hours spent discussing the depths of migration, human rights law, and the implications of various migration policies not only shaped my thesis but also transformed my way of thinking and viewing the world. He has provided invaluable feedback on many chapters of the original version of this book, sparking ideas and reflections I would never have had otherwise. Thank you to all my friends for their unwavering support, encouragement, friendship, and thoughtful feedback.

I extend my heartfelt thanks to Linus Mührel, Esra Demir Gürsel, Heike Krieger, David Cantor and the series reviewers for their invaluable feedback on both earlier drafts and this version of the book. Their insights and critiques have significantly enriched the final work. A special thank you goes to Brill, and in particular to Akiko Hakuno, whose tireless support and thoughtful feedback throughout the writing and publishing process have been instrumental in bringing this book to fruition.

My Ph.D. would not have been possible without the crucial institutional support I received along the way. I am deeply grateful to the Yale Fox Fellowship, the Heinrich-Böll Stiftung, and the Ernst-Reuter Stiftung. Their financial assistance and institutional backing provided me with the time and space necessary to complete my work.

The last person I want to thank is my partner David Cerero Guerra, for his unconditional love and support, always. He stood by me throughout the long and often challenging process of writing this book, always knowing exactly how to encourage and uplift me. His unwavering support helps me overcome any obstacle in life. His critical, interdisciplinary perspective and insightful questions about migration topics and my work have been invaluable in sharpening my thoughts, arguments, and understanding of migration from a non-legal viewpoint. His kindness and dedication to making the world a better place, as well as to academia, inspire me every day. Life is so much more fun with you by my side. Thank you for being there for me, always.

Abbreviations

ACHPR	African Charter on Human and Peoples' Rights (Banjul Charter)
AComHPR	African Commission on Human and Peoples' Rights
ACtHPR	African Court on Human and Peoples' Rights
ACHR	American Convention on Human Rights (Pact of San José)
AComHR	American Commission on Human Rights
ACtHR	American Court of Human Rights
AU	African Union
CAT	Convention against Torture and Other Cruel, Inhuman or Degrading Treatment or Punishment
CEDAW	Convention on the Elimination of All Forms of Discrimination against Women
CERD	Committee on the Elimination of Racial Discrimination
CHRC	Commonwealth of Independent States Convention on Human Rights and Fundamental Freedoms
CHRCoE	Commissioner for Human Rights of the Council of Europe
CIS	Commonwealth of Independent States
CJEU	Court of Justice of the European Union
CMW	Committee on the Protection of the Rights of All Migrant Workers and Members of their Families (Migrant Worker Committee)
CoE	Council of Europe
ComAT	Committee against Torture
ComEDAW	Committee on the Elimination of Discrimination against Women
CPSI	Project Children's Protection and Security International
CPT	European Committee for the Prevention of Torture and Inhuman or Degrading Treatment or Punishment
CRC	Committee on the Rights of the Child
ECHR	European Convention on Human Rights
ECOE	European Convention on Establishment
ECOMHR	European Commission of Human Rights
ECRE	European Council for Refugees and Exiles

ECtHR	European Court of Human Rights
EU	European Union
EUChFR	Charter of Fundamental Rights in the European Union
GC	Grand Chamber (European Court of Human Rights)
Global Compact on Migration (GCM)	UN Global Compact on Safe, Orderly, and Regular Migration
HRC	Human Rights Committee
HRC CIS	Human Rights Commission of the Commonwealth of Independent States
ICCPR	International Covenant on Civil and Political Rights
ICESCR	International Covenant on Economic, Social and Cultural Rights
ICPPED	Convention for the Protection of all Persons from enforced Disappearance
IHRDA	Institute for Human Rights and Development in Africa
ILC	International Law Commission
ILC Draft Articles	Draft Articles on the expulsion of aliens
IOM	International Organization for Migration
MPP	Migrant Protection Protocols
OAU	Organisation of African Unity
OAU Refugee Convention	OAU Convention Governing the Specific Aspects of Refugee Problems in Africa
OHCHR	United Nations Office of the High Commissioner for Human Rights
TFEU	Treaty on the Functioning of the European Union
UNCH	Charter of the United Nations
UNCRC	United Nations Convention on the Rights of the Child
UNCRMW	International Convention on the Protection of the Rights of All Migrant Workers and Members of Their Families (UN Migrant Worker Convention)
UNGA	United Nations General Assembly
UNHCR	United Nations High Commissioner for Refugees
VCLT	Vienna Convention on the Law of Treaties

CHAPTER 1

Setting the Stage: The Prohibition of Collective Expulsion as Guarantor of Migrants' Rights

In her timeless essay, "*We Refugees*" of 1943, philosopher Hannah Arendt a stateless refugee herself at that point, explored the paradox of her circumstances and the refugee's plight in general. Stripped of rights and agency, refugees become "unwelcome guests", she writes, caught in limbo at the edges of political communities that deny them belonging and identity.[1] Likewise, in "*The Rights of Man: What Are They?*",[2] which contains her much debated and interpreted concept of "the right to have rights",[3] Arendt poignantly continues this discourse and describes vividly the vulnerability of stateless individuals and refugees.[4] In this essay, she explores the essential human need to belong to a political community that acknowledges and protects their rights. Written in 1946 in the wake of the displacement and destruction following World War II, Arendt's work underscores how, without political recognition, individuals are left without access to fundamental protections. The author argues that human rights cannot truly be realized without the "right to have rights", which is a right to be part of a community that upholds one's humanity and dignity through legal and political inclusion.[5]

The prohibition of collective expulsion embodies Arendt's concept of the "right to have rights" by ensuring that migrants and asylum seekers are

---

1 Arendt, Hannah *We Refugees* Menorah Journal 31, No. 1, January 1943, pp. 69–77.

2 Hannah Arendt's essay *The Rights of Man: What Are They?* was initially published in 1946 as a response to Hermann Broch's proposal for an "International Bill of Rights" and was later republished in both German and English in 1949. See: Hamacher, Werner and Mendoza-de Jesus, Ronald *On the Right to Have Rights: Human Rights; Marx and Arendt* The New Centennial Review, Vol. 14, No. 2, 2014, pp. 169–214.

3 For a very detailed overview and analysis of the various interpretations thereof, see: Kesby, Alison *The Right to Have Rights: Citizenship, Humanity, and International Law* (Oxford University Press 2012).

4 For an analysis of Arendt's essay and its historical context, see: Faghfouri Azar, Leina *Hannah Arendt: The Right to Have Rights* Critical Legal Thinking, 12 Jul 2019, available at: https://criticallegalthinking.com/2019/07/12/hannah-arendt-right-to-have-rights/. All online sources in this book were last accessed on 10 June 2025.

5 Arendt, Hannah *The Rights of Man: What Are They?* American Labor Conference on International Affairs, Modern Review, 1949, pp. 24–37.

 | DOI:10.1163/9789004535077_002

afforded a fundamental legal safeguard: The right to have their claims for protection heard and assessed individually. This principle affirms the inherent dignity of migrants by recognizing them as rights-bearing individuals whose humanity must be acknowledged by the legal systems of states. In providing migrants the opportunity to present their case, the prohibition takes a critical step toward inclusion, offers a pathway for individuals to seek belonging within a political community that upholds their rights.

This book *The Prohibition of Collective Expulsion: Protecting against Arbitrary Expulsion in Human Rights Treaty Law*[6] is anchored in Arendt's insight, focusing on the rights of migrants and asylum seekers in expulsion scenarios, where individuals are either recognized as rights-bearers or excluded from protections entirely. It examines one of the most foundational principles that upholds the procedural rights of migrants and asylum seekers, the prohibition of collective expulsion. This principle is not only essential for ensuring due process, but it also serves as a gateway to accessing other fundamental rights, as it requires individual assessment and consideration of the specific circumstances. Beyond its procedural importance, the prohibition of collective expulsion exemplifies the growing centrality of human rights in legal and political efforts to safeguard migrants' rights. This reflects a broader trend of "humanrightization", where law, politics, and everyday practices increasingly integrate human rights principles.[7] As Bast highlights, this integration has created a framework for articulating far-reaching demands for the inclusion of migrants through recognized legal arguments, empowering both migrants and social actors to challenge restrictive migration controls effectively.[8]

In this context broader context of human rights trends, the prohibition of collective expulsion, as explored in the following chapters, has become a cornerstone of various regional and international human rights instruments, underscoring its foundational role in shaping migration governance through a human rights lens. These instruments – from the European Convention on Human Rights to the Inter-American Convention, the African Charter, the Migrant Worker Convention, and the International Covenant on Civil and Political Rights – recognize the prohibition of collective expulsion as

6 The basis for this book is the author's dissertation supervised by Helmut Aust at Freie Universität Berlin which was published open access in 2020 at Freie Universität Berlin's online archive Refubium.

7 Bast, Jürgen *The Rise of Human Rights Limits to Migration Control – A European Perspective* AJIL Unbound, Vol. 118, 2024, pp. 208–213.

8 *Ibidem.*

an essential safeguard for migrants' rights. In a nutshell, this prohibition reflects an understanding that each person, regardless of status, should have the right to due process and individual assessment before expulsion, rather than being subject to blanket removal. The book further delves into the evolving interpretation of this principle across jurisdictions and over time, examining how it has been shaped by shifts in migration patterns, control policies, and judicial decisions. By exploring the jurisprudence of international and regional courts, as well as human rights bodies, this analysis reveals the interconnectedness of the prohibition of collective expulsion within these systems. The approach is both comparative and comprehensive, offering insights into judicial developments and dialogues that influence the protection standards across different regions and legal frameworks.

Given the global challenges of migration today, this book provides a resource for scholars of refugee and migration law, as well as practitioners, courts, tribunals, and policymakers. It equips readers with the legal insight, detailed background, and comparative perspectives needed to apply and understand minimum protections for migrants in expulsion contexts. By examining the principle's role within varying human rights regimes, the book sheds light on both shared and distinct approaches across regions, highlighting how judicial dialogue contributes to a coherent, evolving framework that contains the rights of migrants and refugees worldwide. As this book will show, the prohibition of collective expulsion stands as a cornerstone in ensuring the protection of migrants and asylum seekers, against arbitrary removal, safeguarding their fundamental rights even in the most vulnerable circumstances. This principle is not only essential for guaranteeing the right to an individual examination within a state's territory but, as recognized by instruments such as the European Court of Human Rights and the Inter-American Court of Human Rights, also applies in cases of denial of entry at borders, underscoring its role in upholding human rights at every stage of migration. Borders, however, are not natural phenomena but human-made constructs, designed and sanctioned as instruments for controlling behavior.[9] In this context, the following chapters attempt to challenge the idea that border zones, whether along the Mediterranean, at the fences between Spain and Morocco, Poland and Belarus, or Chile and Venezuela, are beyond legal regulation, where states can exercise unchecked authority over migration.

---

9 Towfigh, Emanuel V. and Weyl, Niklas T. *Borders, Citizenship, and Global Inequality: What Barriers, Pushbacks, and Passport Controls Reveal About Our Understanding of the Equality of Humankind* German Law Journal, published online 2024, p. 6.

On the contrary, this book argues that every person within these contexts holds a right to seek protection, rooted in the prohibition of collective expulsion. This prohibition, enshrined in both regional and international treaties and reinforced by binding international law, underscores that states cannot disregard individual rights simply because individuals are seeking entry and protection. The analysis here seeks to clarify the real-world implications of this right: What procedural guarantees must be upheld for asylum seekers at the border? How do courts and treaty bodies interpret and apply these protections? What has driven changes in these interpretations over time, and are there significant regional variations?

Following Arendt's insights on the essential "right to have rights", we turn to the general context of migration today, where the right to protection for migrants and asylum seekers remains critically relevant. Over the past fifty years, this number has risen significantly by 128 million since 1990 and more than threefold since 1970.[10] This upward trend reflects both the increasing interconnectedness of our world and the diverse factors driving people to move across borders. As contemporary migration patterns grow increasingly complex and prominent, with an estimated 281 million international migrants worldwide representing 3.6 percent of the global population,[11] the role of human rights law, including the prohibition of collective expulsion, remains vital in safeguarding the rights of migrants and ensuring that states consistently uphold their obligations.

When moving beyond the numbers and looking at the impacts, it becomes clear that migration presents a wide spectrum of economic, social, and humanitarian opportunities, benefiting both individuals and host states. However, it also introduces profound challenges to national identities, social cohesion, stability, and the capacity of legal and policy frameworks to respond effectively. These complexities have led to a noticeable "politicization of migration issues",[12] affecting both public discourse and legal interpretations. As the movement of people across borders has grown, so too has the role of human rights protections, particularly at the regional level, in

10 International Organization for Migration *2024 World Migration Report* PUB2023/047/L*, 2024 p. 21.

11 *Ibidem.*, p. 4.

12 Migration and border control were amongst the most pressing topics throughout the regions in the global super-election year 2024. This has been the case in the EU parliamentary elections in June 2024 and in the US elections in November 2024, see: Pew Research Center *Immigration attitudes and the 2024 election* 6 June 2024, available at: https://www.pewresearch.org/politics/2024/06/06/immigration-attitudes-and-the-2024-election/.

establishing minimum standards for migrants' rights and limiting the otherwise broad sovereignty of states to control cross-border movement. It is thus little surprising that policies, conventions and agreements governing issues of such movement have developed in parallel.

In this context, one of the most significant international frameworks addressing the protection of fleeing across borders due to persecution is the 1951 Refugee Convention and its 1967 Protocol.[13] Together, they form the cornerstone of refugee protection to this day. With 147 states party to at least one of these instruments, the Convention upholds fundamental protections for refugees, including the principle of *non-refoulement*, which prohibits returning individuals to places where their lives or well-being would be at risk. It also sets forth the definition of "refugee" and prohibits the arbitrary expulsion of legally residing refugees. However, the Convention's protections are limited to those meeting its specific definition: Individuals persecuted based on race, religion, nationality, political opinion, or membership in a particular social group. This may exclude other vulnerable groups, such as internally displaced persons, economic migrants, people displaced by climate change,[14] and those fleeing war or violence, leaving significant gaps in protection.[15]

---

13 UN General Assembly, *Convention Relating to the Status of Refugees*, 28 July 1951, United Nations, Treaty Series, Vol. 189, p. 137, Convention entry into force 22 April 1954. UN General Assembly *Protocol Relating to the Status of Refugees* 31 January 1967, United Nations, Treaty Series, Vol. 606, p. 267, Protocol entry into force 4 October 1967.

14 Matthew Scott takes a more positive view in this regard. He argues that refugee status determination in the context of disasters and climate change has been inconsistently applied by judicial bodies. Drawing on disaster anthropology and political ecology, which highlight discrimination as a factor in vulnerability to disaster, Scott advocates for a revised approach that moves beyond the dominant human rights-based interpretation of the refugee definition. See: Scott, Matthew *Climate Change, Disasters, and the Refugee Convention* (Oxford University Press 2020).

15 Some regional and domestic laws governing asylum extend this protection to other categories of migrants. In the European Union, for example, people fleeing from war receive "subsidiary protection" which constitutes a less extensive form of protection compared to the "refugee" status. Domestic legislation in Africa and Latin America often extends the definition of a refugee, influenced by regional instruments such as the 1969 OAU Convention and the 1984 Cartagena Declaration. For example, Uganda's 2006 Refugee Act (Section 4) includes individuals fleeing external aggression, occupation, foreign domination, or events seriously disturbing public order. Similarly, Egypt's Law 164 of 2024 and Guatemala's Acuerdo de Autoridad Migratoria Nacional No. 2-2019 incorporate threats to public security and gender-based persecution. Colombia's Decree 1067 of 2015 expands protection to those at risk of torture, widespread violence, or mass human rights violations, showcasing the influence of regional frameworks in shaping broader protections at the national level.

These limitations left migrants without adequate international protection for many years. For example, the European Convention on Human Rights (ECHR), drafted in 1950, initially contained no provisions explicitly addressing migrants' rights. It was not until the 1955 Convention on Establishment that expulsion protections for foreigners appeared at the regional level, albeit with a limited scope that extended only to citizens of other member states.[16] This gap in migrant protections would later drive developments in regional human rights instruments, which now play a crucial role in safeguarding migrants' rights across borders.

Through this lens, this book critically examines the prohibition of collective expulsion as a fundamental legal safeguard in today's complex migration landscape and its interpretative evolution in different regions and on the international level. By exploring the prohibition's application and interpretation across various human rights regimes, this book addresses how human rights law and courts have sought to fill the gaps in protection left by traditional refugee frameworks and early human rights instruments. In this context, this first chapter introduces the broader context of the prohibition of collective expulsion in public international law, establishing the book's framework. It begins with an analysis of the reciprocal relationship between state sovereignty and human rights in the context of the admission and expulsion of foreigners (section 1). Following this, section 2 offers a brief historical overview of the prohibition's significance. Section 3 provides an initial look at the various regional and international codifications of the prohibition, highlighting the principle's broad reach globally. The next section (4) explores the different terminology used to describe the prohibition of collective expulsion and evaluates their distinctions. Finally, section 5 outlines the general framework and objectives of the thesis.

1 Balancing State Sovereignty and Migrants' Rights in International Law

State sovereignty is a cornerstone of international law, granting states the authority to regulate the admission and expulsion of foreigners based on their domestic laws. Martti Koskenniemi describes it as a central concept in international law, comparing it to "liberty" in domestic liberal

---

16 Council of Europe *European Convention on Establishment and Protocol thereto*, 529 UNTS 141, ETS No. 19, opening of the treaty on 13 December 1955, entry into force 23 February 1965.

discourse.[17] He characterizes it as "the critical property an entity must possess in order to qualify as a State".[18] However, since the end of World War II, the protection of individuals has gained prominence in international law, increasingly limiting the absolute principle of state sovereignty. This evolution has sparked debates, particularly around the limits of expulsion, asylum, and migration control.

Scholars often engage with the apparent tension between state sovereignty and individual rights, reflecting on how the growth of migrants' rights has constrained state authority in these areas. A central question in these discussions is how far migrants' rights can limit state sovereignty regarding admission and expulsion, and how states have responded to these developments.[19]

In this debate, John Rawls criticizes this development arguing in favor of states' strong sovereign rights to control admission and expulsion. Rawls justifies this approach by stipulating that a democratic society constitutes "a complete and closed social system". As a system that is "self-sufficient and has a place of all the main purposes of human life. It is also closed [...] in that entry into it is only by birth and exit from it is only by death".[20] The large movement of refugees from Kosovo and Bosnia at the time of his writing in the early 1990s may have triggered Rawl's state-centric perspective. In his later work, "The Law of Peoples", Rawls seemingly builds on his previous findings. He justifies a state's absolute prerogative to decide who gets to enter and who by stating that it is a people's government's responsibility to control "the size of their population".[21] In a footnote, he clarifies that this remark "implies that a people has at least a qualified right to limit immigration" as a government must "protect a people's political culture and its constitutional principles".[22] Thus, Rawls rejects the idea of diminishing state sovereignty in the area of migration arguing for a state's continuous right to control admission and expulsion. In contrast, Hannah Arendt famously

17 Koskenniemi, Martti *From APOLOGY to UTOPIA The Structure of International Legal Argument* (Cambridge University Press reissued 2009), p. 300.

18 *Ibidem.*

19 See, for example: Goodwin-Gill, Guy and McAdam, Jane *The Refugee in International Law* (Oxford University Press 3rd edn. 2007), introduction; Gammeltoft-Hansen, Thomas *Access to Asylum: International Refugee Law and the Globalisation of Migration Control* (Cambridge University Press paperback edn. 2013), pp. 11–13.

20 Rawls, John *Political Liberalism* (Columbia University Press 1993), p. 41.

21 Rawls, John *The Principles of the Law of Peoples* (Harvard University Press 2nd edn. 2000), p. 39.

22 *Ibidem.*

proclaimed in "The Origins of Totalitarianism", the decline of the nation-state and the principle of state sovereignty driven by evolving human rights.[23] Echoing Arendt's conclusions, Seyla Benhabib explains that "[o]ne of the cornerstones of Westphalian sovereignty, namely that states enjoy ultimate authority over all objects and subjects within their circumscribed territory, has been delegitimized through international law".[24] However, she is, just like Rawls, skeptical about the success of this development when it comes to migrants' rights. However, in her view, the reason for this bastion of sovereignty in migration lies in states' unwillingness to adhere to certain guarantees. She concludes that developments in human rights law "ironically [...] end up encouraging states to use detention and deportation tactics to avoid their responsibilities under international law" as states are not willing to give up power in this area.[25] In a similar vein, Thomas Gammeltoft-Hansen and Tanja Aalberts argue that recent migration control trends show that states react to a limitation of their sovereign right to control migration by expanding their (restricted) power instead in the space just outside their territories.[26]

The two authors see irregular migration as one of the main drivers for states' "return" to sovereignty in the area of migration.[27] To illustrate this claim, they refer to the high sea, which used to be "a space of non-sovereignty per se" and now has "become the venue for a range of competing claims and disclaims to sovereignty and responsibility".[28] They conclude that by moving migration control outside a state's territory and by outsourcing it to private actors and third states, countries evade their obligations under international law while containing the power to regulate admission into their territories.[29]

Looking at this issue from a philosophical standpoint, Jürgen Habermas comes to a similar conclusion on the relationship between state sovereignty and migrants' rights in today's world as Gammeltoft-Hansen and Aalberts.

---

23 Arendt, Hannah *The Origins of Totalitarianism* (Schocken Books 1951), p. 267.

24 Benhabib, Seyla *The Rights of Others: Aliens, Residents and Citizens* (Cambridge University Press 2013), p. 12.

25 Benhabib, Seyla *Exile, Statelessness and Migration: Playing Chess with History from Hannah Arendt to Isaiah Berlin* (Princeton University Press 2018), p. 122.

26 Gammeltoft-Hansen and Aalberts *Search and Rescue as a Geopolitics of Int. Law* p. 196. The authors draw on the example of an expansion of Search and Rescue Zones outside territorial waters to highlight their point.

27 *Ibidem.*, p. 188.

28 *Ibidem.*, p. 194.

29 *Ibidem.*, p. 197.

He highlights states' reluctance to give up sovereignty in migration and concludes that this field of international law resembles one of the last bastions of state sovereignty. In his view, this tendency entails long-term effects that shape societies and the composition of peoples.[30] Habermas then concludes that this current political system is not fit for today's realities of the movement of people across borders.[31]

Going beyond the analysis of today's realities of people on the move, E. Tendayi Achiume reexamines migration through the lens of decolonization.[32] Building on critiques of state sovereignty, she challenges the dominant understanding of sovereignty as granting states an almost unfettered right to exclude non-nationals, especially economic migrants.[33] Achiume contends that the historical legacies of colonialism, marked by European domination and the exploitation of "Third World" peoples,[34] impose ethical obligations on former colonial powers to open their borders.[35] Migration from the Global South to the Global North, she argues, is not simply a pursuit of better opportunities but a decolonial act that seeks redress for historical injustices.[36] To do so in practice, she suggests reframing sovereignty as an interconnected and ethical concept, where states must recognize their shared responsibility for global inequalities and include migrants as co-sovereigns in a collective political order.[37] Achiume's reframing of sovereignty as an ethical and interconnected concept challenges traditional notions of state control over borders by highlighting historical injustices and the need for shared responsibility in addressing global inequalities. Building on this critique, Towfigh and Weyl extend the discussion by examining how borders and citizenship laws function as mechanisms that perpetuate systemic inequality, calling for a reimagining of governance frameworks that align with principles of global justice and equality. Addressing this notion of global justice and equality, the two authors argue that states rely on physical and legal constructs like borders and citizenship laws to

30 Habermas, Jürgen *The European Nation-State: On the Past and Future of Sovereignty and Citizenship*. (MIT Press. Cambridge 1998) and Benhabib, Seyla *The Rights of Others*.

31 *Ibidem.*, p. 237.

32 Achiume, E. Tendayi *Migration as Decolonization* Stanford Law Review, Vol. 71, June 2019, pp. 1509–1574.

33 *Ibidem.*, p. 1515.

34 *Ibidem.*, p. 1518.

35 *Ibidem.*, p. 1553.

36 *Ibidem.*, pp. 1553–1566.

37 *Ibidem.*, pp. 1566–1573.

restrict access to resources and opportunities to those they want to exclude.[38] These tools perpetuate inequality as they bind individuals to specific territories, often determining their life chances in ways that challenge fundamental principles of justice.[39] In this context, borders in their functional dimension "cannot be justified in terms of fundamental considerations of justice and equality".[40] In this view, current border regimes necessitate a shift toward more universal and equitable governance frameworks.[41]

In sum, as these discussions show, despite the broader trend toward limiting state sovereignty through the development of human rights law, the regulation of migration remains one of the most steadfast expressions of state sovereignty in today's globalized world. States continue to assert their prerogative to control borders and regulate migration, often resisting binding international rules that would limit their sovereign rights. This resistance is evident in instruments like the non-binding New York Declaration for Refugees and Migrants,[42] which, while a step forward in articulating the global commitment to refugee protection, lacks the binding force of treaty law. States' reluctance to subject themselves to robust international norms governing migration underscores the persistent tension between the evolving norms of human rights protection and the enduring claims of state sovereignty. This tension becomes especially apparent in the realm of migration control as showcased in recent jurisprudence on the prohibition by the European Court of Human Rights, the Inter-American Court of Human Rights but also by treaty bodies such as the Committee against Torture.[43] Here, the principle of sovereignty intersects with the rights of migrants, creating an intricate balancing act. States' control over who enters and who remains within their borders is often seen as a manifestation of their

---

38 Towfigh, Emanuel V. and Weyl, Niklas T. *Borders, Citizenship, and Global Inequality: What Barriers, Pushbacks, and Passport Controls Reveal About Our Understanding of the Equality of Humankind* German Law Journal, published online 2024, pp. 8–10.

39 *Ibidem.*, pp. 9–12.

40 Towfigh, Emanuel V. *Borders of Equality or: What Barriers and Pushbacks Reveal about our Understanding of the Equality of all Human Beings* Verfassungsblog, 15 March 2022, available at: https://verfassungsblog.de/os5-borders-of-equality/.

41 Towfigh, Emanuel V. and Weyl, Niklas T. *Borders, Citizenship, and Global Inequality: What Barriers, Pushbacks, and Passport Controls Reveal About Our Understanding of the Equality of Humankind*, pp. 20–21.

42 United Nations General Assembly *New York Declaration for Refugees and Migrants* Resolution adopted by the General Assembly on 19 September 2016, A/RES/71/1 available at: http://www.un.org/en/ga/search/view_doc.asp?symbol=A/RES/71/1. All internet sources in this thesis last accessed on 20 January 2025.

43 See, for example chapters 2 and 3.

sovereignty, yet the increasing recognition of migrants' rights requires states to consider the human impact of their policies. This complex dynamic leads to the question of how international law can mediate between the legitimate sovereign interests of states and the rights of individuals on the move. While states may resist international legal frameworks that constrain their sovereign control over migration, there is a recognition, as showcased by the many court decisions examined in this book, that certain safeguards must be in place and monitored continuously to prevent the abuse of power by states. It is here that the international legal framework, particularly the prohibition of collective expulsion, becomes relevant. This prohibition serves as an essential check on states' authority, especially in border scenarios, ensuring that expulsions are carried out with respect to individual rights and not in a manner that violates fundamental principles or due process. In this context, international and regional human rights law seeks to find a balance, ensuring that state sovereignty is not unduly encroached upon while protecting individuals from arbitrary and unjust treatment.

2 Tracing the Historical Significance of the Prohibition of Collective Expulsion

Throughout history, violent conflicts, persecution and displacement affected various marginalized groups across the globe. In this context, the following section provides a brief overview of how expulsions have played a role throughout history, emphasizing the significance of their prohibition in contemporary times. In this context, it is important to recall that collective expulsions are not only a phenomenon of our days, but that states have historically used banishments and (collective) expulsions as tools for nation-building, isolation, and deterrence. Moreover, throughout history, collective expulsions have often been linked to xenophobia, antisemitism, and racism.[44] When looking at the history of reported collective expulsions its long and tragic trajectory with hundreds of millions of expelled nationals, foreigners, and stateless around the world for various, yet similar reasons becomes apparent. One of the earliest reported practices of collective expulsion occurred in ancient Sparta. "Xenelasia", the practice of expelling all foreigners jointly that were deemed injurious to the public welfare,

44 Weiner, Myron *Ethics, national sovereignty and the control of immigration* International Migration Review, Vol. 30, No. 1, 1996, pp. 171–197.

served as an instrument of social control.[45] Similarly, in ancient Iceland, "thing", or "Alþing" founded in 930, which claims to be the longest running parliament, served as an early version of a juridical system that dispensed justice.[46] The "Alþing" could declare guilty criminals as "outlaws", which led to their loss of the right to property, hospitality, and even the right to remain within the borders of Iceland.[47] The core of this practice was not the expulsion of foreigners *en masse*, but it epitomizes the common practice throughout history and cultures to ban "unwanted", "outlaws", people that were not seen as a part of the host society, but "others" from a foreign territory. Besides this "regulatory" practice of controlling the composition of societies, collective expulsions have also played a significant role when it comes to nation-building throughout history. As Randall Hansen explains

> Borders are basic to the construction and creation of refugee movements in both historical and contemporary contexts. In the former, nation states have been built through mass flight and mass expulsions. In this sense, Europe's interwar period, in which there was a valiant and failed effort to match borders to people, was the exception. Both before and after the 1919–39 period, the norm was to match, through expulsion and murder, people to borders.[48]

This historical perspective underscores how the interplay between borders, expulsions, and nation-building has shaped not only the formation of states but also the identities of those included and excluded. It highlights the enduring legacy of these practices in contemporary border regimes, where exclusion continues to serve as a powerful tool for defining and regulating membership in political communities.

Another example in this regard is the forceful collective expulsion of around 750,000 Palestinian Arabs from Israeli territory between 1947 and 1949.[49] Similarly, the birth of India and Pakistan went hand in hand with

---

45 Figueira, Thomas *Xenelasia and Social Control in Classical Sparta* The Classical Quarterly, Vol. 53, No. 1, 2003, p. 44.

46 Government of Iceland *Alþing Information brochure* available at: https://www.althingi.is/pdf/Althingi2018_enska.pdf, p. 6.

47 Hathaway, Oona and Shapiro, Scott *The Internationalists: How a Radical Plan to Outlaw War Remade the World* (Simon & Schuster 2017), p. 374.

48 Hansen, Randall *State Control: Borders, Refugees, and Citizenship* in: Fiddian-Qasmiyeh; Loescher; Long and Sigona *The Oxford Handbook of Refugee and Forced Migration Studies* (Oxford University Press 2014), p. 255.

49 *Ibidem.*

the expulsion of 8 million people.[50] States like Poland and Czechoslovakia expelled 12 million Germans in the aftermath of the second world war as part of the creation of their new nation-states.[51] Not just in phases of nation-building do states turn to collective expulsions. Expulsions are also a measure to ensure that those who do not "belong", are forced to leave. States invoke collective expulsion to control their population and to remove those who are not or no longer wanted within the territory or to put pressure on other states. Historical examples of such expulsions are the mass expulsion of 60,000 Iranians from Iraq in 1971; the large-scale expulsion of Rwandans from Uganda in the 1980s; the forceful expulsion of 72,000 Muslims from the northern province of Sri Lanka in the 1990s, the collective expulsion of undocumented migrant workers from Malaysia in 2004 or of Qataris by Bahrain, the United Arab Emirates (UAE) and Saudi Arabia in 2017 due to political tensions between Qatar and its neighbors.[52] The practice of expelling people in large numbers is the embodiment of state power over foreigners: the ruling government decides who enters, who stays, and who must leave and under which circumstances. Other common phenomenon linked to collective expulsions is racism and xenophobia. The earliest reported example was the expulsion of large groups of Jews from England in 1290.[53] Some minority groups were mainly affected by collective expulsion in past centuries. The members of such targeted groups possessed different common denominators such as religion, nationality, ethnic background, being stateless, or foreigners. Jews, who were in many instances denied citizenship in Europe, were one of the main targets of collective expulsions until the 20th century.[54] Another historically targeted and persecuted group is the Romani peoples. Reports on their collective expulsions date back to the 15th century.[55] In 1416, for example, groups of Roma were expelled from the Meissen region in Germany. In 1493 entire Roman families were expelled from Milan and in 1504 France's King Louis XII. banished all Roma

50 *Ibidem.*

51 *Ibidem.*

52 *Saudi Arabia cuts off Qatar* The Economist, 10 June 2017, available at: https://www.economist.com/news/middle-east-and-africa/21723018-kingdom-raising-tensions-its-immediate-neighbours-well-iran.

53 Korinek, Karl and Holoubek, Michael *Österreichisches Bundesverfassungsrecht* (Springer 2003), p. 2.

54 Howley, Jacob *Unlocking the Fortress: Protocol No. 11 and the Birth of Collective Expulsion Jurisprudence in the Council of Europe System* Georgetown Immigration Law Journal (2006), Vol. 21, Issue 111, p. 112.

55 *Ibidem.*, p. 112.

from the state's territory. This history of persecution and expulsion found a horrifying peak during the nazi-era. All foreign-born and stateless Roma were collectively murdered or expelled.[56] Collective expulsions of Romani peoples continued to occur in Europe in the 21st century as well as in our recent history. France's and Italy's collective expulsion of Romani in the early 2000s exemplify this.[57] In 2009, 10,000 Romani people were deported by French authorities to Romania and Bulgaria, followed in 2010 by another 8,300 deported individuals. These expulsions were part of a government program to repatriate Romani allegedly to go against illegal camps.[58] Many of these expelled did receive 300 Euro in exchange for the signing of an agreement never to set foot on French territory again.[59] The *Commissioner for Human Rights of the Council of Europe* reported that French police officers confiscated identity papers of "voluntary returnees" until they had reached their country of origin. This act made it impossible for them to change their minds.[60] For these reasons, it is doubtful if such returns were indeed voluntary and in accordance with international law and EU law.[61] This is also evidenced by the decision *Centre on Housing Rights and Evictions v. France* of the European Committee of Social Rights where it condemned these practices in 2011 as discriminatory and contrary to human rights.[62]

---

56 The Patrin Journal: Romani Culture and History *Patrin Timeline of Romani History* (1998), available at: http://www.oocities.org/patrin/timeline.htm. The journal provides a comprehensive timeline of Romani history in Europe from before 400 AD to 1998.

57 Severance, Kristi *France's Expulsion of Roma Migrants: A Test Case for Europe* Migration Policy Institute, 21 October 2010, available at: https://www.migrationpolicy.org/article/frances-expulsion-roma-migrants-test-case-europe.

58 Suddath, Claire *Who Are Gypsies, and Why Is France Deporting Them?* TIME magazine, 26 August 2010, available at: http://content.time.com/time/world/article/0,8599,2013917,00.html.

59 ROMEA *France Resumes deportation of Roma people from Romania* Czech Press Agency, 13 2010, available at: http://www.romea.cz/en/news/world/france-resumes-deportation-of-roma-peple-from-Romania.

60 European Union Agency for Fundamental Rights *The situation of Roma EU citizens moving to and settling in other EU Member States* 2009, available at: http://fra.europa.eu/en/publication/2010/situation-roma-eu-citizens-moving-and-settling-other-eu-member-states, p. 29.

61 For a legal analysis see: Gunther, Caitlin *France's Repatriation of Roma: Violation of Fundamental Freedoms?* Cornell International Law Journal, Vol. 45, 2012, p. 205–212. The author finds that "France's repatriation program would likely have been found to violate its international legal obligations".

62 European Committee of Social Rights *Centre on Housing Rights and Evictions* (COHRE) *v. France* Complaint No. 63/2010, decision on the merits of 28 June 2011.

Another paradigmatic pattern is the link between expulsions and the movement of people across borders. Throughout history, citizens and state representatives perceived migrants as "strangers", "barbarians", or "aliens". Siep Stuurman describes this phenomenon in the following, giving it a positive spin

> From earliest times, people have crossed boundaries and frontiers. Travelers had to come to terms with the unfamiliar customs and ideas of "other" people. People beyond the frontier could be regarded as uncouth barbarians, vile enemies, or even as barely human, but it was also thinkable to see them as fellow humans with whom it would be possible to communicate, trade and collaborate.[63]

The following chapters build on this "two-sides-of-a-coin" idea related to visions of migration. They explore two facets of the migration issue: On one side, the longstanding practice of exclusion, and on the other, the principle of hospitality, which calls for welcoming strangers and providing asylum to those fleeing persecution. This latter phenomenon is for example visible in the inclusion of principles such as the prohibition of collective expulsion in numerous human rights treaties in the last decades. At the same time, migration, as an age-old phenomenon, has always been accompanied by the exclusion of "the other". This dynamic has shaped the relationships between societies and perceived outsiders to this day. This power to determine who is allowed entry, who is integrated, and who remains excluded has traditionally rested in the hands of the receiving society, supported by the principle of state sovereignty. However, this power has been increasingly constrained in the post-World War II era, particularly with the increasing acceptance of human rights. These developments mark a shift toward balancing state control over borders with the protection of individuals fleeing persecution. Nevertheless, during times of instability or perceived "crisis",[64] states often resort to collective expulsions, which serve multiple purposes. Collective expulsions are used to consolidate societal cohesion, pressure migrant-sending

---

63 Stuurman, Siep *The Invention of Humanity Equality and Cultural Difference in World History* (Harvard University Press 2017), p. 3.

64 For an assessment of how "crisis" have become the "new normal" in migration law, see: Moreno-Lax, Violeta *The "Crisification" of Migration Law: Insights from the EU External Border* in: Cope, Kevin; Burch Elias, Stella, and Goldenziel, Jill (eds.) *Oxford Handbook of Comparative Immigration Law* (Oxford University Press 1 ed.), forthcoming, pp. 1–30.

states, leverage political influence on the international stage, or respond to public demands for the removal of foreign nationals. As the examples in this book illustrate, the practice of collective expulsions has evolved over time. Both the legal frameworks and the methods employed for such expulsions have changed, reflecting a growing awareness of human rights protections and international law. Today, international law restricts states' ability to carry out arbitrary collective expulsions, and in response, states continuously adjust their practices.[65]

In this context, states now seek to justify collective expulsions, often constructing legal or political frameworks to support their actions. One example of this is Spain's push-back policy at the Moroccan border, justified by domestic needs, despite being controversial under international human rights standards but not deemed a violation of the prohibition of collective expulsion in this concrete context.[66] Likewise, recently, collective expulsions have become increasingly linked to broader geopolitical dynamics. For instance, at the border between Belarus, Latvia, Lithuania, and Poland, these three latter countries have justified the collective expulsion of migrants and asylum seekers by framing the situation as a response to "hybrid threats" posed by Belarus.[67] They argue that Belarus is using migration as a tool of political leverage, "instrumentalizing" the movement of migrants as part of a broader geopolitical strategy. In this context, these states claim that their expulsions are a necessary defense against this perceived manipulation, further complicating the balance between state sovereignty and migrants' rights. Moreover, states in the Global North, particularly European Union members, the United States, Canada, and Australia, have developed an elaborate system of extraterritorialization and outsourcing of migration control.[68] This system allows these countries to prevent "undesired" migrants from reaching their borders in the first place, often by collaborating with third countries or deploying deterrent measures. At

65 This includes shifting their borders outside their territories, declaring zones as extraterritorial, or cooperating with third states to ensure that migrants and asylum seekers do not reach their territory.

66 See the Grand Chamber decision *N.D. and N.T. v. Spain* ECtHR, [GC] Appl. Nos. 8675/15 and 8697/15, 13 February 2020.

67 See Chapter 5.

68 See, for example: Gammeltoft-Hansen, Thomas *Access to Asylum: International Refugee Law and the Globalisation of Migration Control* (Cambridge University Press paperback edn. 2013), or Moreno-Lax, Violeta and Lemberg-Pedersen, Martin *Border-induced displacement: The ethical and legal implications of distance-creation through externalization* Questions of International Law, Zoom-in 56 (2019) pp. 5–33.

the same time, they limit legal pathways for migration, offering resettlement options to only a select few. These practices underscore the tension between upholding human rights protections and maintaining stringent border controls, reflecting the continuing challenge of balancing state sovereignty with migrants' rights in a complex, globalized world. As this book will explore in greater detail, the evolving nature of collective expulsions and the legal justifications behind them highlight the ongoing struggle between state control over migration and the international human rights commitment to protecting vulnerable individuals.

3 The Application of the Prohibition of Collective Expulsion on a Global Level

One important element of the prohibition of collective expulsion is its vast applicability around the globe as it binds 173 states through regional and international treaty law. These states have either ratified the International Covenant on Civil and Political Rights,[69] the UN Migrant Worker Convention,[70] the Commonwealth of Independent States Convention on Human Rights and Fundamental Freedoms,[71] the 2004 Arab Charter on Human Rights,[72] the European Convention on Human Rights,[73] the EU Fundamental Rights Charter,[74] the African Charter on Human and Peo-

69 As of December 2024, 174 States are parties to the ICCPR. Human Rights Committee in its *General Comment No. 15: The Position of Aliens Under the Covenant* 11 April 1986, (*General Comment No. 15*) determined that the prohibition can be derived from Article 13 ICCPR, para. 10.

70 As of December 2024, 60 States are parties to the UN Migrant Worker Convention. The prohibition of collective expulsion is codified in Article 22(1) of the Convention.

71 As of December 2024, 9 States are parties to the Commonwealth of Independent States. Armenia, Azerbaijan, Belarus, Kazakhstan, Kyrgyzstan, Moldova, Russia, Tajikistan, and Uzbekistan However, as of 2024, only four states are party to the CIS Human Rights Convention: Belarus, Kirgizstan, Russian Federation, and Tajikistan. The prohibition of collective expulsion is codified in Article 25(4) of the Convention.

72 As of December 2024, 18 States are parties to the 2004 Arab Charter on Human Rights. The prohibition of collective expulsion is codified in Article 26(2) of the Charter.

73 As of December 2024, 4 States of the 47 Member States of the Council of Europe have not ratified the additional protocol no. 4 to the ECHR (Greece, Switzerland, Turkey and the United Kingdom).

74 As of December 2024, all EU member states are bound to the Charter. The prohibition of collective expulsion is codified in Article 19(1) of the Charter.

ples' Rights[75] or the American Convention on Human Rights.[76] In contrast to this, only twenty-five states[77] have not signed or ratified any of these treaties. Examples in this regard are Nauru, Myanmar, China, and Cuba. The other states are simultaneously bound to the prohibition by several treaties.[78] If one counts those states that ratified the Convention against Torture, then the prohibition of collective expulsion binds 183 states.[79] As argued below, Article 3 Convention against Torture implicitly contains the prohibition of collective expulsion. Following this line of argument, 183 states have ratified one or several conventions that contain the principles guaranteed by the prohibition of collective expulsion. Interestingly, some states like Libya, Algeria, or Syria that do have a low human rights record signed five human rights treaties that codify the prohibition of collective expulsion. This observation is no surprise in light of Oona Hathaway's finding on the relationship between human rights records and a state's likeliness to join human rights treaties. She found that states with adverse human rights records are more likely to join human rights treaties. Their ratification is of low cost internally and great benefit internationally.[80]

Former Special Rapporteur on the expulsion of "aliens" of the International Law Commission Maurice Kamto even describes the nature of the

---

75 As of December 2024, 54 States have ratified the African Charter on Human and Peoples' Rights. The prohibition of 'mass' expulsion is codified in Article 12(5) African Charter.

76 As of December 2024, 25 States have ratified the Inter-American Convention on Human Rights. Trinidad and Tobago and Venezuela subsequently denounced the ratification in 1998 and 2012 respectively. The prohibition of collective expulsion is codified in Article 22(9) of the Convention.

77 States acknowledged by the United Nations.

78 There is no comparable and binding regional Human Rights instrument for Asia governing migration. The non-binding South Asia Declaration on Refugees which was adopted in January 2004 by the Eminent Persons Group does not contain the prohibition of collective expulsion. The Declaration is available here: http://shodhganga.inflibnet.ac.in/bitstream/10603/28291/17/17_appendices.pdf.

79 The countries that are only bound by the prohibition of collective expulsion as implicitly contained in Article 3 CAT are: Antigua and Barbados, China, Cuba, Cambodia, Holy See, Kiribati, Maldives, Nauru and Fiji. Fiji has however placed reservations limiting severely the applicability of the Convention against Torture. For a list of all member states and reservations see: United Nations Treaty Collection *Convention against Torture and Other Cruel, Inhuman or Degrading Treatment or Punishment* New York, 10 December 1984, available at: https://treaties.un.org/pages/ViewDetails.aspx?src=TREATY&mtdsg_no=IV9&chapter=4&clang=_en#5.

80 Hathaway, Oona *Why Do Countries Commit to Human Rights Treaties?* The Journal of Conflict Resolution, (2007), Vol. 51, No. 4, pp. 588–621.

prohibition of collective expulsion as a general principle of international law.[81] He drew this conclusion after a "study of treaty practice and case law, both national and international, in particular, that of regional human rights courts".[82] Kamto's summary of governments' reaction to the draft provision containing the prohibition of collective expulsion (then Article 10) in his ninth report reflects the overwhelming acknowledgment of the principle as binding. Australia was seemingly the only state rejecting the claim that it constituted binding law. The majority of states that had expressed views on the draft provision acknowledged the principle's status as binding law.[83] This firm status of binding law and its continuous relevance on the global level is also evident in the principle's inclusion in the 2018 Global Compact for Safe, Orderly and Regular Migration (GCM).[84] In Objective 21, the GCM calls on states to respect the safe return of migrants by "upholding the prohibition of collective expulsion".

However, despite its widespread codification and recognition as a general principle of international law, the prohibition is often overlooked, with the *non-refoulement* principle receiving much more attention.[85] Therefore, this book aims to highlight the importance of the prohibition of collective expulsion and contribute to its prominence in the discourse on migrants' rights, with a particular focus on developments in human rights treaty law that have shaped and expanded the understanding and application of this prohibition. To better understand the principle's legal implications, the next section explores the nuances of terminology, particularly the distinction between "collective" and "mass" expulsions, and examines how these terms are used in different legal and political contexts. This is crucial as a

81 Kamto, Maurice *Third report on the expulsion of aliens* A/CN.4/581, 19 April 2007, para. 115.

82 *Ibidem.*, para.27.

83 Kamto, Maurice *Ninth report on the expulsion of aliens* A/CN.4/670, 25 March 2014, para. 39.

84 UNGA *Global Compact for Safe, Orderly and Regular Migration*, A/RES/73/195, 18 December 2018.

85 It must be noted, however, that there have been several important contributions on the prohibition. See, for example, Goodwin-Gill, Guy *The Limits of the Power of Expulsion in Public International Law* British Yearbook of International Law, Issue 47, 1976, pp. 55–156 or Ilyer Krishna *Mass Expulsion as Violation of Human Rights* Indian Journal of International Law, Issue 13, 1974, pp. 169–175. One recent key contribution on the prohibition in the ECHR is Anselm Zölls's book *The Prohibition of Collective Expulsion under Art. 4 Protocol No. 4 of the European Convention on Human Rights. Prohibition of Discriminatory and Arbitrary Expulsions* (in German), Mohr Siebeck, 2021.

foundation for the upcoming chapters' use of the term collective expulsion and the analysis of the prohibition's scope of protection.

4 The Distinction between Collective and Mass Expulsion: Unpacking the Terminology

The European Convention, the Inter-American Convention, and the 2004 Arab Charter, amongst other treaties, speak of "collective" expulsion, its African counterpart refers instead to "mass expulsion". Jean-Marie Henkaerts' leading reference work on the topic, his book *Mass Expulsion in Modern International Law and Practice* seemingly uses these terms interchangeably. Is there a normative or semantic difference between the two terms? The following section will unpack this enigma. An analysis of the literature on these issues, judgments, and other legal documents reveals that there is no clear answer that fits every example. On the one hand, some examples call for a distinction based on the size of the group and the duration of the expulsion. The *Secretariat of the International Law Commission*, for example, holds both forms of expulsion to be governed by different legal regimes.[86] The reason for this distinction lies in the size of a group of expelled foreigners to count as "collective" expulsion. Dieter Deumeland, for example, argued that "collective expulsions" require that states expel several foreigners jointly based on their membership to a particular group.[87] In his view, "collective expulsion" may also refer to expulsions of a small group of individuals as long as they share a common characteristic.[88] In the same vein, Jean-Marie Henckaerts criticizes this distinction-drawing sharply. In his view, such differentiation would lead to the unacceptable situation that there would be two different standards. In his perspective, this would be "detrimental for the protection of human rights" if there are different levels of protection attributed to the term "collective" and the term "mass".[89]

The only provision expressly referring to both mass and collective expulsion and that also distinguishes both situations, is Article 13 ICCPR. The Human Rights Committee found in its General Comment No. 15 that this

86 International Law Commission *Expulsion of Aliens* Memorandum by the Secretariat, A/CN.4/565, 58th session, 2006 p.2.

87 Henkaerts, Jean-Marie *Mass Expulsion in Modern International Law and Practice* p. 185.

88 *Ibidem.*

89 *Ibidem.*, pp. 18–19.

provision contains both, the prohibition of both mass and collective expulsion. Why the Committee concluded this remains unknowns, as the comment is silent in this regard. It only states that "article 13 would not be satisfied with laws or decisions providing for collective or mass expulsions".[90] In contrast, the analysis of various regional human rights treaties below suggests that such a clear distinction is not universally upheld. Examining the wording of regional conventions that codify the prohibition of collective expulsion, we find that this distinction is indeed noticeable. The European Convention on Human Rights (Article 4 of Protocol 4), Article 19(1) of the Charter of Fundamental Rights of the European Union, Article 26(2) of the 2004 Arab Charter on Human Rights, Article 22(9) of the Inter-American Convention on Human Rights, and Article 25(4) of the Commonwealth of Independent States Convention all refer to an absolute prohibition of collective expulsion. The African Charter on Human and Peoples' Rights (Banjul Charter), however, takes a different approach in Article 12(5), where it prohibits the "mass (emphasis added) expulsion of non-nationals". Additionally, the Banjul Charter uniquely emphasizes prohibiting mass expulsions based on discrimination, specifically targeting those "aimed at national, racial, ethnic, or religions [sic] groups". Interestingly, only the English version of the African Charter employs the term "mass expulsion". In its official French, Portuguese, and Arabic texts, the Charter uses "collective expulsion". For instance, the French version uses "l'expulsion collective" rather than the term for mass expulsion, "l'expulsion massive". Similarly, the Portuguese version uses "expulsão coletiva" instead of "expulsão em massa". According to Article 33(1) VCLT, when interpreting a treaty, which is available in several authentic language versions, "the text is equally authoritative in each language" unless the treaty or the parties agree on an exception. Concerning the African Charter, the authentic texts are English, French, and Arabic.[91] As the translations are equally authoritative according to the Charter, Article 33(4) VCLT offers further guidance. This subparagraph stipulates that in case of discrepancies between different versions, the interpreter shall first rely on Article 31 and 32 VCLT. If the uncertainty remains, "the meaning which best reconciles the texts, having regard to the object and purpose of the treaty, shall be adopted".

Such an interpretation in good faith and in accordance with the ordinary meaning of the terms is not expedient here. It would be pure speculation if the term "mass" or "collective" better suits the object and purpose of the

90 Human Rights Committee *General Comment No. 15* para. 10.

91 African Charter on Human and Peoples' Rights UNTS 26263, front page.

Charter. Thus, one ought to refer to supplementary means of interpretation, such as preparatory work and the circumstances of the conclusion as requested by Article 32 VCLT. The preparatory work remains silent on the reasons for such divergences between the different translations of the texts. An Amnesty International paper of 1961 on the Organization of African Unity and Human Rights may offer some insights into this question. Here, the NGO pointed out that there "is no entirely satisfactory text of the African Charter in any of the official languages of the OAU. The original text in French has minor typographical errors, and the English and Arabic texts contain translation errors".[92] Concluding from this, the French version directly translated should have correctly used the term "collective" instead of "mass expulsion". A simple translation error explains this difference. The fact that the rapporteurs to the Charter were French, and therefore French would have been the base language supports this finding. Also, the English translations were inferior, as the translators were not well equipped for such a task.[93] These circumstances led to the discrepancy between several drafts. Even after the adoption of the Charter, several changes were made mainly about style, sense, and the inclusion of missing items. Sometimes even substantive changes were made.[94] This finding further strengthens the argument that the terminology used in the various regional conventions is more similar than it appears at first sight. Unfortunately, the available *travaux préparatoires* of the African Charter are silent about this dissonance in terminology.

However, this finding shows that the approach chosen in the African Charter is not as distinct from other regional and international instruments as it may seem at first. It may even be inferred from this, that there is no legal difference between "mass" and "collective" expulsion and that either term refers to the same size of the group. The dissonance in terminology between "mass expulsion" and "collective expulsion" in the African Charter is further complicated by recent resolutions and guidelines issued by the African Commission on Human and Peoples' Rights. The Commission's language choices in these documents appear to treat the terms as interchangeable,

---

92 Amnesty International *Protecting human rights: International procedures and how to use them (A Series of Amnesty International Papers): 2. The Organization of African Unity and human rights* (1991), available at: https://www.amnesty.org/en/documents/ior63/001/1991/en/, p.6.

93 *Ibidem.*

94 I want to thank Dr. Nathaniel Rubner for these insights. He is an expert on the drafting history of the African Charter on Human and Peoples' Rights. The relevant documents are on file with the author.

adding to the ambiguity around Article 12's intended scope. Notably, the Commission's 2017 Resolution 371 on the Implementation of the New York Declaration on Refugees and Migrants recalls Article 12 of the African Charter, emphasizing "the right to freedom of movement and residence for all individuals and prohibit[ing] the mass expulsion of non-nationals". This resolution references Article 12 in general rather than specifically addressing Article 12(5) and uses "mass expulsion" without elaborating on why this terminology was chosen over "collective expulsion". This broad phrasing implies that the Commission perceives the prohibition as encompassing a wider interpretation of Article 12, applicable to all aspects of freedom of movement within the African Charter.

Further ambiguity arises when assessing documents by the African Commission on Human and Peoples' Rights (AComHPR), and other authoritative actors that interpret the Charter of past years containing references to mass and collective expulsion. For example, in the 2021 *Resolution 484 on the Principle of Non-Refoulement for Asylum Seekers and Refugees*, the Commission reminds states to bear "in mind Article 12(3) of the African Charter which prohibits the **collective** expulsion of aliens [emphasis added]" in light of rising numbers of *refoulement* without clarifying its relevance to the prohibition on expulsion.[95] Unlike Article 12(5), which directly addresses expulsion, Article 12(3) pertains to the right to seek asylum, making this reference unusual and unexplained. By linking *non-refoulement* to Article 12(3) rather than the expulsion-focused Article 12(5), the Commission again appears to adopt a more flexible approach, positioning the prohibition on mass or collective expulsion as a principle embedded within the broader right to movement and asylum without precise textual boundaries. Interestingly, Resolution 486 on *Missing Migrants and Refugees in Africa*, which was adopted by the same Commission on the very same day[96] reinforces this flexible approach by mentioning "mass expulsion" but without specifying the legal basis under Article 12. The Commission used the same approach and wording in a previous resolution of 2017 on the adoption of the *New York*

95 ACHPR *Resolution on the Respect for the Principle of Non-Refoulement of Asylum Seekers and Refugees* ACHPR/Res. 484 (EXT.OS/XXXIII), 28 July 2021, available at: https://achpr.au.int/en/adopted-resolutions/484-resolution-respect-principle-non-refoulement-asylum-seekers, para. 3.

96 ACHPR *Resolution on missing migrants and refugees in Africa and the impact on their families* ACHPR/Res. 486 (EXT.OS/XXXIII), 28 July 2021, available at: https://achpr.au.int/en/adopted-resolutions/486-resolution-missing-migrants-and-refugees-africa-and-impact-their-fa, para. 11.

Declaration for Refugees and Migrants.[97] The lack of specificity in these resolutions regarding why "mass expulsion" or "collective expulsion" is used further blurs the lines between these terms. Moreover, the Commission's varying references across the provisions of Article 12 ACHPR suggest an intent to apply the prohibition broadly across different migration-related rights, without strictly confining it to the text of Article 12(5).

This trend extends to the Commission's and Special Rapporteur on Refugees, Asylum Seekers, Internally Displaced Persons and Migrants in Africa's joint *General Comment No. 5 On the African Charter on Human and Peoples' Rights: The Right to Freedom of Movement and Residence (Article 12(1))*. The comment stresses the prohibition of "arbitrary" and "mass expulsions" of migrant workers and their families without referring specifically to Article 12(5). Instead, the comment invokes Article 12(1) ACHPR, which covers the general right to freedom of movement and residence.[98] Here, too, "mass expulsion" is mentioned without explanation, potentially indicating that the prohibition is considered inherent to Article 12's overall protections on movement rather than limited to expulsion under Article 12(5) ACHPR. What is more is that the 2023 *African Guiding Principles on the Human Rights of All Migrants, Refugees, and Asylum Seekers* presented by the Commission further emphasizes this dual terminology.[99] Principle 20, section 7, states that "the mass or collective expulsion of migrants shall be prohibited", defining "mass expulsion" as targeting specific groups based on national, racial, ethnic, or religious identity.[100] The guidance does not distinguish when "collective" versus "mass" expulsion applies, but instead treats both terms as part of a general principle within Article 12 ACHPR's framework. This interchangeable use, combined with the absence of any textual clarification, suggests that the Commission and the Special Rapporteur are

---

97 ACHPR *Resolution on the Implementation of the New York Declaration for Refugees and Migrants* ACHPR/Res.371(LX), 22 May 2017, available at: https://achpr.au.int/en/adopted-resolutions/371-resolution-implementation-new-york-declaration-refugees-and-mi, para. 2.

98 ACHPR *General Comment No. 5 On the African Charter on Human and Peoples' Rights: The Right to Freedom of Movement and Residence (Article 12(1))* October 2021, available at: https://achpr.au.int/sites/default/files/files/2021-10/generalobservationno5ontherightoffreedomonmovementandresidence.pdf, para. 71.

99 ACHPR *African Guiding Principles on the Human Rights of All Migrants, Refugees, and Asylum Seekers* April 2023, available at: https://www.google.com/url?sa=t&source=web&rct=j&opi=89978449&url=https://achpr.au.int/en/soft-law/african-guiding-principles-human-rights-all-migrants-refugees&ved=2ahUKEwixjJflgN2JAxWMTTABHSVjMG4QFnoECBYQAQ&usg=AOvVaw3yzA7rf8p5GyqDUYTi1O-k.

100 *Ibidem.*, principle 20, section 7.

adopting a practical interpretation, recognizing both terms as valid and applicable across all guarantees related to freedom of movement in Article 12 of the Charter. Overall, the Commission's approach in these recent resolutions, guide and the General Comment reflects an overarching view of the prohibition on expulsion of groups as a broad principle under the African Charter, regardless of the specific terminology used or the sub-article referenced. This flexible interpretation appears to affirm that both "mass" and "collective" expulsion are prohibited under Article 12 as a whole, reinforcing the protection of non-nationals against unjust expulsions as a fundamental aspect of the right to freedom of movement in the African Charter.

Furthermore, as will be shown below, "collective expulsions" in Article 4 Protocol 4 ECHR, as interpreted by the ECtHR covers both, expulsions of large and small groups of foreigners. The prohibition also protects summarily expelled foreigners at the border and long-term residents irrespective of the fact that officials expel them immediately or over an extended period constituting a prohibition of arbitrariness[101] in expulsion settings. In addition, the scope of protection of the prohibition of mass expulsion in the African Charter is congruent with its European counterpart (see Chapter 2 and Chapter 3). Both the prohibition of mass expulsion and the prohibition of collective expulsion aim at ensuring that each expelled foreigner of a group receives the possibility to bring forward their claims. The underlying notion of this guarantee is that the higher the number of expelled individuals, the higher the probability that not every individual receives a personalized examination. The larger the designated group, the stronger the assumption that a prohibited collective/mass expulsion has occurred.[102]

In conclusion, international legal instruments, such as the European Convention, the Inter-American Convention, and the Arab Charter, use the term "collective expulsion", while the African Charter refers to "mass expulsion". While some scholars and institutions have attempted to distinguish between "collective" and "mass" expulsion based on the size of the group or the legal regime governing them, the distinction is not consistently upheld in practice. The term "mass expulsion" in the African Charter is likely a

101 For a detailed assessment of this argument in relation to Article 4 Protocol 4 ECHR, see Zölls, Anselm *The Prohibition of Collective Expulsion under Art. 4 Protocol No. 4 of the European Convention on Human Rights. Prohibition of Discriminatory and Arbitrary Expulsions* (in German), Mohr Siebeck, 2021.

102 For similar findings see: Pöschl, Magdalena *Artikel 4 4. ZPEMRK* in: Korinek and Holoubek *Österreichisches Bundesverfassungsrecht Textsammlung und Kommentar* (Springer 2003) para. 18; Henkaerts, Jean-Marie *Mass Expulsion in Public International Law and Practice* p.14.

result of translation errors, and the terms are often used interchangeably in international and regional legal contexts. The prohibition of both forms of expulsion aims to protect individuals from arbitrary expulsions, ensuring that each case is examined on its merits, regardless of the group size or the terminology used. Therefore, the two terms are interchangeable. Nevertheless, it seems that "collective expulsion" is preferably used in a legal context, whereas "mass expulsion" is also relied upon in a broader context, especially by public media,[103] to describe the phenomenon of expelling a large number of people.

5 The Aim and Roadmap of This Book

This book has thus far introduced foundational elements that shape the prohibition of collective expulsion, guided by Hannah Arendt's concept of the "right to have rights". This framework offers a lens to understand both historical and contemporary challenges in protecting migrants' rights, emphasizing the importance of human rights in the context of migration. For this reason, the analysis centers on the evolution of human rights treaty law concerning collective expulsion, a principle that addresses states' obligations to protect individuals from arbitrary removal and blanket denial of entry into a state's territory. This focus on human rights treaty law allows to witness how the evolving legal framework around collective expulsion has been shaped by a fundamental tension between state sovereignty and the protection of individual rights. It is this tension that underscores the critical need for effective redress mechanisms and raises important questions about the role of human rights treaty law in limiting states' discretion in expulsion cases. In this context, key legal questions arise, such as what procedural and substantive rights can individuals invoke when facing collective expulsion? Do regional and international legal frameworks offer consistent protections? How do these frameworks balance the interests of states with the rights of individuals? To address these questions, this book explores the prohibition

---

103 See for example: Alon, Amir *UN human rights experts say mass expulsion violates international law* Ynetnews, 3 March 2018, available at: https://www.ynetnews.com/articles/0,7340,L-5143004,00.html; JapanTimes Myanmar to send envoys to Rohingya camps in Bangladesh to tell refugees they can go home, Japan Times Online, 2 July 2019, referring to *mass expulsion* of the Rohingya, available at: https://www.japantimes.co.jp/news/2019/07/02/asia-pacific/social-issues-asia-pacific/myanmar-send-envoys-rohingya-camps-bangladesh-tell-refugees-can-go-home/.

of collective expulsion within regional and international human rights law, aiming to clarify its role, scope, and relevance across various human rights instruments – both in theory and in practice. Through a thorough analysis of court decisions, third-party interventions, preparatory works, academic scholarship, historical documents, grey literature, and relevant treaties, the book provides a comprehensive examination of how the prohibition functions across different jurisdictions. Despite recent judgments that have renewed attention to the prohibition, it remains relatively underexplored in human rights scholarship. Given its broad protective reach and its role in safeguarding migrants' procedural rights, this limited focus is unjustified. Therefore, this book aims at elevating the principle to the forefront of debate alongside its sister-provision, the *non-refoulement* principle when we talk about removals of foreigners or push-backs. In doing so, throughout this book, I adopt a comparative approach to analyzing the prohibition of collective expulsion, with a particular focus on the European, African, and Inter-American human rights systems. This methodology is rooted in the belief that comparative analysis not only highlights similarities and differences but also fosters mutual learning and judicial dialogue between regional human rights bodies, academics, and practitioners. By focusing on the examination of the jurisprudence of the European Commission and Court of Human Rights, the Inter-American Commission and Court of Human Rights, and the African Commission on Human and Peoples' Rights, this approach seeks to uncover shared principles and innovative practices that can inform and inspire courts, academics, and policymakers beyond their respective regions.

Another crucial aim of this comparative analysis is to encourage a more reciprocal judicial dialogue. As mentioned above, while the African and Inter-American human rights bodies frequently and explicitly refer to ECtHR jurisprudence to develop complementary protections for asylum seekers and migrants, the reverse is less common. The ECtHR rarely engages explicitly with the rich jurisprudence of its sister courts, which limits the potential for cross-regional influence and hinders the development of a cohesive global framework. As former ECtHR President Róbert Spanó acknowledged, it is essential for human rights courts to learn from each other to advance the universal protection of fundamental rights.[104] This chapter aims to promote such dialogue, particularly by spotlighting the Inter-

104 ECtHR *Human rights protection in the time of the pandemic: new challenges and new perspectives* Dialogue between Judges 2022, 2022, available at: https://www.echr.coe.int/documents/d/echr/dialogue_2022_eng, p. 5.

American system, which has emerged as a leader in protecting migrants' rights, even under the pressures of large migration flows and so-called "crises". Moreover, this comparative approach serves to give greater visibility to human rights systems that are often overlooked in Europe and the Global North. Both the African and Inter-American systems have contributed significantly to the evolution of migrants' rights, yet they remain underrepresented in global discussions. By dedicating substantial attention to these systems, this book seeks to challenge Eurocentric perspectives and enrich the broader discourse on the prohibition of collective expulsion. For instance, while the African system presents challenges for analysis due to limited case law and shorter recommendations, it offers valuable insights into the intersection of human rights protections and resource constraints. Similarly, the Inter-American system has demonstrated notable progressiveness in addressing migrants' rights, often outpacing its European counterpart in recent years.[105]

Finally, a comparative analysis is particularly relevant in light of pressing global challenges such as climate-induced migration,[106] which demands coordinated and harmonized legal approaches. The shared goal of all regional human rights bodies – to further and protect human rights – provides a solid foundation for fostering dialogue and developing common standards for the protection of migrants, asylum seekers, and refugees. By examining the African and Inter-American systems alongside the European framework, I hope to start a broader conversation about the role of judicial dialogue in shaping a more unified and effective global response to the challenges of migration and the prohibition of collective expulsion. This endeavor is not only an academic exercise but also a personal commitment to educating myself about underexplored regions and systems, recognizing the value they bring to global human rights law. Despite the challenges of limited resources and case law in some systems, the insights gained from such comparative analyses are invaluable for understanding the nuanced and interconnected nature of human rights protections across borders. With this conclusion on the aim and methodology of the book, I will now turn to

---

105 Cantor, David James and Barichello, Stefania Eugenia *The Inter-American human rights system: a new model for integrating refugee and complementary protection?* The International Journal of Human Rights, Vol. 17, No. 5, 2013, p. 694.

106 For an analysis of a potentially groundbreaking advisory opinion on this matter pending at the IACtHR, see: Riemer, Lena and Scheid, Luca *Leading the WayThe IACtHR's Advisory Opinion on Human Rights and Climate Change* Verfassungsblog, 18 January 2024, available at: https://verfassungsblog.de/leading-the-way/.

the roadmap of the six chapters exploring the prohibition's foundational aspects, analyzing its nature, scope, and legal significance.

In detail, Chapters 2 and 3 form a unit dedicated to the scope of protection under the prohibition of collective expulsion. Chapter 2 addresses its material elements while Chapter 3 focuses on the prohibition's nature as a procedural safeguard against arbitrary group expulsions. Together, these chapters examine the procedural and substantive protections in both regional and international human rights law, assessing the consistency of guarantees across various frameworks. Chapter 4 examines the prohibition within the broader landscape of human rights, particularly as it pertains to migrants. This chapter analyzes its intersection with other rights, including non-refoulement and fair trial guarantees, providing a contextual explanation for the evolving interpretation of the prohibition in relevant treaties. Finally, Chapter 5 summarizes the key insights from each chapter, offering concluding thoughts on the role of the prohibition of collective expulsion within today's complex migration landscape and the ongoing challenge of safeguarding migrant rights in an era of heightened border controls. In sum, this book seeks to illuminate both the legal and practical significance of the prohibition of collective expulsion. It focuses on its development within human rights treaty law to address evolving jurisprudence around the globe closely connected to changing state practices of collective expulsions and denials of entry. It advocates for the prohibition's critical role in protecting vulnerable groups and ensuring fundamental procedural guarantees in an increasingly restrictive global migration context.

CHAPTER 2

Defining the Substance: Key Elements of the Prohibition of Collective Expulsion

After having approached the prohibition of collective expulsion in more general terms including in Chapter 1, this Chapter unpacks the essential components that structure this core principle across various human rights instruments, addressing its scope in terms of persons, subject matter, and place of application. By comparatively analyzing these elements within regional and international conventions, this chapter highlights the commonalities and divergences that shape the prohibition's implementation across different legal frameworks. The latter part of the chapter explores the theoretical dimensions of the prohibition, positioning it as an intersection of individual and collective rights, and assessing how this unique structure informs the balance of state interests with fundamental human rights protections.

In detail, the first section of this chapter begins by defining its personal scope of application (1). Here, the chapter examines which individuals fall under the protection against collective expulsion, providing a foundation for understanding who is safeguarded under this principle and offers a critical assessment of the terminology used in many of its codifications. Moving to the "collective" element (2), the chapter then explores what constitutes a "group" within the meaning of the prohibition, analyzing which factors are essential in establishing the existence thereof in the sense of the prohibition of collective expulsion. This assessment considers both the size and the characteristics of groups covered by the prohibition, alongside contextual factors influencing these determinations. The following section then turns to the "prohibition" element (3), evaluating whether states can justify exceptions or derogations from the principle of non-collective expulsion, and, if so, identifying the specific circumstances under which such deviations may be allowed. This includes a review of relevant legal standards and the degree of flexibility, if any, that may be applied by states in restrictive border contexts. Next, the chapter delves into the term "expulsion" (4), analyzing how courts and treaty bodies interpret this element uniquely across different legal instruments. This part assesses whether "expulsion" strictly refers to the physical removal of a foreigner from a state's territory or if it also includes cases of non-admission. To contextualize these interpretations, the

 | DOI:10.1163/9789004535077_003

section further discusses the broader debate on extraterritorial human rights applicability, comparing different regional and international regimes' approaches to expulsion and non-admission.

The final section of this chapter (5) synthesizes the insights from the examination of each material element and offers conclusions on the prohibition as codified across various regional and international human rights frameworks. This concluding part highlights commonalities and divergences among the instruments and assesses the broader implications for interpreting and enforcing the prohibition in diverse legal contexts.

1 The Definition of the Personal Scope of Protection of the Prohibition of Collective Expulsion

As examined in detail in chapter 1, the prohibition of collective expulsion is commonly codified across regional and international human rights treaties with a brief statement asserting that the collective expulsion of "aliens" is prohibited, seemingly extending protection to all foreign nationals. Before delving into the details on the scope of protection *ratione personae* of the prohibition, I want to first contextualize the decision to avoid the term "alien" in this book, despite its presence in many legal provisions on collective expulsion.[1] This choice reflects a commitment to more humane and accurate language in the discussion of migration and membership. As political theorist Seyla Benhabib argues, the boundaries of political membership often categorize individuals as either members or outsiders, with terms like "alien" underscoring the idea that membership holds value by distinguishing insiders from those perceived as outsiders.[2] This emphasis on exclusion is closely tied to state sovereignty, yet the words chosen in legislation and conventions frame our understanding of non-citizens and can either reinforce or challenge perceptions of difference.

1 Hanaa Hakiki and Delphine Rodnik likewise "avoid using the term "alien", despite its inclusion in the text of the ECHR and frequent use in the Court's jurisprudence, to not replicate its dehumanizing effect on the categorization and perception of non-nationals". See: Hakiki, Hanaa, and Rodnik, Delphine *Accessing borders, accessing justice? The European Court of Human Rights' jurisprudence on pushbacks at land borders* Asyl 1/2023 p. 3–17.

2 Benhabib, Seyla *The Rights of Others: Aliens, Residents and Citizens* (Cambridge University Press 2013), p. 1.

The term "alien", in place of "foreigner", or "non-citizen" carries significant baggage.[3] While "foreigner" implies a simple distinction of nationality or residency, "alien" dehumanizes, conjuring an image of someone inherently different, strange, or out of place due to their perceived "otherness".[4] This is a deliberate framing choice that can shape societal perceptions, making individuals seem as though they do not belong. Therefore, legislators and policymakers who aim to avoid entrenching prejudicial perspectives must consider the implications of such terms. When applied to laws governing migration, admission, and expulsion, the term "alien" often does more than define legal status; it fosters a narrative that positions individuals as fundamentally "other".

This view is supported by scholars such D. Carolina Núñez who argues that the term "alien" perpetuates a framework of exclusion and otherness that can dehumanize and criminalize individuals based on their immigration status.[5] Núñez highlights how "alien" linguistically positions non-citizens as inherently different and, by implication, unwelcome.[6] Besides that "alien" carries associations with threats or enemies, often linked to ideas of invasion or criminality.[7] This framing can evoke hostility, portraying individuals not as participants in a shared social space but as intruders who disrupt it.[8] These concerns are not only found in academia as the ninth report of Rapporteur Maurice Kamto highlights. Kamto highlights in this regard concerns raised by countries like Peru and South Africa[9] over the term's use in the ILC draft articles. Both nations argued that "alien" detracts from the reality that migration law concerns real human beings and, in effect, deflects attention from their rights and humanity.[10] Yet, despite these objections, the ILC maintained its use of "alien", signalling a reluctance to revise its language despite the opportunity to set a more inclusive standard

3 Goodwin-Gil, Guy *Expulsion in Public International Law* UN lecture series, video available at: http://legal.un.org/avl/ls/Goodwin-Gill_IML_video_3.html, from 38:59 min on.

4 *Ibidem.*

5 Núñez, D. Carolina *War of the Words: Aliens, Immigrants, Citizens, and the Language of Exclusion* BYU Law Review, Volume 2013, Issue 6, Discretion & Deference: Immigrants, Citizens, and the Law, pp. 1518–1561.

6 *Ibidem.*, pp. 1525–1528.

7 *Ibidem.*, pp. 1529–1544.

8 *Ibidem.*, pp. 1543–1544.

9 South Africa suggested the use of the term "migrant" or "foreign national" instead, see: United Nations General Assembly *Sixty-seventh session, official records* A/C.6/67/SR.19, 4 December 2012, para. 79.

10 Kamto, Maurice *Ninth report on the expulsion of aliens* A/CN.4/670, 2014, A/CN.4/670 ILC report, A/69/10, 2014, Chap. IV, para. 13–16.

for future discussions stating that even though this debate "is understandably valid, it seems pointless to dwell on this matter[,] which did not give rise to much debate".[11] This decision not to revise the language of the ILC Draft Articles triggered criticism by international law scholar Guy Goodwin-Gill.[12] He argues that although "alien" has historical roots in legal terminology, its continued use is not only outdated but harmful, carrying negative connotations absent in languages like French ("étranger") or German ("Ausländer"), where terms more neutrally signify someone from abroad.[13] According to Goodwin-Gill, non-citizens should not be labelled "aliens" but rather recognized as human beings who possess inherent rights regardless of citizenship.[14] His position emphasizes that framing matters: Language can either affirm the shared humanity of all individuals or, conversely, contribute to their marginalization.

For these reasons, this analysis avoids the term "alien" except when directly referencing legal provisions or original sources. By choosing language that respects the humanity of non-citizens, this book seeks to avoid perpetuating exclusionary narratives that this term implicitly supports. While terms in official texts may remain unaltered here for accuracy, the choice to adopt more inclusive terminology underscores a recognition of the power of language to either humanize or alienate individuals, an awareness essential to discussions of migration, rights, and belonging. After clarifying this important linguistic element, we will now turn to the material content of the prohibition and turn to question who is covered by it?

Even though the text of the provisions containing the prohibition throughout the various conventions and charters does not address explicitly who falls into the category of "alien", case law and interpretations by courts and other bodies clarified that the prohibition indeed applies universally to all foreigners, regardless of their nationality or residency status. At the same time, the protection under these conventions is explicitly limited to foreigners excluding nationals from the prohibition's scope. This limitation is, for example, visible in the European Convention on Human Rights and the EU Charter of Fundamental Rights. The ECHR offers two separate provisions containing guarantees against arbitrary expulsions. Article 3 Protocol 4 ECHR covers nationals, Article 4 Protocol 4 ECHR covers foreigners.

---

11 *Ibidem.*, para. 16.

12 Goodwin-Gil, Guy *Expulsion in Public International Law* UN lecture series, video available at: http://legal.un.org/avl/ls/Goodwin-Gill_IML_video_3.html, from 38:59 min on.

13 *Ibidem.*

14 *Ibidem.*

Only the EU Charter of Fundamental Rights covers both nationals and non-nationals in one provision. This exclusion of nationals from the scope of protection is explained by the fact that in practice expulsion orders are usually guided to non-citizens as most domestic systems prohibit the expulsion of nationals in the first place.[15]

The International Law Commission (ILC) reached a similar conclusion regarding the scope of the prohibition of collective expulsion, affirming that it applies exclusively to foreigners, not nationals, and extending it to stateless persons.[16] This interpretation was reflected in the ILC's 2014 Draft Articles on the Expulsion of Aliens (ILC Draft Articles), marking the culmination of a decade of work by the Commission on this issue.[17] The ILC first added "expulsion of aliens" to its work agenda at its 2830th meeting on August 6, 2004, appointing Maurice Kamto as Special Rapporteur.[18] In 2005, Kamto presented his preliminary report, which provided an outline for the project and identified key issues for further exploration, including the scope of the prohibition against collective expulsion.[19]

In general, Kamto's reports played a significant role in the development of the ILC Draft Articles, examining the prohibition of collective expulsion and its treatment in regional and international treaty law and help us clarify the scope of protection *ratione personae* of the prohibition of collective expulsion. The ILC Draft Articles, under Article 2(b), include "any individual who does not have the nationality (non-nationals and stateless persons) of the State in whose territory he or she is present" into the provision's scope of protection. Article 7 further specifies that the Draft Articles "are without prejudice to the rules of international law relating to stateless persons, and in particular to the rule that a State shall not expel a stateless person lawfully in its territory save on grounds of national security or public order".

---

15 Doehring, Karl *Die Rechtsnatur der Massenausweisung – unter besonderer Berücksichtigung der indirekten Ausweisung* ZaöRV, Issue 45 1985, p. 1.

16 International Law Commission *Draft articles on the expulsion of aliens with commentaries*, adopted by the International Law Commission at its sixty-sixth session, (2014), A/69/10, *Yearbook of the International Law Commission 2011* Vol. II, Part Two, p. 1.

17 The United Nations General Assembly subsequently endorsed the ILC Draft Articles in resolutions passed in 2014 and 2017. However, these draft articles remain provisional, as they have not yet been adopted as an international convention. They are thus binding only to the extent that they codify universally recognized principles of international law.

18 International Law Commission *Yearbook 2004, Vol. II, Part Two*, A/CN.4/SER.A/2004/Add. 1, para. 364.

19 Kamto, Maurice *First report on the expulsion of aliens* A/CN.4/554, ILC Report, A/60/10, (2005), Chap. VIII, paras. 245–274.

This assessment is in line with the personal scope of protection under all regional human rights instruments codifying the prohibition of collective expulsion as the following section will show. The principle in all these instruments extends to stateless persons, migrants, refugees, and asylum seekers without differentiating on the basis of nationality, residency status, or other criteria.

1.1 *The European Convention on Human Rights*

We will now assess the scope of *ratione personae* protection under the prohibition of collective expulsion in the three major regional human rights instruments, beginning with the European frameworks.

While Article 4 Protocol 4 ECHR also speaks of the prohibition of collective expulsion of foreigners, Article 19(1) Charter of Fundamental Rights in the European Union (EUChFR)[20] states that "collective expulsions are prohibited". The latter provision corresponds to the content of Article 4 Protocol 4 ECHR according to the explanations prepared under the authority of the EU's Praesidium of the Convention.[21] The explanations further clarify that the personal scope of protection of Article 19(1) EUChFR is broader than the scope of Article 4 Protocol 4 ECHR and covers foreigners as well as nationals[22] as the scope of protection of Article 19(1) ChFREU is the result of the ECtHR's developing case law.[23] Neither the ECtHR nor the European Commission on Human Rights ever defined foreigner in the sense of Article 4 Protocol 4. ECHR.[24] The ECtHR however has clarified in several cases the

---

20 Charter of Fundamental Rights in the European Union, 2000 O.J.(C 364) 1, Article 47.

21 Praesidium of the Convention *Draft Charter of Fundamental Rights of the European Union explanations* prepared by the Praesidium, Charte 4473/00 Convent 49, p. 21.

22 *Ibidem.* "Its purpose is to guarantee that every decision is based on a specific examination and that no single measure can be taken to expel all persons having the nationality of a particular State (see also Article 13 of the Covenant on Civil and Political Rights)."

23 Guild, Elspeth *Art 19-Protection in the Event of Removal* in: Peers/Hervey/Kenner/Ward (eds.) *The EU Charter of Fundamental Rights A Commentary* (Hart Publishing 2014), para. 19.07.

24 For a recent assessment of the personal scope of application of the prohibition in Article 4 Protocol 4 ECHR, its extraterritorial applicability and its collective nature see: Gatta, Francesco Luigi
The Problematic Management of Migratory Flows in Europe and its Impact on Human Rights: The Prohibition of Collective Expulsion of Aliens in the Case Law of the European Court of Human Rights in: Bruno, Palombino and Di Stefano (eds.) *Migration Issues before International Courts and Tribunals* (Consiglio Nazionale delle Ricerche 2019), pp. 119–146.

question of who is covered by the scope of protection, granting protection to

> all those who have *no actual right to nationality* in a State, whether they are *merely passing through a country* or *reside or are domiciled* in it, whether they are *refugees* or entered the country on their *own initiative*, or whether they are *stateless* or possess *another nationality* [emphasis added].[25]

The term "alien" in the English version or "étranger" in the French version of Article 4 Protocol 4, as well as the Explanatory Report to the Fourth Protocol, show that the scope of protection includes stateless.[26] In February 2020, the Grand Chamber of the ECtHR reiterated and supplemented this statement in *N.D. and N.T. v. Spain* by stating that the prohibition of collective expulsion applies to all foreigners irrespective of the lawfulness of the person's stay, the length of time he or she has spent in the territory, the location in which he or she was apprehended, his or her status as a migrant or an asylum-seeker and his or her conduct when crossing the border.[27]

Furthermore, a comparison of the wording of Article 4 Protocol 4 ECHR and other *Convention* rights, such as the freedom of movement in Article 2 Protocol 4 and Article 1 Protocol 7 shows that the intention of the drafters was to establish a broad personal scope for the prohibition of collective expulsion encompassing *all* migrants.[28] Judge Pinto de Albuquerque, in his concurring opinion in *Hirsi Jamaa and Others v. Italy* acknowledges this difference in scope between the prohibition of collective expulsion and Article 1 Protocol 7 ECHR stating that

> Article 4 of Protocol 4 and Article 1 of Protocol No. 7 are of the same nature: both are due procedure provisions, but they have substantially different personal scope. The due procedure provision of Article 4 of Protocol No. 4 is of much broader personal scope than the one

25 *Hirsi Jamaa and Others v. Italy* [GC] Appl. No. 27765/09, 23 February 2012, para. 174, with references to the *travaux préparatoires* of Protocol No. 4; *Georgia v. Russia I* [GC], (merits), Appl. No. 13255/07, 3 July 2014, para. 168.

26 Praesidium of the Convention *Fundamental Rights Draft Charter explanations* para. 32.

27 *N.D. and N.T. v. Spain* ECtHR, [GC], para. 185.

28 In contrast to Article 4 Protocol 4 ECHR which refers to foreigners in general, Article 2 Protocol 4 speaks of the freedom of movement of persons "lawfully within the territory of a State", and Article 1 Protocol 7 codifies procedural safeguards for "lawfully resident [foreigners] in the territory of a State".

> provided for in Article 1 of Protocol No. 7, since the former includes all aliens regardless of their legal and factual status and the latter includes only aliens lawfully resident in the expelling State.[29]

Here, Judge Pinto de Albuquerque verifies his claim on the broad scope of application *ratione personae* with reference to the case law of the Inter-American Court, the Inter-American Commission, and the African Commission.[30] This approach is remarkable, as the ECtHR in its case law had never before referred to its regional counterparts when interpreting the prohibition of collective expulsion. The African Commission and the Inter-American Court of Human Rights, in contrast, reference the interpretation of the prohibition of collective expulsion of each other and the ECtHR.[31]

In addition, delving deeper into the case law of the ECtHR by assessing the backgrounds of the applicants in collective expulsion cases at the ECtHR, the personal scope of application is once more confirmed. The applicants in cases such as *Čonka v. Belgium*[32], *Sultani v. France*,[33] and *Georgia v. Russia*[34] were lawful residents of the expelling state before their expulsion. In

29 Pinto de Albuquerque, Paulo *Concurring Opinion Hirsi Jamaa and Others v. Italy* section "the prohibition of collective expulsion".

30 Judge Pinto de Albuquerque refers specifically to *Inter-American Court of Human Rights*, Provisional Measures requested by the *Inter-American Commission on Human Rights* in the matter of the Dominican Republic, case of *Haitian and Dominicans of Haitian origin in the Dominican Republic*, order of the court of 18 August 2000, and African Commission on Human and Peoples' Rights, *Rencontre Africaine pour la Défense des Droits de l'Homme v. Zambia*, Communication No. 71/92, October 1996, paragraph 23, and *Union Inter-Africaine des Droits de l'Homme et al. v. Angola*, Communication No. 159/96, 11 November 1997, para. 20.

31 As third-party interventions have submitted reports that summarize in detail the interpretation and findings of the African Commission, the Inter-American Court, the Human Rights Committee and the International Law Commission on the prohibition of collective expulsion, the ECtHR is arguably well aware of thereof even though it does not mention these sources in its judgements. See for example: Third-party interventions by Coordination Francaise pour le droit d' asile, the Mc Gill Centre, the AIRE Centre and ECRE, *Khlaifia and Others v. Italy* ECtHR [GC] Appl. No. 16483/12, 15 December 2016, paras. 230–236.

32 *Čonka v. Belgium* ECtHR, Appl. No. 51564/99, 5 February 2002.

33 *Sultani v. France* ECtHR, Appl. No. 45223/05, 26 September 2007.

34 *Georgia v. Russia I* ECtHR, [GC]. On 31 January 2019, the Grand Chamber of the Court ruled on the question of just satisfaction in accordance with Article 41 ECHR. By sixteen votes to one, the court ruled that Russia had to pay Georgia 10,000,000 EUR in respect of non-pecuniary damage suffered by a group of at least 1,500 Georgian nationals. The amount was ordered to be distributed to the individual victims by paying EUR 2,000 to the Georgian nationals who had been victims only of a violation of Article 4

contrast, the claimants in *Hirsi Jamaa and Others v. Italy*[35] and *Khlaifia and Others v. Italy*,[36] and the applicants in *N.S. and N.D. v. Spain*[37] were irregular migrants and either never reached the expelling state's territory or stayed only for a brief period within the territory. In *Sharifi and Others v. Italy and Greece*, the Court expressly rejected the respondent's claim that the scope of Article 4 Protocol 4 ECHR excludes foreigners that previously entered a member state's territory irregularly.[38]

In conclusion, based on the assessment of the personal scope above, the prohibition of collective expulsion extends to every non-national and stateless person irrespectively of the legality of their stay and the reasons for their movement across borders. In comparison to Article 1 Protocol 7 ECHR or Article 32 *1951 Refugee Convention*, which protect legal residents/refugees against arbitrary expulsion, Article 4 Protocol 4 ECHR is broader in its ambit of protection *ratione personae*. This is one of several reasons why the prohibition of collective expulsion is one of the most relevant minimal protections for all foreigners against arbitrary treatment contained in the European Convention on Human Rights. This is also one of the reasons why the ECtHR has been deemed – at least in the past – as "point of reference for the generous interpretation of human rights".[39]

However, this conclusion warrants a cautious interpretation taking into consideration the Court's jurisprudence since its *Khlaifia* judgment and even more so since *N.D. and N.T.*[40] In its recent case law, the ECtHR has subtly, though not explicitly, signaled a possible shift towards narrowing the scope of Article 4 of Protocol 4 ECHR to prioritize asylum seekers over other categories of non-citizens.[41] Although the wording of Article 4 Protocol 4

Protocol 4 ECHR (collective expulsion), and 10,000 EUR to 15,000 EUR to those who had also been victims of a violation of Article 5(1) (unlawful deprivation of liberty) and Article 3 ECHR (inhuman and degrading conditions of detention), see para. 77.

35 *Hirsi Jamaa and Others v. Italy* [GC].

36 *Khlaifia and Others v. Italy* [GC].

37 *N.D. and N.T. v. Spain* ECtHR, [GC] Appl. Nos. 8675/15 and 8697/15, 13 February 2020.

38 *Sharifi and Others v. Italy and Greece* ECtHR, paras. 210–213.

39 Thym, Daniel *The End of Human Rights Dynamism? Judgments of the ECtHR on 'Hot Returns' and Humanitarian Visas as a Focal Point of Contemporary European Asylum Law and Policy* International Journal of Refugee Law, Vol. 32, Issue 4, December 2020, p. 573.

40 For an analysis of the restrictions on the scope of Article 4 Protocol 4 ECHR and its broader implications at Europe's borders, see: Sardo, Alessio *Border Walls, Pushbacks, and the Prohibition of Collective Expulsions: The Case of N.D. and N.T. v. Spain* European Journal of Migration and Law, Vol. 23, 2021, pp. 308–331.

41 For the same line of argument, see: Kienzle, Isabel and Jonathan Kießling *Evidently unlawful, yet difficult to evidence: M.A. and Z.R. v. Cyprus advances Strasbourg's case*

ECHR refers broadly to all non-citizens regardless of their status, recent cases such as *N.D. and N.T. v. Spain* (GC, 2020) have shown a tendency to distinguish the protection afforded to asylum seekers from that provided to migrants more generally.[42] In this decision, the Strasbourg Court on the one hand stressed that "expulsion" under Article 4 Protocol 4 ECHR includes anyone who was removed

> irrespective of the lawfulness of the person's stay, the length of time he or she has spent in the territory, the location in which he or she was apprehended, his or her status as a migrant or an asylum seeker and his or her conduct when crossing the border.[43]

At the same time, the Court here already seemed to have deemed the fact that "the applicants' complaints under Article 3 ECHR were declared inadmissible by the Chamber",[44] when it assessed an exception to the prohibition as an element in favor of the inapplicability of the protection of Article 4 Protocol 4 ECHR.[45]

Likewise, the Court's approach in subsequent cases such as *A.A. and Others v. North Macedonia*[46] of 2022 *M.A. and Z.R. v. Cyprus*[47] of 2024 suggests an emerging emphasis on asylum claims in the assessment of

---

law on pushbacks Strasbourg Observer, 22 October 2024, available at: https://strasbourgobservers.com/2024/10/22/evidently-unlawful-yet-difficult-to-evidence-m-a-and-z-r-v-cyprus-advances-strasbourgs-case-law-on-pushbacks/.

42 For a critical assessment of the implications of this Grand Chamber judgment for migrants at European borders, see: Raimondo, Giulia *N.D. and N.T. v Spain: A Slippery Slope for the Protection of Irregular Migrants* Border Criminologies Blog, 20 April 2020, available at: https://blogs.law.ox.ac.uk/research-subject-groups/centre-criminology/centreborder-criminologies/blog/2020/04/nd-and-nt-v-spain.

43 ECtHR *N.D. and N.T. v. Spain* [GC], para. 118.

44 *Ibidem.*, para. 206.

45 The Grand Chamber noted in its assessment of whether it was the "culpable conduct" of the applicants that led to the non-examination of their claims that "[i]n any event, the Court observes that the applicants' representatives, both in their written observations and at the Grand Chamber hearing, were unable to indicate the slightest concrete factual or legal ground which, under international or national law, would have precluded the applicants' removal had they been registered individually". Here, the Chamber insinuates that would the applicants have been asylum seekers, the assessment may have differed on the existence of effective and genuine asylum procedures at the Spanish border. See: ECtHR *N.D. and N.T. v. Spain* [GC], para. 230.

46 ECtHR *A.A. and Others v. North Macedonia* Appl. Nos. 55798/16 and 4 others, 5 April 2022.

47 ECtHR *M.A. and Z.R. v. Cyprus* Appl. No. 39090/20, 8 October 2024.

collective expulsion, despite Article 4's lack of an explicit limitation to asylum seekers. In *M.A. and Z.R.*, the Court's reasoning seemingly was influenced by the fact that the applicants had requested asylum, echoing *N.D. and N.T.*'s link between Article 4 and Article 3 of the ECHR, where protection against collective expulsion under Article 4 was tied to preventing risks of ill-treatment.[48] In *M.A. and Z.R.*, the Court found that the applicants' return from Cyprus constituted an "expulsion" carried out without individual assessments, yet the decisive factor bolstering their complaint was their status as asylum seekers.[49] The judgment further refined the "own culpable conduct" exception from *N.D. and N.T.*, applied when individuals bypass genuinely accessible legal entry routes.[50] Here, the Court rejected the argument that the applicants could have applied for an entry visa, noting that this option was neither genuine nor effective for asylum-seeking applicants.[51] This contrasts with cases where economic migrants, as in *N.D. and N.T.*, or foreigners in transit, as in *A.A. v. North Macedonia*, were deemed able to access other entry channels.[52] Such reasoning underscores the Court's focus on asylum-seeking status in assessing entry accessibility, raising questions on how this approach might shift if applicants' asylum status were less evident. This approach contributes to a widening gap in the Court's treatment of collective expulsion claims involving asylum seekers versus those involving other migrants, as demonstrated by *M.A. v. Latvia*, where potential asylum seekers were unsuccessful in their claim due to insufficient proof of having requested asylum at the border.[53]

1.2 *The African Charter on Human and Peoples's Rights*

Turning now to the African Charter, we find that its personal scope of protection is even broader than that of the ECHR, offering a more inclusive framework that does not reflect the restrictive tendencies seen in recent ECtHR interpretations. A draft version of Article 12(5), which contains the

48 *Ibidem.*, para. 87.

49 *Ibidem.*, paras. 65, 80.

50 ECtHR, *M.A. and Z.R. v. Cyprus* paras. 117–119.

51 *Ibidem.*, para. 117.

52 ECtHR *AA. and Others v. North Macedonia* para. 121. However, and as an important clarification to *A.A. and Others v. North Macedonia*, the ECtHR stressed in *J.A. and Others v. Italy* of 2023, that transiting a country without seeking protection there does not "free" a state from its obligation to conduct individual assessments. Here, the Court underscored that procedural safeguards must apply even if individuals do not intend to seek asylum in the host country. See: ECtHR *J.A. and Others v. Italy* Appl. No. 21329/18, 30 June 2023, paras. 107–116.

53 ECtHR *M.A. and Others v. Latvia* Appl. No. 25564/18, 29 March 2022, paras. 63–69.

prohibition, was even more extensive in its protection covering all forms of mass expulsion without exception.[54] The personal scope of protection against mass expulsion in Article 12(5) African Charter on Human and Peoples' Rights as interpreted by the African Commission on Human and Peoples' Rights (AComHPR) is even more extensive than Article 4 Protocol 4 ECHR.

The African Union Migration Policy Framework for Africa and the Plan of Action (2018–2030) highlights the ongoing importance of this provision for all foreigners stating that

> [h]istorically, migrants have often been deprived of their rights and subjected to discriminatory and racist actions and policies including xenophobia, exploitation, mass expulsion, persecution, and other abuses. Safeguarding the human rights of migrants implies the effective application of norms enshrined in human rights instruments of general applicability, as well as the ratification and enforcement of instruments specifically relevant to the treatment of migrants.[55]

As mentioned in chapter 1 and as will be shown in more detail in chapter 3, the prohibition of "mass expulsion" in the African Charter differs in its wording from its regional counterparts. However, the African Commission on Human and Peoples' Rights has complemented the scope of protection of the prohibition in several cases, converging its scope with that of its counterparts. The African Commission, together with the African Court on Human and Peoples' Rights, now named the African Court of Justice and Human Rights were created to monitor and protect the functions of the African Charter.[56] The Court delivered its first judgment in 2013 but, at the time of writing, had not yet examined any case of mass expulsion.[57] When it comes to the rights of non-citizens, the Special Rapporteur on Refugees, Asylum Seekers, Internally Displaced Persons and Migrant in Africa,

---

54 Murray, Rachel *The African Charter on Human and Peoples' Rights: A Commentary* (Oxford University Press 2019), p. 335.

55 African Union *Migration Policy Framework for Africa and the Plan of Action (2018–2030)* 2018, available at: https://au.int/sites/default/files/documents/35956-doc-au-mpfa-executive-summary-eng.pdf, p. 71.

56 The mandate of the Commission is to be found in Articles 45 ACHPR ff., the functions of the Court are to be found in Article 2 Protocol on the Statute of the African Court of Justice and Human Rights.

57 For all decisions by the Court, see its database available at: https://www.african-court.org/cpmt/.

established in 2004, is tasked to focus on these groups and seek, receive, examine, and act upon violations of their rights.[58] As neither the Court, nor the Special Rapporteur have addressed the prohibition of "mass expulsion" in the African Charter, the subsequent analysis is limited to the Commission's jurisprudence.

As Rachel Murray notes, although "the position of refugees was placed on the African Commission on Human and Peoples' Rights' agenda from a very early stage" and even led to a dedicated conference, the Commission initially paid limited attention to their situation.[59] Similarly, the prohibition of collective expulsion under the African Charter, much like that under the ECHR, remained largely dormant in practice; it was only in 1996 that the Commission decided its first case addressing this issue. Nevertheless, since the Commission's inauguration, it has examined a total of five cases regarding allegations of mass expulsions of non-nationals since then.[60] These

58 The Special Rapporteur on Refugees, Asylum Seekers and Internally Displaced Persons was established by the ACHPR at its 35th Ordinary Session, 21 May to 4 June 2004. Resolution 72 adopted at the 36th Ordinary Session, 23 November – 7 December 2004, laid out the mandate of the Special Rapporteur, which calls for him or her to *inter alia* seek, receive, examine, and act upon the situation of refugees, asylum seekers and internally displaced persons in Africa; undertake studies, research and other related activities to examine appropriate ways to enhance the protection of refugees, asylum seekers, and internally displaced persons; undertake fact-finding missions, investigations, and visits to refugee camps and camps for internally displaced persons; assist Member States of the African Union to develop appropriate policies, regulations and laws for the effective protection of refugees, asylum seekers, and internally displaced persons; etc. Resolution 95 of the 39th Ordinary Session, held in Banjul, in May 2006, extended the mandate of the Special Rapporteur to also include migration issues. For details and all reports and resolutions see: ACHPR *Special Rapporteur on Refugees, Asylum Seekers, Internally Displaced Persons and Migrant in Africa* available at: https://achpr.au.int/en/mechanisms/special-rapporteur-refugees-asylum-seekers-internally-displaced-persons-and-migrant.

59 Murray, Rachel *Refugees and Internally Displaced Persons and Human Rights: The African System Refugee* Survey Quarterly, Vol. 24, No. 2, 2005, p. 58.

60 The first case was *Organisation Mondiale Contre la Torture and Others v. Rwanda* dealt with mass expulsions of Burundian Refugees from Rwanda, ACHPR, 27/89-46/91-49/91-99/93, 1996. The Commission found Rwanda to have violated the African Charter, namely of the right to respect for one's life and integrity, the right to the respect of the dignity inherent in a human being and to the recognition of his legal status, the right to liberty and security, the right to have one's case heard, the right to seek asylum, the right to a decision before being expelled and the prohibition of mass expulsion (enshrined in Articles 4, 5, 6, 7, 12(3) and 12(4) and 12(5) of the Charter) The Commission then urged the government of Rwanda to adopt measures in conformity with this decision. The second case was *Rencontre Africaine pour la Défense des Droits de l'Homme v. Zambia* AComHPR, Communication 71/92, 1996. Here, the

cases assessed jointly offer insight into the African Commission's interpretation of the prohibition of mass expulsion. This assessment reveals that the Commission interpreted the provision in Article 12(5) ACHPR's scope of protection in a manner approximating that of its regional counterparts, in particular Article 4 Protocol 4 ECHR.

At first sight, the personal scope of Article 12(5) ACHPR resembles its counterpart in the EU Charter of Fundamental Rights covering both nationals and foreigners. The wording of Article 12(5) ACHPR only explicitly refers to the prohibition of expulsion of "non-nationals". However, through interpretation, the African Commission expanded the scope of protection *ratione personae* to nationals and foreigners alike.[61] The Commission held in its *Rencontre Africaine pour la Défense des Droits de l'Homme v. Zambia* decision that states ought "to secure the rights protected in the Charter to all persons within their jurisdiction, nationals or non-nationals".[62]

Another closely connected question is the list of prohibited reasons for discrimination in Article 12(5) ACHPR. Comparing the explicit attributes of discrimination in the general prohibition in Article 2 and Article 12(5) ACHPR, the list in Article 2 is considerably broader at first sight. Article 2 ACHPR prohibits *inter alia* discrimination based on colour, sex, language, and political opinion, mentioning explicitly "all forms of discrimination" and only lists some attributes that are "particularly" noteworthy, indicating that the list is not exhaustive. In contrast, the list in Article 12(5) ACHPR appears to be self-contained.[63] However, despite its narrow wording, the

---

Commission found that the expulsion of 517 West Africans from Zambia violated the prohibition of mass expulsion.

The third case was *Union Inter Africaine des Droits de l'Homme, Fédération Internationale des Ligues des Droits de l'Homme and Others v. Angola, African Commission on Human and Peoples' Rights* ACHRR, Comm. No. 159/96, 1997. The fourth case was *African Institute for Human Rights and Development v. Guinea* ACHPR, 2004 and the final case *Institute for Human Rights and Development in Africa v. Republic of Angola* ACHPR, Communication 292/2004 23rd and 24th Activity Reprot of the ACPR, Annex II, 2008.

61 Olaniyan, Kolawole *Civil and Political Rights in the African Charter: Articles 8–14* in: Evans and Murray *The African Charter on Human and Peoples' Rights: The System in Practice 1986–2006* (Cambridge University Press 2008), p. 232.

62 *Rencontre Africaine pour la Défénse des Droits de l'Homme v. Zambia* AComHPR, Communication 71/92, October 1996, para. 22.

63 The wording of Article 12(5), second sentence ACHPR suggests that it only prohibits mass of foreigners based on nationality, race, ethnicity or religion. The provision stipulates: "Mass expulsion shall be that which is aimed at national, racial, ethnic or religions [sic!] groups".

Commission expanded this list of grounds in *Union Inter-Africaine des Droits de l'Homme and others v. Angola*. It explicitly stipulated that Article 12(5) ACHPR applies to "any category of persons, whether on the basis of nationality, religion, ethnic, racial, or other considerations".[64] This clarification combined the prohibited reasons for discrimination of Article 12(5) ACHPR and Article 2 ACHPR.

This finding is in line with the approach taken by the African Commission in all five cases on mass expulsion. In all of them, the African Commission found a violation of both provisions. In *Malawi African Association and Others v. Mauritania*, the Commission held that Article 2 ACHPR lays down a principle that is essential to the spirit of this convention, one of whose goals is the elimination of all forms of discrimination and to ensure equality amongst all human beings.'[65] The African Commission's approach to extent the list of attributes in Article 12(5) ACHPR in accordance with Article 2 ACHPR reflects its commitment to protecting the Charter's essential principle to prohibit any form of discrimination. This combined approach is of particular importance as in past decades, there have been reports on mass expulsions from several African states based on unemployment, increased crime rates, and even as the result of unfavourable football matches.[66] To ensure that all possible reasons for mass expulsions of foreigners are covered by the prohibition in Article 12(5) ACHPR, the scope of protection ought to be as broad and flexible as in Article 2 ACHPR. In conclusion, the scope of protection *ratione personae* of the prohibition of mass expulsion in the African Charter is thus congruent with its regional counterparts.

1.3 *The Inter-American Convention on Human Rights*

The same is true regarding the personal scope of protection of the prohibition in Article 22(9) Inter-American Convention as interpreted by the Inter-American Commission and Court. Like its ECHR counterpart, the provision states that "the collective expulsion of aliens is prohibited".[67] Besides

---

64 *Fédération Internationale des Ligues des Droits de l'Homme v. Angola* AComHPR, para. 17.

65 *Malawi African Association and others v. Mauritania* AComHPR Communications 54/91, 61/91, 164/97-196/97, 210/98, Thirteenth Activity Report 1999–2000, Annex V, para. 131.

66 Umozurike, Oji *The African Charter on Human and Peoples' Rights* (Nigerian Institute of Advanced Legal Studies 1992), p. 7.

67 For a comprehensive commentary on the IACHR in Spanish see: Steiner, Christian and Uribe, Patricia (eds.) *Convención Americana sobre Derechos Humanos comentada* (Suprema Corte de la Nación (México) and Konrad Adenauer Foundation 2014). A

this prohibition, Article 22 Inter-American Convention on Human Rights (IACHR) also guarantees the freedom of movement and residence of "every person".

The IACHR, also known as the "Pact of San José",[68] was adopted on 22 November 1969 in San José, the capital of Costa Rica. The Convention entered into force only nine years after its adoption with the eleventh ratification by Grenada on 18 July 1978. As of December 2024, 23 states are parties to the Convention. Trinidad and Tobago[69] and Venezuela,[70] both former member states, have withdrawn from the instrument.[71] Others, such as the United States[72] have signed but never ratified it, while some, such as Belize, Canada, and Guyana, have done neither.

In contrast to its European counterpart, the prohibition in the Inter-American Convention has played a smaller role in the case law on violations of the Pact of San José. As of January 2025, the Inter-American Court of Human Rights (Corte Interamericana de Derechos Humanos), also based in San José, has only dealt with the prohibition of collective expulsion in its case law in one advisory opinion and a few cases, the last of 2016.[73]

---

commentary on the prohibition of collective expulsion is found therein by Rodrigo Uprimny Yepes and Luz María Sánchez Duque, pp. 550–551.

68 UN registration on August 27, 1979, No. 17955.

69 Trinidad and Tobago's withdrawal became effective on 26 May 1999 over a query on the death penalty, OAS *Press release* E-056/99ie, 26 May 1999, available at: http://www.oas.org/OASpage/press2002/en/Press99/0526991.htm.

70 Former president Hugo Chavez announced the withdrawal on the basis of the governments dissatisfaction of certain decisions of the Inter-American Court of Human Rights, see: Ku, Julian *Venezuela Formally Withdraws from American Convention on Human Rights, Blames the U.S.* OpinioJuris, 11 September 2013, available at: http://opiniojuris.org/2013/09/11/venezuela-formally-withdraws-american-convention-human-rights-blames-u-s/.

71 List of signatures and ratifications provided by the *Inter-American Commission on Human Rights,* available here: https://www.cidh.oas.org/basicos/english/Basic4.Amer.Conv.Ratif.htm.

72 Interestingly, the USA were part of the Conferencia Especializada Interamericana Sobre Derechos Humanos that drafted the Convention. The representative also offered observations on the Human Rights project as can be seen in the *travaux préparatoires* of the Convention. Organization of American States (OAS), *Conferencia Especializada Interamericana Sobre Derechos Humanos*, San José, Costa Rica, OEA/Ser.K/XVI/1.2, pp. 7–22 November 1969, pp. 92–98. The documents do not give any indicator as to the unwillingness of the USA to become a state party in the future.

73 For a holistic database on the jurisprudence and relevant documents related to migration, asylum and the prohibition of collective expulsion, see the Court's official

Nevertheless, the Court has demonstrated a notably progressive approach to protecting migrants' rights. Unlike the ECtHR, which often views migrants primarily as "foreigners" within the framework of state sovereignty, the Inter-American system emphasizes the human dignity of migrants, treating them first and foremost as human beings.[74] This fundamental difference in perspective shapes the Inter-American Court's jurisprudence, particularly in its robust application of due process guarantees to asylum and migration cases.[75] As Cantor and Barichello highlight, the Inter-American system consistently applies Articles 8(1) and 25 ACHR to claims for asylum, extending due process rights and judicial protection to migrants.[76] Moreover, the system has established that legal aid must be provided when necessary to ensure effective access to justice, especially in cases involving the risk of *refoulement*.[77] Besides, by prioritizing equality and the principle of *jus cogens*, as seen in Advisory Opinions 16/99 and 18/03, the IACourtHR's jurisprudence sets a high standard for the treatment of migrants, ensuring that their rights are fully respected even in contexts of heightened state control.[78]

This commitment to viewing migrants as rights-bearers rather than merely as outsiders exemplifies the potential of the Inter-American system to lead in the development of progressive norms for migration governance – especially in a time in which the ECtHR seemingly takes a continuously regressive stance on migrants' rights restricting the scope of protection of the prohibition of collective expulsion.

Returning to the Inter-American Court, the following section will first provide some context of its functions and role before turning to its most relevant jurisprudence on the prohibition of collective expulsion. Starting with its functions, it is relevant to highlight that the Court is tasked with monitoring, interpreting, and applying the IACHR. As a human rights tribunal, it

---

jurisprudence database: https://jurisprudencia.corteidh.or.cr/search/jurisdiction:EA/expulsi%C3%B3n+colectiva.

74 Dembour, Marie-Bénédicte *When Humans Become Migrants Study of the European Court of Human Rights with an Inter-American Counterpoint* (Oxford University Press 2015), pp. 283–312.

75 Cantor, David James and Barichello, Stefania Eugenia *The Inter-American human rights system: a new model for integrating refugee and complementary protection?* The International Journal of Human Rights, Vol. 17, No. 5, 2013, p. 694.

76 *Ibidem.*

77 *Ibidem.*

78 Dembour, Marie-Bénédicte *When Humans Become Migrants Study of the European Court of Human Rights with an Inter-American Counterpoin*, p.312.

has jurisdiction over the American Convention on Human Rights, as well as other treaties adopted within the Inter-American system. Its functions range from interpreting and applying the Convention (Article 62(1)), adjudicating cases, issuing provisional measures (Article 63) to providing advisory opinions (Article 64). If deemed necessary, it can rule on remedies in case of violations of the Convention per Articles 62 and 63 IACHR.

Interestingly and also relevant for the purpose of our analysis, the Court's advisory function[79] is quite extensive[80] (Article 64 IACHR) and in the Court's view binding on its members.[81] The advisory function goes beyond the regionally applicable treaties and extends to "other treaties [emphasis added] concerning the protection of human rights in the American States". The Court has made extensive use of this broad approach, turning to other courts' or treaty bodies' interpretations as well as to international human rights instruments to interpret the Convention "regardless of the principal purpose of such a treaty and whether or not non-Member States of the Inter-American system are or have the right to become parties thereto".[82]

Under Article 61(1) of the Inter-American Convention only member states and the Inter-American Commission on Human Rights can bring

79 For a holistic analysis on this function of the Court in all its dimensions, historial context, evolution, and current debates, see: Benz, Eleanor *The Advisory Function of the Inter-American Court of Human Rights* (Nomos 2024).

80 Advisory opinions have historically played a significant role, with the Court issuing eight advisory opinions within its first eight years after its establishment in 1979, while not deciding a single contentious case. This initial popularity of the advisory tool faded towards the mid-1980s until it regained popularity in 2017 when the Court wowed the world with its Advisory Opinion 23. The opinion acknowledged extraterritorial jurisdiction for transboundary environmental harm; the autonomous right to a healthy environment; and state responsibility for environmental damage. The currently pending opinion is intended to build on this by further strengthening the link between the protection of the environment and respect for human rights. See: Riemer and Scheid *Leading the Way The IACtHR's Advisory Opinion on Human Rights and Climate Change* Verfassungsblog, 2024.

81 Remarkably, and in contrast to the International Court of Justice, for example, the IACtHR's advisory opinions have a strong legal effect on state parties. The Court indicated that all member states should follow its proclaimed opinions as it has "undeniable legal effects" (see: "The Right to Information on Consular Assistance in the Framework of the Guarantees of the Due Process of Law", OC-16/99, para 48). Moreover, while the Convention itself does not expressly state the opinions' bindingness, the Court stressed that states must act per its interpretations (see, e.g., *Almonacid-Arellano et al. v. Chile*, para 124). See: Riemer and Scheid *Leading the Way The IACtHR's Advisory Opinion on Human Rights and Climate Change* Verfassungsblog, 2024.

82 *"Other Treatie" Subject to the Consultative Jurisdiction of the Court* Advisory Opinion, IACourtHR, OC-1/82, requested by Peru, 24 September 1982, p. 12.

cases to the Inter-American Court of Human Rights, while the power to request advisory opinions is limited to member states under Article 64(1). In contrast, individuals and groups of people have the right to lodge complaints directly with the Inter-American Commission on Human Rights,[83] based in Washington, D.C., as provided by Article 44 of the IACHR. Together, the Court and the Commission monitor member states' compliance with the Inter-American Convention, as outlined in Article 33. The Commission, in particular, has a broad mandate that includes promoting human rights awareness (Article 41(a)), issuing recommendations to member state governments (Article 41(b)), conducting studies and reports (Article 41(c)), requesting information on measures adopted by governments (Article 41(d)), providing advisory services (Article 41(e)), acting on petitions and other communications (Article 41(f)), and submitting annual reports to the General Assembly of the Organization of American States (Article 41(g)). This comprehensive set of functions enables the Commission to play a central role in advancing and safeguarding human rights across the Americas.

Relating to the rights of foreigners, the Court importantly declared in its 2003 Advisory Opinion *The Juridical Condition and Rights of Undocumented Migrants* that the fundamental principle of equality and non-discrimination as *jus cogens* norms in international law and affirmed that these principles apply fully to migrants, regardless of their legal status.[84] With direct reference to the prohibition of collective expulsion, the Court held that every foreigner enjoys the right to an individualized examination of their claims before an expulsion.[85] As this opinion shows, when it comes to the personal scope of protection of the prohibition of collective expulsion, the Court explicitly followed the approach of the ECtHR in interpreting the prohibition. This is also true regarding the approach of the Inter-American Commission. In *Nadege Dorzema and Others v. Dominican Republic*, the Court

83 See for example: IAComHR *Second Progress Report of the Rapporteurship on Migrant Workers and Members of Their Families in the Hemisphere*, para. 97.5. Also: IAComHR *Benito Tide Méndez et al. (Dominican Republic) Report on the Merits No. 64/12* Case 12.271, 29 March 2012, para. 253 and IAComHR *Annual Report of the Inter-American Commission on Human Rights 1991* OEA/Ser.L/V/II.81 Doc. 6, rev. 1, February 14, 1992. Chapter V: Situation of Haitians in the Dominican Republic. Also: IAComHR *Report on the Situation of Human Rights in the Dominican Republic* OEA/Ser. L/V/II.104 Doc. 49 rev. 1, October 7, 1999, para. 366.

84 *The Juridical Condition and Rights of Undocumented Migrants* Advisory Opinion, IACourtHR OC-18/03, requested by México, 17 September 2003, paras. 97–101.

85 *Ibidem.*, para. 21.

stated that the prohibition of collective expulsion must apply to **all foreigners**, irrespective of the legality of their stay.[86] The Court further highlighted that no distinction in the proceedings should be made "on grounds of nationality, color [sic!], race, sex, language, religion, political opinion, social origin or other status."[87]

It can be inferred from this that Article 22(9) IACHR protects all collectively expelled foreigners, including stateless persons, migrants, asylum seekers, and refugees, that is, individuals with and without a valid residence permit. The scope of protection *ratione personae* is thus congruent among all regional human rights instruments in as far as these groups of foreigners are covered.[88] It is noteworthy that the Inter-American Court of Human Rights, in both its 2003 Advisory Opinion and its case law, emphasizes the intrinsic relationship between the prohibition of collective expulsion and the prohibition of discrimination. By declaring equality and non-discrimination as *jus cogens* norms, the Court underscores that all foreigners, regardless of their legal status, are entitled to individualized assessments before expulsion, thereby ensuring protection against discriminatory practices. This link was further reinforced in *Nadege Dorzema and Others v. Dominican Republic*, where the Court explicitly stated that the prohibition of collective expulsion applies universally, prohibiting distinctions based on nationality, race, or other status in expulsion proceedings. As shown above, this integrative approach closely mirrors the African human rights system, which similarly connects these principles by prohibiting "mass" expulsions targeting specific groups based on discriminatory grounds.

In contrast, as will be shown in Chapters 3 and 4, the European Court of Human Rights has traditionally framed the prohibition of collective expulsion as a due process right which prevents arbitrary expulsions, often overlooking its deep connection to non-discrimination. The Inter-American system's recognition of this linkage not only strengthens the procedural guarantees for migrants but also aligns the prohibition with broader human rights principles. This more holistic approach offers additional protection for vulnerable populations – that often face discriminatory policies in the migration and expulsion context. Due to this, such a linkage serves as a compelling example of where the ECtHR could benefit from turning to its sister courts in Africa and Latin America, to adopt a

86 *Nadege Dorzema and others v. Dominican Republic Merits, Reparations and Costs* IACourtHR, Judgment of 24 October 2012, Series C, No. 251, paras. 156–159.

87 *Nadege Dorzema v. Dominican Republic* IACourtHR, para. 175.

88 The African Charter goes beyond this in its application by also covering nationals.

more holistic interpretation that fully integrates the prohibition of collective expulsion with the principle of non-discrimination. This more inclusive approach arguably would do justice to the realities at European borders.[89]

With these findings, we turn to two regional human rights conventions that receive little attention in academia and practice but that likewise contain the prohibition of collective expulsion, these are the Arab Charter on Human Rights and the Commonwealth of Independent States Convention on Human Rights and Fundamental Freedoms.

1.4 *The Arab Charter on Human Rights and the Commonwealth of Independent States Convention on Human Rights and Fundamental Freedoms*

The Arab Charter on Human Rights (2004) is both the most recent and one of the most debated regional human rights instruments.[90] After significant revisions to the 1994 version, which never entered into force due to insufficient ratifications, the updated Charter became effective in 2008.[91] As of December 2024, sixteen states are parties to the Charter: Algeria, Bahrain, Egypt, Iraq, Jordan, Kuwait, Lebanon, Libya, Mauritania, Palestine, Qatar, Saudi Arabia, Sudan, Syria, the United Arab Emirates, and Yemen. Notably, Syria has been suspended from the organization since 2011.[92] To monitor compliance with the Charter, the 2004 version established the Arab Human Rights Committee. This body reviews state reports submitted one year after

89 For criticism of the European Courts' "blind eye" on issues like colonialism, racism, etc., see: de Vries, Karin and Spijkerboer, Thomas *Race and the Regulation of International Migration. The Ongoing Impact of Colonialism in the Case Law of The European Court of Human Rights* Netherlands Quarterly of Human Rights, Vol. 39, No. 4, 2021, pp. 291–307 or Spijkerboer, Thomas *Bifurcation of People, Bifurcation of Law: Externalization of Migration Policy before the EU Court of Justice* Journal of Refugee Studies, Vol. 31, No. 2, 2018, pp. 216–239.

90 See for example: Allam, Wael *The Arabic charter on human rights: Main features* Arab Law Quarterly, 2014, Vol. 28, No. 1, pp. 57–63. Also: Osterhaus, Juliane *The Arab Human Rights System* Deutsche Gesellschaft für Internationale Zusammenarbeit and Deutsches Institut für Menschenrechte, 2017, pp. 2–3. Also, in 2015, the International Commission of Jurists called on member states of the Arab League of States not to ratify the Statute of the Arab Court of Human Rights unless and until it is comprehensively amended. ICJ *Arab Court of Human Rights: comprehensive amendments required before ratification* 8 April 2015, available at: https://www.icj.org/arab-court-of-human-rights-comprehensive-amendments-required-before-ratification-new-report/.

91 Osterhaus, Juliane *The Arab Human Rights System* p. 2.

92 International Justice Resource Center *Middle East and North Africa* January 2021, available at: https://ijrcenter.org/regional/middle-east-and-north-africa/.

ratification and subsequently every three years.[93] However, it does not have the authority to receive individual or inter-state complaints.

When it comes to the prohibition of collective expulsion, it is noteworthy that the initial 1994 version of the Charter did not address it. Only the 2004 revision explicitly incorporated this principle in Article 26(2), stating that "[c]ollective expulsions are prohibited in all cases". The wording of this provision suggests a broad scope of protection, encompassing all foreigners regardless of their residency status. Despite this, available sources, such as monitoring reports or information from the official website, are exclusively in Arabic, which the author does not speak, and are limited in scope, leaving key interpretive questions unanswered.[94] Translated summaries of these reports fail to shed further light on the personal scope of the prohibition or other interpretive aspects. Consequently, the effectiveness of the prohibition of collective expulsion under the Arab Charter remains ambiguous and underexplored.

Comparable challenges exist when it comes to the assessment of the Commonwealth of Independent States Convention on Human Rights and Fundamental Freedoms (Commonwealth Human Rights Convention, CHRC).[95] The CHRC, to which only four CIS states are parties as of December 2024, explicitly contains the prohibition of collective expulsion in Article 25(4). This provision states that the '[c]ollective expulsion of aliens shall be prohibited.' The Human Rights Commission of the Commonwealth of Independent States (HRC CIS) is tasked with monitoring the implementation of the Convention under Article 34. However, this provision does not specify the Commission's powers or clarify who can bring forward claims. As of December 2024, the Commission has not officially commenced its monitoring work.[96] Moreover, publicly available information about the Commission and the Convention is exclusively in Russian, limiting broader analysis and accessibility.[97]

93 Allam, Wael *The Arabic charter on human rights: Main features* pp. 62–63.

94 The English version of the official webpage of the League of Arab States is under construction and thus also not available, see: http://www.leagueofarabstates.net/ar/Pages/default.aspx.

95 I would like to thank Vitaly Beloborodov for helping me translate and navigate the documents relating to the Commonwealth Convention.

96 Huntley, Svetlana *The CIS Human Rights Court: a possible alternative to the ECHR?* ECHR and Promotion of Human Rights in Russia, 5 October 2011, available at: http://echrrussia.blogspot.com/2011/10/cis-human-rights-court-possible.html.

97 Commonwealth of Independent States *official webpage* available at: http://cis.minsk.by/page.php?id=11326.

The wording of the provision codifying the prohibition of collective expulsion suggests that its scope extends to all foreigners, regardless of their legal status within member states. However, a review of Russian-language sources, such as Commission reports, provides no additional insight into how this interpretation or other elements of the prohibition are understood. Consequently, this thesis emphasizes a detailed examination of the prohibition in other human rights instruments where more comprehensive information is available. Nevertheless, future research is necessary to comprehensively analyze the prohibition of collective expulsion under the Arab Charter and the CIS Human Rights Convention, particularly to clarify their scope, interpretive frameworks, and practical implementation. Such an examination could, for example, address not only the prohibition of collective expulsion but also existing gaps in accessibility, monitoring mechanisms, and the broader implications for regional human rights protection.

With this call for further research into the Arab Charter and the CIS Human Rights Convention, we will now leave the regional level and turn to the international level to examine the differences and similarities of the personal scope of protection of the prohibition of collective expulsion starting with the UN Migrant Worker Convention.

1.5 *The Migrant Worker Convention*

As a starting point, the Convention, its scope, and even its existence deserve a closer look before we delve into its approach to the prohibition of collective expulsion as it counts with some particular features and is contested to this day. This debate is already reflected in the Convention's rocky start in the 1970s when only after the economic downturn states and other actors realized that international and bilateral agreements regulating employment migration were not sufficient to protect all migrants against abuse and discrimination.[98] The goal to protect migrants with irregular statuses turned out to be particularly contentious amongst participating states, leading to a drafting process lasting from 1980 to 1990.[99] Finally, in December 1990, the United Nations General Assembly adopted the International Convention on the Protection of the Rights of All Migrant Workers and Members of Their Families (UNCRMW), which was opened for signature by all member

98 European Parliament Directorate-General for External Policies *Current Challenges in the Implementation of the UN International Convention on the Protection of the Rights of all Migrant Workers and Members of their Families* EXPO/B/DROI/2013/05, 2013, p. 6.

99 Office of the United Nations High Commissioner for Human Rights *Travaux Préparatoires of Part III of the Convention* 2003, p.1.

states. Despite its early adoption, the Convention only entered into force in July 2003 due to missing ratifications. As of January 2025, 60 states have ratified the Convention, with an additional 20 states having signed it,[100] all of them of the Global South.

Another remarkable element of the UNCRMW is its broad personal scope of protection. Article 1(1) clarifies that the rights and guarantees of the convnetion apply to "all migrant workers and members of their families without distinction of any kind". Subparagraph 2 further clarifies that this protection extends to the entire migration process, including preparation, departure, transit, stay, remunerated activity in the state of employment, and return. Article 2(1) complements this provision by defining a "migrant worker" as "a person who is to be engaged, is engaged or has been engaged in a remunerated activity in a State of which he or she is not a national". While the Convention broadly protects both documented and undocumented migrant workers and their families – which in itself is a fact worth highlighting, certain rights are reserved exclusively for documented migrants. For instance, the right to form associations and trade unions (Article 40) and the right to participate in public affairs and elections in their country of origin (Article 44) are limited to those with regular residence status. These distinctions reflect the UNCRMW's attempt to balance its inclusive approach with the principle of state sovereignty over immigration control.

Importantly, Article 22(1) UNCRMW, which codifies the prohibition of collective expulsion, is not subject to such limitations. This provision applies universally to all migrant workers and their families, regardless of their residence status. The broad application of this guarantee has been explicitly recognized by the Migrant Worker Committee (CMW), the independent body monitoring the implementation of the Convention. In General Comment No. 2, the Committee affirmed that Article 22(1) guarantees procedural safeguards against collective expulsion for both regular and irregular migrants and their families.[101] This inclusive approach underscores the Convention's commitment to ensuring basic human rights protections for all migrants, irrespective of their legal status. By extending procedural safeguards to both documented and undocumented individuals, Article 22(1) reinforces the principle that no person should be subjected to arbitrary or collective expulsion without due process.

---

100 *Ibidem.*

101 CMW *General comment No. 2 on the rights of migrant workers in an irregular situation and members of their families* (2013), CMW/C/GC/2, 28 August 2013, para. 49.

Despite the broad procedural guarantees provided under Article 22(1) UNCRMW, its personal scope appears narrower compared to other human rights instruments analyzed, as it explicitly applies only to "migrant workers and their families". This limitation is further clarified in Article 3 UNCRMW, which explicitly excludes refugees and stateless persons unless their inclusion is provided for by relevant national legislation or applicable international instruments. Consequently, the protection offered by the prohibition of collective expulsion under the UNCRMW does not extend to these vulnerable groups, creating a notable gap in its protective framework. The exclusion of refugees and stateless persons raises important questions about the intent behind the drafting of the Convention. Unfortunately, the *travaux préparatoires* provide no insight into the rationale for this exclusion, leaving the decision unexplained.[102]

This omission is particularly striking given the overlapping vulnerabilities faced by refugees, stateless individuals, and undocumented migrant workers, all of whom are at heightened risk of collective expulsion. By limiting its personal scope, the Convention fails to address the full spectrum of individuals who may require protection against arbitrary or collective expulsion, underscoring the need for complementary protections under other international and regional instruments. Assessing exceptions to the scope of protection under the UN Migrant Worker Convention requires a clear distinction between the legal terms "migrant", "asylum seeker", and "refugee". This differentiation is crucial to determine which individuals fall within the Convention's protective framework. The drafters of the UNCRMW appear to have intentionally drawn a distinction between migrants who cross borders for economic reasons, such as seeking employment, and those who flee persecution. While the former group is protected under the Convention, the latter is explicitly excluded. One possible rationale for this distinction lies in the fact that, at the time of drafting the UNCRMW, the 1951 Refugee Convention and its 1967 Protocol already granted refugees certain rights, including the right to work. For instance, Article 17 of the 1951 Refugee Convention ensures refugees the right to "wage-earning employment". Furthermore, Article 32 of the same Convention prohibits the expulsion of refugees without a decision "reached in accordance with due process of law". These

102 The *travaux préparatoires* of the Convention only stipulate that there was a lively debate about the inclusion of undocumented migrants in the scope of protection of the Convention in general. The issue of stateless and refugees is not mentioned. Office of the United Nations High Commissioner for Human Rights *Travaux Préparatoires of Part III of the Convention* 2003, pp. 1–2.

existing provisions likely influenced the exclusion of refugees from the UNCRMW's scope, emphasizing complementary rather than overlapping protections. In contrast, the UNCRMW does not contain a comparable guarantee, though both Article 32 of the Refugee Convention and Article 22(1) UNCRMW include protections against arbitrary expulsion. Given that the 1951 Refugee Convention and its Protocol already offered a more comprehensive framework for refugees at the time, extending protections to refugees under the UNCRMW could have diluted these existing standards.

While this distinction between "refugees" and "migrants" appears logical from the perspective of the Convention's focus on economic migration, it is challenging to apply in practice. The reasons for migration are often complex and overlapping, making it difficult to categorize migrants strictly as either economic migrants or refugees.[103] A similar rationale may explain the exclusion of stateless persons from the UNCRMW's scope of protection. The 1954 Convention Relating to the Status of Stateless Persons[104] and the 1961 Convention on the Reduction of Statelessness[105] already provide specific rights and guarantees for individuals without nationality. For instance, Article 17 of the 1954 Convention guarantees the right to work, similar to Article 17 of the 1951 Refugee Convention, and Article 31 of the 1954 Convention prohibits the expulsion of stateless persons.

In conclusion, the personal scope of protection under the UNCRMW is more limited than those of its regional and international counterparts. While it includes individuals with both "regular" and "irregular" status, it explicitly excludes refugees and stateless persons. This exclusion may reflect the fact that, by the time the Migrant Worker Convention was drafted in the 1980s, more specific legal regimes protecting refugees and stateless individuals were already in place. The 1951 Refugee Convention and its 1967 Protocol, as well as the 1954 and 1961 Statelessness Conventions, offered these groups more extensive protection, particularly with regard to the right to work, than the UNCRMW did.

---

103 Alan Desmond comes to a similar conclusion stating that the distinction between migrants, refugees and asylum-seekers when it comes to the scope of protection by the Migrant Worker Convention is in practice "opaque". See: Desmond, Alan *Shining new light on the UN Migrant Workers Convention* (Pretoria University Law Press 2017), p. 80.

104 United Nations General Assembly *Convention Relating to the Status of Stateless Persons* 28 September 1954, UNTS Vol. 360, p. 117.

105 United Nations General Assembly *Convention on the Reduction of Statelessness* 30 August 1961, UNTS Vol. 989, p. 175.

With this, we turn to another important international convention that contains the prohibition of collective expulsion, albeit implicitly: the International Covenant on Civil and Political Rights (ICCPR).

1.6 *The International Covenant on Civil and Political Rights*

Within this UN instrument, it is Article 13 ICCPR that implicitly addresses the prohibition of collective expulsions. The Human Rights Committee (HRC), a body of eighteen independent experts monitoring the implementation of the ICCPR,[106] has acknowledged this by stating that "Article 13 would not be satisfied with laws or decisions providing for collective or mass expulsions".[107] The Committee serves an important monitoring role when it comes to the implementation and applicability of the Covenant in the domestic spheres of the member states. States that are parties to the ICCPR are required to submit reports to the HRC detailing the measures taken to implement the rights enshrined in the Covenant.[108] The HRC reviews these reports and may issue its conclusions, along with general comments on specific topics or provisions.[109]

When it comes to the prohibition of collective expulsion in Article 13 itself, the provision appears to limit its scope of protection to foreigners lawfully residing within a state's territory, except in cases where the individual's life is at risk.[110] In this context, "lawfully resident" refers to individuals who have entered a state's territory in compliance with domestic immigration laws.[111] Sarah Joseph and Melissa Castan assess this limited scope of application, arguing that Article 13 offers little protection for asylum seekers who are forced to flee their home states suddenly and without authorization, unless a state recognizes procedural rights for asylum seekers under its domestic law.[112] They suggest that asylum seekers' only recourse against deportation in such cases might lie in invoking Article 7

---

106 Articles 28–39 ICCPR.

107 Human Right Committee *General Comment No. 15: The Position of Aliens Under the Covenant* 11 April 1986, para. 10.

108 Article 40(1) ICCPR.

109 Article 40(4) ICCPR.

110 *Ibidem.*, para. 9. For further details see analysis below on definition of "expulsion" in the ICCPR.

111 Carlson, Scott and Gisvold, Gregory *Practical Guide to the International Covenant on Civil and Political Rights* (Transnational Publishers 2003), p. 99.

112 Joseph, Sarah and Castan, Melissa *The International Covenant on Civil and Political Rights: Cases, Materials, and Commentary* (Oxford University Press 3rd edn. 2013), p. 421.

of the ICCPR, which prohibits expulsion to a state where a person's life would be at risk (the *non-refoulement* principle).[113]

However, a broader review of the HRC's Concluding Observations[114] and General Comment[115] on collective expulsion reveals that the personal scope of protection under Article 13 is more nuanced than Joseph and Castan suggest. In its General Comment No. 15 (1986) on the Position of Aliens under the Covenant, the HRC clarifies that the particular rights of Article 13 apply only to those aliens who are lawfully within the territory of a state party.[116] This means that national law regarding the requirements for entry and stay must be considered in determining the scope of protection, effectively excluding illegal entrants and those who have overstayed their permits.The only possibility in these authors' view for asylum seekers not to be deported in such situations is the invocation of Article 7 ICCPR – prohibiting the expulsion of people to a state where their life is at risk (*non-refoulement* principle).[117]

On the other hand, the HRC further elucidates in the same paragraph that

> if the legality of an alien's entry or stay is in dispute, any decision on this point leading to his expulsion or deportation ought to be taken in accordance with article 13. It is for the competent authorities of the State party, in good faith and in the exercise of their powers, to apply and interpret the domestic law.[118]

Based on this finding, it can be concluded that state parties must consider the guarantees outlined in Article 13 of the ICCPR when determining a foreigner's lawful residency, especially when such a determination is linked to their potential expulsion or deportation. In cases where there is uncertainty regarding the individual's lawful residency, the procedural safeguards provided by the prohibition in Article 13 must be respected by the relevant authorities. This conclusion stems from the following understanding: The

---

113 *Ibidem.*

114 Human Rights Committee *Concluding Observations: Dominican Republic* (2001), CCPR/CO/71/DOM, 3 April 2001; *Concluding observations: Dominican Republic* (2017), CCPR/C/DOM/CO/6, 27 November 2017; *Concluding Observations: Estonia* (2003), CCPR/CO/77/EST, 15 April 2003.

115 HRC *General Comment No. 15.*

116 *Ibidem.*, para. 9.

117 *Ibidem.*

118 *Ibidem.*

scope of protection under Article 13 ICCPR appears to be limited to foreigners who are lawfully residing in the territory of a state (except in cases where their life is at risk). "Lawfully resident" in this context refers to individuals who have entered the state in accordance with its domestic laws.

The HRC's 2003 Concluding Observations on the Dominican Republic further contributed to the ambiguity surrounding the personal scope of Article 13 ICCPR. The report expressed serious concern over ongoing reports of collective expulsions of ethnic Haitians, even when they were nationals of the Dominican Republic. The Committee stated that it is

> gravely concerned at the continuing reports of mass expulsions of ethnic Haitians, even when such persons are nationals of the Dominican Republic. It holds mass expulsions of non-nationals to be in breach of the Covenant since no account is taken of the situation of individuals for whom the Dominican Republic is their own country in the light of article 12, paragraph 4, nor of cases where expulsion may be contrary to article 7 given the risk of subsequent cruel, inhuman or degrading treatment, nor yet of cases where the legality of an individual's presence in the country is in dispute and must be settled in proceedings that satisfy the requirements of article 13. The State party should guarantee the right of every Dominican national not to be expelled from the country and ensure that all persons facing deportation proceedings are covered by the safeguards established in the Covenant.[119]

This statement is unclear regarding whether the prohibition of collective expulsion under Article 13 applies only to foreign nationals who are lawfully residing in the country, or whether it also extends to nationals of the expelling state. The Committee's focus on expressing concern over collective expulsions of nationals from the Dominican Republic does not clearly assert that such expulsions violate Article 13 ICCPR. This lack of explicit language leaves the issue unresolved.

Additionally, in the same paragraph, the HRC called on the Dominican Republic to ensure that its nationals are not arbitrarily expelled in the future, but without referencing Article 13 ICCPR.[120] This omission is significant because, while the Committee condemned violations of Article 13 in

119 HRC *Concluding Observations: Dominican Republic 2001* para. 16. The same concern was raised in the most recent report by the Human Rights Committee in its *Concluding observations: Dominican Republic 2017* paras. 23–24.

120 HRC *Concluding Observations: Dominican Republic 2001* para. 16.

relation to foreign nationals,[121] it did not apply the same legal framework to the expulsion of nationals. Moreover, the Concluding Observations do not clarify whether all the foreign nationals facing expulsion were legally residing in the Dominican Republic. This ambiguity suggests that the HRC may have intended to broaden the application of Article 13 ICCPR beyond "legally residing aliens" to include nationals in the case of collective expulsion. It may also have sought to extend these guarantees to foreigners whose legal residency status is disputed, to protect their right to challenge expulsion. However, the Committee's statements on this matter remain unclear. Foreigners staying irregularly and whose status is not contested are excluded from this protection. Thus, the scope of protection against collective expulsion under Article 13 ICCPR is more limited than its regional counterparts.

1.7 *Conclusions on the Definition of the Personal Scope of Protection*

This section has demonstrated that the prohibition on collective expulsion is an important safeguard in international law, ensuring protection for all non-nationals, including stateless persons, refugees, asylum seekers, and migrants, irrespective of nationality or residency status. This broad applicability underscores the relevance of the prohibition in diverse expulsion contexts, although it explicitly excludes nationals, as most legal systems already prohibit their expulsion. Regional instruments, such as the European Convention on Human Rights, reinforce this protection, offering separate guarantees against arbitrary expulsions for nationals and non-nationals. Similarly, the International Law Commission confirms the prohibition applies exclusively to non-nationals, including stateless persons.

The ECHR's Article 4 Protocol 4 offers expansive protection, applying to all non-nationals regardless of legal status. This provision stands in contrast to more limited instruments like Article 1 Protocol 7 of the ECHR or Article 32 of the 1951 Refugee Convention, which safeguard specific groups. Yet, recent judgments, such as *N.D. and N.T. v. Spain*, indicate a potential shift in focus, where the European Court of Human Rights may prioritize the protection of asylum seekers over other migrants, reflecting an evolving judicial approach.

Other regional systems, such as the African Charter and the Inter-American framework, also recognize the prohibition on collective expulsion but diverge in scope. Article 12(5) of the African Charter explicitly bans

121 *Ibidem.*

the mass expulsion of non-nationals, with an expanded interpretation occasionally including nationals. Meanwhile, the Inter-American Court has emphasized non-discrimination, ensuring the prohibition applies to all foreigners, regardless of legal status, as illustrated in *Nadege Dorzema v. Dominican Republic*. Both systems stress the importance of individualized assessments and condemn discriminatory practices in expulsion cases.

Beyond these, instruments like the Arab Charter and the Commonwealth Human Rights Convention similarly prohibit collective expulsions. However, challenges such as limited enforcement mechanisms and interpretive ambiguities hinder their effective implementation. Despite these hurdles, the provisions suggest a wide scope of protection for foreigners, albeit with uncertain enforcement in practice.

On the international level, the UN Convention on Migrant Workers offers additional safeguards, prohibiting collective expulsion under Article 22 and extending protection to migrant workers regardless of their legal status. However, it excludes refugees and stateless persons, creating concerning protection gaps for these vulnerable populations, who face analogous risks of expulsion. Finally, we learned that Article 13 of the ICCPR prohibits collective expulsion but limits its application to foreigners lawfully residing in a state. The Human Rights Committee has clarified that procedural safeguards must be respected even for individuals with contested legal status. While the Committee's commentary implies a narrow scope, its observations on collective expulsions suggest potential for a broader interpretation. This ambiguity highlights the complexities and evolving challenges in applying Article 13 to contemporary expulsion cases. With this conclusion on the personal scope, we now turn to the second element of the prohibition, the definition of "collective".

2 The Definition of "Collective" in the Prohibition of Collective Expulsion

The Oxford Dictionary of Current English defines "group" as "a number of people or things located, gathered, or classed together".[122] This definition contains two decisive elements that serve as a starting point for the assessment of this element: The size of the group and the connective element between the individual members of the group expressed by the term

122 Waite, Maurice and Stevenson, Angus *Concise Oxford English Dictionary* (Oxford University Press 12th edn. 2011).

"together" in the definition. This definition provides a foundation for analyzing how the size and cohesion of a group influence the interpretation of the term "collective" within the ambit of the prohibition of collective expulsion.

This ambit of protection is dependent on the definition of the term "collective"[123] and thus on the question of whether the expelled group requires a specific size to fall under the provision's scope. In this debate, some scholars argue that every foreigner, irrespective of being expelled individually or as part of a group, ought to enjoy the same level of procedural guarantees.[124] Otherwise, a sports team or an orchestra consisting of foreigners could enjoy protection against collective expulsion; an individual foreign athlete or musician, however, would not fall under the scope of protection of the prohibition.[125] The authors admit that this interpretation would expand the scope of the prohibition immensely, rendering its collective notion irrelevant.[126] Jean-Marie Henckaerts supports this broad interpretation of "collectivity" and supports the extension of the procedural guarantees to all expelled individuals.[127] However, as Henckaerts admits, the issue of how to distinguish "group expulsions" from several simultaneously occurring individual expulsions of foreigners and the required size of such a group for a collective expulsion remains unanswered.[128]

2.1 *Determining Factors for the Collective Nature of an Expulsion*

This section will address these questions and propose a definition of collective expulsion by analyzing relevant case law from regional and international courts and treaty bodies. Key factors will be examined, including the uniformity of expulsion orders, group size, the duration of the foreigners' stay in the expelling state, and their nationality and ethnicity. Additionally, the section will explore factors not related to the individual foreigner, but rather to the expulsion process itself, specifically when expulsions occur without a reasonable and objective assessment of each person's circumstances.

---

123 Van Dijk, Pieter and Van Hoof, Fried *Theory and Practice of the European Convention on Human Rights* (Intersentia 4th edn. 2006), p. 676.

124 *Ibidem.*, pp. 677–678.

125 *Ibidem.*

126 *Ibidem.*

127 Henkaerts, Jean-Marie *Mass Expulsion in International Law and Practice* (Martinus Nijhoff 1995), pp. 13–15.

128 *Ibidem.*

2.1.1 Identical Terms of Expulsion Orders

The question of whether identical terms of expulsion orders inherently signify a violation of the prohibition of collective expulsion provision has been of debate since the prohibition's first interpretation by the European Commission. Both, the Commission and the Court have chosen similar approaches to this issue highlighting that while identical wording in expulsion orders may raise concerns, the decisive factor remains whether each individual's case was genuinely and fairly assessed. This section explores how the courts have addressed this issue, from early cases that dismissed violations based solely on identical terms, to more recent judgments clarifying the need for individualized evaluations, and how these principles apply to complex scenarios involving large-scale expulsions/denials of entry at the border.

This evolution of approaches started initially, in two early *European Commission of Human Rights* cases on Article 4 Protocol 4 of 1977 and 1978, namely *K.G. v. the Federal Republic of Germany* and *O. et autres c. Luxembourg*. Here, the Commission dismissed a violation of the prohibition of collective expulsion as the fact that the applicants' "expulsion orders are held in identical terms is not in itself evidence that they are being expelled collectively and there is no corroboration for any such inference".[129] Years later, the ECtHR reaffirmed this approach in several judgments.[130]

One of these later judgments that addressed this question in length was *M.A. v. Cyprus*. Here, the Court emphasized that such uniformity alone does not automatically constitute a violation of the prohibition of collective expulsion.[131] It further explained that the use of formulaic and identical language in deportation orders and corresponding letters, without specific reference to earlier asylum decisions, is not, in itself, indicative of a collective expulsion.[132] The key determinant is whether each case was individually examined and decided based on its unique facts. Building on this, the Court also noted that even if the deportation orders did not explicitly reference individual status-determining procedures, their issuance could still be valid if grounded in a prior reasonable and objective assessment of the applicants'

129 Council of Europe *Digest of Strasbourg Case-Law relating to the European Convention on Human Rights* Vol. 5 (Carl Heymanns Verlag 1985), p. 890.

130 See for example the following ECtHR cases: *Čonka v. Belgium* para. 62; *Khlaifia and Others v. Italy* [Chamber], paras. 153–154; *Sultani v. France* para. 81 or *Hirsi Jamaa and Others v. Italy*, [GC], para. 184.

131 *M.A. v. Cyprus* ECtHR, para. 254.

132 *Ibidem.*

situations.[133] While acknowledging that mistakes were made in relation to the status of some individuals, including the applicant, the Court held that such errors, though regrettable, do not necessarily demonstrate a collective expulsion. Instead, the focus remained on the procedural safeguards ensuring that each individual was afforded a genuine opportunity to have their case reviewed on its merits.[134] A similar finding was reiterated in *Georgia v. Russia (I)*, where the Grand Chamber found that the systemic use of identical expulsion orders, issued via standard forms with only names and dates changed, indicated a failure to objectively assess the circumstances of each case. In this instance, the lack of procedural safeguards and individual consideration amounted to a violation of Article 4 of Protocol 4.[135]

This vision on the scope of protection on the prohibition in Article 4 Protocol 4 ECHR and the necessity of an individual interview that has been continuously promoted by the Commission and Court for decades was however reduced in the *Khlaifia* Grand Chamber decision. While the Court in *M.A. v. Cyprus* emphasized that identical terms in expulsion orders do not automatically constitute a collective expulsion, it placed significant weight on whether each case was individually assessed prior to the issuance of such orders. The Court clarified that the procedural fairness of the expulsion process depends on whether the authorities conducted a genuine and objective review of each individual's circumstances, regardless of the uniformity in the language of the orders.[136] In contrast, the Court's analysis in *Khlaifia v. Italy* highlighted a restrictionist shift in that regard as the applicants, despite having expulsion orders couched in identical terms and did not undergo any meaningful individual assessment before their removal, had not been deprived of the guarantees of the prohibition of collective expulsion.[137] The Court appeared to retrospectively evaluate that none of the applicants were entitled to protection,[138] a conclusion that fell short of addressing whether the national authorities had fulfilled their responsibility to examine each applicant's circumstances prior to the expulsion and incompatible with the core idea of the prohibition of collective expulsion which guarantees an examination for all foreigners. These contrasting findings underline a consistent theme in the Court's jurisprudence: While

133 *Ibidem.*
134 *Ibidem.*
135 *Georgia v. Russia (I)*, [GC], ECtHR, para. 164.
136 *Khlaifia and Others v. Italy* ECtHR, [GC], para. 213.
137 *Ibidem.*, para. 253.
138 *Ibidem.*

identical expulsion orders do not inherently violate the prohibition of collective expulsion, they raise a strong presumption of procedural deficiencies. States must rebut this presumption by demonstrating that each case was subject to individualized examination. Thus, the prohibition of collective expulsion ultimately hinges on the integrity of the individualized review process conducted by national authorities. With this finding we now turn to the question of the size of a group to constitute a "collective" expulsion in the sense of the prohibition.

2.1.2 Size of the Group

The term "collective" in the prohibition of collective expulsion might suggest that the size of the group is a determining factor. However, as we will explore, this is not the case. Various regional human rights bodies, including the European Court of Human Rights and the Inter-American Court of Human Rights, have clarified that what matters is not the size of the group but whether individualized assessments are conducted. For example, in its 2020 *N.D. and N.T. v. Spain* judgment, the ECtHR's Grand Chamber clarified that the term "collective" refers to a "group" without requiring a minimum number of individuals while the group's size is not a determining factor in whether Article 4 Protocol 4 has been violated. This clarification, drawing on previous case law and the ILC Draft Articles, marks the first time the Court explicitly stated that the group's size is irrelevant.[139] Likewise, in its 2012 judgment in *Nadege Dorzema and Others v. Dominican Republic*, the Inter-American Court explicitly referred to the ECtHR's ruling in *Hirsi Jamaa and Others v. Italy*, emphasizing that "the sheer number of aliens subject to expulsion decisions is not the essential criterion for characterizing an expulsion as collective".[140] This is an example of interjudicial dialogue,

139 *N.D. and N.T. v. Spain* ECtHR, [GC], para. 194.

140 *Nadege Dorzema and others v. Dominican Republic Merits, Reparations and Costs* IACourtHR, Judgment of 24 October 2012. Series C, No. 251, (*Nadege Dorzema v. Dominnican Republic*), para. 172. The Court reiterated this finding in its second case relating to collective expulsion from the Dominican Republic *Case of expelled Dominicans and Haitians v. Dominican Republic Preliminary objections, merits, reparations and costs* IACourtHR, Judgment 28 August 2014. Series C No. 282, para. 361. The original judgment stipulates that the fundamental criteria for the determination of collectiveness of an expulsion is not the number of expelled foreigners, but that the expulsion is not based on an objective examination of the individual circumstances of every foreigner. The original text reads: "el criterio fundamental para determinar el carácter "colectivo" de una expulsión no es el número de extranjeros objeto de la decisión de expulsión, sino que la misma no se base en un análisis objetivo de las circunstancias individuales de cada extranjero".

as the Inter-American Court turns to the ECtHR's jurisprudence to ensure a uniform interpretation of the scope of the prohibition of collective expulsion across jurisdictions. In a similar vein, the African Commission on Human and Peoples' Rights did not address the size of the expelled group at all in five of its cases on the prohibition. It has focused instead on the arbitrary nature of expulsions.[141] These examples show that the prohibition of collective expulsion aims to protect non-nationals from arbitrary expulsion, particularly when expelled as part of a group. It covers foreigners within clearly defined, vaguely defined, or inconclusively defined groups, all expelled under similar circumstances.

Nevertheless, past cases demonstrate that the size of the expelled group can play a significant role in determining a violation of the prohibition of collective expulsion, for example in showing the scale of violations of expulsions without individualized assessments. For instance, in *Georgia v. Russia (I)*, the ECtHR examined the expulsion of a clearly defined group of Georgian nationals under a government policy. The Court later estimated the number of expelled individuals – at least 1,500 – to calculate just satisfaction under Article 41 ECHR, highlighting that the prohibition of collective expulsion had been violated on a substantial scale.[142] This is also true in situations where the size of the group cannot be precisely determined due to practical constraints. For example, in cases of "summary" collective expulsions, such as those described in *N.D. and N.T. v. Spain*[143] at the Spanish-Moroccan border, estimating the exact size of the expelled group is inherently unfeasible. Here, the issue involves not only the group's size but

141 See for example: *Rencontre Africaine pour la Défense des Droits de l'Homme v. Zambia* AComHPR Communication 71/92, 1996. Here, the *African Commission* found that the expulsion of 517 West Africans from the territory of Zambia violated the prohibition of mass expulsion. This finding was not based on the number of expelled foreigners, but on the fact that they were not granted a fair procedure before being removed.

142 *Georgia v. Russia I (Just Satisfaction)* ECtHR, Appl. No. 13255/07, 31 January 2019, para. 71.

143 In the case of the collective expulsions at the Spanish-Moroccan border, the common attribute the individuals share is that they are all from Sub-Sahara Africa due to a racial profiling strategy conducted by Morocco which effectively deters people coming from that region to reach the border post to claim asylum. Alami, Aida *African Migrants in Morocco Tell of Abuse* New York Times, 28 November 2012, available at: https://www.nytimes.com/2012/11/29/world/middleeast/african-migrants-in-morocco-tell-of-abuse.html, issue also addressed at ECtHR Grand Chamber public hearing in case *N.D. and N.T. v. Spain*, Appl. No. 8675/15, 26 September 2018, available at: https://www.echr.coe.int/Pages/home.aspx?p=hearings&w=867515_26092018&language=en.

also the connective element between its members, which will be discussed in the next section.

In cases of large-scale and continuous summary expulsions, each expelled foreigner becomes part of an ever-expanding and undefined group that includes all individuals intercepted and expelled in the past, present, and future. This fluid and ongoing nature of the group highlights that the prohibition of collective expulsion does not depend on whether all affected individuals are removed simultaneously or gradually over time. Even when expulsions occur one by one, the prohibition remains applicable if those individuals are part of a broader group collectively targeted by an overarching expulsion policy. This reflects a fundamental principle upheld consistently across cases and courts: Individualized assessments must be conducted in every instance, regardless of the size of the group or the timeline of the expulsions, to ensure compliance with the prohibition.

This finding is true for all the examined regional instruments containing the prohibition. For example, the African Commission on Human and People's Rights also examined this question in its case *Rencontre Africaine pour la Défense des Droits de l'Homme v. Zambia*. Here, the respondent disputed the characterization of the expulsions of foreigners as collective by pointing out that the deported were arrested over two months, at different places, and served with deportation orders on different dates.[144] This line of argument was, however, rejected by the Commission, which found a violation of the prohibition of mass expulsion. The mere fact that Zambia expelled 517 West Africans based on removal orders did not constitute a violation of collective expulsion. The circumstance that the group of foreigners could not contact their lawyers or appeal against the expulsion order was, however, sufficient for the collective nature of the expulsions.[145] The Commission clarified that the fact that several arrests and deportations of non-nationals took place over several months did not negate the *en masse* element of the expulsion.[146] The size of the expelled group is not a determining factor in classifying an expulsion as collective. Both the European and Inter-American Courts have emphasized that the number of individuals expelled together does not automatically make an expulsion collective. Instead, the focus is on whether the expulsion is arbitrary and involves a group subjected to similar circumstances or a coordinated policy. The size of the expelled group is not a determining factor in classifying an expulsion as

---

144 *Rencontre Africaine pour la Défense des Droits de l'Homme v. Zambia* ACHPR, para. 27.

145 *Ibidem.*, paras. 27–28.

146 *Ibidem.*, paras. 25–27.

collective. Both the European and Inter-American Court have emphasized that the number of individuals expelled together does not automatically make an expulsion collective. Instead, the focus is on whether the expulsion is arbitrary and involves a group subjected to similar circumstances or a coordinated policy.

In conclusion, the "collective" element of the prohibition encompasses any group expelled under similar conditions, irrespective of its size. This principle ensures protection against arbitrary removal, even when the group's size is undefined or the expulsion occurs over an extended period. Importantly, cases such as *Georgia v. Russia (I)* and *Rencontre Africaine pour la Défense des Droits de l'Homme v. Zambia* demonstrate that segmented deportations do not negate the collective nature of expulsions if individualized assessments are not conducted. While the size of the group may be relevant in some contexts, it is not the decisive factor in determining a violation of the prohibition. Instead, the focus remains on the absence of proper consideration for individual circumstances. With this conclusion, we now turn to the question of whether the courts deem some type of connective element between the expelled foreigners necessary to find a violation of the prohibition raising questions like whether the group must be homogeneous to fulfill the "collective" element? Is there a common denominator that all members of the group should share?

2.1.3 Connective Element

Such questions are not purely academic thought games, but have been raised in court. Most prominently, in the *N.D. and N.T. v. Spain* Grand Chamber hearing, judge María Elósegui asked the applicants' defendants these questions. In detail, during the hearing on 26 September 2018, Judge Elósegui asked the applicants' representatives to provide information on how many individuals had been expelled alongside the two applicants and whether the expelled individuals shared any common characteristics, such as nationality, race, or ethnicity. Her question about the composition and size of the group went unanswered.[147] Nevertheless, it highlights a prevailing assumption that some degree of homogeneity among expelled individuals may be necessary to establish a violation of the prohibition of collective expulsion. To gain clarity of this assumption we now turn to examine the connective elements that determine whether an expulsion qualifies as

147 ECtHR Grand Chamber public hearing in case *ND and NT v. Spain*, no. 8675/15, 26 September 2018, available at: https://www.echr.coe.int/Pages/home.aspx?p=hearings&w=867515_26092018&language=en, questions posed by judge Elósegui from 1:41:05 on.

collective under the prohibition. This analysis delves into various possible connectors, including shared characteristics such as nationality or ethnicity, as well as the absence of a reasonable and objective examination of individual circumstances. By exploring these elements, we aim to better understand how the drafters of the codification of the prohibition and courts assess the collective nature of expulsions and ensure adherence to the principle of individualized assessment.

2.1.3.1 *Common Nationality*

We begin our examination of the connective element by exploring nationality as a potential decisive factor. The explanations accompanying Article 19(1) EU Charter of Fundamental Rights, which codifies the prohibition of collective expulsion, provide a useful starting point. These explanations highlight that nationality can play a significant role in determining whether expulsions violate the prohibition due to the absence of individualized assessments. As Article 19(1) EUChFR mirrors the content of Article 4 of Protocol 4 ECHR, this finding extends to the latter.[148] The explanations further clarify that the purpose of Article 19(1) EUChFR is "to guarantee that every decision is based on a specific examination and that no single measure can be taken to expel all persons having the **nationality of a particular State** [emphasis added]".[149] While this underscores the importance of avoiding blanket measures targeting individuals based solely on their nationality, the explanations also make it clear that the prohibition does not strictly require the expelled individuals to belong to a narrowly defined group sharing the same nationality. Instead, the focus lies on ensuring individualized examinations before any expulsion decision and protecting against collective measures that seek to expel all non-nationals based on shared nationality.

This distinction becomes even clearer when analyzing the composition of expelled groups in cases before international courts. Looking at the ECtHR jurisprudence, it becomes evident that the homogeneity of the expelled group is not a prerequisite for determining a violation of the prohibition.

---

148 *Draft Charter of Fundamental Rights of the European Union explanations prepared by the Praesidium*, Charte 4473/00 Convent 49, p. 21.

149 European Union Agency for Fundamental Rights (FRA) *Explanations relating to the Charter of Fundamental Rights* available at: https://fra.europa.eu/en/charterpedia/article/19-protection-event-removal-expulsion-or-extradition, p. 21. The FRA points out that these explanations do not have the status of law, they are intended to serve as a tool for interpretation and shall clarify the scope and content of each provision of the Charter. The explanations were originally drafted by Praesidium of the Convention which also was in charge of drafting the Charter itself.

While some cases involved groups where all individuals shared the same nationality, such as *Čonka v. Belgium* (all Slovakian nationals), *Georgia v. Russia (I)* (Georgians), and *Abdi Ahmed and Others v. Malta* (Somalis), the Court did not treat this uniformity as a compulsory element for finding a violation. Instead, it focused on the lack of individualized assessments and procedural safeguards. This principle is reinforced by cases involving groups with diverse nationalities. For instance, in *Hirsi Jamaa and Others v. Italy,* the applicants were Somali and Eritrean nationals. In *Sharifi and Others v. Italy and Greece,* the applicants came from a wide range of backgrounds, including Afghan, Sudanese, and Eritrean nationalities. Similarly, in *N.D. and N.T. v. Spain,* the applicants from Mali and Ivory Coast were summarily expelled alongside a group of approximately 70 to 80 individuals with differing, undefined nationalities. In none of these cases did the nationality of the expelled individuals serve as a decisive factor for establishing collectivity.

The approach of the African Commission on Human and Peoples' Rights further supports this interpretation. In *Rencontre Africaine pour la Défense des Droits de l'Homme v. Zambia,* Zambia argued that the simultaneous expulsion of 517 individuals from different West African countries did not constitute "mass expulsion".[150] However, the African Commission rejected this argument, emphasizing that "simultaneous expulsion of nationals of many countries does not negate the charge of discrimination".[151] It clarified that the focus should be on the deprivation of a fair process and the right to appeal, not on the homogeneity of the group.[152] Likewise, in *Fédération Internationale des Ligues des Droits de l'Homme v. Angola,* the African Commission condemned the mass expulsion of foreigners based on economic conditions.[153] It ruled that economic hardship does not justify collective measures targeting foreigners, regardless of whether the group shares a common nationality or comprises individuals from multiple states.[154]

In conclusion, nationality is not a decisive denominator for determining the collective nature of expulsions. While a shared nationality among the expelled group may indicate a policy targeting certain foreigners, it is neither a necessary nor sufficient condition for establishing collectivity.

150 *Rencontre Africaine pour la Défense des Droits de l'Homme v. Zambia* AComHPR, para. 24.

151 *Ibidem,* para. 25.

152 *Ibidem.*, paras. 25–28.

153 *Union Inter Africaine des Droits de l'Homme, Fédération Internationale des Ligues des Droits de l'Homme and Others v. Angola, African Commission on Human and Peoples' Rights* AComHPR para. 16.

154 *Ibidem.*

Ultimately, the focus remains on ensuring procedural safeguards and individualized assessments, which lie at the heart of the prohibition of collective expulsion.

2.1.3.2 *Common Ethnicity*

A similar finding applies to ethnicity as a connective element between the expelled individuals of a group. An analysis of the judgments of the European Court of Human Rights on Article 4 Protocol 4 ECHR reveals that the ethnicity of applicants in cases regarding the prohibition only played a role in very particular circumstances.

The most prominent example in this regard is *Čonka v. Belgium*. Here, the four applicants, their spouses, and children were all of Roma ethnicity. Belgium expelled them collectively with approximately 70 other Roma individuals. Although the Roma ethnicity of the collectively expelled was mentioned five times in the judgment,[155] according to the Court, it did not play a role in the determination of collectivity. However, their shared ethnicity indicated a potential absence of an individual, reasonable, and objective examination prior to expulsion. The Court found that the Roma applicants faced widespread discriminatory policies in Belgium, including the existence of a government policy aiming at expelling them on a large scale. Here, the ECtHR made an explanatory statement on the background of expulsion procedures, which was reiterated several times in subsequent cases. It clarified that even though an expulsion of a group

> is taken on the basis of a reasonable and objective examination of the particular case of each individual alien of the group [...] That does not mean, however, that where the latter condition is satisfied the background to the execution of the expulsion orders plays no further role in determining whether there has been compliance with Article 4 of Protocol No. 4.[156]

Thus, the ethnicity of the applicants did not directly serve as a requirement to determine the "connective element" between the expelled individuals. However, the ethnicity of the expelled individuals played a role insofar as they were targeted for this reason by the government campaign to expel Roma collectively from the state's territory.

155 *Čonka v. Belgium* ECtHR, Appl. No. 51564/99, 5 February 2002, paras. 7, 18, 20, 44, 56.
156 *Ibidem.*, para. 59.

In a previous case, *Andric v. Sweden*, the ethnicity of the applicant, Vedran Andric, an ethnic Croat, had played a similar role. Andric argued that his ethnicity would put him at risk in case of his expulsion to his Bosnian home district which was dominated by Muslims.[157] Even though the case was declared inadmissible as the Court found that the authorities had objectively and individually examined the applicant's claims, it illustrates that the claimant's ethnicity, despite being addressed by the court, did not play any role in determining whether or not the expulsion was collective, as there was no policy to expel ethnic Croats from Sweden behind the applicant's particular expulsion order. In other cases, such as *N.D. and N.T. v. Spain* or *Hirsi and Others v. Italy*, ethnicity did not play a role at all. This finding is reflected in the Grand Chamber decision in *N.D. and N.T. v. Spain*, for example. Here, the Court for the first time elaborated in clear terms on the collectivity element in collective expulsion cases and did not find such a connective element in the ethnicity of the applicants.[158] Similarly, the African Commission has emphasized that the prohibition of collective expulsion is not concerned with the ethnicity of the expelled individuals, but rather with the broader question of whether the expulsion process respects human rights and provides individual assessments. For example, in *Union Inter Africaine des Droits de l'homme and Others v. Angola,* the African Commission drew similar conclusions, making the general clarifying proclamation that

> whatever the circumstances may be, however, such measures [of mass expulsion] should not be taken [to] the detriment of the enjoyment of human rights. Mass expulsions of any category of persons, whether on the basis of nationality, religion, ethnic, racial or other considerations constitute a special violation of human rights.[159]

This clear statement of the African Commission reinforces the strong principle that collective expulsions, regardless of the grounds for categorization – be it nationality, religion, ethnicity, or race – represent a significant human rights violation that undermines the fundamental right to individual protection. This finding stretches across jurisdictions showing that, in general, ethnicity does not constitute a connective element between expelled individuals as required by the prohibition of collective expulsion. Ethnicity,

157 *Andric v. Sweden* ECtHR, Appl. No. 45917/99, 23 February 1999, p. 3.

158 *N.D. and N.T. v. Spain*, ECtHR, [GC], para. 195.

159 *Union Inter Africaine des Droits de l'Homme et al. v. Angola* AComHRR, para. 16.

however, is one of several decisive factors in determining whether the background of expulsion procedures suggests that an applicant's examination was not objective and individual.

2.1.3.3 *Absence of Reasonable and Objective Examination of Individual Circumstances*

Building on the analysis of ethnicity as a potential connective element, we now turn to another critical aspect in determining collective expulsion: The absence of a reasonable and objective examination of individual circumstances. In doing so, we first turn to *N.D. and N.T. v. Spain*, as the ECtHR defined here collectivity in terms of the failure to conduct such individualized assessments, thereby recognizing this procedural safeguard as essential to ensuring the protection of applicants' rights. Thus, when assessing whether an expulsion of a group was indeed "collective" in nature, the Court examines whether the state in question respected the procedural guarantees implicitly contained in the prohibition.[160] *Ergo*, in case the expelling state did not conduct a reasonable and objective examination of each foreigner of the group as required by the prohibition, the expulsion is deemed collective. As will be explained below, the level of these guarantees depends on the concrete circumstances of the expulsion, including *inter alia* whether the individuals were identified, or their conduct evaluated prior to the expulsion.

2.1.3.4 *Indicators for the Determination of the Absence of a Reasonable and Objective Examination*

As the decisive question for the determination of the collective nature of an expulsion is the absence of a reasonable, individual, and objective examination of each group member's circumstances, this section provides the indicators which the ECtHR and the EComHR relied upon to determine whether the expulsion in question was collective.[161]

The relevance of the circumstances to the expulsion orders became first apparent in the *Human Rights Commission*'s *Becker v. Denmark* case in 1975. In the submissions, the applicant Becker urged the Commission to consider the circumstances surrounding the return of 200 children to Vietnam. In his view, the Government could not be trusted to have conducted individual

160 These guarantees are assessed in great detail in Chapter 3.

161 The Court and the Commission previously assessed these indicators under the heading "background to the execution of the expulsion order", see: *Čonka v. Belgium* ECtHR Appl. No. 51564/99, 5 February 2002, para. 59.

assessments as it had publicly declared that "the majority of the children should be sent back."[162] He further explained that "for political reasons the Government could not afford to change their decision".[163] Even though the Commission did not explicitly address this background information regarding the pending expulsion of the children, such circumstances became a decisive indicator for the determination of the existence of a violation of the prohibition in subsequent cases by the Court. In general, the Court typically applies a two-step approach to assess the collective nature of an expulsion. First, it examines whether the individual circumstances of each member of the group were objectively and personally considered. If there is any uncertainty regarding this, the Court looks at additional factors related to the expulsion's execution. This second step either resolves the doubts or strengthens the argument that the expulsions were collective, thus violating Article 4 of Protocol 4 ECHR. Background factors that may influence this determination include identical expulsion orders or government policies targeting specific groups. Although the ECtHR has not formally labeled this as a two-step test, it has implicitly applied this approach in several cases, beginning with *Čonka v. Belgium*[164] in 2002.

In subsequent cases, such as *Hirsi Jamaa and Others v. Italy* and *N.D. and N.T. v. Spain* (in the Chamber and Grand Chamber judgment), the fact that the authorities in charge did not conduct any form of identification before the applicants' removal served as an indicator for the Court to determine the collective nature of the expulsion.[165] However, over time, the Court has relied on different terms for the same issue. Whereas the Court spoke of "background to the expulsion" in *Čonka v. Belgium*, it referred to a "general context"[166] in *Georgia v. Russia (I)*, the "same set of circumstances specific to that group" in the Chamber judgment in *N.D. and N.T. v. Spain*,[167] and the "general context" in the Grand Chamber judgment of the same case.[168] In that judgment, the Court implicitly relied on background indicators to determine the collective nature of the expulsion, extending previous case law by making the applicants' behavior before the expulsion a key factor.

162 *Becker v. Denmark* EComHR, p. 232.

163 *Ibidem.*

164 *Čonka v. Belgium* ECtHR, para. 59.

165 *Hirsi Jamaa and Others v. Italy* ECtHR [GC], para. 185 and *N.D. and N.T. v. Spain* ECtHR [Chamber], para. 12.

166 *Georgia v. Russia (I)* ECtHR, [GC], para. 171.

167 *N.D. and N.T. v. Spain* ECtHR, [Chamber], para. 102.

168 *Ibidem.*, para. 197.

Irrespective of these differences in terminology, the existence of government policies targeting the expulsion of specific groups of foreigners serves as a key indicator of the absence of an individual and objective examination in cases of collective expulsion. The ECtHR outlined a two-element test to establish such administrative practices in *Georgia v. Russia* (*I*),[169] drawing on earlier Commission case law from 1983. This test requires evidence of both "repetition of acts", defined as a pattern of analogous breaches sufficiently numerous to form a system, and "official tolerance", where authorities fail to prevent or punish such acts, show indifference, or deny fair hearings in judicial proceedings.[170] In *Georgia v. Russia* (*I*), the Court found a coordinated policy targeting Georgian nationals, leading to a violation of Article 4 Protocol 4 ECHR.[171] While *Georgia v. Russia* (*I*)[172] explicitly referenced "administrative practice", similar cases like *Čonka v. Belgium*[173] and *Hirsi Jamaa v. Italy* avoided this terminology despite meeting its criteria. For example, in *Čonka v. Belgium*, the Court identified a government policy aimed at deterring Slovakian nationals,[174] while in *Hirsi Jamaa*, it highlighted public statements by Italian officials about push-back operations as part of a broader migration control strategy.[175] These policies consistently indicated the absence of individualized assessments[176] and formed a systematic approach to collective expulsions, even when the Court's language varied across cases.[177]

The terminology used by the ECtHR to describe such policies, ranging from "administrative practice" to "systematic policy of irregular returns", varies across rulings, as seen in *N.D. and N.T. v. Spain*[178] and *Khlaifia v.*

169 The Commission and the Court relied on these two elements, but never explicitly established it as a two-element test. *France, Norway, Denmark, Sweden and the Netherlands v. Turkey*, Appl. Nos. 9940-9944/82, Commission decision of 6 December 1983, para. 19.

170 *France, Norway, Denmark, Sweden and the Netherlands v. Turkey* EUComHR, para. 19.

171 *Georgia v. Russia* (*I*), ECtHR, [GC], para. 176.

172 *Ibidem.*, paras. 128–159.

173 *Čonka v. Belgium* ECtHR, para. 62. The Belgian "Director-General of the Aliens Office wrote to the Minister of the Interior and the Commissioner-General for Refugees and Stateless Persons to inform them of his intention to deal with asylum applications from Slovakian nationals rapidly in order to send a clear signal to discourage other potential applicants", para. 30.

174 *Čonka v. Belgium* ECtHR, para. 62..

175 *Hirsi Jamaa and Others v. Italy* ECtHR, [GC], para. 177.

176 *France, Norway, Denmark, Sweden and the Netherlands v. Turkey*, Appl. Nos. 9940-9944/82, Commission decision of 6 December 1983, para. 19.

177 *Ireland v. the United Kingdom* EUComHR, Series A, No. 25, 18 January 1978, para. 159.

178 *N.D. and N.D. v. Spain* ECtHR, [Chamber], para. 67.

Italy.[179] Despite these differences, the underlying implication remains consistent which is that the presence of such practices underscores the lack of individualized examination. This consistency suggests a coherent approach by the Court in applying Article 4 Protocol 4 ECHR, even as it employs diverse descriptive terms to fit the contextual nuances of each case.

2.2 *Conclusions on the Definition of "Collective"*

In conclusion, the "collective" element in the prohibition of collective expulsion does not depend on a narrowly defined or numerically limited group size, nor does it require shared nationality, ethnicity, or physical presence among individuals. Instead, the focus lies on the procedural and circumstantial factors surrounding the expulsion. A connection between the claimant's expulsion and other similar expulsions within a brief period, is sufficient to establish collectivity.

The ECtHR has consistently clarified that collective expulsion does not require simultaneous removal or a definable group but emphasizes the absence of individualized assessments as the decisive factor. The jurisprudence underlines that failure to reasonably and objectively examine individual circumstances is the core issue. The prohibition thus protects foreigners expelled under comparable conditions, emphasizing procedural safeguards over group composition.

Likewise, in the African Charter, while terms like "collective" or "mass" may suggest group-specific protections, the provision fundamentally safeguards individuals against arbitrary expulsion practices connected to broader systemic violations. This interpretation aligns with protections in other instruments, such as Article 13 ICCPR, which also emphasize procedural guarantees against both individual and collective expulsions.

3 The Definition of "Prohibition" in the Prohibition of Collective Expulsion

The concept of "prohibition" in the context of collective expulsion remains undefined in the sources analyzed throughout this chapter, leaving its precise meaning open to interpretation. To approach the definition of term, we will first turn to Article 9 ILC Draft Articles on the Expulsion of Aliens suggests that the Law Commission understands "prohibition" is in the strict

179 *Khlaifia and Others v. Italy* ECtHR, [Chamber], para. 156.

sense as not allowing any derogation, except in cases of emergency.[180] Section three of Article 9 stipulates that

> [a] State may expel concomitantly the members of a group of aliens, provided that the expulsion takes place after and on the basis of an assessment of the particular case of each individual member of the group in accordance with the present draft articles.

This finding is in line with the object and purpose of Article 4 Protocol 4 ECHR, as foreseen by the drafters of the additional protocol. The *travaux préparatoires* reveal that the Consultative Assembly of the European Convention initially wished to establish stringent conditions for lawfully residing foreigners in a member state.[181] The initial proposal for Article 4 requested to limit permitted expulsions to cases of danger to national security or violation of the *ordre public* or morality. However, the Committee of Experts did not follow this proposal and changed its scope from protecting lawfully residing foreigners to prohibiting collective expulsions and erased the possible derogations in case of emergency in its entirety.[182] Thus, Article 4 Protocol 4 ECHR, as it stands, can only be restricted under the exceptional circumstances outlined in Article 15 ECHR, which permits derogations solely in times of emergency. The threshold for invoking such a derogation is exceptionally stringent.[183]

The same is true for the prohibition of collective expulsion in the European Charter on Fundamental Rights (Article 19(1)). No limitations or derogations are allowed to the prohibition[184], except in cases of emergency (Article 52(3)(1) EUChFR in conjunction with Article 15 ECHR).

---

180 Article 9(4) of the Draft Articles foresees a derogation in times of war stating that "the present draft article is without prejudice to the rules of international law applicable to the expulsion of aliens in the event of an armed conflict involving the expelling State".

181 Van Dijk and Van Hoof *Theory and Practice of the European Convention on Human Rights* p. 675.

182 Council of Europe *Explanatory Report on the Second to Fifth Protocols to the European Convention for Protection of Human Rights and Fundamental Freedoms* submitted by the Committee of Experts to The Committee of Ministers, Doc H(71) 11 (1971), p. 11.

183 Article 15(1) ECHR reads "In time of war or other public emergency threatening the life of the nation any High Contracting Party may take measures derogating from its obligations under this Convention to the extent strictly required by the exigencies of the situation, provided that such measures are not inconsistent with its other obligations under international law".

184 Guild, Elspeth *Art 19-Protection in the Event of Removal* para. 19.54.

In contrast, the Inter-American Convention on Human Rights does not include a specific restriction or limitation clause for the prohibition of collective expulsion. Instead, the general derogation clause in Article 27(1) IACHR permits "suspensions" in exceptional circumstances such as war, public danger, or other emergencies threatening the independence or security of a state party. However, this provision imposes strict safeguards, allowing derogations only to the extent and for the duration necessary to address the situation. Additionally, any measures must align with other international obligations and cannot involve discrimination based on race, color, sex, language, religion, or social origin. Significantly, subsection two of Article 27 IACHR enumerates a list of non-derogable rights, including the right to life and juridical personality. The prohibition of collective expulsion, codified in Article 22(9) IACHR, is notably absent from this list, leaving it theoretically open to derogation in extraordinary circumstances, provided all other conditions are strictly met. This nuanced framework highlights the interplay between the non-derogable and derogable aspects of human rights protections in different regional systems.

In contrast, the African Charter takes a different approach compared to its European and American counterparts. The Banjul Charter contains so-called "claw-back clauses"[185] that limit rights directly in the respective Charter provision, rather than in general restriction clauses.[186] The fact that Artice 12(5) ACHPR, which codifies the prohibition of collective expulsion in the Banjul Charter, does not contain such a "clawback-clause" signals that states cannot deviate from this principle. Other civil and political rights guaranteed in the Charter, such as the right to liberty and security enshrined in Article 6 ACHPR contain such a clause stipulating that "no one may be deprived of his freedom except for reasons and conditions previously laid down by law".

Another example is Article 12(4) ACHPR, which prohibits the arbitrary expulsion of legally residing non-nationals unless they have received "a decision taken **in accordance with the law**". Thus, the fact that Article 12 (5) is not limited by a "claw-back clause" or by any other form of restriction underscores its relevance within the Charter. Thus, on the regional level, the African Charter is seemingly the only human rights instrument

185 Turack, Daniel *The African Charter on Human and Peoples' Rights: Some Preliminary Thoughts* Akron Law Review, (1984), Vol. 17, No. 3, pp. 18–19.

186 Mapuva, Loveness *Negating the Promotion of Human Rights Through "Claw-Back" Clauses in the African Charter on Human and People's Rights* International Affairs and Global Strategy, Vol. 51, 2016, p. 1.

that does not foresee any limitation/restriction or derogation of the prohibition of collective expulsion. In practice, no state party to any of the other regional human rights conventions that offers the general possibility to derogate from the convention or charter in case of emergency, has invoked such a provision regarding the prohibition of collective expulsion.

On an international level, Article 13 ICCPR contains an explicit limitation to the foreigners' rights to a decision in the provision itself in case of national security.[187] The UN Commission on Human Rights clarified in the 1985 *Siracus Principles* on limitations and derogations in the ICCPR that national security exceptions as "may be invoked to justify measures limiting certain rights only when they are taken to protect the existence of the nation, its territorial integrity or political independence against force or threat of force".[188] Furthermore, the respective state must ensure that the limitations do not endanger the essence of the restricted ICCPR right.[189] Besides limitations to the prohibition of collective expulsion in case of national emergency, member states also have the possibility to derogate from the guarantees in Article 13 ICCPR under the general derogation clause in Article 4(1) ICCPR. This provision sets a high threshold for derogation limiting it to times of public emergency. Here, similarly to the European and Inter-American Convention, section two of the provision also entails a list of non-derogatory rights.

The prohibition of collective expulsion in Article 22(1) UN Migrant Worker Convention, in contrast, can neither be limited nor derogated from under any circumstances. Article 82 UNCRMW stipulates that the "rights of migrant workers and members of their families provided for in the present Convention may not be renounced".

In conclusion, "prohibition" is understood in its generic sense as not being allowed. In all assessed regional human rights treaties, the prohibition of collective expulsion is not limited or restricted specifically. However, the ECHR, the EUChFR, the IACHR contain a general derogation clause in case of emergency, which does not exempt the prohibition. The threshold for such a derogation is high. The provision implicitly

187 Article 13 ICCPR reads: "An alien lawfully in the territory of a State Party to the present Covenant may be expelled therefrom only in pursuance of a decision reached in accordance with law and shall, *except where compelling reasons of national security otherwise require*, be allowed to submit the reasons against his explusion [sic!] […]".

188 United Nations Commission on Human Rights *The Siracusa Principles on the Limitation and Derogation Provisions in the International Covenant on Civil and Political Rights* 28 September 1984, E/CN.4/1985/4, (*Siracus Principles*), principle 29.

189 UNComH *Siracusa Principles* principle 2.

containing the prohibition of collective expulsion in the ICCPR, can be limited for national security reasons as clarified in the provision itself. In addition, member states can restrict this provision under the Covenant's general derogation clause applicable in times of emergency. In contrast, the prohibition of collective expulsion as codified in the ACHPR and the UNCRMW in contrast does not allow any restriction, limitation, or derogation on any grounds. Thus, the prohibition in these two conventions is absolute.

4 The Definition of "Expulsion" in the Prohibition of Collective Expulsion

In this chapter so far we have defined the terms "alien", "collective", and "prohibition" within the context of the prohibition of collective expulsion. We now turn to the most ambiguous element: Expulsion. Compared to the other components of the prohibition, defining "expulsion" poses the greatest challenge due to inconsistent interpretations across regional and international courts and treaty bodies. The central ambiguity lies in whether "expulsion" includes non-admission or applies strictly to groups of foreigners already within a state's territory.

This debate dates back to the drafting of the 1951 Refugee Convention. During its first reading, the Swiss representative emphasized the interpretative challenges of the terms "expel" and "return".[190] The Swiss Government, also representing Liechtenstein, argued that "expulsion" referred specifically to refugees already admitted to a state's territory, while "refoulement" had a broader, more ambiguous scope, excluding individuals who had not yet entered the state's territory.[191] The Netherlands representative supported this distinction, noting that it reflected the majority opinion among states' representatives, including those of Belgium, the Federal Republic of Germany, Italy, and Sweden.[192] This early consensus has not resolved the definitional ambiguity. Today, courts and treaty bodies continue to grapple with whether expulsion encompasses non-admission. Regional human

190 UNHCR *Convention and Protocol relating to the Status of Refugees with commentaries* 2010, p.8.

191 Conference of Plenipotentiaries on the Status of Refugees and Stateless Persons Summary Record of the Sixteenth Meeting A/CONF.2/SR.16, 23 November 1951, p.7.

192 Weis, Paul *The Refugee Convention, 1951 Travaux Préparatoires analysed with a commentary* pp. 239–240.

rights courts and the International Law Commission have taken divergent approaches, keeping the debate alive and leaving the precise boundaries of "expulsion" open to interpretation.

On the one hand, we have the restrictive definition of compelling "someone to leave a territory". Article 2a) ILC Draft Articles on the Expulsion of Aliens[193] takes this approach, stipulating that "expulsion" "means a formal **act or conduct attributable** to a *State*, by which an alien is **compelled to leave the territory of that State**; it does not include extradition to another State, surrender to an international criminal court or tribunal, or the **non-admission** of an alien to a State [emphasis added]." This approach is reflected throughout the entire Draft Articles as the question of non-admission was excluded in its entirety from their scope.[194] On the other hand, we have a more inclusive approach which entails non-admission scenarios. One prominent case in this regard is the 2012 *Hirsi Jamaa and Others v. Italy* case before the ECtHR. Here, the Court offered for the first time a detailed interpretation of the term "expulsion" in the sense of the prohibition of collective expulsion. Here, the Court dealt with "push-backs" practices on the High Sea undertaken by Italian authorities. In a lengthy and detailed assessment, the Court defined "expulsion" in a generic way as to "drive someone away from a place".[195] Thus, the ECtHR found that push-backs can constitute a violation of the prohibition of collective expulsion even though the applicants have never set foot on the member state's territory. Prior to *Hirsi Jamaa and Others v. Italy*, the Grand Chamber laid the basis for this approach for example in *Medvedyev and Others v. France*. Here, the Court highlighted that

> the special nature of the maritime environment relied upon by the Government in the instant case cannot justify an area outside the law where ships' crews are covered by no legal system capable of affording them enjoyment of the rights and guarantees protected by the

193 The issue of the discrepancy between the more restrictive understanding of "expulsion" in the Draft Articles in comparison to the ECtHR's interpretation was addressed several times by ECtHR judges. In the public hearing before the Grand Chamber in *N.D. and N.T. v. Spain* of September 2018 for example, Judge Linos Alexandre Sicilianos (from 1:49:23 on), referred to the ILC's *Draft Articles on the Expulsion of Aliens*. He pointed out that these draft articles do not define 'expulsion' as encompassing non-admission scenarios of foreigners and that the prohibition of collective expulsion generally has a very limited scope. See also the joint dissenting opinion of judges Ravarani and Bošnjak in *M.A. v. Lithuania*, Appl. No. 59793/17, 11 December 2018, para. 5.

194 ILC *Draft Articles on the Expulsion of Aliens with Commentaries* p. 3.

195 *Hirsi Jamaa and Others v. Italy* ECtHR, para. 174.

> Convention which the States have undertaken to secure to everyone within their jurisdiction, any more than it can provide offenders with a "safe haven".[196]

In this context, it must be stressed context that the Court here is generally applying a territorial notion to the issue of jurisdiction which is "presumed to be exercised normally throughout the State's territory".[197] The ECtHR and its predecessor have made clear in numerous cases that ECHR rights apply extraterritorially only in exceptional circumstances, requiring a specific justification.[198] These exceptions can be divided into two main categories: jurisdiction based on effective control over the person in question and overall (military) control over a specific territory. Initially, the European Commission of Human Rights took a rather extensive approach acknowledging a jurisdictional link insofar as the respective state exercised authority over the persons or property in question. This was stressed by the Commission in its 1975 *Cyprus v. Turkey* decision, among others.[199] Here, the EUComHR took on the issue of the Turkish occupation of Northern Cyprus. In its decision, the Commission explained that, in general, the application of rights is limited to the national territory of the member state in question. However, it also stressed that it

> is clear from the language, in particular [from] the French text [*relevant de leur jurisdiction*], and the object of this Article, and from the purpose of the Convention as a whole, that the High Contracting Parties are bound to secure the said rights and freedoms [...] whether that authority is exercised within their own territory or abroad.[200]

Years later, the ECtHR seemingly moved away from the Commission's more flexible approach, highlighting the "territorial notion" of the ECHR in the

---

196 *Medvedyev and Others v. France* ECtHR [GC], Appl. No. 3394/03, 29 March 2010, para. 81.

197 *Assanidze v. Georgia* ECtHR, [GC], Appl. no. 71503/01, 8 April 2004, para. 139 and *Hirsi Hirsi Jamaa and Others* ECtHR, [GC], para. 71.

198 See for example: *Banković and Others v. Belgium and Others* ECtHR, [GC], Appl. No. 52207/99, 12 December 2001, paras. 61, 67, 71. Also: *Catan and Others v. République de Moldova and Russia* ECtHR, [GC], Appl. Nos. 43370/04, 8252/05 and 18454/06, 19 October 2012, para. 104.

199 *Cyprus v. Turkey*, European Commission on Human Rights, Appl. Nos. 6780/74 and 6950/75, 26 May 1975.

200 *Ibidem.*, para. 8

landmark case of *Banković and Others v. Belgium and Others*.[201] However, this case did not settle the issue in question once and for all. Subsequent cases, such as *Issa v. Turkey*[202] in 2004 where the court seemed to have adopted a more flexible approach on the 'control and authority' of the perpetrating state[203], contributed to the continuing debate over what constitutes jurisdiction.[204] In the following years, several cases dealing with the extraterritorial applicability paved the way for the approach of "continuous and exclusive control over persons" taken by the Grand Chamber in *Hirsi Jamaa and Others v. Italy*.[205]

This approach had a far-reaching effect even beyond the reach of the Convention. The UN Migrant Worker Committee in *General Comment No. 2* of 2013 referred explicitly to the *Hirsi Jamaa* judgment, stipulating that the prohibition of collective expulsion in the UN Migrant Worker Convention is also extraterritorially applicable. Other courts and commissions such as the African Commission and the African Court on Human and Peoples' Rights, the Inter-American Commission, and Inter-American Court have not yet dealt with the question of extraterritorial applicability of the prohibition. None of these treaty bodies have ever defined "expulsion" in their cases and reports. Thus, it is difficult to make a reasonable assessment of their understanding of the term. However, the African Commission and the Inter-American Court both seem to have expanded the scope of application of respective human rights treaties beyond the member states' territory in general. In General Comment No. 3, the Commission stipulated that the member states must ensure "accountability for any extraterritorial violation of the right to life".[206] In a similar vein, the Inter-American Court of

201 *Banković and Others v. Belgium and Others* ECtHR, [GC].

202 *Issa v. Turkey* ECtHR, Appl. No. 31821/96, 16 November 2004.

203 *Ibidem.*, paras. 55, 68–82.

204 Kim, Seunghwan *Non-Refoulement and Extraterritorial Jurisdiction: State Sovereignty and Migration Controls at Sea in the European Context* Leiden Journal of International Law, Vol. 30, 2007, pp. 54–55.

205 These are for example, the Grand Chamber judgment in *Öcalan v. Turkey* (Appl. No. 46221/99, 12 May 2005), where the Court appears to follow the *Issa v. Turkey* approach and *Al-Saadoon and Mufdhi v. the United Kingdom* (Appl. No.61498/08, 30 June 2009) where jurisdiction was established based on an exclusive *de jure* and *de facto* control over the applicant by the respondent state. This approach was repeated in the above described *Medvedyev and Others v. France case* (maritime context) and ultimately endorsed by the Grand Chamber in the landmark *Al-Skeini and Others v. the United Kingdom* case (Appl. No. 55721/07, 7 July 2011).

206 AComHPR *General Comment No. 3 on the African Charter on Human and Peoples' Rights The Right to Life (Article 4)* adopted during the 57th ordinary session of the Africa Commission on Human and Peoples' Rights, 4–18 November 2015, para. 18.

Human Rights in its landmark 2017 *Advisory Opinion on the Environment and Human Rights* clarified that the Inter-American Convention might also be extraterritorially applicable if the affected persons are under the jurisdiction of the acting state. This jurisdictional link exists if there is a causal connection between the incident that led to the human rights violation and the acting state. Thus, in general, the rights in the IACHR also apply outside a member state's territory.[207]

This finding, however, only indicates that the courts could interpret "expulsion" in the broader sense. Another indicator is that the African Commission, the Inter-American Court, and Inter-American Commission refer to the *Hirsi Jamaa* judgment in all their case law on the prohibition after 2012. However, the treaty bodies do so to clarify the procedural guarantees contained in the provision and not to define "expulsion". For example, in its 2014 Haitian expulsion case, the Inter-American Court referred to both the ECtHR *Hirsi Jamaa* case and the ILC *Draft Articles* on the expulsion of aliens.

4.1 *The Coercive Element*

Despite these two distinct approaches, one including non-admission, the other not, when it comes to defining "expulsion", they have one decisive element in common: Both require some form of coercion in the expulsion procedure. Indirect collective expulsions in which the group of foreigners leaves the territory due to some form of pressure without an attributable act to state authorities are not covered.

Both, the International Law Commission in its Draft Articles on the Expulsion of Aliens and the ECtHR in *Berdzenishvili and Others v. Russia* dealt with "indirect", "constructive" and "disguised" collective expulsions providing clarity in this regard.[208] These terms describe the same phenomenon of state authorities acting in a manner that forces foreigners coercively *en masse* to leave a state's territory. According to the ECtHR and the International Law Commission, the state authority must have committed a

---

207 *Advisory Opinion Environment and Human Rights* IACourtHR, OC-23/17OF, requested by the Republic of Colombia, official summary issued by the Inter-American Court, 15 November 2017, p. 4.

208 The International Law Commission adopts the term "disguised expulsion" in Article 10 Draft Articles on the Expulsion of Aliens as "it was difficult to find a satisfactory equivalent of the term "constructive expulsion" in other languages, particularly French, as the term might carry an undesirable positive connotation. Consequently, the Commission opted in this context for the term "disguised expulsion"." ILC *Draft Articles on the Expulsion of Aliens with Commentary* p. 16.

"formal act/conduct"[209] or "measure"[210] that compelled the foreigners to leave the territory. Jean-Marie Henckaerts points out in his chapter on indirect mass expulsion that even though the term "measure" is rather vague, it is limited by the second element of the definition, that the measure has to be committed by "the competent authority". He further explains that actions taken by individuals or non-governmental agents are excluded from this definition. However, he also notes that if the government tolerates or even facilitates such actions by private individuals or groups, the state could be held accountable for not preventing the mass expulsion.[211] Similarly, the International Law Commission in its Draft Articles clarifies that the forcible departure of an alien, resulting indirectly from state action or inaction – such as when the state supports or permits acts committed by its nationals or others – would fulfill the requirement for collective expulsion.[212] The commentary to this provision further elaborates that an indirect expulsion must meet a certain threshold of compulsion to force the foreign nationals to leave, and it must be clear that the state's actions were aimed at causing their departure.[213] In addition to the necessity of state intention in indirect expulsion cases, there is also a high threshold for compulsion or coercion associated with such measures. The ILC further clarified this point by referencing the Eritrea-Ethiopia Claims Commission, emphasizing that for an expulsion to be considered indirect, the individuals leaving the country must have experienced extreme conditions so dire that there was no viable alternative but to depart.[214] These conditions must stem from actions or policies of the host government, or be clearly attributable to that government.[215]

In the 2016 *Berdzenishvili and Others v. Russia* case, the ECtHR applied part of the International Law Commission's approach to indirect expulsions,

209 Article 2a) ILC Draft Articles on the Expulsion of Aliens.

210 *Becker v. Denmark*, Decision of the European Commission of Human Rights on the admissibility of Application No. 7011/75, 19 Yearbook European Convention on Human Rights 416, 1976, para. 454.

211 Henckaerts, Jean-Marie *Mass Expulsion in Modern International Law and Practice* p. 109.

212 Article 10(2) ILC *Draft Articles on the Expulsion of Aliens.*

213 *Ibidem.*

214 ILC *Draft Articles on the Expulsion of Aliens with Commentaries* p. 17, referring to Partial Award, Civilians Claims, Ethiopia's Claim 5, Eritrea Ethiopia Claims Commission, The Hague, 17 December 2004, paras. 91, 95, United Nations, Reports of International Arbitral Awards, Vol. XXVI, pp. 285–286.

215 *Ibidem.*

focusing on the need for a coercive element.[216] The judgment, though not widely discussed, is significant for its interpretation of the prohibition of collective expulsion under Article 4 Protocol 4 ECHR. Here, the Court ruled that the provision only covers indirect collective expulsions when a coercive measure is involved.[217] In this case, the Court clarified that an official expulsion order or a comparable coercive act must be present for an action to qualify as an expulsion. The applicants who voluntarily left Russia, fearing expulsion but without any official expulsion order or coercion, did not fall under the protection of this prohibition. Here, the Court's analysis emphasized that merely fearing arrest or expulsion does not qualify as collective expulsion. For the claim to succeed, there must be an official expulsion order or an act of detention. This aligns with the ILC's view that coercive measures must be present for indirect expulsions to be recognized. The Court referred to the *Georgia v. Russia (I)*[218] case to underline the coercion element, where identity checks, arrests, and detention were deemed sufficient for collective expulsion.[219]

Here too, the African Commission on Human and Peoples' Rights drew similar conclusions in *Institute for Human Rights and Development in Africa v. Guinea*. This case dealt with a public speech given by Guinean President Lansana Conté in September 2000, in which he proclaimed over national state radio that Sierra Leonean refugees in Guinea should be arrested, searched, and confined to refugee camps, a process which led to widespread atrocities committed against Sierra Leonean refugees. One of these atrocities was, as the Commission put it, that "Sierra Leonean refugees were forced to decide whether they were to be harassed, tortured and die in Guinea, or return to Sierra Leone in the midst of civil war where they would face an equally harsh fate."[220] This forced eviction of refugees led to the African Commission's finding that mass expulsion had occurred and that Guinea had violated Article 12(5) ACHPR. The collective expulsion of Sierra Leonean refugees is the only example in the African Commission's case law dealing with indirect mass expulsion by which the refugees had left Guinea on their own. However, as the claimants pointed out,

216 *Berdzenishvili and Others v. Russia* ECtHR, Appl. Nos. 14594/07 and 6 others, 20 December 2016, para. 81

217 *Ibidem.*, para. 81.

218 *Georgia v. Russia I.* ECtHR [GC], para. 45.

219 *Berdzenishvili and Others v. Russia* ECtHR, para. 83.

220 *Institute for Human Rights and Development in Africa v. Guinea* AComHPR, paras. 1,7.

"[P]resident Conté's speech not only made thousands of Sierra Leonean refugees flee Guinea and return to the dangers posed by the civil war, but it also clearly authorized the return by force of Sierra Leonean refugees. Thus, the voluntary return of refugees to Sierra Leone under these circumstances cannot be considered as voluntary but rather as a dangerous option available for the refugees."[221]

The Commission's finding shows that even indirect measures can amount to a violation of the prohibition of collective expulsion as long as the act coerces the foreigner into leaving. This threshold requires that the foreigner does not have any real alternative than to leave the country.

In conclusion, the coercive element is central to defining what constitutes an "expulsions". The ILC, the ECtHR and the ACHPR require that state authorities take an official action or measure that compels foreigners to leave a country's territory. Indirect expulsions, where individuals leave due to pressure but without direct state action, do not meet this threshold. The ILC's Draft Articles and the ECtHR's *Berdzenishvili* case emphasize that coercion or compulsion must be evident, either through an official expulsion order, detention, or other state-conducted acts. The ILC further clarifies that indirect expulsions can occur when the state tolerates or supports actions that lead to forced departure, provided these actions are attributable to the state. The *Berdzenishvili* judgment highlights that voluntary departure, driven by fear but without coercion or an official expulsion order, does not constitute collective expulsion. Similarly, the African Commission in the *Institute for Human Rights and Development in Africa v. Guinea* case concluded that indirect measures, like a government speech leading to the coerced return of refugees, can amount to a violation of the prohibition on collective expulsion.

5 Conclusions on the Material Elements of the Prohibition of Collective Expulsion

This second chapter has thoroughly examined the material elements of the prohibition of collective expulsion, focusing on its personal scope, the concept of "collectivity", the term "prohibition", and the definition of "expulsion". It also explored how these concepts are interpreted by a range of scholars, international bodies, and regional courts, including the European

221 *Ibidem.*, para. 48.

Court of Human Rights, the African Commission on Human and Peoples' Rights, and the Inter-American Court and Commission on Human Rights, among others. The analysis reveals that the prohibition protects all non-nationals, including stateless persons, refugees, asylum seekers, and migrants, without discrimination based on nationality or legal status. While nationals are generally protected from expulsion under most legal systems, the prohibition specifically focuses on non-nationals, with instruments like the ECHR providing broad guarantees. Notably, the interpretation of this prohibition varies across regions; for instance, the African Charter extends protection to nationals under specific circumstances, whereas the ICCPR limits protection to foreigners legally residing in a state.

A key takeaway from this chapter is that the term "collective" in the prohibition does not necessitate a specific group size or shared characteristics among those expelled. Instead, the focus is on procedural fairness, particularly the lack of individualized assessments that fail to account for the personal circumstances of the individuals involved. This understanding is consistent across various regional systems, which aim to protect individuals from arbitrary expulsions, even when they occur as part of a broader, systematic expulsion pattern. In terms of the term "prohibition", the chapter examined derogation clauses within regional instruments, which set high thresholds for exceptions, particularly in times of emergency. Some treaties allow limited restrictions, while others, such as the African Charter and the UN Migrant Worker Convention, offer an absolute prohibition with no scope for derogation. The definition of "expulsion" proves to be more complex than the other elements. The central question is whether it should be understood broadly to include non-admission, as interpreted by the ECtHR in *Hirsi Jamaa and Others v. Italy* and recognized by the UN Migrant Worker Committee in its General Comment No. 2, or more restrictively as "compelling someone to leave a territory", as defined by the International Law Commission in its Draft Articles on the Expulsion of Aliens. Despite differences in approach, both interpretations share a common requirement for some form of coercion in the expulsion process. However, indirect collective expulsions, where a group of foreigners departs due to external pressure without a direct act by state authorities, fall outside the scope of either interpretation.

With this conclusion on the material elements of the prohibition of collective expulsion, including its scope, the concept of collectivity, and the definition of expulsion, we now turn to the procedural elements in Chapter 3, which address the safeguards and guarantees necessary to ensure the protection of individuals against arbitrary expulsions.

CHAPTER 3

Procedural Protections against Collective Expulsion

As we transition from the material elements of the prohibition of collective expulsion, which emphasize the substantive aspects of protection, we now turn to the procedural elements that ensure the enforcement and effectiveness of these protections. Due process rights provide the utmost safeguard against violations of the rule of law,[1] playing a crucial role in preventing arbitrary expulsions. The importance of such procedural guarantees extends not only to domestic law but also to the international sphere, where they are integral to upholding human rights providing the utmost protection against violations of the rule of law. Martti Koskenniemi's assessment that modern international law is more procedural than substantive[2] underscores the significance of these rights. Indeed, many international and regional human rights instruments, from the ICCPR to the Inter-American Convention, the European Convention, and the African Charter, codify key due process protections, including the right to a fair trial and the *ne bis in idem* principle.

As we have seen in chapter 2, courts around the globe have stressed that due process guarantees also hold critical importance in expulsion procedures due to their profound and irreversible impact on the expelled individual. This importance becomes even more pronounced during times of large-scale migration and asylum influxes, where ensuring that every foreigner has a fair opportunity to contest their expulsion tests the practical and administrative capacities of states. In such scenarios, the prohibition of collective expulsion emerges as the cornerstone of procedural protection for migrants facing group expulsions. The succinct wording of multiple conventions, which unequivocally declare that "[c]ollective expulsion of aliens is prohibited", prompts a key question: What procedural guarantees does this prohibition encompass? This chapter examines the procedural safeguards embedded in the prohibition of collective expulsion, aimed at preventing

1 Heuman, Lars and Wahlgren, Peter *Procedural Law Court Administrations* Scandinavian Studies in Law, Vol. 51 (Stockholm Institute for Scandidnavian Law 2007), foreword.

2 Koskenniemi, Martti *The Politics of International Law*, 1 European Journal of International Law, Vol. 1, No. 199, pp. 4–32.

 | DOI:10.1163/9789004535077_004

arbitrary group expulsions. It begins by outlining the minimum due process standards applicable to expulsion procedures in general (1). It then provides an overview of the procedural protections associated with the prohibition of collective expulsion as articulated in various regional and international conventions (2). Finally, section 3 synthesizes the findings, offering a comprehensive assessment of the nature and procedural scope of this critical safeguard.

1 Minimum Procedural Protection Standards in Expulsion Procedures

Under international law, every individual – whether a citizen or a foreigner – benefits from a baseline of human rights protections, even when they are outside their home country.[3] This universal minimum standard is grounded in the recognition of fundamental human dignity but remains undefined in its exact scope and content. At a minimum, it encompasses rights such as the right to life, protection of physical integrity, and certain procedural guarantees, all of which uphold the inherent value of every person.[4] The specific application of such guarantees to foreigners, particularly in the context of expulsion or deportation, remains underexplored in legal scholarship. While international law offers robust protections against arbitrary actions, the procedural rights afforded to non-citizens facing expulsion, such as the right to a hearing or the ability to present evidence against their removal, are often less clearly articulated and implemented.

This section begins by examining the foundational principles of due process, exploring what constitutes fair procedural protections under international human rights law. It then turns to the procedural safeguards enshrined in the prohibition of collective expulsion, as established in various regional and international human rights instruments. The analysis seeks to shed light on how these instruments operationalize procedural protections for foreigners, ensuring that expulsion procedures adhere to fundamental principles of fairness, justice, and the rule of law. In doing so, the following section offers an introduction to what constitutes procedural protection before turning to the procedural scope of application of the prohibition in various regional and international human rights instruments.

---

3 Gornig, Gilbert *Menschenrechtlicher Mindeststandard* in: Schöbener (edn.) *Völkerrecht* (C.F. Müller 2014), p. 303.

4 *Ibidem.*, pp. 303–304.

As a starting point, we need to ask ourselves what makes a right a procedural protection guaranteeing due process? The US Supreme Court case *Goldberg v. Kelly of 1970* offers a general definition for the determination of the elements of due process rights.[5] Here, the US Supreme Court established the requirements for guaranteeing procedural due process for a welfare recipient. According to the US Supreme Court, due process guarantees require a hearing, which among other things, entails an impartial decision-maker, the opportunity to be heard, and reasons for the decision.[6]

An alternative approach is provided by Simona Grossi who explains that

> [a]ny democratic judicial system must be built on the principle of *due process*, the fountain *from which* all *procedural rules and doctrines flourish*. The principle carries with it the ideas of *fairness*, *reasonableness*, and *efficiency*, all to be measured, balanced, and applied to the various, changing circumstances that confront a judicial system in a democracy [emphasis added].[7]

What we learn from these two approaches is that procedural rights are the mechanisms through which the principle of due process is realized in administrative, civil, or criminal legal systems. These rights form the backbone of fair and equitable legal proceedings by ensuring that individuals have meaningful opportunities to participate in decisions affecting their rights and interests.[8] As shown in the following, core procedural rights include, but are not limited to, the right to be heard, the right to an effective remedy, the right to legal representation, and the right to access and understand evidence presented in a case. The importance of procedural rights – especially in the context of migrants' rights – lies in their role as safeguards against arbitrary or unjust exercises of power by the state or other authorities. By embedding transparency and accountability into legal and administrative processes, these rights uphold the rule of law. For example, the right to be heard guarantees that individuals can present their arguments and evidence, ensuring that decision-makers consider all relevant perspectives

5 *Goldberg v. Kelly US Supreme Court* 397 U.S. 254 (1970).

6 *Ibidem.*, p. 271.

7 Grossi, Simona *Procedural Due Process* Seton Hall Circuit Review Vol. 13, No. 2 (2017), pp. 155–202.

8 Examples of codifications of such guarantees are to be found in the Universal Declaration of Human Rights, Article 10 which guarantees the right to a fair and public hearing or in Article 14 and 2(3) International Covenant on Civil and Political Rights which contain the rights to a fair trial and an effective remedy.

before reaching a conclusion. Similarly, the right to an effective remedy provides recourse for individuals to challenge decisions that violate their rights, reinforcing the accountability of institutions. Both of these principles are of great importance in expulsion or denial of entry situations where migrants are in a vulnerable position vis-à-vis the acting state.

Procedural rights also serve broader societal functions. They promote trust in legal and governmental systems by demonstrating a commitment to fairness and justice. In democratic systems, they are essential for maintaining legitimacy and public confidence in the impartiality and efficiency of the judiciary and administrative bodies. Additionally, procedural rights are crucial in protecting vulnerable groups, such as migrants or asylum seekers, who may face systemic disadvantages or discrimination. For these groups, procedural guarantees act as a critical tool to ensure that their rights are respected and that they receive equal treatment under the law.[9]

In general, process rights are categorized as due process rights when they are fair, balanced, impartial, reasonable, and efficient. These elements constitute the basis for fair trial rights in criminal and civil procedures. The European Convention on Human Rights,[10] the Inter-American Convention on Human Rights,[11] the African Charter on Human and Peoples' Rights,[12] the 2004 Arab Charter on Human Rights[13] or the International Covenant on Civil and Political Rights[14] all contain fair trial rights and the right to an effective remedy in criminal and most also in civil procedures. Jointly, these

9 For details see: International Organization for Migration *IOM Information Note on Access to Justice: A Migrant's Right* (2019), available at: https://migrantprotection.iom.int/en/resources/article-issuepolicy-brief-journal-blog-etc/iom-information-note-access-justice-migrants.

10 European Convention on Human Rights, 213 U.N.T.S. 222, 1953, as amended by Protocols Nos. 11 and 14, supplemented by Protocols Nos. 1, 4, 6, 7, 12 and 13, 4 November 1950, ETS 5, Articles 6 and 13.

11 Inter-American Convention on Human Rights, O.A.S. Treaty Series No 36, 1992, 1144 U.N.T.S. 123, entered into force July 18, 1978, reprinted in Basic Documents Pertaining to Human Rights in the Inter-American System, OEA/Ser.L.V/II.82 doc.6 rev.1, 25, Articles 8 and 25(1).

12 African Charter on Human and Peoples' Rights 1981, OAU Doc. CAB/LEG/67/3 rev. 5, 21 I.L.M. 58 (1982), Article 7.

13 2004 Arab Charter on Human Rights, 22 May 2004, entry into force 15 March 2008, Articles 12, 13. The first version of the Arab Charter was adopted in 1994, but no Arab League State had ratified it.

14 International Covenant on Civil and Political Rights 1966, GA Res. 2200A (XXI) of 16 December 1966, 21 UN GAOR Supp. (No 16) 52, UN Doc. A/6316 (1966), 999 U.N.T.S. 171, Articles 14(1) and 2(3)(a).

principles form the basis of due process guarantees in domestic, regional, and international law.[15] Article 47 of the Charter of Fundamental Rights in the European Union (EUChFR),[16] in contrast, goes further and extends fair trial guarantees to "everyone" in any proceeding and the right to remedy to anyone "whose rights and freedoms guaranteed by the by the law of the Union are violated".[17]

Other human rights instruments, most famously the ECHR limit their fair trial and effective remedy provisions to civil and criminal procedures while excluding (most) administrative procedures. Thus, these fair trial rights do not cover asylum processes and expulsion procedures on the domestic level.[18] In recent years, a notable development has emerged within the context of procedural guarantees under the ECHR, particularly relevant to the focus on migrants' rights. This trend, often referred to as a "procedural turn", has gained significant attention among scholars.[19]

This development, as explored in the ECtHR case law, reflects a growing emphasis on the quality and fairness of national decision-making processes rather than solely evaluating substantive outcomes.[20] This shift aligns with

15 The Human Rights Committee has acknowledged in its *General Comment No. 32 on Article 14* that the fair trial guarantees in the ICCPR also apply to civil procedures. See Human Rights Committee *General Comment No. 32 Article 14, Right to equality before courts and tribunals and to a fair trial* CCPR/C/GC/32, 23 August 2007, paras. 13, 16. The Arab Charter seemingly only contains fair trial rights in criminal proceedings.

16 Charter of Fundamental Rights in the European Union, 2000 OJ(C 364) 1, Article 47.

17 For a detailed analysis on the relationship between Article 47 EUChFR and Article 6 ECHR and the scope of application of Article 6 ECHR in general see: Schabas, William *European Convention on Human Rights Commentary* (Oxford University Press 2015), pp. 264–327.

18 For more details on the relationship between the prohibition of collective expulsion and fair trial rights in the respective human rights conventions, see below Chapter 4.

19 The phenomenon has been assessed for example by Huijbers, Leonie *The European Court of Human Rights' Procedural Approach in the Age of Subsidiarity* Cambridge International Law Journal, Vol. 6, No. 2, December 2017, pp. 177–201 or Popelier, *Patricia The Court as Regulatory Watchdog: The Procedural Approach in the Case Law of the European Court of Human Rights* in: Popelier; Mazmanyan and Vandenbruwaene (eds.), *The Role of Courts in a Context of Multilevel Governance* (Intersentia 2013) pp. 249–267 or Brems, Eva *The "Logics" of Procedural-Type Review by the European Court of Human Rights from Part 1 – Foundations and Rationales for Procedural Review by Supranational Courts Deciding Fundamental Rights Cases* in: Gerards and Brems (eds.), Procedural Review in European Fundamental Rights Cases (Cambridge University Press 2017), pp. 17–39.

20 Huijbers, Leonie *The European Court of Human Rights' Procedural Approach in the Age of Subsidiarity* pp. 183–185.

the principle of subsidiarity, which underscores the primary role of national authorities in safeguarding human rights while maintaining the Court's supervisory function.[21] By assessing procedural fairness, regularity, and rationality, the ECtHR ensures that national authorities adhere to principles of transparency, accountability, and reasoned decision-making.[22] This procedural focus allows the Court to respect states' discretion while ensuring compliance with human rights obligations particularly in politically sensitive areas such as migration and asylum procedures

In this context, the question arises which procedural safeguards should states provide for every individual to ensure a fair and effective process at the border and in expulsion cases? This question has been highly debated for decades. Atle Grahl-Madsen notes in "Territorial Asylum" of 1980 that a minimum of process rights are desirable, such as "the right to state his position fully-orally or in writing-before a decision is taken".[23] He further promotes the establishment of a global safeguard that grants every migrant the right to an effective remedy.[24] The author had specifically proposed integrating procedural safeguards into the Draft of the United Nations Group of Experts for the Asylum Convention, yet his recommendation went unheeded. Over 40 years later, the majority of states have still not ratified a legally binding international convention that incorporates such procedural protections for migrants. In response to this gap, courts and treaty bodies have stepped in to bridge the void, compensating for the absence of a globally binding framework by expansively interpreting the prohibition of collective expulsion. This judicial creativity underscores the critical role of procedural safeguards in protecting migrants' rights in the absence of comprehensive international agreements as we will see in the following section.

2 Procedural Protection Standards in the Prohibition of Collective Expulsion

In this section, we now turn from the general notion of what is a procedural right to the concrete question of whether the prohibition of collective

21 *Ibidem.*, pp. 198–199.
22 *Ibidem*, pp. 188–191.
23 Grahl-Madsen, Alte *Territorial Asylum* (Oceana Publications 1980), pp. 56–57.
24 *Ibidem.*

expulsion does include procedural guarantees? If so, are these guarantees consistent across various regional and international human rights conventions? And how do they protect foreigners in various expulsion situations? Addressing these questions is essential to understanding how procedural standards are incorporated into this fundamental principle and how they vary or align across different legal frameworks. For this reason, this section undertakes a comprehensive examination of the procedural guarantees embedded in the prohibition of collective expulsion within regional and international treaties. To begin, it explores the European Convention on Human Rights, which has significantly shaped the procedural interpretation of this prohibition (2.1). It then turns to other regional instruments, including the Charter of Fundamental Rights of the European Union (2.2), the Inter-American Convention on Human Rights (2.3), and the African Charter on Human and Peoples' Rights (2.4).

Following this regional analysis, the section delves into international instruments that contain provisions relevant to the prohibition of collective expulsion. It begins with the International Covenant on Civil and Political Rights, a cornerstone of international human rights law (2.5), and continues with the UN Convention on the Protection of the Rights of All Migrant Workers and Members of Their Families (2.6) and the Convention Against Torture and Other Cruel, Inhuman or Degrading Treatment or Punishment (2.7).

In the final part, the section compares the procedural standards across these conventions, highlighting both shared elements and notable differences. By identifying commonalities, such as the emphasis on non-arbitrariness and individual case assessments, the section illustrates the convergence of certain procedural guarantees while also drawing attention to the unique approaches adopted within each framework. This analysis underscores the evolving nature of procedural protections in the prohibition of collective expulsion and their critical role in safeguarding migrants' rights as well as their role in different expulsion scenarios.

2.1 *Article 4 Protocol 4 European Convention on Human Rights*

As we will see in the following, the procedural elements of the prohibition of collective expulsion under Article 4 of Protocol 4 ECHR play a crucial role in ensuring that expulsions are carried out in accordance with fundamental human rights principles. Beyond the material aspects of the prohibition, the ECtHR has increasingly emphasized procedural safeguards as a means to prevent arbitrary and unlawful expulsions. As Itamar Mann has put it, "the European Court of Human Rights […] has in its jurisprudence on unauthorized migration developed some of its most fundamental tenets of human rights law".[25] This observation is particularly evident in the Court's recent jurisprudence, where it has stressed the procedural guarantees inherent in the prohibition of collective expulsion.[26]

One reason for the ECtHR's repeated engagement with the scope of protection of this provision is the changing external migration control policy of ECHR member states since the 1990s. This policy has continuously focused more and more on outsourcing and extraterritorialisation of migration control measures.[27] Since 2002, applicants have increasingly relied on the prohibition of collective expulsion under Article 4 Protocol 4 ECHR in cases extending beyond the traditional context of expelling resident foreigners from a state's territory. This prohibition has also gained significant relevance in scenarios involving non-admission at borders and immediate returns of migrants. Several cases addressing these evolving expulsion contexts are currently pending before the European Court of Human Rights.[28] The outcomes of these cases are expected to have a substantial impact on states' external migration control policies. This growing focus on Article 4 Protocol 4 in recent years has led to a series of important ECtHR rulings that have clarified the scope of the prohibition. These decisions have underscored the procedural safeguards states must adhere to when expelling groups of individuals, ensuring compliance with the principles of fairness and non-arbitrariness. The following sections analyze these procedural guarantees, exploring both their origins as envisioned by the drafters of the Fourth Protocol and their subsequent development through the jurisprudence of the ECtHR and its predecessor.

A semantic analysis of Article 4 of Protocol 4 ECHR reveals that its concise wording encapsulates four key material elements: Collective, expulsion, foreigner, and prohibition. As explored in Chapter 2, these elements define the scope and application of the provision. Some scholars argue that the prohibition of collective expulsion is limited to these material elements and does not implicitly include procedural rights.[29] This interpretation is

---

25 Mann, Itamar *Humanity at Sea: Maritime Migration and the Foundations of International Law* (Cambridge University Press 2016), p. 3.

26 *Ibidem.*, p. 4.

27 For a detailed analysis of such developments see: Gammeltoft-Hansen, Thomas *Access to Asylum* (Cambridge University Press 2011).

28 Three of them against Latvia, Lithuania and Poland, see also outlook in Chapter 5.

29 Brandl, Ulrike *Verbot der Kollektivausweisung von Ausländern* Art 4 EMRK/Prot 4 in: Internationaler Kommentar zur Europäischen Menschenrechtskonvention mit einschlägigen Texten und Dokumenten Pabel/Schmahl (eds.), (Carl Heymanns Verlag 2013), para. 14.

primarily justified by the literal text of Article 4 Protocol 4 and the *travaux préparatoires*.[30] According to this view, the drafting committee deliberately chose not to include explicit individual guarantees, aiming instead to ensure that state officials examine the individual circumstances of each case during expulsion proceedings.[31] This approach was intended to draw a clear distinction between individual and collective expulsions, avoiding overlap between the two categories.[32] However, other scholars contend that Article 4 Protocol 4 implicitly incorporates procedural safeguards.[33] They argue that the very nature of the prohibition requires an individual, reasonable, and objective examination of the circumstances by the competent authorities.[34] This interpretation suggests that the provision inherently mandates a minimum procedural guarantee to treat each individual case distinctly and fairly during expulsion processes.

As will be demonstrated, the prohibition of collective expulsion encompasses both material elements and procedural guarantees. This conclusion is supported by three key lines of reasoning: A historical examination of the *travaux préparatoires*, an analysis of relevant case law, and a systematic contextualization of the provision within the broader framework of the Convention and its additional protocols. Together, these perspectives reveal that procedural safeguards are an integral component of the prohibition, ensuring fairness and preventing arbitrariness in expulsion practices.

2.1.1 Procedural Protections in the Drafting Process of Article 4 Protocol 4 ECHR

First, a close examination of the Explanatory Report to Protocol Four reveals that the Drafting Committee did not dismiss procedural guarantees in their entirety. The report states that "[i]t was also felt that a provision **limited to**

30 Pöschl, Magdalena *Artikel 4 4. ZPEMRK* in: Korinek/Holoubek *Österreichisches Bundesverfassungsrecht Textsammlung und Kommentar* (Springer 2003), para. 14

31 *Ibidem.*

32 *Ibidem.*

33 Van Dijk, Pieter and Van Hoof, Godefridus *Theory and Practice of the European Convention on Human Rights* (Kluwer Law and Taxation Publishers 3rd edn., 1998), pp. 677–678; Henckaerts, Jean-Marie *Mass Expulsion in Modern International Law and Practice* (Martinus Nijhoff 1995), pp. 13–15, *Deumeland,* Dieter *Das Verbot der Xenelasie bei Ausweisung von Ausländern in der Bundesrepublik Deutschland* AWR Bulletin, Vierteljahresschrift für Flüchtlingsfragen, Vol. 22, No. 4, 1984, p.182.

34 Henckaerts *Mass expulsion in Modern International Law and Practice* p. 13.

guarantees of a procedural character would be **insufficient** and that it would be preferable to have no provision at all [emphasis added]".[35]

It seems that the Drafters relied on the vagueness of the chosen language to allow later in the future a broader leeway of interpretation. The Commission had dismissed a previous version of Article 4 Protocol 4 ECHR, which suggested a derogation from the provision in case of a threat to national security. The Commission offered a counterexample instead: Today's version of the prohibition of collective expulsion.[36] Interestingly, the procedural character of the initial proposal of the Drafting Committee resembled Article 3 of the 1955 Convention on Establishment, which was the first Convention by the Council of Europe to include a list of guarantees to prevent arbitrary individual expulsions. However, the Committee decided to adopt an entirely new provision rather than copying the existing example.[37] The reason for this approach was to avoid conflict between the two legal instruments and to create a provision that did not limit the reasons for expulsion.[38]

Thus, the drafting history of Article 4 of Protocol 4 ECHR demonstrates a deliberate effort to create a provision combining material and procedural elements while allowing for flexible interpretation. The Explanatory Report reveals that while purely procedural guarantees were considered insufficient, the drafters did not exclude them entirely. Instead, they crafted language to enable nuanced interpretations over time. By rejecting an earlier draft permitting national security derogations and avoiding direct replication of the 1955 Convention on Establishment, the drafters aimed to create a unique and universal provision. This version avoids conflicts with other legal instruments and maintains broad applicability by not limiting the grounds for expulsion. Article 4 Protocol 4 ECHR thus integrates substantive protections with implicit procedural safeguards, ensuring fairness and preventing arbitrariness, reflecting the drafters' intent to offer a robust yet adaptable safeguard for foreigners' rights.

35 Council of Europe *Explanatory Report to Protocol No. 4 to the Convention for the Protection of Human Rights and Fundamental Freedoms, securing certain rights and freedoms other than those already included in the Convention and in the first Protocol thereto* ETS No. 46, 16. September 1963, para. 33 c).

36 *Ibidem.*, paras. 31–34.

37 Henkaerts *Mass Expulsion in Modern International Law and Practice* p. 10.

38 *Ibidem.*

2.1.2 Procedural Protections in the Case Law on Article 4 Protocol 4 ECHR

As promised above, we now turn to a close examination of relevant cases from *Alibaks and Others v. the Netherlands* of 1988 to the most recent decision in *M.A. and Z.R. v. Cyprus* of 2024 that reveals that the scope of Article 4 Protocol 4 ECHR does contain procedural guarantees. These cases show that the courts determine a violation of the prohibition based on the question of whether authorities upheld certain procedural guarantees. These guarantees include the assessment of whether the applicant/s could bring forward their claims before being expelled[39] and/or the possibility to have their case reviewed in court proceedings.[40]

In all cases concerning Article 4 Protocol 4 ECHR, the Commission and Court assessed whether states upheld procedural rights, even without explicitly acknowledging that the provision includes procedural elements. Between 1968 and 1995, the European Commission of Human Rights frequently addressed the interpretation of the prohibition of collective expulsion. However, it did not find a violation of this prohibition in any of these cases.

In the earliest cases, violations were dismissed outright because the states in question had not ratified Protocol 4. In other instances, the Commission ruled the cases inadmissible, determining that no "collective" expulsion had occurred since state authorities had carried out objective and individualized examinations of the affected individuals.[41] The first case in which the European Commission of Human Rights substantively examined a violation of the prohibition of collective expulsion occurred five years after the drafting of the fourth protocol. Even though the case remains unpublished, one short paragraph available on the case in the Digest of Strasbourg Case-Law

39 *N.D. and N.T. v. Spain* ECtHR Appls. Nos. 8675/15 and 8697/15, 3 October 2017, para. 154.

40 *Alibaks and Others v. The Netherlands* EUComHR, Appl. No.14209/88, Commission decision of 16 December 1988, Decisions and Reports 59, section "THE LAW".

41 The first published case where Article 4 Protocol 4 was alleged to be violated was *X v. the Federal Republic of Germany*, No. 3110/67, Commission decision of 19 July 1968, see also: Dec. Adm. Comp. Ap. 3803/68, 3804/68, 4 October 1968 (unpublished); Digest of Strasbourg Case-Law relating to the European Convention on Human Rights, Vol. 5 (Carl Heymanns Verlag 1985), p. 890, *X contre la Belgique*, No. 5351/72 6579/74, Commission decision of 18 July 1974. *Becker v. Denmark*, No.7011/75, Commission decision of 3 October 1975, Decisions and Reports 4; *K.G. v. Germany*, No. 7704/76, Commission decision of 11 March 1977; *O. and Others v. Luxembourg*, No.7757/77, Commission decision of 3 March 1978; *Alibaks and Others v. the Netherlands*, Appl. No.14209/88, Commission decision of 16 December 1988, Decisions and Reports 59; *Tahiri v. Sweden*, No. 25129/94, Commission decision of 11 January 1995.

relating to the European Convention on Human Rights reveals that Article 4 Protocol 4 ECHR "prohibits collective expulsion of aliens but not expulsion **strictly limited** to individuals".[42] The Commission ruled this case inadmissible, as

> it clearly appears from the applicants' submissions that the decision to expel them was based on *particular circumstances* relating to *each of the applicants* as *individuals*; whereas, therefore, this decision concerned an expulsion strictly *limited to particular individuals* and the said Article is therefore not applicable [emphasis added].[43]

This unpublished case of 1968, together with the Commission's findings on Article 4 Protocol 4 ECHR in *Becker v. Denmark* of 1975, set the basis for today's understanding of the provision's scope of protection. In *Becker v. Denmark*, the Commission defined collective expulsion as "any measure of the competent authority compelling aliens as a group to leave the country, except where such a measure is taken after and on the basis of a reasonable and objective examination of the particular cases of each individual alien of the group".[44] This case concerned the repatriation of a group of about two hundred Vietnamese children by the Danish authorities. The claimant, Henning Becker, a journalist and the director of the Project Children's Protection and Security International (CPSI), alleged the Danish Government to violate the Convention through the then envisaged repatriation of the

42 Dec. Adm. Comp. Ap. 3803/68, 3804/68, 4 October 1968 (unpublished), paragraph reprinted in Digest of Strasbourg Case-Law relating to the European Convention on Human Rights, Vol. 5 (Carl Heymanns Verlag 1985), (Digest of Strasbourg Case-Law), Article 4, Protocol IV, p. 890.

43 Digest of Strasbourg Case-Law p. 890.

44 *Becker v. Denmark* no. 7011/75, Commission decision of 3 October 1975, Decisions and Reports (DR) 4, p. 236. The Convention bodies referred to this finding in several cases as a source for defining collective expulsion amongst others in *K.G. v. the Federal Republic of Germany*, no. 7704/76, Commission decision of 11 March 1977, unreported; *O. and Others v. Luxembourg*, no. 7757/77, Commission decision of 3 March 1978, unreported; *A. and Others v. the Netherlands*, no. 14209/88, Commission decision of 16 December 1988, DR 59, p. 274; *Andric v. Sweden* ECtHR, Appl. No. 45917/99, 23 February 1999 (*Andric v. Sweden*); *Čonka v. Belgium* No. 51564/99, ECHR 2002-I; *Davydov v. Estonia* (dec.), No. 16387/03, 31 May 2005; *Berisha and Haljiti v. "the former Yugoslav Republic of Macedonia"* (dec.), No. 18670/03, ECHR 2005-VIII; *Sultani v. France*, No. 45223/05, ECHR 2007-IV; *Ghulami v. France* (dec.), No. 45302/05, 7 April 2009; and *Dritsas and Others v. Italy* (dec.), No. 2344/02, 1 February 2011); *Hirsi et al v. Italy* [GC], para. 166.

Vietnamese children. Most of the children belonged to the ethnic Montagnard minority and had been brought to Denmark years before for reasons of safety.[45] In this specific case, the main reason for the Commission's finding was that

> it was also laid down that when peace was restored in the Republic of Vietnam, certain Montagnard students, in the care of the applicant's organisation, would return to Vietnam, to take part in the development of their country.[46]

The Danish government argued that returning the group of children constituted repatriation rather than collective expulsion. In contrast, Mr. Becker contended that the planned removal of the entire group amounted to collective expulsion under Article 4 Protocol 4 ECHR, emphasizing that "these children were the only group of Montagnard and Vietnamese refugees in Denmark",[47] making them a clearly identifiable group. However, the Commission rejected Mr. Becker's arguments and declared the case inadmissible. It reasoned that since the Danish government had committed to assessing each case individually and acknowledged that repatriation might be in the best interest of some children, the situation did not constitute collective expulsion.[48] The applicant maintained that the appropriate test for determining the collective nature of an expulsion was whether "a group of persons is expelled without due regard to the individual case".[49] While the Commission accepted this criterion, it did not clarify how authorities should conduct individualized assessments, ultimately dismissing the applicant's claims in just four brief paragraphs. Interestingly, the Commission did not comment on the fact that the applicant submitted the case to the Commission before the expulsion of the children from Denmark. Thus, it seems that the prohibition covers not only post-expulsion cases but also impending expulsions in which the probability is sufficiently substantiated.

Another example in this regard is the ECtHR's 2014 *Abdi Ahmed and others v. Malta* case. The case deals with 102 Somali applicants intercepted by Maltese authorities. The applicants argued that their pending deportation would constitute an arbitrary collective expulsion. They underlined this

---

45 *Becker v. Denmark* EUComHR p. 217.
46 *Becker v. Denmark* EComHR, p. 217.
47 *Ibidem.*, p. 231.
48 *Ibidem.*, p. 890.
49 *Ibidem.*, p. 231.

claim stating that "no assessment of each applicant's situation had been undertaken, other than one based on sex and physical condition".[50] The Court did not follow this line of argument rejecting this claim in its entirety. It justified the inadmissibility as the applicants either had an individual examination in the aftermath of their "almost" expulsion or still have the possibility to bring forward claims.[51]

These two examples show that in collective expulsion cases, state officials must already have conducted the act of collectively expelling the foreigners. In the alternative, the applicants must show that the impediment thereof is sufficiently urgent to pass the admissibility stage. Even though the Commission did not find any violation of Article 4 Protocol 4 in its case law, it interpreted the provision to implicitly contain procedural guarantees. In detail, Article 4 Protocol 4 ECHR protects each foreigner who is not individually expelled but with others under similar circumstances. Each foreigner has the right to an objective and reasonable examination of his or her circumstances. Nevertheless, the relevance of the Commission's interpretation of the prohibition of collective expulsion, which laid the basis for the European Court's interpretation of the provision since the early 2000s, must not be underestimated. The fact that the ECHR continues to refer to these fundamentals in its judgments substantiates this point. Building on the foundation laid by the Commission, the Court further developed the interpretation of the prohibition of collective expulsion through numerous cases between 2002 and 2024. In these cases, the Court examined alleged violations in depth, addressing expulsions of long-term resident foreigners as well as situations involving denials of entry.

Looking at the circumstances of the alleged collective expulsions in these judgments, it becomes apparent why the more detailed interpretation of the procedural guarantees became necessary. The circumstances of the collective expulsions in the cases that reached the Court became more diverse over time. Claimants alleged a violation of Article 4 Protocol 4 in push-backs scenarios on the High Sea,[52] immediate summary expulsions, so-called "hot returns",[53] and non-admission scenarios.[54] These evolving

50 *Abdi Ahmed and Others v. Malta* ECtHR, Appl. No. 43985/13, 16 September 2014, para. 83.

51 *Ibidem.*, para. 84.

52 See: *Hirsi Jamaa v. Italy* ECtHR [GC], Appl. No. 27765/09, 23 February 2012.

53 See: *Khlaifia and Others v. Italy* ECtHR [GC] Appl. No. 16483/12, 15 December 2016.

54 See ECtHR judgments: *N.D. and N.T. v. Spain*, [Chamber] and *Hirsi Jamaa and Others v. Italy* [GC] or *M.K. and Others v. Poland* ECtHR, Appl. Nos 40503/17, 42902/17 and 43643/17, 23 July 2020 or *Shahzad v. Hungary* ECtHR, Appl. No. 12625/17, 8 July 2021.

scenarios have required the Court to refine its approach in distinguishing between different forms of expulsion, taking into account the specific legal and factual circumstances of each case.

To analyze this development, I differentiate between two main categories of collective expulsion that have emerged through the Court's jurisprudence. The first category concerns the expulsion of foreigners who have already resided in a state for an extended period. This form of expulsion, which I refer to as the "original" concept of collective expulsion, aligns most closely with what the drafters of the Convention initially envisioned when drafting Article 4 Protocol 4 ECHR.

The second scenario to which I refer as "expedited" collective expulsion deals with immediate group expulsions of non-nationals. State officials either expel the foreigners upon entry, prevent them from entering or conduct so-called "hot returns". These are physical removals immediately after their entry and interception. The reason for the distinction between these two scenarios is that the ECtHR seemingly treats the two sets of collective expulsion scenarios differently. This distinction becomes visible when it comes to the level of procedural guarantees for the respective foreigners. It seems that in its recent case law the Court has also drawn a distinction between asylum seekers and those migrating for other reasons in this category granting procedural protections to the latter to an even lesser degree.[55]

In "expedited" collective expulsion scenarios, Article 4 Protocol 4 ECHR does not guarantee the right to an interview *per se*. The effective possibility of every foreigner of the group to bring forward her or his claims is

55 As shown in Chapter 2, 1.1, recent ECtHR case law suggests a shift toward prioritizing asylum seekers under Article 4 of Protocol 4 ECHR, though not explicitly stated. While Article 4 Protocol 4 ECHR applies to all non-citizens, cases like *N.D. and N.T. v. Spain* (2020) have differentiated protection for asylum seekers. The Court clarified that "expulsion" under Article 4 applies to anyone removed, but suggested that the inadmissibility of asylum claims under Article 3 may affect Article 4 protection. In cases like *A.A. and Others v. North Macedonia* (2022) and *M.A. and Z.R. v. Cyprus* (2024), asylum claims have influenced the Court's approach to collective expulsion, despite no explicit limitation in Article 4 Protocol 4 ECHR. In *M.A. and Z.R.*, the Court linked Article 4 Protocol 4 protection to the risk of ill-treatment under Article 3, rejecting the argument that applicants could have applied for a visa, noting it wasn't a genuine option for asylum seekers.

This trend highlights a growing distinction between how asylum seekers and other migrants are treated in collective expulsion cases, as seen in *M.A. v. Latvia*, where a lack of evidence of an asylum request led to an unsuccessful claim. This raises questions about how the Court will address cases where asylum status is unclear.

satisfied in these scenarios when the foreigners had at least the **possibility** to bring forward claims. Furthermore, in these cases, Article 4 Protocol 4 ECHR does not guarantee the right of every foreigner to individual legal assistance/assistance of an interpreter. This is not the case in "original" collective expulsion scenarios in which states need to ensure the full scale of procedural guarantees. These include the objective and effective assessment of every foreigner of the group, not just the possibility to bring forward claims. In the "original" scenarios, also the right to legal assistance and an interpreter is guaranteed as well as the right to appeal/review, which triggers the suspensive effect of the expulsion and the right to an effective remedy. The ECtHR does not draw such a clear distinction in its judgments.

In conclusion, the ECtHR's interpretation of the prohibition of collective expulsion under Article 4 Protocol 4 ECHR reveals a nuanced approach that distinguishes between two categories of expulsion scenarios: The "original" form, involving foreigners who have resided in a state for an extended period, and the "expedited" form, which concerns immediate expulsions or non-admissions. This distinction is relevant as it impacts the procedural guarantees afforded to individuals in each scenario. While "original" collective expulsion scenarios trigger a comprehensive set of procedural protections, such as the right to individual assessments, legal assistance, and the right to appeal, "expedited" scenarios offer more limited protections, focusing on the possibility for individuals to raise claims without guaranteeing rights like legal assistance or interpreters. Recent case law also suggests that the ECtHR is increasingly differentiating between asylum seekers and other migrants, granting asylum seekers more procedural safeguards. This evolving trend highlights the Court's shifting approach and the varying levels of protection depending on the nature of the expulsion and the status of the individuals involved. The next section will build on this analysis by examining, in detail, the concrete procedural protections embedded in the prohibition of collective expulsion, drawing from the full range of ECtHR case law. This detailed exploration will clarify the extent to which these procedural guarantees are applied and how they differ across various expulsion scenarios.

2.1.2.1 *Objective and Individual Assessment*

An individual, reasonable, and objective examination of the circumstances of each member of the group before the expulsion is the cornerstone of the prohibition of collective expulsion. The "Twenty Guidelines on Forced Return" adopted by the Committee of Ministers of the Council of Europe in

2005 highlight this.[56] These guidelines are binding upon adoption on the Council of Europe member states.[57] However, as reservation of the United Kingdom to "comply or not" with specific guidelines under the Rules of Procedure[58] shows, some Council member states are reluctant to transfer any authority in migration matters to a regional level.

In the introduction to the Guidelines, the Committee of Ministers emphasizes member states' obligation to grant "every person seeking international protection" due process rights such as

> the right for his or her application to be treated in *a fair procedure* in line with international law, which includes access to an *effective remedy* before a decision on the removal order is issued or is executed [emphasis added].[59]

Furthermore, Guideline 3 even contains the prohibition of collective expulsion stipulating that

> A removal order *shall only* be issued on the basis of a reasonable and objective examination of the particular case of each individual person concerned, and it *shall take into account* the circumstances specific to each case. The collective expulsion of aliens is prohibited [emphasis added].[60]

The Commentary on Guideline 3 further clarifies the scope of this protection, emphasizing that while the logistical coordination of group departures is not inherently prohibited, each removal order must be based on an individualized assessment. Even in cases where individuals share similar administrative situations or common characteristics, decisions must be made on a case-by-case basis.[61] Through these guidelines, the Committee of Ministers reaffirms that member states must grant due process rights to all foreigners

---

56 Council of Europe, Committee of Ministers *Twenty Guidelines on Forced Return* September 2005.

57 Council of Europe *About the Committee of Ministers* available at: https://www.coe.int/en/web/cm/about-cm. The Committee makes clear in the preamble of the Twenty Guidelines on Forced Return that the guidelines reflect existing binding law and serve as a collection of best practice.

58 Council of Europe *Twenty Guidelines on Forced Return* footnote on p. 1.

59 *Ibidem.*, p. 7.

60 *Ibidem.*, p. 16.

61 *Ibidem.*, p. 17.

seeking international protection. This includes not only the right to apply for protection but also the right to a thorough and individualized examination of their claims. These guarantees form part of the scope of protection of the prohibition of collective expulsion. As Guideline 3 uses of "shall" instead of "should", the Committee understands the prohibition of collective expulsion as an obligatory norm. This norm obliges member states to guarantee every foreign individual of a group an assessment of their circumstances before being expelled. To ensure compliance with this obligation, the Commission and the Court established guiding indicators for the determination of whether states have genuinely and individually taken the personal circumstances of each member of the group into account. The Court assesses these indicators under the heading "background to the execution of the expulsion order"[62]. Thus, if the expelling member state does not comply with these procedural guarantees, the court considers this as an indicator that Article 4 Protocol 4 ECHR is violated.[63]

The Court's approach here is a two-step test. First, the judges examine whether the circumstances of the case indicate that there has been an objective and individual examination of each member of the group. If the subsequent procedure casts doubt, other factors on the background to the execution of the expulsion come into play. This second part of the test may either eliminate such doubts or reinforce the notion that the expulsions were collective and thus a violation of Article 4 Protocol 4 ECHR. Such background factors may vary from identical terms of expulsion orders to government policies aiming at the expulsion of a particular group. Even though the ECtHR did not call it a two-step test, such an examination has been implied in several cases, starting with *Čonka v. Belgium*[64] in 2002. However, over time, the Court has relied on different terms for the same issue. Whereas the Court spoke of "background to the expulsion" in *Čonka v.*

62 *Čonka v. Belgium* ECtHR Appl. No. 51564/99, 5 February 2002, para. 59.

63 The relevance of the background to expulsion orders became first apparent in the above-mentioned Human Rights Commission's *Becker v. Denmark* case of 1975. Here, the Commission found that Denmark did comply with the obligation arising from Article 4 Protocol 4 to individually consider the circumstances of every individual of the group of applicants. In the submissions, Becker urged the Commission to consider the surrounding circumstances of the return of 200 children. In his view, the Government could not be trusted to conduct individual assessments as it declared publicly that "the majority of the children should be sent back". He further explained that "for political reasons the Government could not afford to change their decision". See: *Becker v. Denmark* EComHR, p. 232.

64 *Čonka v. Belgium* ECtHR para. 59.

Belgium, it referred to a "general context"[65] in *Georgia v. Russia I*. With this conclusion, we now turn to a key question at the heart of the prohibition of collective expulsion: does the principle encompass the right to an individual interview before the expulsion? Given that the prohibition hinges on the requirement for a case-by-case assessment, it is crucial to examine whether a personal hearing, are covered by the scope of protection of this provision. Therefore, the following section explores how the ECtHR has addressed this issue over time.

2.1.2.2 *Individual Interviews*

Given that the prohibition of collective expulsion is rooted in the need for individual evaluations, it is essential to understand the role of personal interviews in ensuring that everyone's rights and circumstances are properly considered. While the "Twenty Guidelines on Forced Return" adopted by the Council of Europe emphasize the obligation for states to conduct an individualized examination of every foreigner's situation, the question remains as to whether this guarantees a formal personal interview for all individuals subject to expulsion.[66] The Guidelines highlight the importance of evaluating the specific circumstances of each individual, even when they are part of a group, and make it clear that collective expulsion is prohibited, regardless of shared characteristics among group members.[67] However, the ECtHR, in its more recent case law since 2016 has taken a more restrictive approach when it comes to personal interviews as a procedural safeguard for every individual facing expulsion. This section will shed light on the role of personal interviews as a procedural guarantee under Article 4 Protocol 4 ECHR, evaluating how the Court has addressed the necessity and scope of personal interviews in its rulings and its shifting and restrictive approach.

Before the 2016 *Khlaifia* Grand Chamber judgment, this question seemed to have been implicitly answered by the establishment of the individual-examination requirement itself. The applicants in *Khlaifia* brought this question to the table. They highlighted in their submissions "that the key issue in the present case was whether an individual interview was necessary prior to their expulsion"[68] per Article 4 Protocol 4 ECHR. They argued

65 *Georgia v. Russia I* [GC] (merits), Appl. No. 13255/07, 3 July 2014, para. 171.
66 Council of Europe *Twenty Guidelines on Forced Return* pp. 16–17.
67 *Ibidem.*
68 *Khlaifia and Others v. Italy* ECtHR [GC], para. 220.

further that "to exclude the need for an individual interview would render meaningless the procedural safeguard of Article 4 of Protocol 4".[69] However, the majority of judges in the 2016 Grand Chamber *Khlaifia* judgment did not follow this line of arguments by seemingly limiting the right to an interview to "original" expulsion scenarios. In this case, the applicants had argued that Italian officials had failed to conduct personal interviews. Italy rebutted this claim. The respondent argued that each foreigner enjoyed a "genuine individual interview, carried out in the presence of an interpreter or cultural mediator, following which the authorities had filled out an "information sheet" containing personal data and any circumstances specific to each migrant".[70] These sheets, however, could not be presented as a fire destroyed them. Assessing this discrepancy of facts, the Grand Chamber concluded that "the [Italian] Government provided a plausible explanation to justify their inability to produce the applicants' information sheets". The Court further pointed out that at the time in question, numerous translators, social workers, psychologists, and cultural mediators were present. This led to the conclusion that it is "reasonable to assume" that these people conducted individual interviews.[71] Next, the Grand Chamber made a general remark on the necessity of an individual interview per Article 4 Protocol 4. It stipulated that

> *Article 4 of Protocol No. 4 does not guarantee the right to an individual interview in all circumstances*; the requirements of this provision *may be satisfied* where *each* alien has a *genuine and effective possibility of submitting arguments* against his or her expulsion, and where those arguments *are examined* in an appropriate manner by the authorities of the respondent State [emphasis added].[72]

69 *Ibidem.* Denise Venturi raised a similar question in her assessment of the Khlaifia Grand Chamber judgment on the interpretation of Article 4 Protocol 4 ECHR stating that "the Court's conclusion on this aspect leaves several doubts and open questions behind. It appears to undermine the ECHR's guarantees applicable to expulsion; if the right to an individual interview is not provided for by Article 4 Protocol 4, how can a collective expulsion be effectively forestalled? Such interpretation restricts the scope of this provision inevitably". *The Grand Chamber's ruling in Khlaifia and Others v Italy: one step forward, one step back?* Strasbourg Observer, 10 January 2017, available at: https://strasbourgobservers.com/2017/01/10/the-grand-chambers-ruling-in-khlaifia-and-others-v-italy-one-step-forward-one-step-back/#more-3466.

70 *Ibidem.*, paras. 224, 245.

71 *Ibidem.*, para. 246.

72 *Khlaifia and Others v. Italy* ECtHR [GC], para. 248.

Authors like Jill Goldenziel have criticizes the Court for this finding stating that the "decision leaves unclear exactly what a meaningful opportunity for a migrant to challenge his deportation would look like".[73] It seems that the Court wanted to distinguish "original" and "expedited" collective expulsion cases that trigger different levels of procedural guarantees.

However, the Grand Chamber's analysis does little to resolve this uncertainty. Without revisiting the issue of interviews, the Court merely refers to the general possibility for applicants to contest their expulsion – a point asserted by Italy and disputed by the applicants – without elaborating on what meaningful access to such a remedy would entail.[74] What is more is that it seems that the Court deemed the situation to be one that does not require an individual interview. Further, it seems that the Court concludes that each applicant had missed her or his opportunity to bring forward their claims against their expulsion. This finding, in turn, led to the conclusion that Article 4 Protocol 4 was not violated. Next, the Court made a surprising statement given the broad personal scope of application of the provision encompassing **every** foreigner irrespective of their reasons for entering a state's territory.

Summarizing the applicants' situation at hand, the Court concluded that

> the applicants' representatives, both in their written observations and at the public hearing, were unable to indicate the slightest factual or legal ground which, under international or national law, could have justified their clients' presence on Italian territory and preclude their removal.[75]

This *ex post* perspective seemingly contradicts the established broad scope of protection *ratione personae,* which includes **every foreigner**. Article 4 Protocol 4 ECHR equally protects migrants and asylum seekers as clarified in settled ECtHR case law. Thus, it seems unlikely that the Court wanted to draw such a distinction as it did not stipulate that individual interviews are only required in case the foreigner brings forward substantive claims for protection. Stefano Zirulia, the lawyer who represented the applicants in the Grand Chamber proceedings, highly criticized this approach, contending that the Court introduced a new requirement in this paragraph. He asserts

---

73 Goldenziel, Jill *Khlaifia and Others v. Italy – International Decisions* American Journal of International Law, Vol. 112, Issue 2, April 2018, p. 279.

74 *Khlaifia and Others v. Italy* ECtHR [GC], paras. 249, 250.

75 *Ibidem.*, para. 253.

that states are now obligated to conduct individual interviews "only when there are risks to life or physical well-being".[76] Further, Zirulia argues that this interpretation effectively renders Article 4 of Protocol 4 almost redundant, as the same outcome could be achieved by directly applying the principle of non-refoulement.[77] Likewise, Judge Georgios Serghides, in his partly dissenting opinion, criticizes in length the court's approach to limiting the scope of protection to the mere "genuine and effective possibility" to bring forward individual claims for protection. He points out that

> [t]his interpretation departs from the Court's previously established case-law, according to which the aim of Article 4 of Protocol No. 4 is invariably to prevent States from being able to proceed with collective expulsions of aliens without examining, through the procedure of a personal interview, the individual circumstances of each one. In other words, this interpretation disregards the mandatory nature of the procedural obligation of the authorities to conduct personal interviews in all cases engaging Article 4 of Protocol No. 4.[78]

Despite this criticism by some scholars, activists, and even ECtHR judges, it must be acknowledged that the Grand Chamber restricted in *Khlaifia* the obligation of states to conduct a thorough examination of each group member's circumstances before being jointly expelled. It is noteworthy in this regard that this restriction applies only in certain expulsion contexts. In cases of "original" collective expulsion, where individuals are already present within a state's territory for an extended period, the full range of procedural safeguards should apply, including a thorough examination of everyone's circumstances before expulsion. However, in "expedited" expulsion scenarios, such as hot returns, this requirement is less stringent. In these cases, a limited level of procedural guarantees is provided. Specifically, the right to an individual interview is not absolute, but rather reduced to the mere possibility of presenting one's claims for consideration before the expulsion is carried out. This distinction highlights the

76 Zirulia, Stefano *A template for protecting human rights during the 'refugee crisis'? Immigration detention and the expulsion of migrants in a recent ECtHR Grand Chamber ruling* EU Law Analysis, 5 January 2017, available at: http://eulawanalysis.blogspot.com/2017/01/a-template-for-protecting-human-rights.html.

77 *Ibidem.*

78 Jude Serghides Partly Dissenting Opinion in *Khlaifia and Others v. Italy* ECtHR [GC], para. 12.

varying procedural standards based on the specific nature of the expulsion process. At the same time, the Court acknowledged *N.D. and N.T. v. Spain* that governments also need to provide at least for an identification process for everyone in "expedited" collective expulsion cases. The Court noted that "the Government cannot take shelter behind the absence of identification given that they are themselves responsible for it".[79] However, this finding places a significant burden on those being expelled or refused admittance, as it now falls upon them, in the midst of an expedited expulsion process, to recognize that they must raise their claims for protection during the identification phase. This shifts the responsibility to the individuals facing expulsion, requiring them to be aware of their rights and to assert them in a high-pressure, time-sensitive situation. This is particularly problematic in light of the scope, object, and purpose of the prohibition, which is to prevent arbitrary expulsion. The very essence of this prohibition requires an inherent level of equality of power between the state and the individual facing expulsion. However, in such expedited processes, this balance is undermined, as the individual is placed in a vulnerable position where they must navigate complex legal procedures under duress, without adequate support or clear access to remedies.

In conclusion, states satisfy the procedural requirements of Article 4 Protocol 4 ECHR in "original" collective expulsion cases by offering each individual an objective examination of their circumstances. The competent authorities or, if necessary, the domestic courts must conduct this process in an interview or hearing. This requirement is arguably not required in "expedited" collective expulsions scenarios where the granting of the possibility for an individual assessment satisfies Article 4 Protocol 4 ECHR as long as the respective state at least identifies each individual. The ambiguity of the relevant section of the *Khlaifia and Others v. Italy* Grand Chamber judgment and the lack of clear reasoning in this paragraph leads to this conclusion as well as subsequent case law such as *N.D. and N.T. v. Spain*. What is more is that the ECtHR arguably interpreted Article 4 Protocol 4 ECHR in a manner limiting the procedural guarantees in "expedited" collective expulsion cases to the effective possibility to bring forward one's claims. This limited scope of protection includes the right to legal assistance and a translator, as well as the right to an effective remedy/appeal. The right to an appeal against the expulsion is in these scenarios in general without a suspensive effect. An exception to this is at hand when the individual claims

79 *N.D. and N.T. v. Spain* ECtHR [Chamber], para. 60.

asylum, any other form of protection, or that her or his return would violate the *non-refoulement* principle. In contrast, the level of procedural rights in "original" scenarios, namely in cases of collective expulsions of resident foreigners from a state's territory is much more comprehensive. Foreigners in these cases enjoy procedural guarantees such as the right to an individual interview, the right to legal assistance and interpretation, the right to appeal with a suspensive effect, and the right to an effective remedy before domestic courts.

2.1.2.3 *Legal Assistance/Availability of Interpreters*

One other significant factor in collective expulsion cases is the lack of fair process guarantees, particularly concerning access to legal assistance and translators. In cases assessed by the ECtHR, one recurring issue is the difficulty or inability of applicants to contact legal representatives or obtain translation services before being expelled. This lack of support is particularly problematic in collective expulsion scenarios, where individuals may not fully understand their rights, or the procedural steps required to challenge their removal. Given the circumstances surrounding collective expulsions, it is highly likely that the individuals affected require both legal assistance and the services of a translator to ensure that they can properly present their case. It is unrealistic to assume that all migrants are aware of their legal rights or understand how and when to raise claims before the competent authorities. To ensure a fair process, all individuals involved in collective expulsions must have the opportunity to consult with a lawyer and/or translator. This procedural safeguard is part of the minimum standard of due process, which is deeply rooted in both International Refugee Law and Human Rights Law. The fair process is only achieved when individuals are informed of their rights and are given a genuine opportunity to raise their claims. The provision of legal assistance and translation services by the state is therefore a fundamental requirement, enabling individuals to effectively exercise their rights and challenge the legality of their expulsion.

The ECtHR ruled in the 2014 *Sharifi v. Italy and Greece* case for the first time, particularly on collective expulsions from one EU state to another based on the Dublin-system. Here, the ECtHR made the necessary clarification that the Dublin system itself does not justify collective and indiscriminate returns between EU member states.[80] This finding was primarily

80 *Sharifi and Others v. Italy and Greece* ECtHR [Chamber], paras. 214–225.

because the access of the affected migrants and asylum seekers to legal assistance and an interpreter depended on the goodwill of the border police. In most cases, state authorities directly returned the migrants and asylum seekers to the country of first arrivals under the Dublin regulations.[81]

Furthermore, the Court highlighted in *Čonka v. Belgium,* that "it was very difficult for the aliens to contact a lawyer".[82] This circumstance was one relevant factor expressly considered by the Court to determine whether the officials had conducted a genuine, objective, and individual examination. In general, the right to legal assistance and a translator also applies to situations of "expedited" collective expulsions. The former *Commissioner for Human Rights of the Council of Europe* (Human Rights Commissioner) Nils Muižnieks's press release on Spain's hot return policy at the Spanish Moroccan border fence, cited in *N.D. and N.T. v. Spain,* highlighted the absolute necessity of such a basic standard. He summoned the Spanish authorities "to ensure that material and human resources, including adequate numbers of trained police officers, lawyers, and interpreters, are made available" to ensure the adherence to "fundamental human rights safeguards".[83] This press release highlights the urgency of the assistance of a legal counselor and a translator not only in situations of "original" sets of collective expulsions but likewise in "expedited" collective expulsion scenarios. This necessity has become visible for example in the assessment of the circumstances in *Hirsi Jamaa and Others v. Italy*[84] where the applicants did not even have any opportunity to explain their circumstances or to be assisted by lawyers, interpreters or medical personnel.[85] For this reason, the Court found a violation of Article 4 Protocol 4 ECHR. These circumstances led to the Court's overall conclusion that Italy had violated the prohibition of collective expulsion.[86] The Court confirmed this obligation in its subsequent case law repeatedly, highlighting that providing such services form part of the duty to provide genuine and effective procedures for legal entry.[87]

---

81 *Ibidem.* 215.

82 *Čonka v. Belgium* ECtHR, para. 62.

83 *N.D. and N.T. v. Spain* ECtHR [Chamber], para. 42.

84 *Hirsi Jamaa and Others v. Italy* ECtHR [GC], para. 185.

85 *Ibidem.*

86 *Hirsi Jamaa and Others v. Italy* ECtHR [GC], para. 186.

87 See, for example, *N.D. and N.T. v. Spain* ECtHR, [GC], paras. 212–217, *A.A. and Others v. North Macedonia* ECtHR, paras. 116–122; *Shahzad v. Hungary* ECtHR, paras. 63–67; *M.H. and Others v. Croatia* ECtHR, paras. 295–304.

In conclusion, the prohibition of collective expulsion under Article 4 Protocol 4 ECHR guarantees the right to legal assistance and access to a translator. This procedural safeguard is essential for ensuring that individuals facing expulsion, whether they are long-term residents or subject to expedited removal procedures, can fully exercise their rights and present their claims effectively. This guarantee applies equally to both "original" collective expulsion scenarios – where foreigners have resided in the state for a longer period and "expedited" collective expulsions, which involve immediate group removals. In both cases, providing access to legal counsel and translation services is critical to ensuring that the expulsion process remains fair and transparent. These procedural protections enable individuals to understand their rights and navigate the legal process, fostering compliance with the fundamental principles of due process and human rights.

2.1.2.4 *The Right to an Effective Remedy/Suspension of Expulsion*

After having examined the role of legal assistance within the context of the prohibition of collective expulsion, we now turn to the right to an effective remedy, which is equally essential to ensure minimum due process guarantees against arbitrary collective expulsions.[88] The Convention guarantees this right in Article 4 Protocol 4 in conjunction with Article 13 ECHR.[89] The right to an effective remedy plays a critical role in the context of the prohibition of collective expulsion under Article 4 of Protocol 4 ECHR. This procedural guarantee ensures that individuals facing expulsion can challenge their removal before domestic courts. However, while individuals affected by "original" collective expulsions typically benefit from the full scope of procedural protections, including the right to an effective remedy, the situation differs for those subjected to expedited collective expulsions. In the latter case, individuals also retain the right to an effective remedy before national courts, but the jurisprudence of the ECtHR suggests that the expulsion order in these cases does not automatically trigger the suspensive effect of the removal. This raises significant concerns about the timing and accessibility of judicial review in situations where individuals are swiftly expelled

88 For an examination on the relationship between the prohibition of collective expulsion with the right to an effective remedy, see also Chapter 4, 4.2.

89 See for example: *Khlaifia and Others v. Italy* ECtHR [GC], para. 256. The applicants alleged *inter alia* a violation of their right to an effective remedy in accordance with Article 4 Protocol 4 in conjunction with Article 13 ECHR as they were not afforded an effective remedy before a national authority.

without sufficient opportunity to challenge the decision or are denied entry to a territory where they could lodge any appeal.

An analysis of the case law on the prohibition of collective expulsion reveals the particular role of Article 13 ECHR in ensuring comprehensive procedural protection in expulsion cases. This is, for example, visible in the fact that the Court frequently examines alleged violations of Article 4 Protocol 4 before addressing claims under Article 13, recognizing that breaches of the prohibition of collective expulsion often coincide with the absence of effective and accessible remedies. In the landmark case *Georgia v. Russia I*, the Grand Chamber emphasized this connection, holding that a violation of Article 4 Protocol 4 inherently indicates a lack of effective remedies, thereby making a separate assessment under Article 13 unnecessary.[90] This approach highlights the interconnected nature of the procedural safeguards under the Convention, where the absence of adequate protections against collective expulsion typically undermines the availability of effective legal recourse. This section will further explore the relationship between the prohibition of collective expulsion and the right to an effective remedy, focusing on the ECtHR's approach to ensuring that individuals can effectively challenge expulsion orders, particularly in the context of expedited removals.

Already in the early *Čonka v. Belgium* decision, the Court stressed for the first time the relevance of the right to an effective remedy for cases relating to collective expulsion from a state's territory.[91] The relevance of this finding lies mainly in the provision's suspensive effect on the expulsion order under specific circumstances. This suspension is particularly relevant as the removal may potentially be irreversible for practical reasons.

Also in later cases, such as *Hirsi Jamaa v. Italy* and *Sharifi and Others v. Italy and Greece*, the Court found that the inexistence of any domestic remedy for asylum seekers may lead to a violation of Article 4 Protocol 4 in conjunction with Article 13 ECHR.[92]

In *Hirsi Jamaa*, the Court held that the state had violated the applicants' "right to obtain sufficient information to enable them to gain effective access to the relevant procedures and to substantiate their complaints".[93]

---

90 *Georgia v. Russia I* ECtHR [GC], para. 212.

91 *Čonka v. Belgium* paras. 77–85.

92 *Hirsi* Jamaa and Others v. Italy ECtHR, [GC], paras. 201–207 and *Sharifi and Others v. Italy and Greece* ECtHR, Appl. No. 16643/09, 21 October 2014, paras. 240–243.

93 *Hirsi* Jamaa and Others v. Italy ECtHR, [GC], para. 204.

Similarly, in *Sharifi and Others v. Italy and Greece*, the Court underscored the link between collective expulsions and the deliberate obstruction of asylum claims or other legal procedures.[94] The combined protection of Article 4 Protocol 4 and Article 13 ensures that asylum seekers have access to such legal avenues before expulsion.

However, in expedited collective expulsion cases, the right to seek protection does not always trigger a suspensive effect, leaving certain individuals at risk of immediate removal despite potential claims for international protection. The Court acknowledged this conclusion implicitly in *Khlaifia and Others v. Italy*. Here, the Grand Chamber stressed that the automatic suspensive effect of a remedy against an expulsion order is not an absolute obligation. If there is no real risk of a violation of the applicants' rights to be free from inhuman or degrading treatment, the order does not trigger the suspensive effect.[95] The Grand Chamber found that "an effective possibility of challenging the expulsion decision by having a sufficiently thorough examination [...] carried out by an independent and impartial domestic forum" suffices.[96]

It then concluded that an ongoing asylum process or other protection determination procedure could trigger the suspension of the expulsion.[97] While Article 13 ECHR guarantees an effective remedy to prevent irreversible actions like expulsion, the Court has found violations of Article 13 ECHR when applicants with valid claims under Articles 2 or 3 ECHR (due to risks they face upon removal) were prevented from seeking asylum or lacked access to a remedy with automatic suspensive effect.[98]

Concluding from this it has to be noted that the Court has ruled that the absence of a suspensive effect does not automatically violate Article 13 in conjunction with Article 4 Protocol 4 ECHR, provided there is no real risk of harm in the destination country. This distinction creates a divide between asylum seekers, who benefit from stronger procedural safeguards, and other migrants, for whom the Court's restrictive interpretation limits protection. As a result, the suspensive effect is maintained only as long as the asylum procedure is ongoing. However, this safeguard applies exclusively to individuals within a group who have explicitly raised claims for international

94 *Sharifi and Others v. Italy and Greece* ECtHR, paras. 242–243.
95 *Khlaifia and Others v. Italy* ECtHR, [GC], para. 281.
96 *Khlaifia and Others v. Italy* ECtHR, [GC], para. 279.
97 *Ibidem.*, para. 281.
98 *M.K. and Others v. Poland* ECtHR, paras. 212–220; *Hirsi Jamaa v. Italy* ECtHR, paras. 201–207; *Sharifi and Others v. Italy and Greece* ECtHR, paras. 240–243.

protection. Furthermore, it also creates a differentiation of the level of protection depending on the situation of the expulsion. In "original" collective expulsion cases, every individual has the right to an effective remedy before domestic courts, which inherently suspends expulsion while the legal process is pending. This guarantee is a fundamental aspect of the protection offered by Article 4 Protocol 4 in conjunction with Article 13 ECHR. In contrast, "expedited" collective expulsions do not benefit from the same automatic suspension. Here, only an individual's pending asylum application or request for other forms of protection triggers a suspensive effect. Without such a pending claim, expulsion would risk violating the *non-refoulement* principle. Hence, the ECtHR's recent approach to implicitly differentiate between "asylum seekers" and "migrants" and expulsion scenarios creates disparities in protection. Based on this approach, for an act to constitute collective expulsion in the sense of the provision, it must be carried out in a manner that entirely deprives individuals of an objective assessment before removal. However, if an applicant has had the opportunity to challenge their expulsion in a prior proceeding – such as an asylum process – this is generally deemed sufficient to satisfy Article 4 Protocol 4 ECHR. Notably, the provision does not require states to document such assessments or ensure their legal accuracy, leaving room for procedural gaps that may undermine individual rights.

Nevertheless, the examination of the ECtHR's case law reveals that the prohibition of collective expulsion guarantees at least a *minimum* safeguard: Individuals must have a "genuine and effective possibility" to present their claims at some point before removal. The specifics of this assessment remain largely within the discretion of the expelling state. The examination has also shown that despite the absence of explicit procedural guarantees in the text of Article 4 Protocol 4, the Court has interpreted the provision to include key due process rights. These include the right to challenge expulsion, access to legal assistance and a translator, and the availability of an effective domestic remedy – all of which are crucial for meaningful protection. Ultimately, the right to an effective remedy, as guaranteed by Article 4 Protocol 4 in conjunction with Article 13 ECHR, remains a cornerstone of legal protections in collective expulsion cases. While it provides essential safeguards for asylum seekers, its application is more limited for other migrants, raising concerns about the adequacy of procedural guarantees in expedited expulsion cases. As will be further explored below, these procedural protections are also reflected in the regional and international legal frameworks that complement the prohibition of collective expulsion under Article 4 Protocol 4 ECHR.

2.1.3 Conclusions on Procedural Protections in Article 4 Protocol 4 ECHR

After assessing the procedural guarantees contained in the prohibition of collective expulsion under Article 4 Protocol 4 of the European Convention on Human Rights, one has to conclude that the provision serves as a crucial safeguard against arbitrary removals, ensuring that each individual receives a fair and reasonable assessment before expulsion. Beyond the material aspects of expulsion, this provision implicitly guarantees essential procedural rights, including the opportunity for individual examination, access to legal assistance, and the availability of translation services. Without these safeguards, individuals facing expulsion would struggle to understand their rights or effectively challenge their removal, rendering the prohibition of collective expulsion meaningless in practice. To determine these safeguards, one ought to turn to the ECtHR which has played a key role in clarifying the scope of Article 4 Protocol 4 ECHR, emphasizing that the provision is not limited to the material aspects of expulsion but also encompasses procedural protections. The Court's jurisprudence has consistently supported the latter view, recognizing that procedural safeguards are integral to preventing collective expulsions. This aligns with the drafting history of the provision, which, although it did not explicitly incorporate procedural guarantees, left room for a broad interpretation that allows for the progressive development of protections over time.

In detail, to assess whether a collective expulsion has occurred, the ECtHR employs a two-step test. First, it examines whether an individualized, reasonable, and objective assessment was conducted for each person affected. If doubts arise, the Court then considers additional contextual factors, such as the manner in which the expulsion was carried out, the policies governing the removals, and the accessibility of legal remedies. This approach ensures that expulsions are not executed arbitrarily and that affected individuals have a genuine opportunity to present their claims. In addition, also legal assistance and translation services are particularly crucial in cases of collective expulsion. Migrants and asylum seekers often lack knowledge of domestic legal procedures and may face significant language barriers that prevent them from effectively asserting their rights. Without access to legal representation and translation, individuals are at a severe disadvantage, unable to comprehend or navigate the proceedings that determine their fate. The Court has consistently underscored the necessity of these safeguards, recognizing them as minimum due process guarantees rooted in international refugee and human rights law. Several key ECtHR rulings illustrate this. In *Sharifi v. Italy and Greece* (2014), the Court found that collective expulsions under the Dublin system violated Article 4 Protocol 4 because access to legal assistance and interpretation was left to the discretion of border police, an arrangement insufficient to guarantee fair treatment. Similarly, in *Čonka v. Belgium* (2002), the Court held that the applicants had been denied effective legal representation and translation services, reinforcing the importance of procedural fairness in expulsion cases. In *Hirsi Jamaa v. Italy* (2012), the Court ruled that the failure to provide legal assistance, interpretation, or medical support contributed to a violation of the prohibition of collective expulsion, further underscoring that these protections apply equally in both traditional and expedited expulsion contexts.

Next, this section turned to the interconnectedness between the prohibition of collective expulsion with the right to an effective remedy, enshrined in Article 13 ECHR. It showed how the latter principle complements the prohibition of collective expulsion by ensuring that individuals facing removal can challenge their expulsion before domestic courts. However, in recent jurisprudence since 2016 the Court has drawn distinctions between different categories of migrants when determining the scope of this right. The Court seems to suggest that asylum seekers benefit from a stronger application of the suspensive effect of an expulsion order, meaning their removal is generally halted while their asylum claims are under review. In contrast, other migrants, particularly those subjected to expedited removal procedures, face greater obstacles in accessing remedies that would prevent immediate expulsion. This distinction reflects the Court's evolving approach to procedural protections, but it also raises concerns about the adequacy of safeguards for non-asylum-seeking migrants. Nevertheless, the general importance of suspensive remedies in expulsion cases cannot be overstated, particularly when there is a risk that removal could expose individuals to inhuman or degrading treatment. While the Court has affirmed that suspensive effect is a critical component of effective remedies, it has also clarified that this protection is not absolute. Whether an individual can benefit from suspensive effect depends largely on the existence of an ongoing asylum process or a pending claim for international protection. This differentiated approach reflects the tension between state interests in controlling migration and the fundamental rights of individuals facing expulsion.

Irrespective of this restrictive trend in the jurisprudence of the Strasbourg Court, the procedural protections embedded in the prohibition of collective expulsion are essential to ensuring fairness in expulsion cases. The ECtHR's jurisprudence has reinforced the necessity of legal assistance, translation services, and access to effective remedies as fundamental safeguards against arbitrary removals. With this conclusion on the European Convention, we now further examine how these procedural guarantees are applied within regional and international legal frameworks, assessing their effectiveness and consistency across different legal systems. In doing so, we will for now remain in the European context, assessing the approach taken in the EU Charter of Fundamental Rights when it comes to procedural guarantees of the prohibition.

2.2 *Article 19(1) EU Charter of Fundamental Rights*

As the EU's primary human rights instrument, the Charter provides an additional layer of legal safeguards, complementing and, in some respects, expanding upon the protections established under the ECHR. According to the explanation by the Praesidium, the Charter provision corresponds to the content of Article 4 Protocol 4 ECHR.[99] Article 52(3) of the Charter even codifies this finding, stating that "the meaning and scope of those rights shall be the same". As a consequence, the jurisprudence of the ECtHR on Article 4 Protocol 4 ECHR is to be consulted for the determination of the scope in Article 19(1) ChFREU.[100] However, while the Charter aligns with the ECHR in many aspects, its approach to the prohibition of collective expulsion reflects certain structural and substantive differences that warrant closer analysis. One key distinction is the wording and scope of Article 19(1) ChFREU, which explicitly states that "collective expulsions are prohibited". This provision is notable for its broader personal scope, as it applies not only to foreigners but also to nationals of the expelling state[101] – a departure from most other codifications of the prohibition. Additionally, unlike the ECHR, which separates protection against arbitrary expulsion of lawfully residing foreigners into a distinct provision, the Charter consolidates both protections within a single article.[102] As the protection granted in Article 19(1) ChFREU results from the developing case law of the ECtHR,[103] the provision can be seen as the advancement of the

99 Praesidium of the Convention *Draft Charter of Fundamental Rights of the European Union explanations prepared by the Praesidium*, Charter 4473/00 Convent 49, p. 21.

100 Guild, Elspeth *Art 19-Protection in the Event of Removal* in: Peers/Hervey/Kenner/Ward (eds.) The EU Charter of Fundamental Rights A Commentary (Hart Publishing 2014), para. 19.37.

101 Article 4 Protocol 4 ECHR for example only covers the scope of protection of foreigners.

102 Brandl *Art 1 Prot 7* in: Pabel and Schmahl (eds.) *Internationaler Kommentar zur Europäischen Menschenrechtskonvention mit einschlägigen Texten und Dokumenten* (Carl Heymanns Verlag 2013), para. 51.

103 *Ibidem.*, para. 19.07.

prohibition in Article 4 Protocol 4 ECHR. Following this line of argument, the fact that there is no provision similar to Article 1 Protocol 7 ECHR in the EU Charter may be an indicator that the line of the jurisprudence of the Strasbourg Court concerning the prohibition turned the provision implicitly into a process right. Furthermore, in contrast to Article 4 Protocol 4 ECHR, the personal scope of Article 19(1) EU Charter includes not only foreigners but also nationals of the expelling state. Thus, the provision in the EU Charter constitutes a comprehensive development of the original version of the prohibition comprising material and process rights for foreigners and nationals in one provision. The practical implementation and development of the prohibition in Article 4 Protocol 4 ECHR by the European Court of Human Rights has thus led to a comprehensive evolution of the scope of protection of Article 19(1) EU Charter.

When delving into the examination on the procedural guarantees of Article 19(1), it becomes apparent that the EU Charter of Fundamental Rights establishes procedural guarantees relevant to collective expulsion cases, which are generally applicable to all administrative procedures. These guarantees include the right to good administration (Article 41), the right to be heard and to a fair legal process (Articles 47 and 48). Articles 47 and 48 of the Charter ensure respect for the rights of the defense and the right to a fair trial in judicial proceedings. Meanwhile, the right to good administration, codified in Article 41(1), stipulates that "every person has the right to have his or her affairs handled impartially, fairly, and within a reasonable time". Specific guarantees under this provision include the right to an effective remedy (Article 41(3)), access to one's file (Article 41(2)), the obligation for the administration to provide reasons for its decisions (Article 41(2)), and the right to be heard (Article 41(2)).

The Court of Justice of the European Union (CJEU) has emphasized the importance of the right to be heard in several judgments, reinforcing its critical role in ensuring fairness and procedural justice in administrative proceedings, including those involving migration and expulsion.[104] Unlike the limited wording of Article 41(1) of the EU Charter, which binds only "institutions, bodies, offices, and agencies of the Union", the CJEU expanded its applicability in *Mukurubega* and *Boudjlida*.[105] The Court clarified that

---

104 See for example: *M. M. v Minister for Justice, Equality and Law Reform and Others* CJEU, C-277/11, 22 November 2012, paras. 82–83 or *Sophie Mukarubega v Préfet de police und Préfet de la Seine-Saint-Denis* CJEU, C-166/13, 5 November 2014, para. 43.

105 *Mukarubega v Préfet de police* CJEU, paras. 45–50; *Khaled Boudjlida v Préfet des Pyrénées-Atlantiques* CJEU C-249/13, 11 December 2014, para. 34.

the right to good administration, including the right to be heard, extends to all member state officials when they act within the scope of EU law, as the right to be heard reflects a fundamental principle of EU law.[106] According to the CJEU, this right ensures that individuals affected by adverse decisions can present their claims to the competent authorities.[107] Moreover, member states must consider these submissions carefully and impartially, examining all relevant aspects of the individual case and providing a detailed statement of reasons for their decisions.[108] The reasoning must be sufficiently specific and concrete to enable the affected individual to clearly understand the grounds for rejection, a requirement rooted in the principle of respect for the rights of the defense.[109] Some scholars argue that this duty to provide reasons also applies to member states in expulsion cases, requiring authorities to give due consideration to the particular circumstances of the individual concerned before issuing a removal decision.[110] These procedural obligations align closely with those imposed by the European Court of Human Rights, which similarly requires member states to conduct a "reasonable and objective examination of the particular case of each individual" in collective expulsion scenarios.[111]

This conclusion triggers the question whether this finding that the member states are bound to the right to be heard is also applicable to collective expulsion cases? A key argument against this assumption is that the expulsion of non-nationals falls within the national competence of member states, albeit constrained by obligations under international and European law. However, the Court of Justice of the European Union addressed this issue in the *Mukarubega* case, clarifying that when a matter falls under the scope of national law, it is the provisions of that law that are decisive. It stressed that

> provided that the rules adopted to that effect are the same as those to which individuals in comparable situations under national law are

106 *Boudjlida v Préfe des Pyrénées-Atlantiques* CJEU, para. 37.
107 *Ibidem.*, para. 38.
108 *Ibidem.*
109 *Ibidem.*
110 Carlier, Jean-Yves; Leboeuf, Luc *Collective expulsion or not? Individualisation of decision making in migration and asylum law* EU migration law blog, 8 January 2018, available at: http://eumigrationlawblog.eu/collective-expulsion-or-not-individualisation-of-decision-making-in-migration-and-asylum-law/.
111 *Alibaks v. the Netherland* EComHR, p. 274; reaffirmed in *Andric v. Sweden* ECtHR, p. 4.

> subject (the principle of equivalence) and that they do not make it impossible in practice or excessively difficult to exercise the rights conferred by the European Union legal order (the principle of effectiveness).[112]

Thus, every case of expulsion from the territory of an EU member state needs to be under the general principles of EU law, such as the right for every non-national facing expulsion to "a fair and transparent procedure".[113] The European Commission, in its proposal on common removal standards, likewise acknowledged these guarantees and highlighted that the basis for fair procedures is the issuance of expulsion orders. The proposal states that "due to the fact that Member States do not systematically issue return decisions in connection with the termination of legal stay, the proposal clarifies the need to issue a return decision immediately after a decision rejecting or terminating the legal stay is taken".[114] Furthermore, the proposal by referring to the case-law of the European Court of Justice highlights that the suspensive effect of the expulsion is also necessary to secure a fair process.[115]

In conclusion, the procedural guarantees contained in Article 19(1) EU Charter in cases of collective expulsions are equivalent to those contained in Article 4 Protocol 4 ECHR. However, also the right to good administration in Article 41 EU Charter comes into play when member states act within the scope of the EU, including expelling foreigners. Article 41 EU Charter spells out and clarifies the procedural guarantees that form the right to be heard in the prohibition of collective expulsion. The prohibition of collective expulsion in Article 19(1) ChFREU contains the right to bring forward claims against the expulsion, the right to legal assistance/translator, and the right to an effective remedy/appeal with a suspensive effect. With this conclusion, we now turn from the European regional system to the Inter-American Convention, which, while offering less case law to draw from, provides more extensive procedural guarantees.

---

112 *Mukurubega v Préfet de police* para. 51.

113 *Ibidem.*, para. 61.

114 European Commission, *Proposal for a Directive of the European Parliament and the Council of common standards and procedures in Member States for returning illegally staying third-country nationals (recast) A contribution from the European Commission to the Leaders' meeting in Salzburg on 19–20 September 2018*, COM(2018) 634 final, 12 September 2018, p.7.

115 *Ibidem.*

2.3 *Article 22(9) Inter-American Convention on Human Rights*

The Inter-American Convention on Human Rights provides a distinct approach to the prohibition of collective expulsion, embedding it within a broader framework of migration-related protections. While its jurisprudence is less developed compared to the European system, the procedural guarantees it establishes are notably expansive. Article 22(9) explicitly prohibits the collective expulsion of foreigners, reinforcing the broader right to freedom of movement and residence for all individuals under its jurisdiction. These protections adopted on 22 November 1969, which succinctly state "es prohibida la expulsión colectiva de extranjeros"[116], are fundamental in safeguarding the dignity and autonomy of migrants and displaced persons. However, the practical enforcement of these guarantees was delayed, following Grenada's eleventh ratification on July 18, 1978. The delay in the Convention's entry into force highlights the complexities of establishing regional human rights frameworks, particularly when consensus among diverse member states is required. Once in force, Article 22 became a cornerstone for protecting individual rights in migration contexts across the Americas.

As examined in Chapter 2, in contrast to its European counterpart, the prohibition in the Inter-American Convention has played a smaller role in the case law on violations of the Pact of San José. As of 2024, the Inter-American Commission and the Inter-American Court of Human Rights, have only in a few cases and advisory opinions dealt with the prohibition of collective expulsion. In its case law, both the Commission and Court continuously highlighted that the prohibition of collective expulsion is inherently tied to procedural guarantees that ensure a reasonable, objective, and individualized assessment of each person's circumstances.[117] The Inter-

116 For a comprehensive commentary on the IACHR in Spanish see: Steiner, Christian and Uribe, Patricia (eds.) *Convención Americana sobre Derechos Humanos comentada* (Suprema Corte de la Nación (Mexico) and Konrad Adenauer Foundation 2014). A commentary on the prohibition of collective expulsion is found therein by Rodrigo Uprimny Yepes and Luz María Sánchez Duque, pp. 550–551. Interestingly only the English version uses the problematic term "alien", the Spanish version refers to "foreigners".

117 See, for example, *Nadege Dorzema and others v. Dominican Republic* Merits, Reparations and Costs IACourtHR, judgment of 24 October 2012, Series C, No. 251 or IAComHR *Debido proceso en los procedimientos para la determinación de la condición de persona refugiada, y apátrida y el otorgamiento de protección complementaria* OEA/Ser.L/V/II., Doc. 255, 5 August 2020, para.174; or IAComHR *Movilidad humana y obligaciones de protección: Hacia una pespectiva subregional* OEA/Ser.L/V/II., Doc. 194, 21 July 2023, para. 197.

American Commission made one of its most significant pronouncements on the prohibition of collective expulsions under Article 22(9) ACHR in the context of the collective expulsions of Haitians and Dominican-Haitians from the Dominican Republic during the 1990s.[118] Here, the Commission strongly condemned collective expulsions as a severe violation of international law and emphasized the need for individual expulsions to be conducted in a manner consistent with basic standards of justice, offering adequate procedural safeguards to prevent errors and abuses.[119] The IAComHR further highlighted that the absence of such guarantees not only violates fundamental principles of international law but also constitutes a form of arbitrariness incompatible with basic standards of justice.[120] Expulsion decisions must therefore be based on individualized processes that adequately assess the rights and circumstances of each person, ensuring that no indiscriminate or collective measures are implemented.[121]

Building on this, the Inter-American Court of Human Rights, in *Nadege Dorzema and Others v. the Dominican Republic*, examined the procedural protections required under Article 22(9) ACHR.[122] Referencing the European Court of Human Rights' interpretation of Article 4 Protocol 4 ECHR, the Court affirmed that every foreigner is entitled to an individualized assessment of their circumstances before expulsion.[123] Without such an analysis, the act constitutes an arbitrary expulsion, violating the prohibition of collective expulsions.[124] The Court further stressed that policies targeting the collective removal of foreigners must fully respect the guarantees inherent in the prohibition of collective expulsion.[125] These include the procedural rights derived from the principles of due process and judicial protection, as required under Article 22(9) in conjunction with Article 8(1) ACHR.[126] Article 8(1) ACHR provides for fair trial guarantees, including the right to a hearing conducted with due safeguards,

118 IAComHR *Report on the Situation of Human Rights in the Dominican Republic* OEA/Ser. L/V/II.104 Doc. 49 rev. 1, October 7, 1999.

119 *Ibidem.*, para. 366.

120 IAComHR *Resolución 04/19, Principios interamericanos sobre los derechos humanos de todas las personas migrantes, refugiadas, apátridas y víctimas de la trata de personas* 7 December 2019, Section XVI, principle 72.

121 *Ibidem.*

122 *Nadege Dorzema and others v. Dominican Republic* IACourtHR, para. 171.

123 *Ibidem.*

124 *Ibidem.*

125 *Ibidem.*, para. 155.

126 *Ibidem.*

within a reasonable time, and overseen by an impartial and independent authority.[127] It explains its conclusion with reference to the interpretation of the Human Rights Committee's *General Comment No. 15*; the African Commission's *Union Inter Africaine des Droits de l'homme et al v. Angola*, and the International Law Commission's *Draft Articles on the Expulsion of Aliens*.[128] The Court further concludes that states should not distinguish on the grounds of "nationality, color, race, sex, language, religion, political opinion, social origin or, other status".[129] In a later case against the Dominican Republic in 2014, the Court repeated its previous findings on the obligation to conduct individualized assessments without discrimination to comply with the prohibition of collective expulsion.[130]

Building on this, the Court went a step further by explicitly outlining the specific procedural guarantees that must be upheld to ensure compliance with the prohibition of collective expulsion under the Inter-American Convention.[131] According to the Court, these are the right to receive information on the charges and reasons for the expulsion, including information on the individual's rights; the possibility to bring forward claims against the charges; the possibility of requesting and receiving consular assistance; legal assistance; assistance from a translator and the right to appeal to the competent authorities.[132] This appeal triggers the suspensive effect of the expulsion until the appellate body reaches a reasoned decision.[133] On the right to have the possibility to bring forward claims, the Court stressed that this included at least the identification of each individual and the specific evaluation of their migratory situation,[134] with particular attention to their need for international protection.[135] Interestingly, the Inter-American Court reached its conclusions regarding the "possibility to bring forward claims" as early as 2012, several years before the European Court of Human Rights

127 *Ibidem.*, paras. 156–159.

128 *Ibidem.*

129 *Ibidem.*, para. 175.

130 *Expelled Dominicans and Haitians v. Dominican Republic Preliminary Objections, Merits, Reparations and Costs* IACourtHR, judgment 28 August 2014, Series C No. 282, para. 171.

131 *Nadege Dorzema v. Dominican Republic* IACourtHR, para. 175.

132 *Ibidem.*

133 *Ibidem.*

134 IAComHR *Debido proceso en los procedimientos para la determinación de la condición de persona refugiada, y apátrida y el otorgamiento de protección complementaria* OEA/Ser.L/V/II., Doc. 255, 5 August 2020, para. 175.

135 *Expelled Dominicans and Haitians v. Dominican Republic* IACourtHR, para. 381.

adopted this exact terminology in its 2016 *Khlaifia* Grand Chamber decision. However, unlike the ECtHR, the Inter-American Court did not elaborate further on the specific procedural requirements that this "possibility" entails. Subsequently, the Court has continued to use this phrasing in its later decisions, reaffirming the importance of providing individuals subject to expulsion with an opportunity to present their claims.[136] Yet, these later references have also lacked a deeper exploration of the practical measures or procedural safeguards necessary to fulfill this obligation comprehensively. This leaves room for interpretation and reliance on complementary principles, such as due process and non-discrimination, to clarify the scope of protection under the Inter-American system.

Irrespective of this ambiguity, the Court continuously underscored the importance of the prohibition of collective expulsion, for example in its 2014 Advisory Opinion on family separation.[137] The Court emphasized that any administrative or judicial body deciding on family separation due to the expulsion of one or both parents based on their migratory status must ensure that the decision is individualized and considers the specific circumstances of the case.[138] This individualized assessment must adhere to the principles of due process and prioritize the child's best interests, considering the parameters established in the opinion.[139] The Court explicitly linked this obligation to the prohibition of collective expulsion, reinforcing that measures impacting families and children in migration contexts require a thorough and case-specific evaluation to avoid arbitrary or discriminatory practices.[140] By aligning family separation decisions with the prohibition of collective expulsion, the Court highlighted the broader implications of procedural safeguards in protecting fundamental human rights in migration processes. Moreover, like the ECtHR, the Commission has underscored that these procedural guarantees extend to measures that aim to prevent migrants from reaching a state's borders or push them toward

---

136 *Expelled Dominicans and Haitians v. Dominican Republic Preliminary Objections, Merits, Reparations and Costs* IACourtHR, Judgment 28 August 2014. Series C No. 282, (*Expelled Dominicans and Haitians v. Dominican Republic*), para. 381 and IAComHR *Debido proceso en los procedimientos para la determinación de la condición de persona refugiada, y apátrida y el otorgamiento de protección complementaria* OEA/Ser.L/V/II., Doc. 255, 5 August 2020, para. 175.

137 *Advisory Opinion on family separation* IACourtHR, OC–21/14, 19 August 2024, requested by Argentina, Brasil, Paraguay and Uruguay, para. 281 and footnote 553.

138 *Ibidem.*

139 *Ibidem.*, para. 280–282.

140 *Ibidem.*, para. 281.

another state.[141] This principle applies to actions taken within a state's territory as well as extraterritorially, such as interdictions on the High Sea.[142] Collective expulsions, even in these contexts, must adhere to processes that provide effective defense mechanisms, including the right to be heard, access to judicial remedies, and the provision of legal assistance and translators where necessary.[143] These guarantees ensure that any expulsion decision respects the human rights of migrants and avoids arbitrary or large-scale violations of their fundamental rights across regions.

In conclusion, the procedural guarantees under Article 22(9) ACHR underscore the Inter-American Court and Commission's dedication to safeguarding migrants' rights in "original" expulsion context as well as in situations of denial of entry. The Court mandates individualized assessments for each person subject to expulsion, considering their unique circumstances and potential need for international protection. Procedural safeguards include the right to receive information, legal and consular assistance, access to translators, the opportunity to contest expulsion decisions, and the suspensive effect of appeals. These measures prevent arbitrary expulsions and uphold due process and non-discrimination principles. The ACHR's guarantees closely align with those in Article 4 Protocol 4 of the European Convention on Human Rights. Both emphasize individualized assessments and protections against arbitrary expulsions, including extraterritorial actions like interdictions and denials of entry. However, Article 22(9) ACHR offers additional protections, such as the right to consular assistance, and explicit protection against discrimination, making its scope broader. While the ACHR provides a more expansive framework, the ECtHR's detailed jurisprudence offers valuable insights for refining procedural safeguards. Together, these systems reinforce the importance of protecting migrants' and asylum seekers' rights across regions.

2.4 *Article 12(5) African Charter on Human and Peoples' Rights*

The prohibition of collective expulsion in Article 12(5) African Charter, also referred to as "Banjul Charter", takes a distinct approach in comparison to

141 IAComHR *Informe sobre la situación de derechos humanos de familias, niños, niñas y adolescentes no acompañados refugiados y migrantes en los Estados Unidos de América* OAS/Ser.L/V/II.155, Doc. 16. 24 July 2015, para. 105 and IAComHR *Debido proceso en los procedimientos para la determinación de la condición de persona refugiada y apátrida, y el otorgamiento de protección complementaria,* para. 176.

142 *Ibidem.*

143 *Ibidem.*

its regional counterparts when it comes to its wording, but also procedural guarantees. At first sight, it becomes apparent that Article 12(5) differs in wording and structure. The provision states: "The mass expulsion of non-nationals shall be prohibited. Mass expulsion shall be that which is aimed at national, racial, ethnic, or religions [sic!] groups". The reasons for the terminology "mass" instead of "collective" and its focus on non-discrimination were already assessed in detail above in Chapters 1 and 2.

The following section will start with examining the unique structure of the prohibition in the African Charter, which appears to emphasize the discriminatory nature of the measure rather than the absence of procedural guarantees.[144] This is supported by the African Commission on Human and People's Rights description of non-discrimination in *Good v. Botswana* as a fundamental principle of international human rights law "whose respect is essential to the exercise and enjoyment of all human rights".[145] This finding is remarkable, given the fact that the mentioned provisions differ immensely in their scope and nature.[146] In order to understand the specific design of this prohibition, one has to keep in mind the political and cultural situation and circumstances during the drafting period of the charter.[147] The prohibition of mass expulsion was included in the charter after the continent had experienced several mass expulsions of non-nationals from African countries during the 1960s and 1970s. Governments denationalized and expelled the descendants of immigrant groups *en masse*.[148] One of the most well-known examples was the mass expulsion of the vast majority of the Asian

144 Similar argument see: Bekker, Gina *Mass expulsion of foreign nationals: A 'special violation of human rights' – Communication 292/2004 Institute for Human Rights and Development in Africa v Republic of Angola* African Human Rights Law Journal, Vol. 9, No. 1, 2009, pp. 268–269.

145 *Good v. Botswana* ACHPR, Communication 313/05, (2010) 28th Activity Report, Annex iv; 2010, para. 218.

146 Some are designed as equal-protection clauses, others are restricted to specific rights, some provisions provide a non-exhaustive list of grounds on which basis a discrimination is prohibited, others are self-contained. An example of such a self-contained provision is Article 12(5) African Charter prohibiting mass expulsion based on a restricted list of grounds such as nationality, religion, ethnicity, and race.

147 The *travaux préparatoires* of the African Charter used for this section stem from my archival work at the United Nations Archives and the Archives of the International Labor Organization in Geneva in May 2018 together with Dr. Misha Plagis.

148 Manby, Bronwen *Struggles for Citizenship in Africa: Mass denationalization and expulsion*, (ZED books 2009), Chapter 4, p. 1.

population from Uganda by the government of Idi Amin, which was triggered by racial tensions.[149]

When the African Charter was adopted under the auspices of the Organisation for African Unity (OAU), now the African Union (AU), the idea was to establish an instrument that specifically deals with human rights issues on the African continent and to promote and protect human rights and fundamental freedoms for all African citizens.[150] However, over time, the African Commission has gradually aligned the scope of protection under the African Charter with that of its regional counterparts.[151] While the initial emphasis was on the non-discriminatory nature of collective expulsion, the Commission has increasingly highlighted the procedural guarantees inherent in the prohibition. It has underscored the interconnectedness of these guarantees with broader principles of due process and fair trial rights, as explored in Chapters 2 and 4.[152] This evolution reflects a broader recognition within the African human rights system that effective protection against collective expulsions requires not only the prevention of discrimination but also the implementation of robust procedural safeguards to ensure fairness and accountability. One of the reasons for this initial focus on non-discrimination is to be found in the genesis of the convention. The drafters highlighted that they "thought it prudent not to deviate much from the international norms solemnly adopted in various universal instruments by the different member states of the OAU".[153] This finding is true for many provisions. However, this is not the case concerning the final version of the prohibition of mass expulsion enshrined in Article 12(5) ACHPR, which entails a quite distinct approach. Previous draft versions of the provisions resembled heavily the provision codified in the fourth additional protocol to the ECHR.[154]

---

149 For a detailed analysis on the correlation between the mass expulsion of Asian decendents from Uganda and the development of Article 12(5) African Charter see: Henckaerts, Jean-Marie *Mass Expulsion in Modern International Law and Practice* pp. 22–24.

150 Mapuva, Loveness *Negating the Promotion of Human Rights Through "Claw-Back" Clauses in the African Charter on Human and People's Rights* International Affairs and Global Strategy, Vol. 51, 2016, p. 1.

151 See Chapter 2, 1.2.

152 See Chapter 2, 1.2 and Chapter 4, 4.3.

153 *Part II, No. 1 (a) Preliminary draft of the African Charter prepared during the Dakar Meeting of Experts at the end of 1979* CAB/LEG/67/3/Rev. 1, reprinted in Human Rights Law in Africa Vol. 4 (1999), p. 81.

154 Article 12(4) of the last draft before adoption, the Banjul draft of 1980 (CAB/LEG/67/3) red: "The collective expulsion of foreigner shall be prohibited".

However, despite its distinct wording and structure, the African Commission has interpreted Article 12(5) ACHPR by drawing from the interpretation of the European Court of Human Rights and the European Commission on Human Rights. The African Commission referred explicitly to the relationship between the prohibition in the European Convention and the African Charter in *Institute for Human Rights and Development in Africa v. Angola.*

Here, the Commission held that

> The African Charter is not unique in prohibiting mass expulsions. The European Convention on Human Rights provides some protection against expulsion. The fourth Protocol to the same Convention *similarly* [emphasis added] prohibits collective expulsion of aliens as well as the expulsion of nationals from their own state. Its seventh Protocol prohibits expulsion of an alien lawfully resident in a state except when a decision to that effect is taken in accordance with law. Here, the person concerned is entitled to submit reasons against the expulsion, have the case reviewed and be represented for these purposes before a competent authority.[155]

This paragraph illustrates that the African Commission closely monitors the developments and codifications in other regional human rights systems. By drawing from the jurisprudence of other treaty bodies, the Commission has revealed that, despite the distinct wording of the provisions in the Banjul Charter, the scope of protection is remarkably similar across regions. The emphasis on the discriminatory nature of collective expulsions in Article 12 (5) of the African Charter aligns with the Charter's broader structure, which repeatedly highlights the principle of non-discrimination. The Preamble to the African Charter stresses the commitment of Organization of African Unity members to eliminate all forms of discrimination, particularly those based on race, ethnicity, color, sex, language, religion, or political opinions. Article 2 of the Charter further extends these protections to all individuals, without distinction.

As explained above, since the Charter's entry into force, the African Commission on Human and Peoples' Rights complemented the scope of protection of the prohibition in several cases. An assessment of this jurisprudence signals a move away from the formal requirements established in

---

155 *Institute for Human Rights and Development in Africa v Republic of Angola* AComHR Comm. No. 292/04 (2008), para. 70.

Article 12(5) ACHPR.[156] The African Commission's conclusion in *Institute for Human Rights and Development in Africa v Republic of Angola* illustrate this move towards a reading of the provision as containing procedural guarantees.[157] By examining a violation of Article 1 ACHPR,[158] the Commission explicitly referred to the obligation of all member states to the Charter to grant due process rights to all non-nationals before being expelled as a group. The Commission highlighted that "there is nothing in the African Charter that requires member states of the African Union to guarantee for non-nationals an absolute right to enter and/or reside in their territories".[159] However, the AComHPR also pointed out that this does "not in any way mean that the African Charter gives member states the free hand to unnecessarily and **without due process** [emphasis added] deal with non-nationals to such an extent that they are denied the basic guarantees".[160]

Another argument is that the African Commission herself sees the prohibition of discrimination as a guarantor for due process. An indication for these findings is to be found in the *Principles and Guidelines on the Right to a Fair Trial and Legal Assistance in Africa* adopted by the *African Commission on Human and Peoples' Rights* in 2003.[161] Here, the Commission defined the duties of a prosecutor to ensure the due process rights for everyone. The Commission stipulated that due process is guaranteed *inter alia* if prosecutors "carry out their functions impartially and avoid all political, social, racial, ethnic, religious, cultural, sexual, gender or any other kind of discrimination".[162] It follows that non-discrimination is a prerequisite for due process. Besides that, the principle stipulated that prosecutors ought to "act with objectivity [...] and pay attention to all

156 Bekker, Gina *Mass expulsion of foreign nationals* pp. 269–270.

157 *Ibidem.*

158 Article 1 African Charter reads: "The member states of the Organisation of African Unity, parties to the present Charter shall recognise the rights, duties and freedoms enshrined in the Charter and shall undertake to adopt legislative or other measures to give effect to them."

159 *Institute for Human Rights and Development in Africa v Republic of Angola* AComHR, para. 84.

160 *Ibidem.*

161 AComHR *Principles and Guidelines on the Right to a Fair Trial and Legal Assistance in Africa* adopted by the African Commission on Human and Peoples' Rights in accordance with its mandate under Article 45(c) of the African Charter on Human and Peoples' Rights "to formulate and lay down principles and rules aimed at solving legal problems relating to human and peoples' rights and fundamental freedoms upon which African states may base their legislation", 2003, C. b).

162 *Ibidem.*, principle F. h); i).

relevant circumstances [and] consider the views and concerns of victims".[163] Therefore, due process rights as enshrined in the African Charter require an individual and impartial decision free from discriminatory motives. Thus, Article 12(5) ACHPR also contains due process rights such as the right to an individual decision.

The Commission, however, does not mention whether Article 12(5) ACHPR also contains the right to legal assistance and an interpreter and the right to an appeal/effective remedy as guaranteed in other regional human rights instruments. The Commission has made it clear that the prohibition on collective expulsions obliges states to ensure that certain procedures are followed to uphold the rights of those subject to expulsion.[164] In *Union Interafricaine des Droits de l'Homme* of 1997 the Commission emphasized that deportations can only take place after a court decision.[165] This means that expulsions must be based on a judicial process, where the individual's case is subject to examination and determination by the courts. In *Rencontre Africaine pour la Défense des Droits de l'Homme v. Zambia* the Commission reinforced this approach, clarifying that states have the right to take legal action against individuals who are unlawfully within their borders.[166] However, the Commission stressed that this right must be exercised under the principles of fairness and justice, ensuring that the affected individuals have access to legal remedies and that their rights are not violated in the expulsion process.[167] This shows that the ACHPR underscores the importance of procedural safeguards in expulsion procedures, linking the right to expel non-nationals with the need for judicial oversight, effective remedies, and protection against arbitrary decisions. Likewise, a contextual reading of the prohibition of collective expulsion within the *Banjul Charter* reveals that each foreigner in case of mass expulsion enjoys these guarantees. The often-succinct analysis by the Commission on the scope of application of Article 12(5) ACHPR makes it challenging to assess the origins of these requirements.

---

163 *Ibidem.*

164 Murray, Rachel *The African Charter on Human and Peoples' Rights: A Commentary* p. 335, see also: Ouguergouz, Fatsah *The African Charter on Human and Peoples' Rights A Comprehensive Agenda for Human Dignity and Sustainable Democracy in Africa* (Kluwer Law International 2003), p. 131.

165 *Union Inter Africaine des Droits de l'Homme, Fédération Internationale des Ligues des Droits de l'Homme and Others v. Angola* AComHPR, Comm. No. 159/96, 1997, para. 20.

166 *Rencontre Africaine pour la Défense des Droits de l'Homme v. Zambia* AComHPR, Communication 71/92, 1996, para. 31.

167 *Ibidem.*

In conclusion, despite its distinct approach in wording and nature, the prohibition of collective expulsion in the African Charter contains procedural guarantees against arbitrary expulsions for all foreigners. These guarantees include the right of every member of the group to an individual examination of her or his circumstances, the right to legal assistance and an interpreter as well as the right to an effective remedy. Having examined the procedural guarantees against collective expulsion at the regional level, we now turn to the international framework to assess how these protections are established and enforced on a broader scale. The International Covenant on Civil and Political Rights (ICCPR) plays a central role in this regard, setting out fundamental safeguards for the expulsion of foreign nationals.

2.5 *Article 13 International Covenant on Civil and Political Rights*

To start with this assessment, we first take a general look at the procedural safeguards for the expulsion of foreign nationals are enshrined in several key provisions of the ICCPR. Article 5(2) ICCPR establishes a fundamental obligation for states to uphold a minimum standard of human rights. While states have the authority to extend the scope of each provision of the Covenant through domestic law, they are prohibited from offering rights to a lesser extent than those guaranteed at the international level. Besides that, Article 13 of the ICCPR provides procedural safeguards for the expulsion of lawfully resident foreigners from a state's territory. It requires that expulsions be carried out "in pursuance of a decision reached in accordance with law" and guarantees individuals the right to challenge their expulsion by submitting reasons against it and the right to appeal the decision. This provision is also the one where the prohibition of collective expulsion comes into play as Article 13 ICCPR implicitly contains this principle according to the Human Rights Committee in *General Comment No. 15*. The Committee has made it clear that collective expulsions cannot satisfy the procedural guarantees outlined in Article 13 and, therefore, must be prohibited under this provision.[168] This finding in *General Comment No. 15* is relevant for expulsion procedures as its inclusion of procedural guarantees provides a framework for substantive accountability.[169] The inclusion of these guarantees in the prohibition ensures that states cannot expel individuals based on

168 HRC *General Comment No. 15* para. 9.

169 Joseph, Sarah and Castan, Melissa *The International Covenant on Civil and Political Rights Cases, Materials, and Commentary* (Oxford University Press 3rd edn. 2013), p. 419.

immutable characteristics, such as race, and guarantees due process protections for all foreigners in group expulsion cases, free from discrimination.[170] The same principles apply to the prohibition of collective expulsion as indirectly reflected in Article 13 of the ICCPR. Importantly, this implicit prohibition of collective expulsion under the ICCPR holds more significance than it might initially appear. With 173 state parties bound to the Covenant, including countries such as Switzerland, the United States, Israel, Australia, Iran, and Japan, many of which are not subject to this prohibition under any other treaty, its global impact is considerable.[171]

When comparing Article 13 ICCPR with its regional counterparts, a key structural difference becomes evident: Unlike most regional instruments, it integrates two core principles within a single provision – the prohibition of collective expulsion and the protection against expulsion without due process for lawfully residing foreigners.[172] At its core, Article 13 ICCPR is primarily a procedural safeguard, ensuring due process for foreign nationals facing expulsion.[173] The Human Rights Committee reinforced this interpretation in *General Comment No. 15*, emphasizing that the provision guarantees each individual a case-by-case assessment, making collective or mass expulsions inherently incompatible with its requirements.[174] The Committee further clarified that this protection extends beyond a mere formal entitlement, requiring effective access to procedural guarantees such as the right to present arguments against expulsion, the right to have the decision reviewed by a competent authority, and the right to legal representation.[175] Notably, the HRC underscored that these procedural safeguards may only be waived in exceptional cases where "compelling reasons of national security" justify such a departure.[176]

Over a decade after the publication of this first general comment that clarified the implicit codification of the prohibition of collective expulsion in Article 13, the Human Rights Committee once again reaffirmed in 2003 the importance of individual assessments in expulsion cases, emphasizing

170 *Ibidem.*

171 United Nations Human Rights Office of the High Commissioner *ICCPR Status of Ratification Dashboard*, available at: http://indicators.ohchr.org/.

172 HRC *Concluding Observations: Dominican Republic* (2001), CCPR/CO/71/DOM, 3 April 2001, para. 16.

173 Guild, Elspeth *Art 19-Protection in the Event of Removal* para. 19.08.

174 HRC *Concluding Observations: Dominican Republic* (2001), CCPR/CO/71/DOM, 3 April 2001, para. 16.

175 *Ibidem.*

176 *Ibidem.*

that collective expulsions violate the protections outlined in the ICCPR. Underscoring the necessity of procedural safeguards for all individuals facing deportation, the HRC in its *Concluding Observations on the Dominican Republic* expressed its concerns about

> the continuing reports of mass expulsions of ethnic Haitians, even when such persons are nationals of the Dominican Republic. It holds *mass expulsions of non-nationals to be in breach of the Covenant since no account is taken of the situation of individuals* for whom the Dominican Republic is their own country in the light of article 12, paragraph 4, nor of cases where expulsion may be contrary to article 7 given the risk of subsequent cruel, inhuman or degrading treatment, nor yet of cases where the legality of an individual's presence in the country is in dispute and must be settled in proceedings that satisfy the requirements of article 13.
>
> The State party should guarantee the right of every Dominican national not to be expelled from the country and *ensure that all persons facing deportation proceedings* are *covered by the safeguards* established in the *Covenant* [emphasis added].[177]

This emphasis on individualized assessments and procedural safeguards in the case against the Dominican Republic is not unique as the Human Rights Committee has consistently reaffirmed this principle in its review of state practices of the past decade. For example, the Committee came to a similar conclusion on the importance of an individual assessment of the circumstances of every claimant in its *2003 Concluding Observations on Estonia*. The Committee stressed that states should conduct individual asylum determination procedures before removing migrants coming from so-called "safe countries".[178] The Committee expressed openly its concern that Estonia "may deny the individual assessment of a refugee claim when the applicant is considered to come from a "safe" country".[179] The Committee then went on to point out that member states

177 *Ibidem*. The same concern was raised in the most recent report by the Human Rights Committee in its *Concluding observations on the sixth periodic report of the Dominican Republic* (2017), CCPR/C/DOM/CO/6, 27 November 2017, paras. 23, 24.

178 *Ibidem*.

179 *Ibidem*.

> in order to afford effective protection [...] of the Covenant, applications for refugee status should always be assessed on an *individual basis* and that a decision declaring an application inadmissible should not have restrictive procedural effects such as the *denial of suspensive effect of appeal* (articles 6, 7 and 13 of the Covenant) [emphasis added]".[180]

This conclusion once again shows that Article 13 ICCPR contains procedural guarantees such as the right to be heard by a competent authority, the right to review, and the right to the assistance of a legal counsel.[181] The right to be heard by a competent authority also refers to administrative authorities. The Human Rights Committee implicitly acknowledged this in *Maroufidou v. Sweden*.[182] In addition, Article 13 ICCPR in conjunction with Articles 6 and 7 ICCPR guarantees the suspensive effect of an appeal against an expulsion order.[183] The HRC continuously reaffirmed its approach to the prohibition of collective expulsion and the importance of individualized assessments, for example in its 2024 *Concluding Observations on Greece's third periodic report*.[184] In these observations, the Committee expressed concern over Greece's pushback practices at its sea and land borders, highlighting violations of the *non-refoulement* principle and the prohibition of collective expulsion.[185] The HRC specifically addressed the excessive use of force, ill-treatment, and the lack of procedural safeguards during pushback operations, as well as the detention of third-country nationals without any real prospect of return.[186] It then called on Greece to cease the collective expulsion of migrants, insisting that expulsions must be preceded by individualized assessments of protection available in "safe third countries".[187] The Committee further emphasized the need for Greece to enforce the *non-refoulement* principle effectively and

180 Human Rights Committee *Concluding Observations: Estonia* (2003), CCPR/CO/77/EST, 15 April 2003, para. 13.

181 Human Rights Committee *Denmark: Concluding Observations on Denmark* (2000), CCPR/CO/70/DNK, 15 November 2000, para. 17.

182 Joseph and Castan *ICCPR* with reference to: Human Rights Committee *Maroufidou v. Sweden* Communication No. R.13/58, 9 April 1981.

183 *Ibidem.*

184 Human Rights Committee *Concluding observations on the third periodic report of Greece* CCPR/C/GRC/CO/3, 7 November 2024, para. 20.

185 *Ibidem.*, paras. 19–20.

186 *Ibidem.*

187 *Ibidem.*, para. 20.

ensure fair and efficient asylum procedures for all asylum seekers, irrespective of their entry method.[188] These recommendations underscore the HRC's consistent emphasis on ensuring that collective expulsions are conducted in line with international human rights standards, including adequate procedural guarantees.

In conclusion, this list of guarantees highlights the similarities between the prohibition outlined in Article 13 of the ICCPR and those found in its regional counterparts discussed above. The scope of protection, both *ratione personae* and about the procedural guarantees it contains, is largely comparable across the ICCPR and other regional and international human rights instruments. Furthermore, we established that Article 13 ICCPR implicitly contains procedural guarantees against collective expulsion. The Human Rights Committee acknowledged this finding in its *General Comment No. 15*. The scope of application *ratione personae* of the provision includes any foreigner who is expelled *en masse*, contrary to the wording of the provision, which only speaks of lawfully residing foreigners. The core of the prohibition in the ICCPR is to guarantee every foreigner the possibility to bring forward her or his claims against the expulsion. In detail, the procedural guarantees contained in Article 13 ICCPR encompass the right to be heard by a competent authority. Administrative procedures satisfy this obligation. Furthermore, the prohibition contains the right to review/appeal by/to a competent authority. The right to review also guarantees a suspensive effect of the expulsion proceedings (Article 13 in conjunction with Articles 6 and 7 ICCPR). The provision also guarantees the right to the assistance of legal counsel. The prohibition of collective expulsion in the ICCPR further contains material elements prohibiting the discriminatory treatment of foreigners based on attributes such as race, religion, nationality, etc. With these findings, we conclude our assessment of the procedural guarantees under the ICCPR's prohibition of collective expulsion and turn to another significant international instrument: The UN Migrant Worker Convention. As we will learn in the following, the procedural safeguards enshrined in this convention play a relevant role in strengthening the protection of migrant workers and their families against collective expulsion.

2.6 *Article 22(1) UN Migrant Worker Convention*

The relevance of the procedural guarantees contained in the prohibition of collective expulsion in the United Nations International Convention on the

188 *Ibidem.*, paras. 19–20.

Protection of the Rights of All Migrant Workers and Members of Their Families (UNCRMW or Migrant Worker Convention) is noteworthy for several reasons. First, its global reach distinguishes it from its regional counterparts. States from all continents are parties to the UN Migrant Worker Convention,[189] which makes it a truly international protection mechanism. However, migrant-receiving states such as the USA, Australia, France, Germany, or Great Britain have not ratified the Convention. Migrant-sending states such as Mexico, Morocco, or the Philippines, in contrast, are parties to the Convention. Second, the personal scope of protection of most provisions of the Convention is quite extensive. It protects every migrant and their family throughout the entire migration process and thus, even before reaching the territory of another state.[190] In general, the Convention draws distinctions between regular and irregular migrants.[191] Irregular migrants enjoy fewer rights than regular migrants in the Convention. In contrast, the provision containing the prohibition of collective expulsion does not draw such a distinction. The prohibition in the UNCRMW guarantees a fair and genuine expulsion procedure to every migrant irrespective of the individual's legal status. The Committee on the Protection of the Rights of All Migrant Workers and Members of their Families (CMW) acknowledged this finding explicitly in its *General Comment No. 2* of 2013. Here, the CMW offered further insight into its understanding of the scope of the prohibition of collective expulsion stressing that

> Article 22 of the Convention prohibits collective expulsion and provides *procedural safeguards* in *individual expulsion* proceedings with

---

189 United Nations Office of the High Commissioner for Human Rights *Status of Ratification International Convention on the Protection of the Rights of All Migrant Workers and Members of their Families* Interactive Dashboard, available at: http://indicators.ohchr.org/.

190 The personal scope of protection of the UN Migrant Worker Convention is established in its Article 1(1) which extends the umbrella of protection that "all migrant workers and members of their families without distinction of any kind". Subparagraph two of Article 1 clarifies that this protection is guaranteed during "the entire migration process of migrant workers and members of their families, which comprises preparation for migration, departure, transit and the entire period of stay and remunerated activity in the State of employment as well as return to the State of origin or the State of habitual residence". Article 2(1) UNCRMW complements this notion of the personal scope by defining the term "migrant worker" as "a person who is to be engaged, is engaged or has been engaged in a remunerated activity in a State of which he or she is not a national".

191 See, for example, in Articles 35–37 and Articles 67–69.

> respect to *both regular and irregular migrant workers and members of their families* [emphasis added].[192]

This is particularly notable as the Committee explicitly extends the scope of protection to individuals with irregular status, an approach that aligns with the realities of migration but one that states are often reluctant to recognize. This stance reflects the broader approach of the UN Migrant Worker Convention, which seeks to frame migrant workers first and foremost as human beings, emphasizing their dignity and vulnerability rather than solely their legal status.[193] The prohibition in the UN Migrant Worker Convention is thirdly noteworthy as the content of procedural guarantees contained in Article 22 UNCRMW is equivalent to the one in its regional counterparts. The provision provides procedural guarantees against arbitrary expulsion. This recognition of procedural safeguards aligns with the broader understanding that migrant workers require specific protections. As ILC Special Rapporteur on the "expulsion of aliens", Maurice Kamto, explains, "the case of migrant workers falls within a special regime",[194] highlighting the distinct legal framework designed to safeguard their rights. He further stresses that this "special" regime guarantees

> [e]ach case of expulsion should be examined and decided *individually*. The procedure to be followed in cases of expulsion, which is described in minute detail, reinforces the guarantees that protect the rights of expellees, including sheltering them from mere administrative decisions. It guarantees the expellees' *right to receive information*, to *submit*

---

192 CMW *General comment No. 2 on the rights of migrant workers in an irregular situation and members of their families* CMW/C/GC/2, 28 August 2013, para. 49.

193 The UN Migrant Worker Convention explicitly frames migrant workers as human beings, emphasizing their dignity and vulnerability throughout its text. The Preamble underscores "the need to respect the basic human rights of all migrant workers", reaffirming fundamental human dignity regardless of migration status. Article 16(1) affirms their right to liberty and security, while Article 25 explicitly recognizes the rights of irregular migrant workers, stating that they "shall enjoy treatment not less favorable than that which applies to nationals" concerning remuneration and working conditions. Additionally, Article 68 urges states to take measures to prevent irregular migration in a way that respects the fundamental rights of all migrants. Together the preamble and these provisions reflect the Convention's overarching approach to centering the human dignity and vulnerability of migrant workers, irrespective of their legal status.

194 Kamto, Maurice *Preliminary report on the expulsion of aliens* A/CN.4/554, 2 June 2005, para. 25.

> *arguments* against their expulsion and to be *compensated* if a decision of expulsion that has already been executed is subsequently annulled [emphasis added].[195]

This emphasis on procedural fairness ensures that migrant workers are not only informed of expulsion decisions but can also meaningfully challenge the process. By explicitly requiring that decisions be communicated in a language the migrant understands, Article 22 UNCRMW strengthens accessibility and due process, setting a higher standard for procedural guarantees compared to many regional instruments. This standard includes the right to receive a decision from a competent authority (subparagraph 2). This decision must be in a language the migrant understands (subparagraph 3). Subparagraph 4 guarantees the migrants' right to submit reasons against their expulsion and the right to an appeal, which triggers the suspension of the expulsion. Lastly, the provision guarantees the right to seek compensation (subparagraph 5).

Unfortunately, however, as the UNCRMW's individual complaint mechanism has not yet entered into force due to a lack of ratifications,[196] individuals cannot yet claim a violation of Article 22 UNCRMW or its due process guarantees. As a result, the Committee on Migrant Workers remains the sole body with the authority to interpret this provision.[197] Its role is limited to reviewing state reports on the implementation of the Convention and issuing concluding observations.[198] An analysis of the CMW's annual and sessional reports from 2004 to 2024 suggests that the issue of collective expulsion has not been a focal point of its oversight. Notably, the reports

195 *Ibidem.*

196 United Nations Office of the High Commissioner *Communications procedures Committee on the Protection of the Rights of All Migrant Workers and Members of their Families* available at: https://www.ohchr.org/en/treaty-bodies/cmw/communications-procedures. Neither the inter-state communications procedure nor the individual complaint mechanism have yet entered into force. Article 76 of the International Convention on the Protection of the Rights of All Migrant Workers and Members of Their Families gives the Committee on Migrant Workers competence to receive and consider communications by a state party alleging violations of the Convention by other states parties who made the necessary declaration under Article 76. This inter-state complaint mechanism will become operative when 10 states parties have made the necessary declaration under Article 76.

197 United Nations Office of the High Commissioner of Human Rights *Committee of Migrants Workers general information on the work of the Committee* available at: https://www.ohchr.org/EN/HRBodies/CMW/Pages/CMWIntro.aspx.

198 *Ibidem.*

from 2012 to 2019 make no mention of collective expulsions, individual expulsions, or Article 22 UNCRMW, highlighting a significant gap in the Convention's practical enforcement.[199] In contrast, while the reports from 2008 to 2012 frequently address individual expulsion practices, the 2020/2021 and 2022/2023 reports only briefly mention the prohibition of collective expulsions. The 2020/2021 report, in particular, underscores the Committee's recognition of collective expulsions as a significant challenge to the protection of migrant rights, especially during the COVID-19 pandemic. It further shows that in discussions with state parties, international organizations, and civil society, the Committee highlighted the detrimental effects of such expulsions and stressed the necessity of adhering to procedural safeguards to prevent violations of migrants' rights.[200] Likewise, in the 2022/ 2023 report, the Committee continued to draw attention to collective expulsions as a pressing concern.[201] On International Migrants Day 2022, the Committee, alongside other human rights bodies, condemned the role of restrictive border management policies, including collective expulsions and pushbacks, in the disappearance and deaths of migrants.[202] The Committee identified such practices as contributing to violations of the principle of *non-refoulement* and exacerbating the vulnerabilities of migrants, particularly women and unaccompanied children.[203] These recurring references highlight the Committee's commitment to ensuring that collective expulsion practices are scrutinized and that migrants' rights are upheld, especially at member states borders,[204] as well as when concluding readmission agreements.[205] Earlier reports had already reminded state parties of their duty to

---

199 All annual/sessional reports of the Committee on the Protection of the Rights of All Migrant Workers and Members of Their Families from 2004 to 2024 are available on the webpage of the UN High Commissioner for Human Rights: https://tbinternet.ohchr.org/_layouts/treatybodyexternal/TBSearch.aspx?Lang=en&TreatyID=7&DocTypeID=27.

200 CWM *Thirty-second session* (6–16 and 29–30 April 2021), General Assembly, Official Records, Seventy-sixth Session, Supplement No. 48, A/76/48, para. 56.

201 CMW *Thirty-fifth session* (19–30 September 2022) and *thirty-sixth session* (27 March–6 April 2023) General Assembly, Official Records, Seventy-eighth Session, Supplement No. 48, A/78/48, para. 54.

202 *Ibidem.*

203 *Ibidem.*

204 CMW *Thirteenth session (22 November–3 December 2010), fourteenth session (4–8 April 2011)* General Assembly, Official Records, Sixty-sixth session, Supplement No. 48, A/66/48, (2010/12 Committee Report).

205 CMW *2010/11 Committee Report* para. 36. In the specific case, the Committee was concerned about such agreements between Albania and several countries of origin of

ensure procedural safeguards for expelled migrant workers and their families, including the right to appeal an expulsion order before an administrative body and to have access to a first-instance court in all expulsion scenarios.[206] Additionally, the Committee raised concerns about certain states' expulsion, detention, and deportation practices, which it argued violated the principles enshrined in Article 22 of the Convention.[207] One noteworthy example in this regard is the Committee's consideration of Albania's state report under Article 74 of the UNCRMW. Here, the experts found that Albania had violated the prohibition on collective expulsions by forcibly expelling Sub-Saharan African migrants.[208] The Committee criticized Albania for its failure to respond to reports of multiple instances of collective expulsions, despite its assurances that adequate safeguards were in place.[209] As a result, the Committee recommended measures to ensure that every individual facing expulsion is granted the right to an objective examination by competent authorities, aligning with the case law of regional human rights bodies.[210]

Moreover, the Committee reminded member states of their obligation to establish a legal framework governing expulsion and deportation procedures in accordance with Articles 22 and 23 of the Convention.[211] Reflecting obligations similar to those set forth by the European Commission on Human Rights, the Committee reiterated that the prohibition of collective expulsions includes the right of every migrant to present reasons against their expulsion.[212] It further clarified that Article 22 obliges states to take effective measures to provide redress to victims and to prevent such expulsions in the future.[213]

---

migrant workers and suggested to establish "appropriate procedural guarantees for migrants".

206 CMW *2010/11 Committee Report* para. 23.

207 CMW *2010/11 Committee Report* paras. 29, 30.

208 CMW *Eleventh session (12–16 October 2009), twelfth session (26–30 April 2010), General Assembly, Official Records sixty-fifth Session, supplement No. 48* (2009/10 Committee Report), paras. 22–34.

209 CMW *2009/10 Committee Report* para. 22.

210 CMW *2009/10 Committee Report* para. 23.

211 *Ibidem.*

212 See first case pertaining to Article 4 Protocol 4 ECHR *X and Y v. Sweden* ECtHR on the Admissibility of Applications 3803/68 and 3804/68, 4 October 1968.

213 *CMW 2009/10 Committee Report* para. 23. The ECtHR similarly established the duty of Member States to provide for measures of redress. It did so, for example, in *Čonka v. Belgium, Hirsi Jamaa and Others v. Italy, Sharifi, and Others v. Italy and Greece,* or *N.D. and N.T. v. Spain.*

However, to conduct a comprehensive analysis of the scope of the provision, it is essential to consider sources beyond the recommendations provided by the Committee in its annual reports. One such valuable source is the General Comments issued by the Committee on the Protection of the Rights of All Migrant Workers and Members of Their Families, which offer further insight into the scope of Article 22 of the Migrant Worker Convention. In total, the Committee published six General Comments between February 2011 and January 2025.[214] The General Comments dealt with issues ranging from migrant domestic workers,[215] migrant workers in irregular situations,[216] human rights of children in the context of international migration[217] to the convergence of the Convention and the Global Compact for Safe, Orderly and Regular Migration.[218] In its *General Comment No. 2* of 2013, the CMW offered further insight into the scope of Article 22(1) UNCRMW stating that

> Article 22 of the Convention prohibits collective expulsion and provides *procedural safeguards* in *individual expulsion* proceedings with respect to *both regular and irregular migrant workers and members of their families*. While article 22 regulates only the procedure and not the substantive grounds of expulsion, its purpose is to *prevent arbitrary expulsions* and to provide *substantive protection against expulsions* in certain situations. Article 22 applies to all procedures aimed at the

---

214 All General Comments are available here, UN Office of the High Commissioner for Human Rights https://www.ohchr.org/en/treaty-bodies/cmw/general-comments.

215 CMW *General Comment No. 1 on migrant domestic workers* CMW/C/GC/1, 23 February 2011.

216 CMW *General Comment No. 2 on the rights of migrant workers in an irregular situation and members of their families* CMW/C/GC/2, 28 August 2013.

217 See two joint General comments of the Migrant Worker Committee and Committee on the Rights of the Child: *Joint general comment No. 4 (2017) of the Committee on the Protection of the Rights of All Migrant Workers and Members of Their Families and No. 23 (2017) of the Committee on the Rights of the Child on State obligations regarding the human rights of children in the context of international migration in countries of origin, transit, destination and return* CMW/C/GC/4 and *Joint general comment No. 3 and No. 22 of the Committee on the Rights of the Child on the general principles regarding the human rights of children in the context of international migration* CMW/C/GC/3, both of 16 November 2017.

218 See: CMW *General Comment No. 6 The Convergence of the Convention and the Global Compact for Safe, Orderly and Regular Migration*. As of January 2025, the General Comment is still in its draft status since 2022.

> obligatory departure of migrant workers whether described in national law as expulsion or otherwise [emphasis added].[219]

These elaborations of the Committee on the prohibition of collective expulsion highlighting the procedural nature of the prohibition and its aim to prevent arbitrary expulsions strongly resemble the findings drawn above on the scope of the prohibition in regional contexts. This is also visible in the language and findings of the Committee when it obliges states to examine and decide each case individually stressing that states "have an obligation to ensure that their expulsion procedures provide *sufficient guarantees* to ensure that the *personal circumstances* of each migrant worker are *genuinely and individually* taken into account [emphasis added].[220] This procedural understanding of the provision's scope was again confirmed four years later by the Migrant Worker Committee in *General Comment No. 3*. Here, it recalled that the Migrant Worker Convention prohibits collective expulsions and that the member states must provide safeguards against arbitrary group expulsions.[221] The Committee's emphasis on individual case examination and the provision of safeguards against arbitrary expulsions reflects a consistent approach that aligns with the procedural guarantees found in both regional and international legal frameworks. By reaffirming these principles in *General Comment No. 3*, the Committee further solidifies the understanding that the prohibition of collective expulsions extends beyond merely preventing mass expulsions to ensuring the protection of individual rights through fair and non-arbitrary procedures.

This emphasis on procedural safeguards and the prevention of arbitrary expulsions not only mirrors regional practices but also highlights the intersection of the prohibition of collective expulsions with broader principles of international law. In particular, the Committee's focus on ensuring protection against arbitrary expulsions draws a clear connection to other key procedural principles, notably the *non-refoulement* principle. This relationship becomes even more evident when examining how Article 22 of the UNCRMW enshrines both protections, underscoring their intertwined nature.[222]

In conclusion, Article 22 of the UN Convention on the Rights of Migrant Workers and Members of Their Families offers migrants and their families a

---

219 CMW *General Comment No. 2* para. 49.

220 *Ibidem.*

221 CMW *Joint General Comment No. 3 and No.* 22 para. 47.

222 For a detailed assessment on the relationship between both principles see chapter 4.

comprehensive framework of procedural safeguards against arbitrary expulsions. Unlike other instruments that address the prohibition of collective expulsions, Article 22 explicitly outlines these procedural rights, including access to an interpreter, legal counsel, the right to present claims, and the right to have one's case reviewed. These provisions ensure a level of protection comparable to those enshrined in major regional human rights instruments. Similarly, the European Convention on Human Rights, the African Charter, and the Inter-American Convention provide similar protections, safeguarding all foreigners, regardless of their legal status, against arbitrary collective expulsions. Notably, the Migrant Worker Committee's reference to the European Court of Human Rights' jurisprudence on the prohibition of collective expulsion highlights the growing alignment between international and regional human rights systems. This convergence underscores a global consensus that the prohibition of collective expulsion is a fundamental due process right, integral to upholding core procedural guarantees in migration contexts. This alignment between international and regional human rights systems not only reinforces the procedural safeguards against collective expulsions but also sets the stage for the next examination of similar protections in Article 3 of the Convention Against Torture. This examination will once more highlight the various frameworks of procedural safeguards aimed at preventing human rights violations in the context of migration and expulsions on the international level.

2.7 *Article 3 Convention against Torture*

In contrast to the UN Migrant Worker Convention, the Convention against Torture (CAT) does not contain the prohibition of collective expulsion implicitly. However, the Committee against Torture (ComAT) reads the principle's guarantees into the *non-refoulement* principle of Article 3(1) CAT by calling it the prohibition of "collective deportation" or "collective return". To examine this terminology, it is noteworthy to stress that generally, "return" covers the removal of a foreigner from a state's territory to their country of origin[223] and that "expulsion" and "removal" can be used interchangeably.[224] Whereas "deportation" is understood as the removal act of a

223 Hamdan, Eman *The Principle of Non-Refoulement under the ECHR and the UN Convention against Torture and Other Cruel, Inhuman or Degrading Treatment or Punishment* (Brill/Nijhoff 2016), p. 106, fn. 169.

224 European Commission *Migration and Home Affairs expulsion definition* available at: https://ec.europa.eu/home-affairs/what-wedo/networks/european_migration_network/glossary_search/expulsion_en.

foreigner who has been deemed deportable.[225] Leaving aside these semantic questions and returning to Article 3(1) CAT it becomes apparent that the provision stipulating that "[n]o State Party shall expel, return ("refouler") or extradite a person to another State where there are substantial grounds for believing that he would be in danger of being subjected to torture" resembles that of Article 33(1) 1951 Refugee Convention. This resemblance emphasizes the shared commitment across instruments to prevent return to places where individuals face grave risks. In this context, return and expulsion under Article 3(1) of the CAT refer to actions that physically remove individuals from a state's territory, even if such non-admission places the expelled individual at risk of torture.[226]

As in the previous sections, here too, we examine the specific interpretations and developments provided by committees overseeing their implementation. This means that we now turn to the Committee Against Torture which is composed of ten experts,[227] which in 1996 established a working group to assess questions concerning both Article 3 and Article 22 of the Convention Against Torture (CAT)[228]. This move stemmed from the Committee's recognition of the need to clarify the scope of protection under these provisions.[229] Based on the findings of the working group, the Committee adopted its first general comment on Article 3 in November 1997, which focused primarily on issues related to evidence and the burden of proof, rather than directly addressing the prohibition of collective return or deportation.[230] However, two decades later, General Comment No. 4 of 2017 began to touch upon the prohibition of collective deportation, subtly incorporating it within the broader context of the Committee's interpretation of Article 3(1).[231] Here, the Committee

225 Hamdan, Eman *The Principle of Non-Refoulement under the ECHR and the CAT* p. 106, fn. 169.

226 *Ibidem.*, p. 105.

227 For a list of the current experts, see here: https://www.ohchr.org/en/treaty-bodies/cat/membership.

228 Article 22 CAT deals with the possibility of individuals to communicate violations of a provision of the CAT to the Committee against Torture.

229 United Nations General Assembly *Report of the Committee against Torture* Supplement No. 44, A/53/44, 1998, pp. 25–26.

230 See: Committee against Torture *Annex IX of the Report of the Committee against Torture* Supplement No. 44 A/53/44, 1998, pp. 52–53.

231 Committee against Torture *General Comment No. 4 (2017) on the implementation of article 3 of the Convention in the context of article 22* (2018), CAT/C/GC/4, 4 September 2018, para. 13.

explained in detail that the scope of Article 3(1) CAT entails the obligation to examine each case

> *individually*, impartially and independently [...] through competent administrative and/or judicial authorities, in conformity with essential *procedural safeguards*, notably the guarantee of a prompt and transparent process, a *review* of the deportation decision and a *suspensive effect* of the appeal [emphasis added].[232]

Further, the Committee established that the expelling state should ensure that

> [i]n each case, the person concerned should be informed of the intended deportation in a timely manner. *Collective deportation, without* an *objective examination* of the *individual cases* with regard to personal risk, should be considered as a *violation of the principle of non-refoulment* [emphasis added].[233]

These excerpts of the General Comment show that the Committee Against Torture emphasized that the scope of Article 3(1) CAT requires that each case be examined individually, impartially, and independently by competent authorities, ensuring essential procedural safeguards, such as a prompt and transparent process, a review of deportation decisions, and the suspensive effect of an appeal closely tying the prohibition with the *non-refoulement* principle.

Comparing the language and specific terms in this general comment with the language of the ECtHR and the EComHR on Article 4 Protocol 4 ECHR, the resemblance is evident. As shown above, the two bodies interpreted the prohibition of collective expulsion to contain the safeguards the Committee highlighted in its comment. Even the terminology such as "objective examination" and "individual examination through competent authorities" is equivalent. There are however two significant differences. First, the Committee refers to "collective deportation" instead of "collective expulsion". Second, the Committee found that a violation of the prohibition of collective deportation constitutes a violation of the *non-refoulement* principle and not a violation of a separate, independent concept. However, a closer look

232 *Ibidem.*
233 *Ibidem.*

at the General Comment reveals that the two concepts are the same, only labeled differently. The relevant footnote referencing "collective deportation" refers to the paragraph of the Human Rights Committee's *General Comment No. 15* in which the Committee clarifies that Article 13 ICCPR contains the prohibition of collective expulsion.[234] The footnote provided for by the ComAT further refers to Article 22(1) UNCRMW which protects migrants from "measures of collective expulsion" and highlights that "[e]ach case of expulsion shall be examined and decided individually". This direct reference shows that the *Committee against Torture* is well aware of the existence and the scope of application of the prohibition of collective expulsion in international conventions. Why the Committee chose the term "collective deportation" instead of "collective expulsion" remains unknown as the official documents are silent on this point. Maybe, the reason for the different use of terminology is deliberately chosen to highlight the Committee's distinct approach to the relationship between the prohibition of collective expulsion and the *non-refoulement* principle.

What makes these questions even more difficult to answer is the fact that in its concluding observations on Italy of 2017, the Committee mentioned for the first time the prohibition of "collective return" as a distinct concept that forms part of the guarantees protected by Article 3 CAT (*refoulement* and collective return). The Committee expressed its concerns about allegations that Italy "may have acted in breach of the principle of *non-refoulement* and carried out collective returns".[235] Therefore, the ComAT urged the state party to guarantee "that all asylum seekers have the opportunity for an individual review and are protected from refoulement and collective return".[236] Similarly, in its concluding observations on Greece of 2019, the Committee raised "serious concerns" about ongoing situations of "collective returns" of foreigners. The Committee referred to reports that raise

> repeated allegations of *summary forced returns* of asylum seekers and migrants –including Turkish nationals– intercepted at the sea and at the land border with Turkey in the northeastern Evros region, with

234 Office of the High Commissioner for Human Rights *General Comment No. 15, The Position of Aliens Under the Covenant* adopted by the Human Rights Committee on 11 April 1986, para. 15.

235 Committee against Torture *Concluding observations on the fifth and sixth periodic report of Italy* (2017), CAT/C/ITA/CO/5–6, 21 November 2017, para. 20.

236 *Ibidem.*, para. 21.

> *no prior risk assessment of their personal circumstances* [emphasis added].[237]

Based on this report, the Committee recommended that Greece ensures that every migrant has "the opportunity for an **individual review**, with automatic suspensive effect against expulsion decisions, and are **protected from refoulement *and* collective return** [emphasis added]".[238] The Committee had highlighted these guarantees in prior reports on Greece without mentioning the term "collective return". The fifth and sixth report of 2012, for example, highlights that member states must follow the established due process guarantees when expelling foreigners. These include access to legal remedies or access to the asylum procedure, free legal aid, or effective information provided through interpretation services and the right to an effective appeal.[239] Overall, the Committee does not use the terms "collective deportation/return" in a consistent manner in cases on group expulsions of migrants without a thorough process. However, in all cases in which the Committee dealt with group expulsions, the core procedural guarantees against expulsion *en mass* were highlighted. The ComAT's 2005 considerations on the periodic report of Ukraine are one example in this regard. Here, the Committee expressed its concern about group removals of migrants to a place where they "would be in danger of being subjected to torture".[240] The ComAT highlighted once again that

> [u]nder no circumstances should the State party *expel*, return or extradite a person to a State where there are substantial grounds for believing that the person would be in danger of being subjected to torture. When determining the *applicability of its obligations under article 3* of the Convention, the State party should *examine thoroughly* the merits of each *individual* case, ensure that adequate *judicial mechanisms* for reviewing the decision are in place, sufficient *legal defence* is available

237 Committee against Torture *Concluding observations on the seventh periodic report of Greece* (2019), CAT/C/SR.1779, 7 August 2019, para. 16.

238 *Ibidem.*, para. 17.

239 Committee against Torture *Consideration of reports submitted by States parties under article 19 of the Convention Concluding observations of the Committee against Torture* CAT/C/GRC/CO/5–6, 27 June 2012, para. 19.

240 Committee against Torture *Consideration of Reports submitted by States Parties under Article 19 of the Convention Conclusions and recommendations of the Committee against Torture: Ukraine* (2007), CAT/C/UKR/CO/5, 3 August 2007, para. 19.

> for each person subject to extradition, and that effective post-return monitoring arrangements are established [emphasis added].[241]

Likewise in the *General Comment No. 4* of 2017 the Committee, affirmed once more the existence of procedural guarantees in Article 3 CAT against arbitrary (collective) expulsions. These are the right to an individual assessment of each foreigner's circumstances by the competent authorities, the right to legal assistance, a translator as well as the right to effective remedy with suspensive effect. The Committee reminded state parties once more that they "should take legislative, administrative, judicial and other preventive measures" to ensure these guarantees.[242]

In conclusion, the Committees against Torture's considerations and recommendations on Article 3 CAT suggest that the provision offers a combination of the *non-refoulement* principle and procedural guarantees, such as an objective examination of the individual circumstances before an expulsion (prohibition of collective expulsion). The procedural guarantees contained in Article 3 CAT are comparable to the ones in other regional and international human rights treaties containing the prohibition of collective expulsion namely the right for every foreigner before their expulsion to an individual examination of their circumstances, the right to legal assistance and a translator as well as the right to an appeal.

3 Conclusion on Procedural Protection Standards against Collective Expulsion

This chapter has examined the procedural guarantees against collective expulsion in the various regional and international human rights instruments containing it. In doing so, it has argued that due process guarantees offer the essential protection against arbitrary state actions including expulsions. When properly implemented, process rights ensure that procedures remain fair, balanced, impartial, reasonable, and efficient. Such guarantees underpin fundamental rights in both criminal and civil contexts, forming the basis of fair trial rights. Key human rights instruments, including the European Convention on Human Rights, the Charter of Fundamental Rights of the European Union, the Inter-American Convention on Human Rights, the African Charter on Human and Peoples' Rights and the International

241 *Ibidem.*

242 Committee against Torture *General Comment No. 4* (2017) para. 18.

Covenant on Civil and Political Rights, enshrine the right to fair trial and an effective remedy, particularly in criminal matters. However, these safeguards are not universally applied in administrative expulsion procedures which limits migrants' rights in such circumstances significantly.

When it comes to the concrete procedural guarantees provided for by the prohibition of collective expulsion, we started our examination on the regional level before turning to international human rights instruments. The first analysis of this chapter turned to Article 4 Protocol 4 ECHR. This provision, despite its wording does not suggest so implicitly, includes specific procedural guarantees such as the right to individual examination, legal assistance, and translation services. All of these guarantees are key safeguards in preventing arbitrary expulsions. The examination of the jurisprudence of the European Court of Human Rights has shown that the Court has reinforced the importance of these protections, making clear that procedural safeguards are inseparable from the prohibition itself. Through its jurisprudence, notably in cases like *Čonka v. Belgium* and *Hirsi Jamaa v. Italy*, the Court has emphasized the need for both individual assessments and a broader contextual evaluation to prevent collective expulsions. Legal assistance and translation services are essential in these cases, ensuring fairness, especially for migrants who may be unaware of their rights or unable to assert them effectively. The right to an effective remedy, enshrined in Article 13 ECHR, further strengthens these safeguards by allowing individuals to challenge expulsion decisions in domestic courts. However, the Court has limited the suspensive effect of such appeals in expedited expulsion cases, particularly for non-asylum seekers, revealing discrepancies in the procedural protections offered based on migration status. The second European human rights instrument analyzed, the EU Fundamental Rights Charter, likewise presented an important guarantee of procedural rights across various expulsion procedures.

This convergence of procedural protections across different human rights instruments highlights the universal importance of safeguarding due process rights in the context of collective expulsions. Regional and international treaty bodies have consistently interpreted this principle to provide at least minimum procedural guarantees for all individuals facing expulsion. In this regard, the African Charter, despite initially focusing more on the discriminatory nature of expulsions, has evolved in its interpretation of collective expulsion, aligning more closely with the procedural safeguards found in other human rights frameworks. Compared to its sister conventions in Europe and Africa, the Inter-American Convention on Human Rights goes even further, offering not only procedural protections but also the right to consular assistance in cases of collective expulsion. This standardization in the interpretation of the prohibition of collective expulsion across different treaties is unsurprising, given the mutual influence and shared interpretations between regional human rights bodies. For instance, the Inter-American Commission and the UN Migrant Worker Committee have both drawn on the ECtHR *Hirsi Jamaa* judgment in their interpretation of the prohibition of collective expulsion.

On the international level, both the ICCPR and the UN Migrant Worker Convention enshrine procedural guarantees in cases of collective expulsion, including the right to challenge expulsion decisions, the right to legal assistance and translation, and the right to an effective remedy with a suspensive effect on the expulsion. These procedural safeguards align with those found in regional treaties, ensuring that no individual is expelled without due process. Furthermore, Article 3 of the Convention against Torture while primarily focused on the *non-refoulement* principle, implicitly includes the prohibition of collective expulsion. The CAT Committee's guidance reinforces this interpretation, highlighting the importance of assessing individual circumstances before any expulsion is carried out.

Overall, this chapter has shown in detail that the prohibition of collective expulsion emerged as a fundamental due process right designed to protect individuals from arbitrary group expulsions. The procedural guarantees inherent in this prohibition, including the right to contest expulsion, the right to legal assistance and translation, and the right to an effective remedy, are consistent across regional and international human rights treaties. This convergence underscores the vital role of procedural safeguards in protecting migrants' rights and ensuring fairness in the expulsion process. It also showcases the relevance of inter-judicial dialogue between regional and international human rights bodies to create a shared understanding and alignment of the standards applicable to the prohibition of collective expulsion, ensuring that procedural safeguards are consistently upheld across various human rights instruments.

CHAPTER 4

The Prohibition in Global Context: The Role of the Principle in Human Rights Law

For many displaced individuals and migrants, gaining entry into other nations represents a difficult, sometimes life-threatening, and rare opportunity. The immense barriers they face, ranging from stringent immigration controls to perilous journeys, make such crossings exceptionally challenging and statistically improbable. In stark contrast, individuals from industrialized nations experience a vastly different reality. Their access to most of the world's borders is facilitated by their privileged citizenship, which often comes with visa-free travel or streamlined application processes. This stark disparity underscores the systemic inequities in global mobility, where one's nationality can significantly dictate their freedom to move and shape their life opportunities.[1]

This stark inequality in global mobility not only highlights systemic inequities but also raises critical questions about the right to seek protection and entry at states' borders. When it comes to the core guarantees in this context, the prohibition of collective expulsion and the *non-refoulement* principle must be mentioned as important cornerstones of human rights law.

This chapter situates the prohibition of collective expulsion within the broader framework of human rights law. It begins by analyzing the nature of the principle as an interrelated individual right, balancing its individual and collective dimensions (1). Building on this, part two addresses the extent to which public international law addresses, or fails to address, the protection of migrants as individuals and when moving across borders in groups (2). The following section (3) explores how the prohibition of collective expulsion, in conjunction with the principle of *non-refoulement*, acts as a safeguard against arbitrary group expulsions, particularly to locations where migrants face life-threatening risks. This section also examines the interplay between these two principles. The third section delves into the relationship

1 For insightful and elaborate analysis of this dichotomy, see: Schmalz, Dana Refugees, Democracy and the Law: Political Rights at the Margins of the State (Routledge 2022) or Shachar, Ayelet *Beyond Open and Closed Borders: The Grand Transformation of Citizenship*, Jurisprudence, Vol. 11, No. 1 (2020), pp. 1–28.

 DOI:10.1163/9789004535077_005

between the prohibition of collective expulsion and other rights enshrined in human rights conventions, with a particular focus on its connection to the prohibition of discrimination (4). This analysis highlights how the relationship between these principles has influenced the evolving interpretation of the prohibition of collective expulsion. It also offers a critical reflection of the prohibition's shortcomings in light of current expulsion policies – often related to racial discrimination. Finally, the chapter concludes by summarizing its key findings (5).

1 The Prohibition of Collective Expulsion as an Interrelated Individual Right: Balancing Individual and Group Dimensions

To contextualize the prohibition of collective expulsion within the broader framework of human rights and due process guarantees at international borders, it is essential to first clarify the nature of this prohibition and determine its legal category. Specifically, the question arises: Is it an individual right, a collective right, or something in between? Understanding this distinction is critical for interpreting how the prohibition functions within legal systems and for ensuring its effective implementation. By exploring its underlying principles, procedural mechanisms, and connections to both individual and collective dimensions, we can better grasp its role in protecting those subjected to collective expulsions.

At first glance, the term "collective" in the prohibition of collective expulsion suggests it may be a group right. However, determining whether it is an individual, collective, or hybrid right requires addressing two key questions: Who is the right-holder? and are the concepts of individual and collective rights mutually exclusive, or can they coexist?

While collective rights (e.g., in the areas of self-determination, land rights, biodiversity) exist in international law, they are less defined than individual rights.[2] For instance, the African Charter on Human and Peoples' Rights

2 Group rights are not nearly as undisputed and clearly defined as the individual rights. Nevertheless, regional and international law offer examples of codified collective rights. The International Labour Organization's Indigenous and Tribal Peoples Convention of 1989 is one example. This Convention protects indigenous and tribal peoples' rights granted to the group as a whole qua existence as a group. International Labour Organization *Convention concerning Indigenous and Tribal Peoples in Independent Countries* Convention No. 169, entry into force on 5 September 1991, adoption in Geneva, at 76th ILC session on 27 June 1989.

explicitly includes collective rights, such as equality, peace, and development. During the drafting of the ACHPR, Guinea, and Madagascar, two socialist-inclined states at that time pushed for the inclusion of such rights, which they saw as distinct characteristics of the African Human Rights system.[3] However, the prohibition of collective expulsion is notably absent from these chapters and instead falls under individual rights provisions, like freedom of movement (Article 12 ACHPR, Article 22(5) IACHR).

What the prohibition in its regional codifications has in common is that it protects foreign individuals jointly expelled under comparable circumstances. While a group may file claims in certain contexts (e.g., Article 34 ECHR, Article 44 IACHR[4]), courts still assess each individual's case independently, ensuring due process. This confirms that the rights-holder is every person of the group, not the group as a legal entity.

The "collective" aspect is necessary to trigger the scope of the prohibition but does not alter its individual nature.[5] The prohibition involves both procedural and material elements: the right to individual assessment is contingent on the collective nature of the expulsion. Therefore, the prohibition is best understood as a hybrid right, combining features of individual rights with material links to group circumstances. This "interrelated individual right" depends on similar violations of multiple individuals but remains fundamentally individual in nature.

What does this categorization mean for the prohibition's practical implementation at borders and Courts' assessment of its violations and remedies?

This categorization has significant implications particularly in cases where systemic patterns of procedural violations occur within a group. As outlined in Chapter 2,[6] government policies targeting specific groups of

3 Viljoen, Frans *The African Charter on Human and Peoples' Rights/The Travaux Préparatoires in the light of subsequent practice* Human Rights Law Journal, Vol. 25, No. 9–12, 2004, p. 317.

4 Article 34 ECHR reads: "Individual applications - The Court may receive applications from any person, non-governmental organisation or group of individuals claiming to be the victim of a violation by one of the High Contracting Parties of the rights set forth in the Convention or the Protocols thereto. The High Contracting Parties undertake not to hinder in any way the effective exercise of this right [emphasis added]". Article 44 American Convention reads: "Any person or group of persons, or any nongovernmental entity legally recognized in one or more member states of the Organization, may lodge petitions with the Commission containing denunciations or complaints of violation of this Convention by a State Party".

5 Bisaz, Corsin *The Concept of Group Rights in International Law* (Brill/Nijhoff 2012), p. 8.

6 See Chapter 2, 2.4 connective element.

foreigners, such as those identified in *Georgia v. Russia (I)*,[7] *Čonka v. Belgium*,[8] and *Hirsi Jamaa v. Italy*,[9] reveal how administrative practices can undermine the right to an individual and objective examination. These policies highlight the challenges posed by systematic violations, which require a careful balance between addressing collective patterns and upholding individual assessments.

When systematic practices are identified, such as patterns of expulsion targeting certain nationalities or migrant groups, the procedural right to an individualized examination risks becoming meaningless. The ECtHR established a two-pronged test in *Georgia v. Russia (I)*[10] to identify such administrative practices, requiring evidence of both the repetition of acts, a pattern of analogous breaches forming a systemic approach, and official tolerance, where authorities fail to prevent, investigate, or rectify these acts. This framework is crucial for uncovering state policies that violate the prohibition of collective expulsion. However, remedies often focus on individual reparations without adequately addressing the systemic issues that perpetuate these violations.

The hybrid nature of the prohibition necessitates safeguards to address group-level violations, such as push-backs at borders or at sea, while preserving the right to individualized assessments. Courts and treaty bodies must navigate the tension between recognizing patterns of systemic violations and ensuring that state officials examine each individual's circumstances or at least grant them the possibility to raise complaints. For example, in *Čonka*, *N.D. and N.T.*, or *M.K and Others v. Poland*,[11] the ECtHR identified systemic policies that affected the individual applicants but were aimed at deterring specific groups in their entirety. This highlights the difficulty of reconciling collective recognition with individualized remedies. The varying terminology employed by the ECtHR, ranging from "administrative practice" in *Georgia v. Russia (I)*[12] to "systematic policy of irregular returns" in *N.D. and N.T.*,[13] to "systemic practice of misrepresenting the statements given by

7 The Commission and the Court relied on these two elements, but never explicitly established it as a two-element test. *France, Norway, Denmark, Sweden and the Netherlands v. Turkey* Appl. Nos. 9940-9944/82, Commission decision of 6 December 1983, para. 19.

8 *Čonka v. Belgium* ECtHR, para. 62.

9 *Hirsi Jamaa and Others v. Italy* ECtHR, [GC], para. 177.

10 *Georgia v. Russia (I)*, ECtHR, [GC], paras. 19, 128–159.

11 *M.K. and Others v. Poland* ECtHR, Appl. Nos. 40503/17, 42902/17, 43643/17, 23 July 2020.

12 *Georgia v. Russia (I)* ECtHR, [GC], paras. 128–159.

13 *N.D. and N.D. v. Spain* ECtHR, [Chamber], para. 67.

asylum-seekers" in *M.K. and Others*[14] illustrates the complexity of these cases. While these terms capture the broader context of collective violations, they often result in remedies focused solely on individual claims,[15] potentially diluting the effectiveness of legal safeguards against large-scale violations of fundamental rights of migrants and asylum seekers.

To strengthen enforcement mechanisms, courts, and treaty bodies could develop enhanced procedural obligations for states engaging in systematic practices, such as independent monitoring of expulsion processes. Recognizing group-level violations explicitly, where systemic practices are proven, could allow for remedies addressing both individual harms and the structural factors enabling such violations. Context-specific recommendations, such as tailored policy reforms, training for border authorities, and penalties for non-compliance, would help ensure more robust protections. By bridging enforcement mechanisms with the principle's dual dimensions, a focus on systemic practices and their structural underpinnings not only reinforces individual protections but also ensures that collective violations are meaningfully addressed within the broader legal framework. Courts should adapt their remedial frameworks to balance individual assessments with the collective patterns that trigger the prohibition. By addressing systemic violations explicitly and recommending structural reforms, the legal framework can better reflect the principle's hybrid nature.

In conclusion, the prohibition of collective expulsion uniquely bridges individual and collective dimensions, complicating its enforcement and application. Although aimed at protecting individuals, its invocation depends on systemic violations targeting groups. Such practices undermine procedural safeguards by disregarding individualized assessments. Courts and treaty bodies must balance addressing these systemic patterns with ensuring individual remedies. Strengthened enforcement mechanisms, such as independent monitoring and tailored policy reforms, can better protect against these violations. Recognizing its hybrid nature calls for a legal framework that ensures individual protections while addressing collective breaches effectively.

---

14 *M.K. and Others v. Poland* ECtHR, para. 174.

15 According to Article 41 ECHR, if "the Court finds that there has been a violation of the Convention or the Protocols thereto, and if the internal law of the High Contracting Party concerned allows only partial reparation to be made, the Court shall, if necessary, afford just satisfaction to the injured party". The Court can award pecuniary damage, non-pecuniary damage, and costs and expenses to the applicants. It has done so in all of the here mentioned expulsion cases where a violation of Article 4 Protocol 4 ECHR has been found.

2 The Protection of Groups of Migrants in Public International Law

Traditionally states were the center of attention in international law. Individuals did not play a role as subjects until far into the 20th century when several treaties introduced civil and political, and economic, social, and cultural rights for individuals on an international level (first and second generation).[16] The rights of collectives form part of the third generation of human rights.[17] Several international and regional human rights instruments contain comprehensive individual civil and political and/or economic, social, and cultural rights. The International Covenant on Economic, Social and Cultural Rights, as well as the African Charter on Human and Peoples' Rights and the 2004 Arab Charter on Human Rights, contain individual and collective rights. While international and regional human rights instruments provide extensive protections for individuals, the question arises as to how these frameworks address the specific needs of groups of migrants, particularly in situations of removal. Although individual rights are well-documented, the protection of migrant groups, especially in collective expulsion scenarios, raises complex questions about their treatment under international law. This leads to important inquiries about how international human rights law, refugee, and migration law specifically safeguard these groups, and what role the prohibition of collective expulsion plays in ensuring their protection.

The following section will address and answer these questions by offering first an overview of the protection of collectives in public international law before turning to the role of this principle for the protection of migrant groups and its distinctive character as an interface between individual and collective protection. To understand how collective protections extend to migrant groups, we will to first explore the broader context of international migration law within public international law, which provides its foundational framework.

International migration law does not constitute a field of law independent of public international law. It rather constitutes the collection of all international legal principles in treaty law and customary law that together form the framework governing the movement of people across borders.[18]

16 Klabbers, Jan *International Law* (Cambridge University Press 2013), p. 107.

17 *Ibidem.*, pp. 115–116.

18 Kotzur, Markus *Migrationsbewegungen als Herausforderung für das Völkerrecht* in: Dethloff, Nolte, Reinisch (eds.) *Migrationsbewegungen Berichte der Deutschen Gesellschaft für Internationales Recht* Vol. 49 (C.F. Müller 2018), p. 321.

This framework includes special regimes only for refugees, such as the 1951 Refugee Convention, the UN Migrant Worker Convention, and international and regional human rights instruments.

Historically, the protection of individuals and particularly of groups has played a minor role in international law. Especially the committal of mass atrocities during the Second World War led to increased international attention for the protection of individuals and collectives as well as to the drafting and adoption of binding rules in this regard. However, already before the Second World War, the Institut de Droit International made a first attempt at codifying human rights with the adoption of the New York Declaration of 1929.[19] However, states did not immediately endorse the declaration's adoption by the Institute or transform it into a binding international treaty.[20] Nevertheless, the New York Declaration is evidence against the narrative that international human rights protection only emerged after the end of the Second World War.[21]

Against the backdrop of the Second World War, states ultimately seemed to be willing to subjugate themselves under binding human rights treaties protecting groups. The drafting process of the Genocide Convention[22] reflects this. In 1948, during the United Nations General Assembly Sixth Committee debate on a draft of the Convention, Mr. Azkoul, the representative of Lebanon, elaborated on his understanding of genocide, stating that it constituted "a new legal category, that of collective crime".[23] However, despite this assertion, a key point of contention during the drafting of the Convention was the definition of "group" or "collective", which remained unresolved for some time. The representatives could not quickly agree on a

19 Aust, Helmut *From Diplomat to Academic Activist: André Mandelstam and the History of Human Rights* European Journal of International Law, (2014), Vol. 25, No. 4, p. 1107. The adopted New York Declaration, which contains six provisions (e.g., the right to life and the duty of states not to withdraw the nationality of their citizens) is annexed to the paper. The declaration does not foresee any provision on the protection of groups.

20 *Ibidem.*, p. 1113.

21 *Ibidem.*, p. 1107.

22 The Convention on the Prevention and Punishment of the Crime of Genocide, adopted by the United Nations General Assembly on 9 December 1948, UNGA resolution 260 A (III). The Convention entered into force on 12 January 1951.

23 UNGA, Sixth Committee 66th Mtg, UN Doc A/C.6/SR.66, para. 32. For an unconventional narrative on the genesis of the concepts genocide and crimes against humanity and the role Hirsch Lauterpacht and Raphael Lemkin played in outlawing them see: Sands, Philippe *East West Street On the Origins of Genocide and crimes Against Humanity* (Weidenfeld & Nicolson 2016).

common understanding of these terms.[24] They described them, for example, as "an abstract concept; [...] an aggregate of individuals; [with] no independent life of its own; [which] was harmed when the individuals composing it were harmed".[25] The final version of Article 2 of the Genocide Convention ultimately defined Genocide as "means any of the following acts committed with intent to destroy, in whole or in part, a national, ethnical, racial or religious group". However, the Convention in its nineteen articles remains silent on what exactly stipulates a group or collective in the sense of Article 2. Even though such debates did not spin around questions of expulsions of groups, they demonstrate the difficulty of defining "groups" in international law.

While this definition may be challenging, international law's primary focus is on large groups of people.[26] Nevertheless, international law itself mostly only provides "individualistic vocabulary" which calls for a more collective dimension of terminologies and concepts in public international law.[27] One explanation for this subsidiary role of groups in international law may be found in the historical evolution of human rights law. During the Cold War era, western states perceived collective, social, economic, and cultural rights as hierarchically subordinate to individual civil and political rights.[28] On an international level, this prioritization of individual civil and political rights had already become apparent in 1966 with the division of the Universal Declaration's rights into two distinct treaties,[29] the International Covenant on Civil and Political Rights and the International Covenant on Economic, Social and Cultural Rights (ICESCR).[30]

---

24 UNGA, Sixth Committee 66th Mtg, UN Doc A/C.6/SR.66, para. 9–91.

25 Statement by Mr. Chaumont, UNGA, Sixth Committee, 73rd Mtg, UN/Doc A/C.6/SR.73, para. 91.

26 Morss, John *International Law as the Law of Collectives: Toward a Law of Peoples* (Ashgate 2013), pp. 2–3.

27 *Ibidem.*

28 Fredman Sandra *Human Rights Transformed: Positive Rights and Positive Duties* (Oxford University Press 2008), pp. 1–4. See also: Lichuma, Caroline *In International Law We (Do Not) Trust: The Persistent Rejection of Economic and Social Rights as a Manifestation of Cynicism* in: Baade et al. *Cynical International Law?* (Springer 2021).

29 For a more detailed analysis of this development see: Bilchitz, David *Poverty and Fundamental Rights: The Justification and Enforcement of Socio-Economic Rights* (Oxford University Press 2007) and Fredman, Sandra *Human Rights Transformed: Positive Rights and Positive Duties* (Oxford University Press 2008).

30 UNGA *International Covenant on Civil and Political Rights* 16 December 1966, UNTS, Vol. 999, p. 171, and UNGA *International Covenant on Economic, Social and Cultural Rights* 16 December 1966, UNTS, Vol. 993, p. 3.

Nevertheless, there are notable examples of collective approaches on the international and regional human rights level. The ICESCR contains collective rights such as the right of all peoples to self-determination in Article 1(1) or the right of all peoples to "freely dispose of their natural wealth and resources" as codified in Article 1(2) ICESCR. The inclusion of collective rights is also common on the regional level as the African Charter on Human and Peoples' Rights and the Arab Charter demonstrate. This collective dimension of rights plays a crucial role in the African Charter. Not only does the title of the treaty itself use collective vocabulary, but also the preamble refers to "people" eight times. Furthermore, six provisions of the Charter (Articles 19–24) contain collective rights. Nevertheless, in both conventions, the collective is not defined.[31] Likeweise, the 2004 Arab Charter on Human Rights also contains several collective rights such as the right to self-determination (Article 2(1)), the right to economic, social and cultural development (Article 2(1)), and the right to resist foreign occupation (Article 2(4)). Similarly, the 2004 Arab Charter contains collective dimensions, which are visible in the use of the terms "all peoples" in the respective provisions.

When turning away from general human rights law and towards international migration law, the role of collectives is notably distinct and carries particular significance. Unlike other areas of international law, where the concept of collectives often lacks a cohesive vocabulary, migration law features widely recognized and frequently used terms such as "mass movement of people across borders", "mass influx", "mass migration", "collective expulsion", and "mass expulsion". Despite the prevalence of these terms, international law provides no definitive thresholds or criteria to determine what qualifies as "mass" or "collective".

A critical distinction emerges when comparing the treatment of collectives in general international law versus international migration law. In broader international law, collectives are often regarded as rights-bearing entities deserving of specific protections. However, this perspective does not seamlessly translate to migrant collectives. While certain principles, like *non-refoulement* and the prohibition of collective expulsion, aim to protect individuals within groups of migrants, the characterization of collectives in migration law remains more ambiguous and contested.

---

31 For a thorough assessment of the collective rights in the *African Charter on Human and Peoples' Rights* see: Baldwin, Clive and Morel, Cynthia *Group Rights* in: Evans and Murray (eds.) *The African Charter on Human and Peoples' Rights: The System in Practice 1986–2006* (Cambridge University Press 2008), pp. 244–288.

States frequently perceive large-scale migration as a potential threat to their sovereignty and security, influencing how they engage with procedural guarantees under international law. Refugee law has acknowledged this tension, allowing for derogations from certain protections in the face of security concerns. For instance, Article 33 of the 1951 Refugee Convention enshrines the principle of *non-refoulement* but includes an exception for individuals who pose a security risk to the receiving state.[32] This concession to national sovereignty has been invoked in practice, as seen in Turkey's derogation from *non-refoulement* during the 1980s, citing the mass influx of Kurdish refugees as a justification.[33]

This duality reflects the hybrid nature of protections like the prohibition of collective expulsion. While firmly rooted in safeguarding the rights of individuals within a collective, these protections are shaped by the broader context of state sovereignty and security concerns. As a result, the interrelated individual character of such norms becomes apparent. Their application requires balancing the procedural guarantees owed to each person with the collective dynamics that often trigger their invocation.

Another phenomenon attributable to the large-scale movement of people across borders is the "assymetry of power"[34] which their crossing creates. The migrants and the receiving states are to varying degrees conferred rights by international law; the state of origin is left "powerless" or "rightless" in this triangular relationship.[35] At the same time, states of origin arguably prefer not to be involved for various reasons.[36] Groups of migrants have the right to leave their home country[37] per Article 13 Universal Declaration of Human Rights or Article 12 ICCPR. The receiving country, in contrast, has

32 Gameltoft-Hansen, Thomas *Access to Asylum International Refugee Law and the Globalisation of Migration Control* (Cambridge University Press 2013), p. 55.

33 Goodwin-Gill, Guy and McAdam, Jane *The Refugee in International Law* (Cambridge University Press 3rd edn. 2007), p. 289.

34 Uepermann-Wittzack, Robert *Ordnung und Gestaltung von Migrationsbewegungen durch Völkerrecht* in: Dethloff, Nolte, Reinisch (eds.) *Migrationsbewegungen Berichte der Deutschen Gesellschaft für Internationales Recht* Vol. 49, (C.F. Müller 2018), p. 244.

35 *Ibidem.*,

36 For example the EU and several member states repeatingly point out that the reason why most irregular migrants cannot be returned to their country of origin is to be found in the identification of the individuals and in the lack of cooperation with these states when it comes to receiving these individuals. See: European Commission *Communication from the Commission to the Council and the European Parliament on EU Return Policy* COM(2014) 199, 28 March 2014, p. 3.

37 For an indepth analysis of the right to leave, especially in the context of externalized migration control see: Markard, Nora *The Right to Leave by Sea* pp. 591–616.

the power to deny their entry, which is limited by human rights principles such as the *non-refoulement* principle and the prohibition of collective expulsion. The country of origin is left without rights and power unless it violates international law. These states must let their citizens leave. This imbalance of power constitutes a "certain asymmetry from an international law point of view".[38]

In this context, the evolution of international law from a state-centered framework to one that incorporates individual and collective rights marks a significant shift in the protection of migrants' rights. While individuals gained recognition as subjects of international law in the 20th century, particularly through civil, political, economic, social, and cultural rights, the rights of collectives emerged later and remained less defined. This gap is particularly evident in migration law, where collectives such as groups of migrants are often addressed through concepts like "mass migration" or "collective expulsion" but without clear thresholds or criteria. Protections such as *non-refoulement* and the prohibition of collective expulsion aim to safeguard individuals within these groups, reflecting the hybrid nature of these principles as both individual and collective guarantees. However, state sovereignty and security concerns often shape their application, creating tensions between procedural guarantees for migrants and state prerogatives. This asymmetry is further complicated by the limited role of states of origin, which are often excluded from the triadic relationship between migrants, receiving states, and international law. Balancing these dynamics requires a nuanced approach that respects individual rights while addressing the collective dimensions of migration.

3 *Non-refoulement* and the Prohibition of Collective Expulsion: Intersecting Pillars of Protection in International Human Rights Law

The *non-refoulement* principle is often described as the "cornerstone" of international refugee law.[39] One reason for this attribution may be found in

---

38 Ueppermann-Wittzack, Robert *Ordnung und Gestaltung von Migrationsbewegungen durch Völkerrecht* p. 244.

39 Gammeltoft-Hansen, Thomas *Access to Asylum* p. 44. Scholars dedicate a lot of attention to the principle, see for example: Goodwin-Gill, Guy and McAdam, Jane *The Refugee in International Law*; also: Moreno-Lax, Violeta and Papastavridis, Efthymios *Boat Refugees and Migrants at Sea: A Comprehensive Approach Integrating Maritime Security*

its codification in the 1951 Refugee Convention. Article 33(1) 1951 Refugee Convention[40] reads

> No Contracting State shall expel or return ('refouler') a refugee in any manner whatsoever to the frontiers of territories where his life or freedom would be threatened on account of his race, religion, nationality, membership of a particular social group or political opinion.

When drafting the 1951 Refugee Convention, states were reluctant to codify everyone's right "to seek and to enjoy in other countries asylum from persecution" as guaranteed in Article 14(1) Universal Declaration of Human Rights. Thus, due to a lack of codifying the right to seek asylum, *non-refoulement* is the strongest binding principle to protect a refugee's life against persecution.[41]

Initially, Article 33 of the 1951 Refugee Convention only protected "refugees" in the sense of its definition in Article 1(a). International and regional human rights courts and monitoring bodies have expanded the principle's personal scope of application over time. The scope of protection thus also applies to anyone who would be subject to torture, cruel or inhuman and degrading treatment or punishment, or to an arbitrary deprivation of her or his right to life or enforced disappearance in case of forceful return.[42] This expansion of the principle's scope by regional human rights bodies led to the situation that the regional refugee law is significantly broader compared to the international level.[43] International, regional, and national human rights bodies and courts also interpreted *non-refoulement* as an "implicit guarantee flowing from the obligations to respect, protect and fulfill human rights".[44]

---

with Human Rights (Brill/Nijhoff 2016) or Gammeltoft-Hansen, Thomas *Access to Asylum International Refugee Law and the Globalisation of Migration Control.*

40 The 1967 Protocol to the Convention lifted the territorial and time restrictions to persecutions within Europe and before 1951. This adjustment elevated the Convention to the status of being the most important treaty for the protection of refugees. 148 states are either members of the Convention, the protocol or both instruments.

41 Gammeltoft-Hansen, Thomas *Access to Asylum* pp. 44–46.

42 Sharpe, Marina *The Regional Law of Refugee Protection in Africa* (Oxford University Press 2018), p. 131.

43 Kotzur, Markus *Migrationsbewegungen als Herausforderung für das Völkerrecht* in: Dethloff, Nolte, Reinisch (eds.) *Migrationsbewegungen Berichte der Deutschen Gesellschaft für Internationales Recht* Vol. 49 (C.F. Müller 2018), p. 308.

44 Committee on the Protection of the Rights of All Migrant Workers and Members of Their Families and Committee on the Rights of the Child *Joint general comment No. 3*

Furthermore, there is broad consensus amongst scholars that this principle applies to all foreigners and enjoys the status of binding customary international law.[45] The United Nations High Commissioner for Refugees[46] and several United Nations General Assembly resolutions[47] support this finding. Only a few scholars reject this conclusion on the principle's nature as customary international law.[48]

On the contrary, other scholars argue even that it constitutes *jus cogens* in the sense of Article 53 Vienna Convention on the Law of Treaties.[49] The

---

(2017) of the Committee on the Protection of the Rights of All Migrant Workers and Members of Their Families and No. 22 (2017) of the Committee on the Rights of the Child on the general principles regarding the human rights of children in the context of international migration CMW/C/GC/3-CRC/C/GC/22, 16 November 2017, para. 45.

45 See for example: McAdam, Jane and Durieux, Jean-Francois *Non-Refoulement through Time: The Case for a Derogation Clause to the Refugee Convention in Mass Influx Emergencies* International Journal of Refugee Law, Vol. 16, Issue 1, 2004, pp. 4–24. Also: Costello, Cathryn and Foster, Michelle *Non-refoulement as custom and jus cogens? Putting the prohibition to the test* in: Heijer and van der Wilt (eds.) Netherlands *Yearbook of International Law 2015* Vol. 46, (T.M.C. Asser Press 2016), (*Non-refoulement as custom and jus cogens? Putting the prohibition to the test*), pp. 273–327 or Gameltoft-Hansen, Thomas *Access to Asylum* p. 55. As well as: Lauterpacht, Elihu and Bethlehem, Daniel *The Scope and Content of the Principle of Non-Refoulement*, in: Feller, Türk, Nicholson *UNHCR Refugee Protection in International Law: UNHCR's Global Consultations on International Protection* (Cambridge University Press 2003).

For a detailed analysis on the status of the non-refoulement principle jus cogens norm see: Allain, Jean *The jus cogens Nature of non-refoulement* International Journal of Refugee Law, (2001), Vol. 13, No. 4, pp. 533–558.

46 UNHCR *Advisory Opinion on the Extraterritorial Application of Non-Refoulement Obligations under the 1951 Convention relating to the Status of Refugees and its 1967 Protocol* 26 January 2007, para. 15. UNHCR's Advisory Opinion is a response to a request for its position on the extraterritorial application of *the non-refoulement* principle of Article 33 of the 1951 Convention Relating to the Status of Refugees and its 1967 Protocol. UNHCR stresses that *the non-refoulement* principle as complemented by international human rights law constitutes customary international law for all persons, not only refugees in the sense of the 1951 Refugee Convention and its protocol.

47 UNHCR *The Principle of Non-Refoulement as a Norm of Customary International Law. Response to the Questions Posed to UNHCR by the Federal Constitutional Court of the Federal Republic of Germany in Cases 2 BvR 1938/93, 2 BvR 1953/93, 2 BvR 1954/93* 31 January 1994, para. 3.

48 James Hathaway rejects the claim that customary international law expands the personal scope of application beyond refugees referring to a lack of state practice and opinio juris. See: Hathaway, James *Leveraging Asylum* Texas International Law Journal, Vol. 45, No. 3, 2010, pp. 503–536.

49 Cathryn Costello and Michelle Foster argue for example that *non-refoulement* has reached jus cogens status due to its universal and non-derogatory character. See: Costello, Cathryn and Foster, Michelle *Non-refoulement as custom and jus cogens? Putting*

first explicit document in which states acknowledged the *jus cogens* status of this principle was the non-binding 1984 *Cartagena Declaration on Refugees* adopted by the Colloquium on the International Protection of Refugees in Central America, Mexico and Panama. This declaration stressed

> the importance and meaning of the principle of non-refoulement (including the prohibition of rejection at the frontier) as a corner-stone of the international protection of refugees. This principle is imperative in regard to refugees and in the present state of international law should be acknowledged and observed as a rule of jus cogens.[50]

A subsequent Executive Committee conclusion of 1996 of the United Nations High Commissioner for Refugees confirmed the principle's *jus cogens* character.[51] Opponents of this view argue that the security exception to the prohibition of returning refugees in Article 33(2) 1951 Refugee Convention and parallel domestic laws contradict this interpretation.[52] The *Canadian Supreme Court*, for example, referred to such an exception in the 2002 *Suresh v. Canada* judgment to justify the return of a Sri Lankan citizen, deemed a security threat.[53] Another example is the above-described case of

the prohibition to the test pp. 273–327. See also: Goodwin-Gill, Guy and McAdam, Jane *The Refugee in International Law* p. 218.

50 Colloquium on the International Protection of Refugees in Central America, Mexico and Panama *Cartagena Declaration on Refugees*, adopted during meeting in Cartagena, Colombia between 19–22 November 1984, para. 5.

51 UNHCR *EXCOM Conclusion No.79 (XLVII)* 11 October 1996. See also: Allain, Jean *The jus cogens Nature of non-refoulement* pp. 533–558 and Goodwin-Gil, Guy and McAdam, Jane *The Refugee in International Law* p. 218.

52 Guy Goodwin-Gill and Jane McAdam do not make this claim, but demonstrate that this argument is brought forward against the categorization of the non-refoulement principle as just cogens norm. See: Goodwin-Gill, Guy and McAdam, Jane *The Refugee in International Law* pp. 218–219. For a general assessment of the relationship between *jus cogens* norms in domestic and international law regarding *refoulement* and the prohibition of torture see: De Wet, Erika *The Prohibition of Torture as an International Norm of jus cogens and Its Implications for National and Customary Law* European Journal of International Law (2004), Vol. 15, No. 1, pp. 97–121.

53 Supreme Court of Canada *Suresh v. Canada (Minister of Citizenship and Immigration)* Case No. 27790, 1 S.C.R. 3, 2002 SCC 1, 11 January 2002, paras. 7, 31. The Inter-American Commission on Human Rights in turn concluded that Canada had violated Mr Suresh's rights stipulating that "While the Commission recognizes the State's right to exclude non-citizens and to protect Canadian society from persons considered to be dangerous, having regard to the foregoing considerations, the Commission finds that the State impermissibly denied Mr. Suresh the right to challenge the legality of his detention without delay [...] and that the State [...] fail[ed] to afford Mr. Suresh

Kurdish refugees which were declared a threat to the security of the region and subsequently refouled by Turkey.[54]

Irrespective of the question of its customary law or *jus cogens* nature, the *non-refoulement* principle is explicitly or implicitly included in several international human rights instruments. Article 3 Convention against Torture and Article 16(1) International Convention for the Protection of all Persons from enforced Disappearance (ICPPED)[55] contain the *non-refoulement* principle explicitly. The International Covenant on Civil and Political Rights[56] as well as in the Convention on the Rights of the Child,[57] the Convention on the Elimination of All Forms of Discrimination against Women (CEDAW),[58] and the UN Migrant Worker Convention contain the principle implicitly.[59]

One significant difference between the *non-refoulement* principle and the prohibition of collective expulsion is the fact that the latter's scope of protection between the regional and international instruments barely differs. This is not the case regarding the scope of protection of the *non-refoulement* principle. There is a significant discrepancy between the regional and international levels.[60] Nevertheless, together, they form the basis of protection for migrants and asylum seekers alike against the arbitrary return to a place where their lives would be at risk.

The prohibition of collective expulsion and the principle of *non-refoulement* are mutually reinforcing. The prohibition of collective expulsion provides procedural safeguards by ensuring that individuals' fears of return are thoroughly evaluated by the relevant authorities. Conversely,

---

adequate or effective protection from deprivation of his basic right to liberty. See: IAComHR *Manickavasagam Suresh v. Canada* Report on the Merits No. 8/16, Case 11.661, 13 April 2016, para. 83.

54 Goodwin-Gill, Guy and McAdam, Jane *The Refugee in International Law* pp. 218–219.

55 UNGA *International Convention for the Protection of all Persons from enforced Disappearance* (ICPPED), 20 December 2006, entry into force 23 December 2010.

56 For a brief, but precise overview of the non-refoulement principle in the ICCPR see: De Week, Fanny *Non-Refoulement under the European Convention on Human Rights and the UN Convention against Torture The Assessment of Individual Complaints by the European Court of Human Rights under Article 3 ECRR and the United Nations Committee against Torture under Article 3 CAT* (Brill/Nijhoff 2017), pp. 48–55.

57 UNGA *Convention on the Rights of the Child* (CRC), 20 November 1989, entry into force 2 September 1990.

58 UNGA *Convention on the Elimination of All Forms of Discrimination against Women* (CEDAW), 18 December 1979, entry into force 3 September 1981.

59 González Morales, Felipe UN Special Rapporteur on the Rights of Migrants *letter to the Representative of the USA regarding the Migrant Protection Protocols* (MPP) 7 March 2019, OL USA 4/2019, p. 3.

60 Kotzur, Markus *Migrationsbewegungen als Herausforderung für das Völkerrecht* p. 308.

the principle of *non-refoulement* secures the substantive implementation of these evaluations, preventing the return of individuals to unsafe conditions if such risks are confirmed. The following section examines the interaction between these two principles across various regional and international human rights instruments.

3.1 *Intersecting Safeguards: The Prohibition of Collective Expulsion and* Non-refoulement *in Regional Human Rights Frameworks*

The prohibition of collective expulsion and the principle of *non-refoulement* are fundamental safeguards in international and regional human rights law. While distinct, these principles are deeply interconnected, mutually reinforcing procedural and substantive protections to prevent individuals from being returned to situations where their life, liberty, or well-being are at risk. Their relevance extends beyond traditional expulsion scenarios to include denials of entry at borders, such as pushbacks, where procedural guarantees constitute minimum legal safeguards.

This section examines the interplay between these two principles, exploring how they function in tandem to provide comprehensive protections. First, the relationship will be analyzed at the regional level across conventions and case law, such as those of the European, Inter-American, and African systems. The discussion will then expand to the international level, considering treaties like the ICCPR, the UN Migrant Worker Convention, and the Convention against Torture, which either explicitly or implicitly embody both principles.

Most regional human rights treaties assessed illustrate this dual structure, with each framework incorporating the prohibition of collective expulsion and, to varying degrees, the principle of *non-refoulement*. This dual structure is, for example, apparent in the **African Charter**. Article 12(5) ACHPR contains the prohibition of "mass" expulsion. As mentioned above, the Charter only implicitly contains the *non-refoulement* principle. The African Commission on Human and Peoples' Rights has suggested in her jurisprudence that Article 5 (prohibition of torture and cruel, inhuman or degrading punishment and treatment) and Article 18 (protection of the family unit) contains the *non-refoulement* principle in removal contexts.[61]

Furthermore, another, more specific African treaty, the 1969 OAU Refugee Convention (in Article 2(3)), contains this principle explicitly.[62]

61 Sharpe, Marina *The Regional Law of Refugee Protection in Africa* p. 133.

62 Organization of African Unity (OAU) *Convention Governing the Specific Aspects of Refugee Problems in Africa* 1001 U.N.T.S. 45, 10 September 1969, entry into force on 20 June 1974.

Thus, Article 12 together with Articles 5 and 18 African Charter constitute two independent legal principles that mutually reinforce each other in cases of arbitrary removals of foreigners to an unsafe place.

The same applies to the Inter-American Convention on Human Rights. Here, Article 22 IACHR explicitly contains both principles. Article 22(8) ensures that

> [i]n no case may an alien be deported or returned to a country, regardless of whether or not it is his country of origin, if in that country his right to life or personal freedom is in danger of being violated because of his race, nationality, religion, social status, or political opinions.

The only regional human rights instrument that contained both principles explicitly at the moment of its adoption was the **Inter-American Convention** which entered into force in 1978. Both, the Inter-American Commission and the Court have stressed that *non-refoulement* is a cornerstone of international protection for all individuals seeking asylum or other forms of international protection, regardless of their legal status or whether they have entered the country formally and undergone immigration control.[63]

The Inter-American Commission on Human Rights has stressed the strong relationship between *non-refoulement* and other provisions.[64] It held that the deportation of a foreigner could constitute a violation of other rights such as the prohibition of being subjected to cruel, inhuman, or degrading treatment, the protection of family life, the rights of children, and the prohibition of collective expulsion.[65] Under the Inter-American protection system, the principle prohibits direct return, rejection at the border, and "chain refoulement", which occurs when a person is sent to a country or territory from which they may subsequently be transferred to a place

63 IAComHR *Movilidad humana y obligaciones de protección Hacia una perspectiva subregional* OEA/Ser.L/V/II. Doc. 194, 21 July 2023, para. 194. See also, IAComHR *Principios interamericanos sobre los derechos humanos de todas las personas migrantes, refugiadas, apátridas y las víctimas de la trata de personas* Resolución 04/19, 7 December 2019, principle 6. IACourtHR *Caso Familia Pacheco Tineo Vs. Bolivia* Serie C No. 272, 25 November 2013, paras. 151–152.

64 IAComHR *Human Rights of Migrants, Refugees, Stateless Persons, Victims of Human Trafficking and Internally Displaced Persons: Norms and Standards of the Inter-American Human Rights System* OEA/Ser.L/V/II.Doc. 46/15, 2015, para. 355.

65 *Ibidem.*, paras. 356, 375.

where their life, liberty, or personal integrity is at risk.[66] The Inter-American Court of Human Rights, drawing on the Human Rights Committee's General Comment No. 31, affirmed in *Wong Ho Wing v. Peru* that the principle applies universally to all forms of transfer to another state, including extradition.[67]

The Convention also explicitly contains the prohibition of collective expulsion in Article 22(9). The provision states succinctly that "[t]he collective expulsion of aliens is prohibited". Article 22(8) IACHR explicitly anchors the *non-refoulement* principle in both, the right to life and the prohibition of torture, cruel and inhuman treatment comparable to the approach taken by the Migrant Worker Committee.

In the **European context**, both the European Convention on Human Rights and the Charter of Fundamental Rights of the European Union follow a dual structure. The *non-refoulement* principle only gained significance in the European context in 1989 with *Soering v. the United Kingdom*.[68,69] The prohibition of collective expulsion in both instruments offers procedural due process guarantees against arbitrary expulsion. Thereby, it constitutes the basis for the assessment of whether a member state can return an individual to another country without violating the *non-refoulement* principle.

Article 19 ChFREU contains both: the prohibition of collective expulsion in subparagraph one and the *non-refoulement* principle in subparagraph two. Article 19(2) ChFREU explicitly stipulates that the *non-refoulement* principle protects any person in case of removal, expulsion, and extradition. The provision, furthermore, mentions explicitly that the scope of protection entails the return to a place "where there is a serious risk that he or she would be subjected to the death penalty, torture or other inhuman or degrading treatment or punishment". The Charter of Fundamental Rights thus also anchors the *non-refoulement* principle in the right to life and the prohibition of torture and cruel, inhuman, or degrading treatment.

---

66 IAComHR *Movilidad humana y obligaciones de protección Hacia una perspectiva subregional* paras. 194–195.

67 *Wong Ho Wing v. Peru* IACourtHR, judgment on reparations and costs, 26 June 2012, Series C, No. 297, para. 135. See also: *Wong Ho Wing v. Peru* IACourttHR, judgment on preliminary objection, merits, reparations and costs, 30 June 2015, para. 130.

68 *Soering v. the UK* ECtHR, Apppl. No. 14038/88, 7 July 1989, para. 88.

69 Fanny de Weck explains that the European Commission of Human Rights already laid the ground for the non-refoulement interpretation by the ECtHR. However, the Court dealt for the first time with an allegation of non-refoulement in *Soering v. UK*. See: De Weck, Fanny *Non-Refoulement under the European Convention on Human Rights and the UN Convention against Torture* p. 18.

In the ECHR, Article 4 Protocol 4 contains the prohibition of collective expulsion, and Article 3 ECHR implicitly encompasses the *non-refoulement* principle. According to the explanation by the Praesidium, Article 19(1) EUChFR corresponds to the content of Article 4 Protocol 4 ECHR.[70] The explanation further clarifies that Article 19(2) EUChFR incorporates the case law from the ECtHR on Article 3 ECHR.[71] Article 52(3) EUChFR codifies this finding, stating that "the meaning and scope of those rights shall be the same". Therefore, the jurisprudence of the ECtHR on Article 4 Protocol 4 ECHR affects the scope of protection of Article 19(1) EUChFR.[72] Thus, in the following, I rely on a closer examination of the relationship between the prohibition of collective expulsion and the *non-refoulement* principle in the European Convention which *ergo* also applies to Article 19 EUChFR.

In *Sharifi and Others v. Italy and Greece* of 2014, the ECtHR highlighted the mutually influential relationship between the two principles and their interpretation in light of each other "ne sont pas non plus dépourvus d'intérêt".[73]

The United Nations High Commissioner for Human Rights in an intervener brief to the ECtHR's *Hirsi et al v. Italy* case confirmed this while the autonomy of the prohibition of collective expulsion as an independent "rule of general international law". It further noted that it

> is distinguishable from the principle of *non-refoulement* in that it is inherently *a due process right* [emphasis added] that entitles every non-national to an individualized examination of *all* arguments militating against his or her expulsion in the first place.[74]

One of the reasons for the categorization of the prohibition of collective expulsion as a due process right was the distinguishability between the *non-refoulement* principle codified in Article 3 ECHR and the prohibition of

70 Praesidium of the Convention *EXPLANATIONS RELATING TO THE CHARTER OF FUNDAMENTAL RIGHTS Official Journal of the European Union* C 303/02, 14 December 2007, p. 8.

71 *Ibidem.*

72 Guild, Elspeth *Art 19-Protection in the Event of Removal* in: Peers/Hervey/Kenner/Ward (eds.) *The EU Charter of Fundamental Rights A Commentary* (Hart Publishing 2014), para. 19.37.

73 *Sharifi and Others v. Italy and Greece* ECtHR, Appl. No. 16643/09, 21 October 2014, para. 211.

74 *Hirsi et al v. Italy* ECtHR intervener brief filed on behalf of the UNITED NATIONS HIGH COMMISSIONER FOR HUMAN RIGHTS. Filed pursuant to leave granted by the Court on 4 May 2011, (*Intervener brief*) p. 1.

collective expulsion. The High Commissioner believes that the prohibition of collective expulsion

> is *essentially a due process requirement* that must be considered in its own regard. *Any State* considering expulsion of a group of non-nationals is *required to consider*, with due diligence and in good faith, the *full range of individual circumstances* that may militate against the expulsion of each particular individual in the group [emphasis added].[75]

As the Court in its *Hirsi and Others v. Italy* Grand Chamber judgment noted, a second intervener brief[76] "pointed out the importance of **procedural guarantees** [emphasis added] in the area of protection of the human rights of refugees". It further clarified that "States were bound to examine the situation of each individual on a case-by-case basis to guarantee effective protection of the fundamental rights of the parties concerned and to avoid removing them while there was a risk of harm".[77]

This second *amicus curiae* brief shares the approach of the first in that the prohibition of collective expulsion, in contrast to the *non-refoulement* principle, contains procedural guarantees.[78]

The UN Special Rapporteur on the Human Rights of Migrants explicitly shares the notion of the two principles being separate legal concepts in an intervention of January 2019.[79] Here, Felipe González Morales highlights the significance and independence of the two principles. In his intervention in the form of a letter to the Representative of the United States of America,

---

75 UNHCHR *Intervener brief* para. 8.

76 Columbia Law School Human Rights Clinic, African Refugee Development Center, Allard K. Lowenstein International Human Rights Clinic at Yale Law School, Center for Social Justice at Seton Hall University School of Law, Florida Coastal School of Law Immigrant Rights Clinic, Institute for Justice & Democracy in Haiti, Migrant and Refugee Rights Project of the Australian Human Rights Centre at the University of New South Wales School of Law, Physicians for Human Rights and Professors James Gathi, Tally Kritzman-Amir, Stephen H. Legomsky and Margaret L. Satterthwaite *Intervener brief in Hirsi Jamaa and Others v. Italy* ECtHR, 17 April.

77 *Hirsi et al v. Italy* ECtHR, [GC] para. 165.

78 Columbia Law School Human Rights Clinic et. al. *2nd Intervener brief in Hirsi Jamaa* para. 22. The intervener brief referred to the codification of the prohibition of collective expulsion in U.N. Human Rights Comm., General Comment No. 15, para. 10 (noting that Article 13 of the ICCPR prohibits arbitrary expulsion and "entitles each alien to a decision in his own case").

79 *Hirsi Jamaa and Others v. Italy* ECtHR, [GC], para. 164.

he criticizes the "Remain in Mexico Policy" invoked in January 2019. This policy obliged migrants entering or seeking admission to the USA to return to Mexico for the duration of their asylum/immigration process. The Special Rapporteur sees therein a violation of the prohibition of collective expulsion, which may as well violate the *non-refoulement* principle in specific cases.[80]

Thus, the *non-refoulement* principle and the prohibition of collective expulsion constitute two individual principles that are interrelated and mutually reinforcing in case of arbitrary removals of foreigners from a member state's territory. The dual structure of the provisions in both conventions reflects this independence of the two principles.

The duality between the two principles is also arguably contained in the 2004 **Arab Charter on Human Rights**. The 2004 version codifies the prohibition of collective expulsion in Article 26(2). Neither the initial nor the redrafted version of the Arab Charter contains the *non-refoulement* principle. If the Charter implicitly contains this principle cannot be conclusively clarified here.[81] The paucity of subsidiary sources that could provide clarity are limited in their scope and only available in Arabic.[82] A summary assessment of these reports by the Arab Human Rights Committee did not reveal whether the Charter contains the *non-refoulement* principle.

A contextual analysis of the 2004 Arab Charter suggests that it provides a limited version of the non-refoulement principle, primarily through the interplay of Articles 28, 5, and 8. Article 28 establishes the right of individuals to seek political asylum to escape persecution, explicitly excluding those prosecuted for ordinary criminal offenses. It further specifies that "[p]olitical refugees shall not be extraditable", indicating recognition of the *non-refoulement* principle for political refugees under certain conditions.

80 González Morales, Felipe UN Special Rapporteur on the Rights of Migrants *Letter to the Representative of the USA regarding the Migrant Protection Protocols* (*MPP*) 7 March 2019, OL USA 4/2019, p. 1.

81 Paroula Naskou-Perraki argues that the Charter does contain the non-refoulement principle which is however only applicable to recognized political refugees and thus even narrower in its scope of application than Article 33 Refugee Convention. See: Naskou-Perraki, Paroula *The Arab Charter on Human Rights: A new start for the protection of human rights in the Arab* world Άρθρο που δημοσιεύτηκε στο Revue Hellenique de Droit International, τεύχος 1,2009, pp. 117–136.

82 The English version of the official webpage of the League of Arab States is under construction and thus also not available, see: http://www.leagueofarabstates.net/ar/Pages/default.aspx.

Additionally, Article 8 obligates member states to protect everyone within their territory from physical or mental torture and from cruel, inhuman, or degrading treatment or punishment. Article 5 guarantees the right to life, though it is not absolute, as Article 6 permits the death penalty for the "most serious crimes" in accordance with national law.

When read together, these provisions imply a prohibition against returning individuals to states where their life or personal integrity is at risk, at least in the case of political refugees who have not committed serious crimes. However, this protection is narrow and excludes broader categories of at-risk individuals. Consequently, the 2004 Arab Charter provides the most limited safeguards among international human rights instruments in terms of procedural guarantees for foreigners.

The **Commonwealth of Independent States Convention on Human Rights and Fundamental Freedoms** adopts a dual-structure approach like that of the 2004 Arab Charter regarding the principles of *non-refoulement* and the prohibition of collective expulsion. Article 25(4) of the Convention explicitly prohibits collective expulsion but does not codify the *non-refoulement* principle. While Article 2(1) guarantees the right to life, its scope is limited as the treaty allows for the death penalty. Additionally, Article 3 prohibits torture and cruel, inhuman, or degrading treatment or punishment.

The interpretation of the *non-refoulement* principle within the Convention's context can be inferred from the 1996 conference declaration by CIS countries and neighboring states on "the Problems of Refugees, Displaced Persons, Other Forms of Involuntary Displacement and Returnees". In this declaration, the participating states agreed to limit the application of the *non-refoulement* principle to refugees as defined in Article 33(1) of the 1951 Refugee Convention.[83] Consequently, both the CIS Convention and the 2004 Arab Charter provide a significantly narrower scope of protection *ratione personae* for the principle of non-refoulement compared to other regional and international human rights instruments.

Despite these limitations, all assessed regional instruments uniformly prohibit collective expulsion without distinction between refugees and migrants. This prohibition applies universally to all foreigners and underscores the

83 Commonwealth of Independent States *Regional Conference to Address the Problems of Refugees, Displaced Persons, Other Forms of Involuntary Displacement and Returnees in the Countries of the Commonwealth of Independent States and Relevant Neighbouring States* 11 June 1996, CISCONF/1996/5, paras. 13 (c), 32, 43, 82.

independence of the two legal principles, *non-refoulement* and the prohibition of collective expulsion.

3.2 *Intersecting Safeguards: The Prohibition of Collective Expulsion and* Non-refoulement *in International Human Rights Frameworks*

On an international level, the picture is less uniform with the ICCPR and the UN Migrant Worker Convention following the dual structure, while the UN Convention against Torture takes a different approach.

The **ICCPR** follows this dual structure between the two principles even though it does not contain any of the two principles in question explicitly. However, the Human Rights Committee interpreted the Covenant to implicitly contain *the non-refoulement* principle *inter alia* in its General Comment No. 20 of 1992 and No. 31 of 2004. The HRC based this principle on the prohibition of torture, cruel, inhuman, and degrading treatment in Article 7[84] and in the right to life in Article 6 ICCPR.[85] In a prior General Comment, the HRC had clarified that Article 13 ICCPR implicitly contains the prohibition of collective expulsion.[86]

The HRC read the prohibition of collective expulsion into the prohibition of arbitrary expulsion of lawfully residing foreigners. One possible reason for this early clarification on the prohibition in 1986, could be the fact that the principle was already explicitly contained in the fourth protocol to the ECHR, in the Inter-American Convention, and in the African Charter.

Besides the ICCPR, the **UN Migrant Worker Convention** has a dual structure between the two principles. The UN Migrant Worker Committee interpreted Articles 9 and 10 UNCRMW to implicitly contain the *non-refoulement* principle.[87] Here again, *non-refoulement* is interpreted as an inherent part of the scope of protection of the right to life (Article 9 UNCRMW). The Committee, however, anchors this principle also in the prohibition of torture and cruel, inhuman, or degrading treatment (Article 10 UNCRMW).

---

84 HRC *General comment No. 20 on Article 7 of the International Covenant on Civil and Political Rights on the Prohibition of Torture, or Other Cruel, Inhuman or Degrading Treatment or Punishment* 10 March 1992, para. 9.

85 HRC *General Comment No. 31 on the nature of the general legal obligation imposed on State Parties to the Covenant* 26 May 2004, CCPR/C/21/Rev.1/Add.13, para. 12. See also: HRC *General Comment No. 36 on article 6 of the International Covenant on Civil and Political Rights, on the right to life* CCPR/C/GC/36, 30 October 2018, para. 31.

86 HRC *General Comment No. 15 The position of aliens under the Covenant* (1986), para. 10.

87 Committee on the Protection of the Rights of All Migrant Workers and Members of Their Families and Committee on the Rights of the Child *Joint general comment No. 3 (2017)* paras. 45–47.

Article 22(1) UNCRMW contains the prohibition of collective expulsion. The provision stipulates that "[m]igrant workers and members of their families shall not be subject to measures of collective expulsion. Each case of expulsion shall be examined and decided individually". The CMW stressed in its *Report on the Global Compact on Migration* the significance of the combination of both principles for migration control policies in line with due process guarantees and other human rights obligations. The Committee mentions the importance and applicability of the two principles in particular when it comes to returns of foreigners to their countries of origin, the management of borders worldwide, and the fight against human trafficking and smuggling.[88] This input paper once more highlights the legal independence and mutual reinforcement of both principles that together ensure minimum due process guarantees against arbitrary expulsion to a place where the foreigner's life is at risk.

Article 3 of the UN Convention against Torture[89] does not explicitly reference the prohibition of collective expulsion, yet the Committee against Torture has effectively integrated its guarantees into the principle of *non-refoulement*.[90] The Committee uses terms like "collective deportation" and "collective return" to address the procedural safeguards necessary to prevent group expulsions without individual assessments.[91] These safeguards include the obligation to examine each case independently, impartially, and with due process, ensuring that no individual is returned to a country where they risk torture, including in cases of admission.[92]

The Committee's interpretation[93] aligns with the principles outlined in other human rights instruments, such as the European Convention on

88 CMW *Input for the Secretary-General's Report on the Global Compact on Migration* 7 September 2017, paras. A., J., M..

89 UN General Assembly *UN Convention against Torture and Other Cruel, Inhuman or Degrading Treatment or Punishment* (CAT) adopted on 10 December 1984, UNTS, vol. 1465, p. 85, entry into force 26 June 1987.

90 Hamdan, Eman *The Principle of Non-Refoulement under the ECHR and the UN Convention against Torture and Other Cruel, Inhuman or Degrading Treatment or Punishment* (Brill/Nijhoff 2016), p. 106, fn. 169.

91 European Commission *Migration and Home Affairs expulsion definition* available at: https://ec.europa.eu/home-affairs/what-we-do/networks/european_migration_network/glossary_search/expulsion_en.

92 *Ibidem.*, p. 105.

93 Committee against Torture *General Comment No. 1* (1998), annex IX of the Report of the Committee against Torture Supplement No. 44 (A/53/44), 1998, pp. 52–53; Committee against Torture *General Comment No. 4* (2017) on the implementation of

Human Rights, though it frames collective expulsions within the broader scope of *non-refoulement* rather than treating them as separate concepts. Observations from cases involving Italy and Greece highlight recurring concerns about pushbacks and summary expulsions without proper risk assessments.[94] Despite inconsistent terminology,[95] the Committee consistently emphasizes the need for procedural guarantees, such as access to legal remedies, information, and appeal rights, to prevent *refoulement* and collective "returns".[96]

Article 3 CAT presents a distinctive approach by combining the protections of the *non-refoulement* principle with procedural safeguards typically associated with the prohibition of collective expulsion. While the Committee against Torture refrains from explicitly using terms like "collective expulsion", it ensures equivalent guarantees through its interpretation of *non-refoulement*. This integrated approach underscores the mutual reinforcement and independent nature of these principles, providing robust protection against expulsion to unsafe conditions while emphasizing due process obligations.

In its broader analysis of these principles in international migration law, the International Organization for Migration (IOM) has affirmed this

---

Article 3 of the Convention in the context of article 22 CAT/C/GC/4, 4 September 2018, para. 13.

94 Committee against Torture *Concluding observations on the fifth and sixth periodic report of Italy* CAT/C/ITA/CO/5-6, 21 November 2017, paras. 20–21; Committee against Torture *Concluding observations on the seventh periodic report of Greece* CAT/C/SR.1779, 7 August 2019, para. 16.

95 Looking more closely at this particular paragraph of the fourth general comment, it seems that the concepts "collective deportation" and "collective expulsion" are the same, only with different labels. The footnote in this paragraph referencing "collective deportation" refers to the Human Rights Committee's general comment No. 15 of 1986. The footnote in question refers specifically to para. 15 of the general comment which clarifies that Art. 13 ICCPR guarantees every foreigner a decision in her or his case as this provision "would not be satisfied with laws or decisions providing for collective or mass expulsions". The footnote further refers explicitly to Article 22(1) UN Migrant Worker Convention, which protects migrants from "measures of collective expulsion" and highlights that "[e]ach case of expulsion shall be examined and decided individually". This direct reference shows that the Committee against Torture is well aware of the existence and the scope of application of the prohibition of collective expulsion in international conventions. Why the Committee chose the term "collective deportation" instead of "collective expulsion" remains unknown.

96 Committee against Torture *Consideration of reports submitted by States parties under article 19 of the Convention Concluding observations of the Committee against Torture* CAT/C/GRC/CO/5-6, 27 June 2012, para. 19.

distinction. The IOM highlights that while both principles are interrelated and mutually reinforcing, they maintain their independent legal character, ensuring complementary safeguards against arbitrary removals and the risks associated with forced returns.

The IOM highlights the legal independence of the two principles while stressing their mutual reinforcement and interdependence.[97] The organization then concludes that the "lack of an individualized assessment of the individual's situation prevents States from adequately verifying whether reasons exist not to expel or return a migrant in observance of the principle of *non-refoulement*.[98]

In conclusion, the prohibition of collective expulsion and the *non-refoulement* principle are closely interrelated yet independent legal safeguards. The prohibition of collective expulsion serves as a procedural foundation, ensuring individuals have the right to present claims against expulsion and have them objectively assessed. This right extends beyond asylum claims to encompass risks to life, well-being, health conditions, or vulnerabilities, such as those faced by unaccompanied minors.

While the *non-refoulement* principle can operate independently, as in cases where returning individuals to unsafe countries constitutes a clear violation, its interdependence with the prohibition becomes evident in individualized scenarios.

Across regional human rights instruments, such as the African Charter, the Inter-American Convention on Human Rights, and the European Convention on Human Rights, these principles demonstrate a dual structure. They are either explicitly codified or implied through provisions on torture, the right to life, and family protection. Regional jurisprudence has emphasized their mutual reinforcement, recognizing *non-refoulement* as a substantive safeguard and the prohibition of collective expulsion as a procedural right, ensuring individualized assessments of every case. Despite these differences, both principles are universally recognized by courts, monitoring bodies, and organizations like the IOM as complementary and mutually reinforcing.

At the international level, instruments like the ICCPR, the UN Migrant Worker Convention, and the Convention against Torture reflect this interplay. The Committee against Torture, for instance, has integrated collective

97 International Organization for Migration *INFORMATION NOTE ON THE PRINCIPLE OF NON-REFOULEMENT* April 2014, p. 9.

98 *Ibidem.*

expulsion safeguards into its interpretation of *non-refoulement*. These instruments collectively highlight the evolving nature of these principles, adapting them to ensure protection in diverse migration scenarios.

Together, they form the cornerstone of protection for migrants, asylum seekers, and refugees against arbitrary removal and return to unsafe conditions.

4 The Interconnectedness of the Prohibition of Collective Expulsion and Other Human Rights

The prohibition of collective expulsion is a cornerstone of human rights law, safeguarding individuals against mass removals without due process. Its significance lies not only in its standalone protection but also in its intricate connection to broader human rights guarantees such as non-discrimination, the right to an effective remedy, and fair trial rights. These interconnections are particularly important in border management and expulsion contexts, where systemic patterns of exclusion or discrimination often emerge.

Courts and treaty bodies have been instrumental in reshaping the prohibition from a simple obligation to refrain from *en masse* expulsions into a complex norm that incorporates procedural safeguards, often read in conjunction with other provisions. This evolution reflects the growing recognition of the prohibition as a dynamic principle that responds to changing forms of collective expulsion practices. It now encompasses fair process guarantees, ensuring that any collectively expelled foreigner has the right to minimum procedural protections before removal. These include the right to be heard, access to legal remedies, and the prevention of discriminatory practices in expulsion decisions. On the discriminatory aspect, especially the African and Inter-American human rights systems serve as role models.

This section explores the relationship between the prohibition of collective expulsion and other rights enshrined in human rights conventions. It examines how these interconnected rights, such as protections against arbitrary expulsion for legally residing individuals, fair trial guarantees, and the prohibition of discrimination have shaped the scope and interpretation of the prohibition. By analyzing this relationship, the discussion highlights the broader human rights framework that underpins and reinforces the scope of protection of the prohibition of collective expulsion – especially in border contexts.

4.1 *The Relationship between the Prohibition of Collective Expulsion and the Prohibition to Expel Lawfully Resident Foreigners*

Several regional human rights Conventions contain two separate provisions that offer protection against expulsion, one to lawful residents and the other to all foreigners irrespective of the legality of their presence or the denial of their entry.[99]

Article 22(6) Inter-American Convention or Article 12(4) African Charter are two examples. These provisions offer protection to foreigners lawfully in the territory against arbitrary expulsions guaranteeing a prior decision reached "in accordance with law".

However, the most prominent example is the European Convention. The ECHR contains two separate provisions in two separate protocols that offer protection against arbitrary expulsion. Article 1 Protocol 7 offers such guaranteesto lawfully residing residents, Article 4 Protocol 4 ECHR, to all foreigners. The scope of protection of Article 4 Protocol 4 ECHR encompasses the scope of Article 1 Protocol 7 ECHR and goes even beyond offering additional procedural safeguards for all foreigners.[100]

Article 25(3)[101] Commonwealth of Independent States Convention and Article 26(2) 2004 Arab Charter on Human Rights[102] equally contain a

---

99 Article 13 ICCPR does not follow this dual structure. Similarly, neither the Fundamental Rights Charter of the EU, nor the UN Migrant Worker Convention show such a dual structure. These conventions all contain only the prohibition of collective expulsion which is broader in its personal scope of application but at the same time more limited as it excludes individual expulsions.

100 Article 4 Protocol 4 ECHR provides broader protections than Article 1 Protocol 7 ECHR, applying to all foreigners regardless of legal status and encompassing all procedural guarantees in Article 1 Protocol 7 while extending to additional rights, such as access to an interpreter and the suspensive effect of an appeal. Unlike Article 4 Protocol 4, which can only be derogated in times of war or national emergency under Article 15 ECHR, Article 1 Protocol 7 allows derogations for reasons of public order or national security, making its threshold for restrictions significantly lower. While Article 1 Protocol 7 emphasizes the right to case review, the Explanatory Report clarifies that it does not mandate suspensive effect during appeals, further highlighting the comprehensive scope of Article 4 Protocol 4 in ensuring procedural fairness. For the Explanatory Report, see: Council of Europe *Explanatory Report Protocol 7* para. 13.2.

101 The subsection stipulates: "Aliens who are lawfully in the territory of any Contracting Party may be expelled only in application of a lawful decision, and they shall have the opportunity of appealing against their expulsion".

102 The subsection stipulates: "An alien lawfully in the territory of a State Party may be expelled only in pursuance of a decision reached according to the law and shall, except where compelling reasons of national security otherwise require, be given the possibility of having his case reviewed by a competent authority. Collective expulsions are prohibited in all cases".

separate provision against arbitrary expulsions for legally residing foreigners. Thus, these two Conventions follow the ECHR's dual approach and contain two separate provisions against arbitrary expulsions, one exclusively for lawfully residing foreigners, and one for collectively expelled foreigners. Given the inexistence of case-law or other documents on the prohibition of collective expulsion in these two conventions, the subsequent section exclusively assesses the relationship between these provisions in the ECHR.

The evolution of procedural safeguards in expulsion cases under the European Convention reveals significant gaps and limitations, particularly in addressing protections for all foreigners. Ulrike Brandl notes that the inclusion of Article 1 Protocol 7 ECHR in 1984 aimed to fill a procedural void, as neither the Convention nor earlier Protocols 1 and 4 explicitly guaranteed safeguards for individual expulsions.[103] However, the drafters of Protocol 4 (1963) had consciously avoided codifying such rights, opting instead for a broad and open prohibition of collective expulsion in Article 4 Protocol 4,[104] to avoid potential conflicts with existing treaties like the European Convention on Establishment (ECoE). In retrospect, these concerns proved unfounded, as the ECoE's scope was limited to protecting lawfully residing nationals of contracting states under specific conditions, whereas the Assembly's initial draft of Article 4 Protocol 4 proposed broader protections for all foreigners.[105]

Protocol 7's attempt to close the procedural gap has been largely ineffective. Article 1 Protocol 7 offers only minimal guarantees for lawfully present foreigners[106] and has not been ratified by all member states, with notable

103 Brandl, Ulrike *Prozeßgarantien in Verfahren zur Ausweisung Fremder* Art 1 EMRK/Prot 7 in: Pabel and Schmahl (eds.) *Internationaler Kommentar zur Europäischen Menschenrechtskonvention mit einschlägigen Texten und Dokumenten* (Carl Heymanns Verlag 2013), para. 1.

104 Council of Europe *Explanatory Report to Protocol No. 4 to the Convention for the Protection of Human Rights and Fundamental Freedoms, securing certain rights and freedoms other than those already included in the Convention and in the first Protocol thereto* ETS No. 46, 16 November 1963, para. 34 a).

105 European Convention on Establishment, and Protocols Thereto ETS No. 19, 13 December 1955, entered into force 23 February 1965.

106 The prohibition of collective expulsion guarantees the procedural rights that are explicitly codified in Article 1 Protocol 7 namely the right of a lawfully resident foreigner in a Member State's territory not to "be expelled therefrom except in pursuance of a decision reached in accordance with law". Article 1 Protocol 7 further clarifies in its subsection one the procedural guarantees such a foreigner enjoys namely the right to submit reasons against his or her expulsion (a), to have her or his case reviewed (b)

abstentions from Germany and the Netherlands.[107] Both countries are nevertheless bound by the international obligation not to arbitrarily expel legally residing foreigners as both countries have ratified the ICCPR, which contains this principle in its Article 13.[108] Even among ratifying states, reservations such as Switzerland's exclusion of cases involving security threats further undermine its scope.[109] Although its content mirrors Article 13 of the ICCPR, which obliges ratifying states to prevent arbitrary expulsion of legally residing individuals, Protocol 7's limited scope fails to address procedural guarantees for all foreigners, particularly those subject to collective expulsions.[110] Scholars, including Mark Villinger, have criticized the provision's inadequacy, labeling it as overly "frugal".[111]

Historical analysis shows that the initial intention of Article 4 Protocol 4 ECHR aligned with the protection of lawfully residing foreigners from arbitrary expulsion. However, the Committee of Experts shifted its focus exclusively to collective expulsions, prioritizing state sovereignty and avoiding international oversight over individual expulsion decisions.[112] This shift created a divergence between Article 4 Protocol 4 and Article 1 Protocol 7, despite their shared origins. While the former now provides safeguards against collective expulsions, the latter offers minimal protections for individual cases, leaving a substantive gap for other categories of foreigners.

---

and lastly "to be represented for these purposes before the competent authority or a person designated by that authority" (c).

107 Council of Europe *Details of Treaty No. 117, Protocol 7 to the Convention for the Protection of Human Rights and Fundamental Freedoms* available at: https://www.coe.int/en/web/conventions/full-list/-/conventions/treaty/117.

108 Germany ratified the ICCPR in 1973, the Netherlands in in 1978. Article 13 ICCPR reads: "An alien lawfully in the territory of a State Party to the present Covenant may be expelled therefrom only in pursuance of a decision reached in accordance with law and shall, except where compelling reasons of national security otherwise require, be allowed to submit the reasons against his expulsion and to have his case reviewed by, and be represented for the purpose before, the competent authority or a person or persons especially designated by the competent authority".

109 Reservation made by Switzerland *Reservations and Declarations for Treaty No.117 – Protocol No. 7 to the Convention for the Protection of Human Rights and Fundamental Freedoms*, Declarations in force as of 1 November 1988, available at: https://www.coe.int/en/web/conventions/full-list/-/conventions/treaty/117/declarations?p_auth=tOkSUelj.

110 Henckaert, Jean-Marie *Mass Expulsion in Public International Law and Practice* p.33.

111 Villinger, Mark *Handbuch der EMRK Garantien der Zusatzprotokolle §31* (Schulthess Polygraphischer Verlag 2nd edn. 1999), para. 691.

112 Council of Europe *Explanatory Report on the Second to Fifth Protocols to the European Convention for Protection of Human Rights and Fundamental Freedoms, submitted by the Committee of Experts to The Committee of Ministers* H(71) 11 (1971), p. 11.

Ultimately, the distinct trajectories of Article 4 Protocol 4 and Article 1 Protocol 7 highlight the ECHR's piecemeal approach to procedural safeguards in expulsion contexts. Despite their differences, the interconnected origins and objectives of these provisions underscore the substantive relationship between the prohibition of collective expulsion and the procedural guarantees embedded in the prohibition of collective expulsion.

In general terms, the relationship between Article 1 Protocol 7 and Article 4 Protocol 4 of the European Convention on Human Rights demonstrates a *lex specialis-lex generalis* dynamic, where the former serves as a specific procedural safeguard for lawfully resident foreigners, while the latter provides broader protections against collective expulsion. Exemplary cases, such as *Sharma v. Latvia*[113] and *Georgia v. Russia I*,[114] reveal that when the personal scope of Article 1 Protocol 7 is not applicable, Article 4 Protocol 4 operates as a residual safeguard. Despite their congruent procedural guarantees, Article 4 Protocol 4 has garnered significantly more judicial attention due to its broader application to all foreigners, irrespective of legal status, and its relevance in addressing mass expulsion practices. The limited impact of Article 1 Protocol 7 stems from its narrow scope and the ECtHR's preference for expansive interpretations of Article 4 Protocol 4 to ensure comprehensive protection against arbitrary expulsions.

The drafting history of Protocol 7 supports this finding. The main reason for drafting Protocol 7 was the reduction of a discrepancy in protection between the ICCPR adopted in 1966 and the ECHR.[115] Thus, the aim of the Committee of Ministers after 1966 was to extend civil and political rights and freedoms of the European Convention.[116] In retrospect, this attempt led to the ECtHR's approach to interpreting the scope of those provisions that were accepted by its members states. This approach led in particular to the Court's extensive interpretation of the prohibition of collective expulsion.

This evolution underscores the importance of preventing discrepancies in protections between lawfully and unlawfully resident foreigners, a goal shaped by the historical development and interpretative expansion of these provisions.

---

113 *Sharma v. Latvia* ECtHR, Appl. No. Appl. No. 28026/05, 24 March 2016, para. 75.

114 *Georgia v. Russia I*. ECtHR, [GC], Appl. No. 13255/07, 3 July 2014.

115 Council of Europe *Explanatory Report Protocol 7* para. 1.

116 *Ibidem.*, paras. 2–3.

4.2 *The Relationship between the Prohibition of Collective Expulsion, Fair Trial, and Due Process Rights*

The prohibition of collective expulsion, as interpreted by courts and treaty bodies, incorporates procedural safeguards aimed at preventing arbitrary expulsions *en masse*. These safeguards align closely with fair trial and due process rights, which are independently enshrined in human rights conventions. Together, these guarantees play a critical role in ensuring a minimum of guarantees for fair procedures, particularly in the context of collective expulsions and denials of entry at borders.

Fair trial and due process rights are fundamental guarantees that ensure individuals can effectively defend their rights in legal and administrative proceedings.[117] These rights encompass procedural safeguards such as the right to be heard, access to legal representation, equality before the law, and protection from arbitrary decisions. In the European Convention, these rights are primarily enshrined in Article 6, which guarantees a fair trial, and Article 13, which provides the right to an effective remedy. The African Charter similarly safeguards these principles through Article 7, which outlines the right to a fair trial. The Inter-American Convention on Human Rights further codifies these rights in Articles 8 and 25, which respectively provide for judicial guarantees and the right to judicial protection.

This section explores the relationship between the prohibition of collective expulsion, fair trial, and due process guarantees across various human rights instruments. By analyzing this interplay, the section highlights the extent to which these combined protections are essential for safeguarding individual rights and preventing systemic violations. It also underscores the differing approaches taken by regional frameworks, with the European Convention on Human Rights adopting a more restrictive stance compared to the broader protections afforded by the EU Charter of Fundamental Rights, the African Charter, and the Inter-American Convention.

The European Convention,[118] the Inter-American Convention,[119] the African Charter,[120] the 2004 Arab Charter on Human Rights,[121] or the ICCPR[122] all contain fair trial rights and the right to an effective remedy in criminal

117 Momsen, Carsten and Willumat, Marco *Due Process and Fair Trial* in: Caeiro; Gless, Mitsilegas, Costa, Snaijer and Theodorakakou (eds.) *Elgar Encyclopedia of Crime and Criminal Justice* (Edgar Elgar 2024), pp. 102–113.

118 *European Convention on Human Rights*, Articles 6 and 13.

119 *Inter-American Convention on Human Rights*, Articles 8 and 25(1).

120 *African Charter on Human and Peoples' Rights*, Article 7.

121 *2004 Arab Charter on Human Rights*, Articles 12, 13.

122 *International Covenant on Civil and Political Rights*, Articles 14(1) and 2(3)(a).

and most also in civil procedures. These rights form the basis of due process guarantees in domestic, regional, and international law.[123]

Article 47 EUChFR,[124] in contrast, goes further and extends fair trial guarantees to everyone in any proceeding and the right to remedy to anyone "whose rights and freedoms guaranteed by the by the law of the Union are violated".[125]

In contrast, Article 6 ECHR does not apply in expulsion or denial of entry scenarios. This provision ensures the right to a fair trial, providing key procedural safeguards for individuals involved in legal proceedings.[126] It guarantees the right to a fair and public hearing by an independent tribunal, within a reasonable time, and includes the right to legal assistance, to be informed of charges, and to examine witnesses (Article 6(1)). It also upholds the presumption of innocence (Article 6(2)) and the right to a defense, including access to evidence and time to prepare (Article 6(3)). However, this protection applies to criminal, civil to some areas of administrative law, such as road-traffic offenses or offences against social-security legislation.[127]

As applicants in collective expulsion cases before the ECtHR, cannot invoke these *general* fair trial rights, they must rely on Article 4 Protocol 4 or Article 1 Protocol 7 ECHR. This limitation may also explain why the Court had to interpret the scope of protection of Article 4 Protocol 4 ECHR to contain procedural guarantees. The Convention itself and previous ECtHR caselaw barred the application of general fair trial rights in collective expulsion cases.

Given the specific wording of the prohibition of collective expulsion in the ECHR and the lack of other provisions offering procedural guarantees

123 The Human Rights Committee acknowledged in its *General Comment No. 32 on Article 14* that the fair trial guarantees in the ICCPR also apply to civil procedures. See: HRC *General Comment No. 32 Art. 14, Right to equality before courts and tribunals and to a fair trial* CCPR/C/GC/32, 23 August 2007, paras. 13, 16. The Arab Charter seemingly only contains fair trial rights in criminal proceedings.

124 *Charter of Fundamental Rights in the European Union*, Article 47.

125 For a detailed analysis on the relationship between Article 47 EUChFR and Article 6 ECHR and the scope of application of Art. 6 ECHR in general see: Schabas, William *European Convention on Human Rights Commentary* (Oxford University Press 2015), pp. 264–327.

126 Nevertheless, Article 4 Protocol 4 ECHR in conjunction with Article 13 ECHR offers the right to an effective remedy in expulsion cases.

127 For details and an exhaustive list of all administrative offences covered by Article 6 ECHR see: Council of Europe, European Court of Human Rights *Guide on Article 6of the European Convention on Human Rights Criminal Limb* 21 August 2019, para. 31.

against arbitrary expulsions for all foreigners, the ECtHR arguably turned to interpret the succinct and vague wording of the provision in Protocol 4.

The limitation of Article 6 ECHR guarantees in expulsion or denial of entry procedures is particularly problematic because it limits the explicit fair trial, and due process guarantees available to individuals facing removal from a state's territory.

As a result, individuals cannot invoke general fair trial rights, such as the right to a public hearing, legal representation, or the right to contest charges, in expulsion proceedings under this provision. Instead, they must rely on more limited provisions like Article 4 Protocol 4 ECHR or Article 1 Protocol 7, which have been interpreted by the European Court to contain procedural guarantees. This limitation has become more pronounced since the ECtHR's rulings in *Khlaifia* and especially *N.D. and N.T.*, where the Court significantly restricted the guarantees of Article 4 Protocol 4 in border contexts, further undermining due process in expulsion scenarios. Having Article 6 ECHR available to individuals in these cases would offer a more holistic safeguard by providing stronger and explicit procedural rights, ensuring a more comprehensive approach to fairness in expulsion processes. To strengthen these protections, the ECtHR should turn to the Inter-American or African human rights systems for inspiration, ensuring a genuine and effective application of human rights guarantees in border and expulsion contexts.

This issue also becomes evident in the application of the right to an effective remedy under Article 4 Protocol 4, in conjunction with Article 13 ECHR. The Court has significantly limited the application of the suspensive effect of an expulsion decision, restricting it primarily to asylum seekers. While Article 13 ECHR ensures the right to an effective remedy that can prevent irreversible measures, such as expulsion, and is widely applied in migration and asylum cases, the Court has found violations of Article 13 in cases where applicants, who had an arguable claim under Articles 2 or 3 ECHR due to risks they faced upon removal, were prevented from seeking asylum or did not have access to a remedy with automatic suspensive effect.[128]

In contrast, the Court ruled that the lack of a suspensive effect does not automatically violate Article 13 combined with Article 4 Protocol 4 if there is no real risk of harm in the destination country.[129] This shows an unjustifiable distinction between asylum seekers and other migrants. While Article

---

128 *M.K. and Others v. Poland* ECtHR, paras. 212–220; *Hirsi Jamaa v. Italy* ECtHR, paras. 201–207; *Sharifi and Others v. Italy and Greece* ECtHR, paras. 240–243.

129 *Khlaifia and Others v. Italy* ECtHR, [GC] para. 281.

13 is applied in asylum contexts, the Court's restrictive interpretation of the suspensive effect in expedited expulsions limits the scope of protection for individuals that do not meet this prerequisite.

The **Inter-American Convention**, alongside its Commission and Court took a distinct and more progressive approach when it comes to fair trial rights in the migration context.

Article 8 and Article 25 of the Inter-American Convention on Human Rights establish fundamental guarantees for the protection of fair trial rights and due process. Article 8 ensures that everyone has the right to a hearing by a competent, independent, and impartial tribunal, as well as the right to be informed of the charges against them and to prepare an adequate defense. It also includes safeguards such as the right to legal assistance, the presumption of innocence, and the prohibition of double jeopardy. Article 25 complements these protections by guaranteeing the right to an effective remedy before a competent authority when an individual's rights are violated, ensuring access to justice even when other legal avenues fail.

In its 2003 Advisory Opinion on the rights of undocumented migrants, the Inter-American Court of Human Rights emphasized the universal applicability of these fair trial and due process rights for all foreigners in all legal proceedings involving its member states.[130] The Court affirmed that due process entails all procedural requirements necessary to ensure individual migrants – irrespective of their status – can adequately defend their rights against any state act or omission, whether administrative, punitive, or judicial in nature.[131]

The Court further highlighted that these rights apply not only to criminal matters but also to civil, labor, and administrative contexts, thereby extending their scope to migration and asylum procedures.[132] Importantly, the Court also underscored the principle of equality before the law and the prohibition of discrimination, requiring states to adopt countervailing measures to address systemic disadvantages faced by migrants.[133] These measures aim to ensure effective access to justice and fair adjudication, not merely formal compliance.[134] The Court also noted that the denial of free legal aid, coupled with risks of deportation or detention during legal proceedings,

130 *Advisory Opinion on Juridical Condition and Rights of Undocumented Migrants* IACourtHR Series A No. 18, requested by México, 17 September 2003, paras. 121–127.

131 *Ibidem.*, paras. 121–124.

132 *Ibidem.*, paras. 123–126.

133 *Ibidem.*, para. 120.

134 *Ibidem.*, paras. 121–122.

constitutes a violation of judicial protection and guarantees.[135] It concluded that due process is a fundamental human right that must be preserved across all state actions affecting individuals, ensuring fair decisions and genuine access to justice.[136]

The Inter-American Court reemphasized the broad application of due process and fair trial guarantees in the context of migration and expulsion procedures in its 2013 decision *Pacheco Tineo v. Bolivia* case.[137] Here, the Court highlighted that the right to seek and receive asylum, when read in conjunction with Articles 8 and 25, guarantees that asylum seekers are heard by the state in a manner that respects due process guarantees through the appropriate procedures.[138] The Court further explained that, given the specific regulation of the right to seek asylum, and relating to the minimum due process guarantees that must be upheld in migration procedures, these protections should be applied to procedures involving refugee status determinations or those potentially leading to the expulsion or deportation of an asylum seeker or refugee.[139]

Finally, the Court outlined specific obligations for states to ensure that asylum seekers have access to a process that guarantees a proper examination of their claims. These obligations include providing necessary support such as legal representation, ensuring impartiality and objectivity in the review process, protecting the confidentiality of the application, and offering the opportunity for appeal if asylum is denied, with the possibility of suspensive effects to allow the applicant to remain in the country while the appeal is processed.[140]

Besides the Court, also the Inter-American Commission on Human Rights has reaffirmed the applicability of fair trial and due process rights in migration and asylum contexts, emphasizing the necessity of minimum procedural guarantees. For example, in its report on the human rights situation of asylum seekers in Canadian detention of 2000, the Commission clarified that while the right to seek asylum under Article 27 XXVI of the American Declaration does not guarantee the granting of asylum, it does require that

135 *Ibidem.*, para. 126.

136 *Ibidem.*, para. 127.

137 See also: IACoutHR *Cuadernillo de Jurisprudencia de la Corte Interamericana de Derechos Humanos No. 2: Personas en situación de migración o refugio* 2020, paras. 154–160.

138 *Pacheco Tineo v. Bolivia* IACourtHR, paras. 128–132.

139 *Ibidem.*, paras. 128–130.

140 *Ibidem.*, paras. 133–136.

claimants have the opportunity to be heard.[141] This right to be heard is intrinsically linked to the principle of due process, which underpins several provisions of the Declaration, including Articles II (equal protection), XVII (recognition of juridical personality and civil rights), XVIII (fair trial), and XXVI (due process) American Declaration.[142] The Commission highlighted that the procedural guarantees necessary to present an asylum claim must be tailored to the specific circumstances of each case.[143] For instance, while a simple records review may suffice to determine whether a prior claim has been rejected, more complex issues, such as assessing potential risks to national security or public order, require detailed fact-finding and legal analysis.[144] The Commission cited cases illustrating how even seemingly administrative decisions, such as determining whether an individual holds refugee status from another country, can involve intricate evaluations of fact and law.[145]

In conclusion, the relationship between fair trial, due process rights, and the prohibition of collective expulsion within the Inter-American System represents a strong framework that prioritizes individual rights and procedural fairness in migration and asylum contexts. The Inter-American Convention on Human Rights, particularly through Articles 8, 22(9), and 25, offers comprehensive protections for migrants, including those facing expulsion or seeking entry to a territory to seek protection. These provisions ensure that migrants, regardless of their legal status, are entitled to fair and impartial hearings, legal assistance, and access to effective remedies.

The Inter-American Court has been instrumental in extending these due process guarantees beyond criminal matters, affirming that they must be upheld in all legal proceedings involving migrants, including administrative and expulsion procedures. These protections are not merely formal; they address systemic barriers to access to justice that migrants often face, such as discrimination[146] and lack of legal aid.

Moreover, the prohibition of collective expulsion, closely tied to these fair trial and due process guarantees, reflects a holistic approach that

141 IAComHR *Report on the Situation of Human Rights of Asylum-Seekers within the Canadian Refugee Determination System* 2000, available at: https://www.cidh.org/countryrep/Canada2000en/canada.htm, para. 60.

142 *Ibidem.*

143 *Ibidem.*

144 *Ibidem.*

145 *Ibidem.*

146 For more details on the interplay between the prohibition of collective expulsion and non-discrimination see the next section below.

protects migrants from arbitrary state actions. The Inter-American Court has stressed that collective expulsion violates individual due process rights, as each case must be considered on its merits, ensuring that migrants are not subjected to group expulsions without adequate legal consideration.

In contrast to the more limited approach of the European Convention on Human Rights, which focuses primarily on criminal law contexts, the Inter-American system offers a broader, more inclusive framework for protecting migrant rights. This approach is not only more comprehensive in scope but also more attuned to the complexities of migration, where due process protections are essential in addressing the unique vulnerabilities migrants face. By intertwining fair trial rights, due process guarantees, and the prohibition of collective expulsion, the Inter-American system provides a more robust and holistic safeguard for migrants' rights.[147] Likewise, the provision governing fair trial and due process guarantees in the **African Charter** (Article 7) does not only apply in civil and criminal matters but also in expulsion cases. Like its Inter-American Counterpart, the African Charter does not exclude administrative acts from its general fair process guarantees. It seems that the prohibition of collective expulsion in the ECHR instruments evolved as a due process guarantee because the general fair process guarantees did not apply to expulsion procedures. In contrast, the prohibition of collective expulsion in the Banjul Charter evolved from a prohibition of discrimination towards a due process right. It underwent this evolution not independent from fair trial provisions but in conjunction with the Charter's general fair trial guarantees. While most human rights treaties contain a provision on the right to remedies, and another on the right to a fair trial, the wording of Article 7(1)(a) ACHPR unifies the two types of protection in one provision.[148] The African Commission clarified this approach in *Zimbabwe Human Rights NGO Forum v. Zimbabwe* stating that "the protection afforded by Article 7 is not limited to the protection of the rights of arrested and detained persons but encompasses the right of every individual to access the relevant judicial bodies competent to have their causes

147 For a similar analysis see: Cantor, David James and Barichello, Stefania Eugenia *The Inter-American human rights system: a new model for integrating refugee and complementary protection?* The International Journal of Human Rights, Vol. 17, No. 5, 2013, p. 694.

148 For a detailed analysis on this exceptional position of Article 7(1)(a) see Plagis, Misha; Riemer, Lena From Context to Content of Human Rights: The Drafting History of the African Charter on Human and Peoples' Rights and the Enigma of Article 7 In: *Journal of the History of International Law*, Vol. 23, (2020), pp. 556–589.

heard and be granted adequate relief."[149] The scope of protection of Article 7(1)(a) ACHPR is quite extensive and entails the right to a first instance decision, to an appeal to a higher tribunal, to compensation, to access to relevant factual information as well as the right to the execution of a judgment.

The African Commission confirmed the latter in its 2005 decision *Antoine Bissangou v. Republic of Congo*. There, the Commission pointed out that it is

> of the view that the right to be heard guaranteed by Article 7 of the African Charter includes the right to the execution of a judgment [...] As a result, the execution of a final judgment passed by a Tribunal or legal Court should be considered as an integral part of "the right to be heard" which is protected by Article 7.[150]

The *Principles and Guidelines on the Right to a Fair Trial and Legal Assistance in Africa* list the right to an effective remedy explicitly as part of Article 7(1)(a) ACHPR.[151] The Commission adopted these principles and guidelines as it found it "necessary to formulate and lay down principles and rules to further strengthen and supplement the provisions relating to a fair trial in the Charter and to reflect international standards".[152] The guarantees entail the right to access justice, reparation, and access to the factual information concerning the violations. The right to access to justice includes both, the right to address a matter in front of a court or similar competent organ as well as the right to an appeal to a second instance.[153]

149 *Zimbabwe Human Rights NGO Forum v. Zimbabwe* ACHPR, Communication No. 245/02, 2006, para. 213.

150 *Antoine Bissangou v. Republic of Congo* AComHPR, Communication No. 252/2002, 2006, para. 75.

151 AComHPR *Principles and Guidelines on the Right to a Fair Trial and Legal Assistance in Africa* 2003. Adopted in accordance with its mandate under Article 45(c) ACHPR "to formulate and lay down principles and rules aimed at solving legal problems relating to human and peoples' rights and fundamental freedoms upon which African states may base their legislation", para. C. b).

152 AComHPR *Principles and Guidelines on the Right to a Fair Trial and Legal Assistance in Africa* Preamble.

153 Manby, Bronwen *Civil and Political Rights in the African Charter on Human and Peoples' Righs: Articles 1–7 in: Evans, Murray The African Charter on Human and Peoples' Rights The system in Practice, 1986–2006* (Cambridge University Press 2nd edn. 2008), p. 200.

The Commission held in *Zimbabwe Human Rights NGO Forum v. Zimbabwe* that Art. 7 contains both: the right to a fair trial and the right to an effective remedy. Here, the African Commission stressed that

> the protection afforded by Article 7 is not limited to the protection of the rights of arrested and detained persons but encompasses the right of every individual to access the relevant judicial bodies competent to have their causes heard and be granted *adequate relief* [emphasis added].[154]

In a later case, the Commission confirmed this finding. In *Kenneth Good v. Republic of Botswana*, the African Commission dealt with the expulsion of an Australian national, teaching at the University of Botswana expelled after having written a critical article about the local government.[155] Here, the African Commission found *inter alia* a violation of Article 7(1)(a) ACHPR as the applicant

> was not afforded any meaningful opportunity to challenge his expulsion either by *way of hearing before* the expulsion order was made, or by *way of appeal after* the order was made. [...] He was neither given *any remedy* in respect of the violations of his rights [emphasis added].[156]

This finding suggests that Article 7(1)(a) ACHPR also contains the right to an appeal and remedies in expulsion cases. The African Commission affirmed the inclusion of the right to an appeal into the scope of protection of Article 7 ACHPR in several subsequent cases.[157]

The African Commission found a violation of the prohibition of collective expulsion and fair trial rights in four out of five cases in which it dealt with expulsion *en masse*. More specifically, the Commission referred to a violation of Article 7(1)(a) ACHPR, the right to an appeal to competent national

---

154 *Zimbabwe Human Rights NGO Forum v. Zimbabwe* para. 213.

155 *Kenneth Good v. Republic of Botswana* AComHPR, Communication No. 313/05, 2010, paras. 2–3.

156 *Ibidem.*, para. 116.

157 See for example: *Egyptian Initiative for Personal Rights and Interights v Arab Republic of Egypt* AComHPR, Communication No. 334/06, 2011, para.205 and *Law Office of Ghazi Suleiman v Sudan* AComHPR, Communication No. 222/98-229/99, 2003, para. 53 and in *Civil Liberties Organisation, Legal Defence Centre, Legal Defence and Assistance Project v. Nigeria* AComHPR, Communication No. 218/98, 2001, paras. 32–33.

organs against acts of violating fundamental rights in all of these cases.[158] The only exception where the Commission did not refer at all to Article 7 is the case *Institute for Human Rights and Development in Africa v. Guinea*.[159] This case dealt with a public speech given by Guinean President Lansana Conté in September 2000, in which he proclaimed over the national radio that Sierra Leonean refugees in Guinea should be arrested, searched, and confined to refugee camps. This announcement led to the widespread commitment of atrocities against Sierra Leonean refugees.[160] This forced eviction of refugees led to the finding of the *African Commission* that Guinea had violated Article 12(5) African Charter. Why neither the applicants nor the Commission invoked Article 7, the right to a fair trial, or Article 12(4) African Charter, procedural guarantees in case of expulsion of legally residing foreigners, remains an enigma. None of the applicants received an expulsion order or had the right to challenge their expulsion on an individual basis. Thus, both provisions would have equally applied.

The fair trial rights enshrined in Article 7(1)(a) ACHPR is of significance in cases of collective expulsion, as the provision grants individuals the possibility to plead their case before the competent national courts".[161] The scope of the provision is quite extensive. It entails the right to a first instance decision in case of expulsion, the right to an appeal, compensation, relevant factual information, as well as the right to the execution of a judgment. Thus, it provides due process rights for all expelled members of a group. In a manner comparable to Article 7(1)(a) ACHPR, the African Commission also relied on other Charter provisions to extend the prohibition's scope of protection. These provisions are Article 2 (prohibition of discrimination) and Article 12(4) ACHPR (protection against arbitrary expulsion of legally residing foreigners).

In conclusion, the African Charter provides a comprehensive framework for the protection of fair trial and due process rights, extending these protections to expulsion cases. Article 7, which unifies the right to a fair trial

158 See for example: *Organisation mondiale contre la torture ets al. v. Rwanda* AComHPR, para. 34; *Rencontre africaine pour la défence des droits de l'Homme v. Zambia* AComHPR, para. 29; *Union interafricaine des droits de l'Homme et. al. v. Angola* AComHPR, para. 19; *Institute for Human Rights and Development in Africa v Angola* AComHPR, paras. 56–60.

159 *Institute for Human Rights and Development in Africa v. Guinea* AComHPR, Communication No. 249/02, 2004.

160 *Institute for Human Rights and Development in Africa v. Guinea* AComHPR, paras. 1, 7.

161 *Union interafricaine des droits de l'Homme et. al. v. Angola* AComHPR, para. 20.

and the right to an effective remedy, ensures that individuals, including migrants, are afforded the opportunity to challenge expulsion decisions, seek judicial review, and access remedies for violations of their rights. Unlike the European Convention, where the prohibition of collective expulsion evolved as a due process guarantee, the ACHPR explicitly links the prohibition of collective expulsion to broader due process and non-discrimination principles.

The African Commission's interpretation of Article 7 ACHPR has extended its scope to include the right to a meaningful opportunity to challenge expulsion decisions, both before and after an expulsion order is made. This includes the right to appeal, access to relevant factual information, and the execution of judgments. These due process guarantees are vital in ensuring that individuals subjected to expulsion, whether collectively or individually, can fully assert their rights before competent judicial bodies.

In conclusion, after having assessed the relationship between the prohibition of collective expulsion, fair trial, and due process rights, their interconnectedness has become visible in expulsion contexts. The prohibition of collective expulsion, as interpreted by various courts and treaty bodies, incorporates essential procedural safeguards that prevent arbitrary expulsions. These safeguards align closely with fair trial and due process rights, which are fundamental guarantees in human rights conventions. These rights ensure individuals can defend their rights in legal and administrative proceedings, encompassing the right to be heard, access to legal representation, equality before the law, and protection from arbitrary decisions. In the European Convention, these rights are primarily enshrined in Article 6, which guarantees a fair trial, and Article 13, which provides for an effective remedy. Similarly, the African Charter and the Inter-American Convention safeguard these principles, with the latter codifying rights to a fair trial and effective remedy in Articles 8 and 25.

However, the European Convention's application of these guarantees in expulsion procedures is more restrictive. While Article 6 ECHR provides a broad range of procedural protections, it does not apply to expulsion or denial of entry cases. This limitation means that individuals facing removal from a state's territory must rely on more limited provisions, such as Article 4 of Protocol 4, which has been interpreted by the European Court to include some procedural guarantees. This contrasts with the broader protections found in the Inter-American and African systems, which apply fair trial and due process rights more expansively in migration contexts. The Inter-American Court, for example, has emphasized that these rights must be upheld in all legal proceedings involving migrants, including expulsion procedures. In contrast, the European Court's restrictive interpretation of the suspensive effect of expulsion decisions limits the scope of protection for non-asylum-seeking migrants. This gap in protection underscores the need for stronger procedural safeguards in expulsion contexts, which the Inter-American and African systems better provide. By combining fair trial rights, due process guarantees, and the prohibition of collective expulsion, these systems offer a more robust framework for protecting migrant rights.

4.3 *The Relationship between the Prohibition of Collective Expulsion and the Prohibition of Discrimination*

The prohibition of collective expulsion is not only inherently linked to fair trial and due process rights, but also to the prohibition of discrimination, as exclusionary practices in migration and border control often perpetuate systemic racial biases.

This relationship is key in understanding the dynamics of border management practices, which are not neutral or unbiased. As numerous scholars[162], studies and reports have shown, human-made laws, including those governing migration, often reflect systemic biases, and border practices can exacerbate discrimination.[163] Simultaneously, too often, international legal frameworks address only surface-level discrimination, without confronting the deeper structures and ideologies that sustain racial hierarchies.[164] As Spain Bradly argues in her concept of "human rights racism", international law must go beyond addressing individual discriminatory acts to tackle the systemic roots of racism as a violation of human rights.[165]

The prohibition of collective expulsion mandates that states assess each individual claim for protection in an objective, neutral, and non-discriminatory manner. However, despite this mandate, reports from across the

162 See, e.g., de Vries, Karin/Spijkerboer, Thomas *Race and the Regulation of International Migration. The Ongoing Impact of Colonialism in the Case Law of The European Court of Human Rights* Netherlands Quarterly of Human Rights, 2021, Vol. 39, No. 4, pp. 291–307 or Spijkerboer, Thomas *Bifurcation of People, Bifurcation of Law: Externalization of Migration Policy before the EU Court of Justice* Journal of Refugee Studies, 2017, Vol. 31, No. 2 or Spain Bradley, Anna Human Rights Racism Harvard Human Rights Journal, Vol. 32, No. 1, 2019, pp. 1–58.

163 For an analysis of the effect of US policies on Indigenous People, see: Kowalski, Joseph *Imaginary Lines, Real Consequences: The Effect of the Militarization of the United States-Mexico Border on Indigenous Peoples* INDIAN Law Journal, Vol. 5, Iss. 2 (2017), pp. 645–648.

164 Spain Bradley, Anna *Human Rights Racism* Harvard Human Rights Journal, Vol. 32, No. 1 (2019), pp. 1–58.

165 *Ibidem.*, pp. 32–33.

globe highlight discriminatory practices, particularly based on race or ethnicity, in expulsion processes.[166] Vulnerable groups such as Black, Indigenous, and Sub-Saharan African migrants are often disproportionately targeted in these expulsions, with practices that violate their fundamental rights to health, physical integrity, and life.[167]

Recent reports have illustrated how such discriminatory practices, particularly against Haitian and African migrants, reflect broader systemic racism within migration policies. These discriminatory expulsion practices are compounded by border externalization measures, such as those involving the U.S. and Mexico, which restrict access to asylum and expose marginalized groups to further violence.[168] International human rights bodies, including the UN Committee on the Elimination of Racial Discrimination, have raised concerns about the racialized nature of these practices and called for active countermeasures by states.[169]

The prohibition of collective expulsion is deeply interconnected with the principle of non-discrimination, as both aim to ensure that the rights of

---

166 Human Rights Watch *Abused and Expelled Ill-Treatment of Sub-Saharan African Migrants in Morocco* 10 February 2014, available at: https://www.hrw.org/report/2014/02/10/abused-and-expelled/ill-treatment-sub-saharan-african-migrants-morocco, OHCHR *UN calls on Algeria to stop expelling thousands of sub-Saharan African migrants* 22 May 2018, available at: https://news.un.org/en/story/2018/05/1010392, or Committee on the Protection of the Rights of All Migrant Workers and Members of Their Families *Concluding observations on the second periodic report of Chile*, CMW/C/CHL/CO/2, 11 May 2021.

167 A comprehensive report prepared for the Inter-American Commission on Human Rights, 186th Period of Sessions in 2023 by an alliance of human rights defenders offers a comprehensive analysis of the interconnectedness of migration and systemic racism by adopting an anti-racist lens when assessing migration control policies across the Americas. See: Black Alliance for Just Immigration (BAJI), the Center for Justice and International Law (CEJIL), the Center for Immigration Law and Policy (CILP) at the UCLA School of Law, Comunidades Indígenas en Liderazgo Organizativo (CIELO), Haitian Bridge Alliance (HBA), Migrant Works Alliance for Change (MWAC), the Promise Institute for Human Rights at the UCLA School of Law, Observatorio de Racismo en México y Centroamérica, RacismoMX, Espacio Migrante A.C, and Cameroonian Action Network *Report for the Inter-American Commission on Human Rights 186th Period of Sessions Public Hearing on the Situation of human mobility from an ethnic-racial approach* 2023, available at: https://promiseinstitute.law.ucla.edu/wp-content/uploads/2023/07/2023-Situation-of-human-mobility-from-an-ethnic-racial-approach.pdf.

168 *Ibidem*, pp. 12–13.

169 Committee on the Elimination of Racial Discrimination *Statement on the Tragic Events at the Moroccon-Spanish Border* No. 3 (2022), 107th Session of CERD, 8–30 August 2022, p. 2.

vulnerable migrants are respected and protected. However, as recent case law and reports demonstrate, expulsion practices often fail to meet these standards, undermining the very protections that the prohibition of collective expulsion is meant to ensure. The persistence of racial profiling and the denial of access to asylum procedures further exacerbates the vulnerability of marginalized migrant groups, highlighting the urgent need for stronger protections against discriminatory expulsion practices.

This section explores the intersection of these principles, focusing on how collective expulsions and border pushbacks disproportionately target marginalized racial and ethnic groups. Regional human rights systems, such as the Inter-American and African instruments, explicitly acknowledge this connection, addressing the interplay between racial discrimination and violations like collective expulsion. By examining these frameworks, the analysis underscores the need for a more comprehensive approach to tackling systemic racial injustice in migration policies.

We turn first to the interconnectedness of the two principles in the **Inter-American Convention.** In *Ricardo Canese v. Paraguay,* the Inter-American Court stressed the relevance and interconnectedness of Article 22 IACHR with other guarantees for the enjoyment of "the free development of the individual".[170] In doing so, the Court showcased that it does not apply this provision in a legal vacuum but sees its interconnectedness with other core principles of the Convention.

When it comes to the prohibition of collective expulsion, Article 1 IACHR is one of these interconnected core principles. Article 1 enshrines two essential duties, first, the obligation to respect the rights and freedoms of all individuals under their jurisdiction, and second, the obligation to guarantee their full and free exercise without any form of discrimination. The provision underscores the principle of equality and non-discrimination, prohibiting differential treatment based on factors such as race, color, sex, language, religion, political opinions, national or social origin, economic status, birth, or any other social condition.

Any form of treatment that can be deemed discriminatory in the exercise of any rights recognized in the Convention is inherently incompatible with its provisions.[171] The Inter-American Court reinforced this interpretation, noting in its Advisory Opinion on the Legal Status and Human Rights of the

170 *Ricardo Canese v. Paraguay* IACourtHR, Series C No. 111, 31 August 2004, para. 115.

171 IACoutHR *Cuadernillo de Jurisprudencia de la Corte Interamericana de Derechos Humanos No. 14: Igualdad y no-discriminación* 2019, para. 53.

Child that non-discrimination is an essential element in guaranteeing the full and free exercise of rights under the Convention.[172]

Article 1 imposes a duty on states to adopt positive measures that prevent discrimination and ensure that all individuals, regardless of their characteristics or conditions, can fully enjoy their fundamental rights.[173]

In its 2003 Advisory Opinion on the rights of undocumented migrants, the Inter-American Court of Human Rights emphasized the principle of equality before the law and the prohibition of discrimination, requiring states to adopt countervailing measures to address systemic disadvantages faced by migrants.[174] In subsequent cases, the Court also emphasized that, while states have the authority to determine the procedures and authorities to be used in these cases, the principles of non-discrimination and due process require that these procedures be predictable, coherent, and objective at every stage to prevent arbitrary decisions.[175]

When it comes to the interplay of non-discrimination and the prohibition of collective expulsion in the Inter-American Convention, the IACourt stressed their interconnectedness, as seen in *Nadege Dorzema v. Dominican Republic*.[176] Here, the Court highlighted that any proceeding leading to the expulsion or deportation of an individual must be conducted on an individual basis and must adhere to the principle of non-discrimination, explicitly prohibiting differential treatment based on nationality, color, race, sex, language, religion, political opinion, social origin, or other statuses.[177]

By linking these principles, the Court affirms that collective expulsion inherently violates non-discrimination because it disregards individualized assessments and often targets groups based on protected characteristics. This interpretation underscores that upholding the prohibition of collective expulsion is not only a procedural safeguard but also a substantive guarantee of equality, ensuring that all individuals, irrespective of their legal status or identity, are treated with fairness and dignity. For this reason, the Court

172 *Advisory Opinion on the Legal Status and Human Rights of the Child* IACourtHR, Serie A No. 17, OC-17/02, 8 August 2002, para. 43.

173 IACoutHR *Cuadernillo de Jurisprudencia de la Corte Interamericana de Derechos Humanos No. 14: Igualdad y no-discriminación* para. 53.

174 *Advisory Opinion on Juridical Condition and Rights of Undocumented Migrants* IACourtHR, Series A No. 18, requested by México, 17 September 2003, paras. 121–127.

175 IACoutHR *Cuadernillo de Jurisprudencia de la Corte Interamericana de Derechos Humanos No. 2: Personas en situación de migración o refugio* 2020, para. 157.

176 *Nadege Dorzema v. Dominican Republic* IACourtHR.

177 *Ibidem.*, para. 175.

then concluded that the Dominican Republic in the case at hand had violated not only the prohibition of collective expulsion, but also the non-discrimination principle by reasons of expelling them due to their Haitian background.[178]

In conclusion, the Inter-American Court of Human Rights underscores the intrinsic connection between the principles of non-discrimination and the prohibition of collective expulsion, as evidenced in its jurisprudence. It affirms that collective expulsion inherently violates the principle of non-discrimination by disregarding individualized assessments and targeting groups based on protected characteristics, thus breaching the substantive guarantees of equality and dignity enshrined in the American Convention.

In a similar vein and an even more poignant example showcasing the interconnectedness of the prohibition of collective expulsion and non-discrimination is the **African Charter.**

The focus on the discriminatory nature of prohibited mass expulsions in Article 12(5) ACHPR fits within the structure of the African Charter as a whole. The African Charter and its preamble mention the principle of non-discrimination several times. The Charter stresses that the members of the Organization of African Unity must eliminate "all forms of discrimination, particularly those based on race, ethnic group, colour, sex, language, religion or political opinions". Article 2 ACHPR repeats this notion and extends the Charter's protections to everyone without distinction.[179]

One reason for the focus on the discriminatory nature of mass expulsion in the African Charter arguably lays in the historical and political context. The OAU focused since its establishment primarily on the questions of mass movement of people across borders and the expulsion of large groups within Africa. The fact that in 1964, the Council of Ministers set up an ad-hoc commission consisting of ten African nations to deal with such issues

178 *Ibidem.*, para. 178.

179 The African Charter is, however, not the only instrument relying on the approach of the prohibition of discrimination in expulsion procedures. The *International Law Association* by attempting to denounce forced transfers of population in their (not legally binding) *1986 Declarations of the Principles of International Law on Mass Expulsions* relied on the non-discrimination approach established in the African Charter in order to define expulsion as "an act or a failure to act [...] with the intended effect of forcing the departure of persons against their will [...] for reason of race, nationality, membership of a particular social group or political opinion. See: International Law Association *Declaration of Principles of International Law on Mass Expulsion*, Report of the sixty-second Conference of the International Law Association, 1986, principle 14.

and find solutions to these problems supports this claim.[180] The United Nations High Commissioner for Refugees, among others, supported this attempt. The outcome was the OAU Convention Governing the Specific Aspects of Refugee Problems in Africa[181] (OAU Convention on Refugees)[182] in 1969.

African states did not only establish the Banjul Charter as an alternative concept to the European Human Rights system but also the 1969 OAU Refugee Convention. The latter aimed at a protection scheme tailored to the needs of post-colonial Africa. Its distinct definition of the term "refugee", for example, supports this finding.

Another reason for the inclusion and the distinct design of Article 12(5) ACHPR may have been the political circumstances in the period between the signature of the OAU Convention on Refugees in 1969 and the adoption of the African Charter on Human and Peoples' Rights in 1981.

In the decade between the two conventions, the need for such a provision had increased on the African continent as states committed several arbitrary mass expulsions. One example of such violations is the expulsion of the Nigerian immigrant community from Ghana in 1969[183] or the mass expulsion of all individuals of Asian descent from Uganda in 1972[184] as well as the expulsion of a large number of Banyarwanda in the early 1980s also from Uganda. Another example is the mass expulsion of several hundred thousand Nigerians from Ghana in 1965 and 1970.[185] In an attempt to prevent further similar mass expulsions, driven by xenophobic sentiments and

---

180 Kannyo, Edward *The Banjul Charter on Human and Peoples' Rights: Genesis and Political Background* in: Meltzer and Welch (eds.) Human Rights and Development in Africa (State University of New York Press 1984), p. 137.

181 *Organization of African Union Convention Governing the Specific Aspects of Refugee Problems in Africa* Adopted by the Assembly of Heads of State and Government at its sixth ordinary session, UNTS No. 14691, entry into force 20 June 1974.

182 Kannyo *The Banjul Charter on Human and Peoples' Rights: Genesis and Political Background* p. 137.

183 For a detailed analysis of the causes and impacts of this mass expulsions see here: Olaosebikan, Aremu and Adeyin, Thesea *Expulsion of Nigerian Immigrant Community from Ghana in 1969: Causes and Impact* Developing Country Studies, Vol. 4, No.10, 2001, pp. 176–186.

184 The government of Idi Amin assured by racial tensions within the country expelled almost the entire Asian population. For a detailed analysis on the correlation between the mass expulsion of Asian decedents from Uganda and the development of Art. 12(5) African Charter see: Henckaerts, Jean-Marie *Mass Expulsion in Modern International Law and Practice* pp. 22–24.

185 Manby, Bronwen *Struggles for Citizenship in Africa* p. 96.

ethnic conflicts, the drafters may have designed Article 12(5) ACHPR in a fashion to prevent future violations thereof.

An argument in favor of this finding is the different approach taken in the earliest drafts (M'Baye draft[186]). The M'baye draft, named after the then president of the International Court of Justice Kéba M'Baye, adopted verbatim the prohibition of collective expulsion as enshrined in Article 22(9) IACHR and Article 4 Protocol 4 ECHR. This approach was utterly lost in the following Dakar Draft,[187] which was the result of the 1979 Dakar Meeting of Experts.

Article 12(5) Dakar Draft stipulates in its first sentence that "[t]he mass expulsion of non-nationals shall be prohibited". In so far, the drafts and the final version are identical in terms. The second sentence to the paragraph, however, differs completely. The adopted provision in the African Charter states that "mass expulsion shall be that which is aimed at national, racial, ethnic or religious groups". The Dakar Draft, in contrast, stipulated that "no economic, political or other reasons would justify such a measure". The difference between these two approaches is significant. The final version contains a prohibition of discrimination, the earlier versions rely on an approach which does not define the term, but instead points out that no derogation of this prohibition is possible.

As Rubner explains, the reason for this change may lay in the drafters' will to point out that the problem of collective expulsion in the African context did not so much stem from the expulsion of the Ugandan Asians during the era of Idi Amin, but rather from other inter-African expulsions.[188]

The drafts of the African Charter, including the prohibition of collective expulsion, underwent significant substantive amendments before its adoption in Banjul, the Gambia, in 1981. The regional character was stipulated even more dominantly, and the prohibition of mass expulsion was adjusted.

186 M'Baye, Kéba *Draft African Charter on Human and Peoples' Rights* (*M'Baye proposal*) prepared for the Meeting of Experts in Dakar, Senegal from 28 November to 8 December 1979, CAB/LEG/67/1.

187 *Guiding Principle 1, No. 3Preliminary draft of the African Charter prepared during the Dakar Meeting of Experts at the end of 1979* CAB/LEG/67/3/Rev. 1, reprinted in Human Rights Law in Africa Vol. 4 (1999), pp. 81–91.

188 Dr. Nathaniel Rubner, yet unpublished monograph. The document is on file with the author. *The African Charter on Human and Peoples' Rights: Political, Intellectual and cultural origins* (provisional title). This section builds on the research and ideas developed in Rubner's doctoral work: Nathaniel Rubner, An Historical Investigation of the Origins of the African Charter on Human and Peoples' Rights, 2008, available at: http://archives.au.int/handle/123456789/2566.

Naldi describes this development as a weakening of the prohibition that "appears totally to undermine the original intention since it seems that ethnic groups could be expelled on economic grounds".[189] This amendment, which restricted the comprehensive scope of protection of the prohibition seems to have been compensated through interpretation by the African Commission.

The Commission applied the prohibition of mass expulsion in all its case-law jointly with the general prohibition of discrimination enshrined in Article 2 of the Charter. This joint application led to the complementation of the prohibition's scope of protection.

The chosen approach in the African Charter arguably suggests that the drafters wanted to stress that every mass expulsion based on xenophobic or ethnic resentments is prohibited. It is not surprising that the drafters decided for this approach in light of the heinous crimes of mass expulsion that had occurred on a widespread level in the 1960s and 1970s in Africa.

In retrospect, this tool aiming at the prevention of collective expulsions turned out to be ineffective, even after the adoption of the Charter in 1981. Before the prohibition of mass expulsion became legally binding for the member states with the Charter's entry into force in 1986, Nigeria expelled two million foreigners in 1983 and about 700,000 in 1985.[190]

Jean-Marc Sore acknowledges the great importance of the prohibition of mass expulsion in the African context. Nevertheless, he also points out that it is questionable if Article 12(5) ACHPR has achieved its aim of preventing such grave human rights violations and claims a "relative weakness of paragraph 12(5) in contrast to similar international instruments".[191]

Nevertheless, the provision is of particular significance in the framework of the African Charter. The fact that the article does not contain a "claw-back-clause" to limit the scope of application emphasizes this finding.

189 Naldi, Gino *The Organization of African Unity: An Analysis of its Role* (Bloomsbury Academic 1999), p. 111.

190 New York Times Nigeria Completes the Second Expulsion of Aliens The New York Times, 26 May 1985, available at: http://www.nytimes.com/1985/05/26/world/nigeria-completes-the-second-expulsion-of-aliens.html.

191 Sorel, Jean-Marc *Article 12* in: Kamto and Collectif *La Charte africaine des droits de l'homme et des peuples et le protocole y relatif portant création de la Cour africaine des droits de l'homme: Commentaire article par article* (Emile Bruylant 2011), p. 306. The original French version reads: "la relative faiblesse du paragraphe 5 de l'article 12 au regard des autres instruments internationaux".

Several provisions in the Banjul Charter contain these clauses to limit their scope of application rather than containing general derogation clauses, as found in other human rights conventions.[192] Thus, the fact that Article 12(5) is not limited by a "claw-back clause" or by any other form of restriction stresses its importance. The provision's non-derogation nature is even more significant given the fact that in general social economic and cultural rights prevail over civil and political rights within the charter. The preamble of the African Charter stipulates in its seventh paragraph the particular focus of the Charter on economic, social, and cultural rights, which are "a guarantee for the enjoyment of civil and political rights". Gittleman stresses that the African Commission has indicated that in case of a collision between economic, social, and cultural rights with civil and political rights, the first-mentioned rights prevail.[193]

In most cases in which the African Commission considered the prohibition of mass expulsion in Article 12 ACHPR, it also referred to Article 2 ACHPR, the prohibition of discrimination.[194] In *Malawi African Association and Others v. Mauritania*, the Commission held that Article 2 "lays down a principle that is essential to the spirit of this convention, one of whose goals is the elimination of all forms of discrimination and to ensure equality amongst all human beings".[195]

Comparing the attributes on which basis discrimination is prohibited in Article 2 and Article 12(5) ACHPR, it becomes apparent that the range of attributes in Article 2 is considerably broader. Article 2 includes "all forms

192 Turack, Daniel *The African Charter on Human and Peoples' Rights: Some Preliminary Thoughts* Akron Law Review, (1984), Vol. 17, No. 3, pp. 365–366. Other civil and political rights guaranteed in the Charter, such as the right to liberty and security enshrined in Art. 6 of the Charter contain such a clause stipulating that "no one may be deprived of his freedom except for reasons and conditions [emphasis added] previously laid down by law". Another example can be found in Article 12(4) ACHPR which prohibits the arbitrary expulsion of legally residing non-nationals unless they have received "a decision taken in accordance with the law".

193 Gittleman, Richard *The Banjul Charter on Human and Peoples' Rights: A legal Analysis* in: Welch and Meltzer Human Rights and Development in Africa (State University of New York Press 1984), pp. 154–155.

194 Olaniyan, Kolawole *Civil and Political Rights in the African Charter: Articles 8–14* in: Evans and Murray *The African Charter on Human and Peoples' Rights: The System in Practice 1986–2006* (Cambridge University Press 2008), p. 232.

195 *Malawi African Association and others v. Mauritania* Communications Nos. 54/91, 61/91, 164/97-196/97, 210/98, Thirteenth Activity Report 1999–2000, Annex V, para. 131.

of discrimination" and only lists some attributes that are "particularly" noteworthy.[196] To ensure that all reasons for mass expulsions of non-nationals are covered, the scope of protection ought to be broad and flexible.

Article 2 ACHPR speaks of granting the "rights recognized and guaranteed" in the Charter to "every individual" "without any distinction". *Ergo*, the prohibition of collective expulsion in Article 12(5) ACHPR also covers other forms of discrimination that go beyond the self-contained list of the provision.

The fact that the African Commission referred in all its judgments on mass expulsion to the non-discrimination clause of Article 2 Banjul Charter supports this finding.[197]

In *Fédération Internationale des Ligues des Droits de l'Homme v. Angola* of 1997, the Commission highlighted this finding by pointing out that economic difficulties do not justify in any way the turn of States to radical measures "aimed at protecting their nationals and their economies from non-nationals". The Commission then proclaimed that

> whatever the circumstances may be, however, such measures should not be taken at the detriment of the enjoyment of human rights. Mass expulsions of *any category of persons*, whether on the basis of nationality, religion, ethnic, racial or **other** *considerations* constitute *a special violation* of human rights [emphasis added].[198]

A similar approach was chosen by the Commission in the case *Malawi African Association and others v. Mauritania*. The Commission held here that Article 2 "lays down a principle that is essential to the spirit of the convention, one of whose goals is the elimination of *all forms of discrimination* [emphasis added] and to ensure equality among all human beings".[199]

---

196 Umozurike, Oji *The African Charter on Human and Peoples' Rights* (Nigerian Institute of Advanced Legal Studies 1992), p. 7.

197 *Organisation Mondiale Contre la Torture et. al. v. Rwanda* ACHPR; *Rencontre Africaine pour la Défense des Droits de l'Homme v. Zambia* ACHPR; *Fédération Internationale des Ligues des Droits de l'Homme v. Angola* ACHPR; *African Institute for Human Rights and Development v. Guinea* ACHPR, and *Institute for Human Rights and Development in Africa v. Republic of Angola* ACHPR.

198 *Union Inter Africaine des Droits de l'Homme et. al. v. Angola* para. 16.

199 *Malawi African Association and others v. Mauritania* ACHPR, Thirteenth Activity Report 1990–2000, Annex V, para. 131.

These cases support the finding that Article 2 ACHPR extends the narrow list of attributes of prohibited discrimination in Article 12(5) ACHPR. To ensure a comprehensive scope of protection against arbitrary expulsions, Article 12(5), Article 2(1), Article 7(1)(a), and Article 12(4) African Charter apply conjunctively. This finding is in line with the African Commission's approach to guarantee comprehensive protection against discrimination concerning all rights and freedoms enshrined in the Charter.

The interconnectedness between the prohibition of collective expulsion and non-discrimination in the Inter-American and African human rights systems underscores the indivisibility of human rights. The Inter-American Court of Human Rights, through its interpretation of Articles 1 and 22 of the American Convention, emphasizes that collective expulsions inherently violate the principle of equality by neglecting individualized assessments and often targeting groups based on protected characteristics. Similarly, the African Charter's Articles 2 and 12(5) reinforce that mass expulsions predicated on discriminatory grounds, such as nationality, race, or economic status, constitute severe violations of human rights. The African Commission, particularly in cases like *Fédération Internationale des Ligues des Droits de l'Homme v. Angola*, affirmed that even economic or social pressures cannot justify measures that disproportionately affect marginalized groups, extending the scope of protection against arbitrary and discriminatory practices.

On the international level, the Migrant Worker Committee and the Committee on the Elimination of Racial Discrimination (CERD) have equally emphasized the critical interconnectedness between the prohibition of collective expulsion and non-discrimination. In its 2021 concluding observations on Chile's second periodic report, the CMW underscored that administrative expulsion procedures must adhere to both individual assessment and non-discrimination principles.[200] This includes ensuring that expulsions are not based on factors such as nationality, skin color, or social origin, and providing guarantees such as the right to appeal and access to legal assistance.[201]

Similarly, CERD, in its General Recommendation No. 30 of 2004, explicitly called on states to ensure that non-citizens are not subject to collective expulsions where personal circumstances have not been considered, thus

200 Committee on the Protection of the Rights of All Migrant Workers and Members of Their Families *Concluding observations on the second periodic report of Chile* CMW/C/CHL/CO/2, 11 May 2021, para. 27.

201 *Ibidem.*, para. 48.

preventing both discriminatory intent and effect.[202] Furthermore, CERD's 2022 statement on the Melilla border "tragedy"[203] highlighted the need for non-discriminatory practices in expulsions and equal access to effective remedies for non-citizens, underscoring the universal application of equality and fairness at borders.[204]

These findings collectively stress the imperative for states to address systemic biases in migration governance by addressing the individual dimension of arbitrary expulsions by relying on the prohibition of collective expulsion and the collective dimension in case of discriminatory practices by examining violations of the non-discrimination principle.

The analysis of this jurisprudence demonstrates that these two regional human rights systems alongside the two international bodies CMW and CERD view the prohibition of collective expulsion not only as a procedural safeguard but also as a substantive guarantee of equality. The African Commission's broader interpretation of Article 2 ACHPR to encompass a wide range of discriminatory attributes, coupled with its insistence on upholding non-discrimination even in challenging circumstances, aligns with the IACourtHR's acknowledgment of interconnected rights. Together, these interpretations offer a framework for preventing the use of collective expulsions as a tool for perpetuating systemic inequality.

The same is true for interpretations of the interconnectedness of the two principles by the Migrant Worker Committee and the Committee On the Elimination of Racial Discrimination.

The interconnectedness of these principles is particularly relevant in expulsion and border contexts, where policies often reflect and amplify discriminatory attitudes, such as racism, xenophobia, and economic exclusion. Border management and migration policies can become mechanisms for targeting specific groups based on nationality, ethnicity, or socio-economic conditions, which not only violate individual rights but also perpetuate

---

202 CERD *General Recommendation No. 30 on the discrimination of non-citizens* CERD/C/64/Misc.11/rev.3, 2004, para. 26.

203 The UN Committee on the Elimination of Racial Discrimination made clear in its "statement on the tragic events at the Moroccan-Spanish Border" on the death of at least 23 migrants at the Melilla border in June 2022 that expulsions at the border "do not discriminate in purpose or effect among non-citizens on grounds of race, colour or ethnic or national origin, and that non-citizens have equal access to effective remedies, including the right to challenge expulsion orders, and are allowed effectively to pursue such remedies". See: CERD *Statement on the Tragic Events at Moroccan-Spanish Border* No. 3, 2022, 107th Session, 8–30 August 2022, p. 2.

204 *Ibidem.*

systemic inequalities. By embedding non-discrimination into the prohibition of collective expulsion, courts ensure that individuals are not reduced to mere representations of their group identity and that states cannot exploit broad categorizations to justify expulsions or non-admission.

The European Court of Human Rights could learn from the Inter-American, African and international systems by adopting a similarly integrated approach in its collective expulsion jurisprudence. Applying Article 14 ECHR, which prohibits discrimination, to complement Article 4 Protocol 4 on collective expulsion, would allow the Court to address not only procedural irregularities but also the underlying discriminatory motivations often driving such policies. This would strengthen protections by acknowledging the collective dimension of rights violations, addressing systemic inequalities, and challenging racist or xenophobic undercurrents in state practices. Strategic litigants before the ECtHR could advance this approach, advocating for the recognition of interconnected rights to ensure comprehensive accountability and protection.

5 Conclusions on the Role of the Prohibition of Collective Expulsion within the Human Rights System

The prohibition of collective expulsion serves as a fundamental safeguard in international human rights law, bridging the protection of individual and collective rights. It underscores the necessity of procedural guarantees, ensuring that each individual's circumstances are assessed fairly and without discrimination before an expulsion or when requesting access at the border.

While its primary aim is to protect individuals from arbitrary or indiscriminate removal, the principle also addresses systemic patterns of exclusion, which often target specific groups. This dual dimension, individual and collective, complicates its enforcement but highlights its importance in maintaining fairness and due process in migration and expulsion contexts.

This prohibition is deeply intertwined with broader human rights principles, such as the right to a fair trial, effective remedies, and protection against discrimination. Regional human rights systems, particularly the Inter-American and African framework, have expanded procedural safeguards for migrants, emphasizing individualized assessments and due process even in administrative contexts. In contrast, the European system, while robust in some areas, offers more limited protections in expulsion procedures, underscoring the need for stronger harmonization of these rights across systems.

The interplay between the prohibition of collective expulsion and the principle of *non-refoulement* further demonstrates their complementary nature. Both aim to protect individuals from harm, yet they operate through distinct mechanisms, *non-refoulement* as a substantive safeguard against return to danger, and the prohibition of collective expulsion as a procedural right ensuring individualized review. Together, they form a cohesive framework addressing the minimum procedural guarantees before expulsions or in non-admission scenarios.

Furthermore, the evolving nature of international human rights law reflects the shift from a state-centered to a rights-based paradigm. This progression underscores the importance of balancing state sovereignty with individual human rights. By addressing both individual and systemic violations, the prohibition of collective expulsion exemplifies the hybrid nature of migration protections, ensuring procedural guarantees for individuals while challenging broader patterns of exclusion and discrimination.

The relationship between the prohibition of collective expulsion and the prohibition of discrimination is a cornerstone of safeguarding procedural guarantees and equality in migration governance. As demonstrated by the jurisprudence of the Inter-American Court of Human Rights and the African Commission on Human and Peoples' Rights, these principles are deeply intertwined, offering both procedural safeguards and substantive guarantees.

The principle of non-discrimination strengthens the prohibition of collective expulsion by addressing systemic inequalities and ensuring individualized assessments, while the prohibition of collective expulsion operationalizes non-discrimination by preventing states from targeting marginalized groups through arbitrary or racially motivated practices.

At the international level, the Migrant Worker Committee and the Committee on the Elimination of Racial Discrimination echo this interconnected approach, emphasizing that expulsions must be free from both discriminatory intent and effect. This dual focus underscores the critical need for migration policies to go beyond formal equality and actively dismantle systemic barriers rooted in racism, xenophobia, and economic exclusion. Courts and treaty bodies should play a key role in dismantling such underlying tendencies by turning both to an assessment of violations of the prohibition of collective expulsion and non-discrimination.

Ultimately, embedding non-discrimination within the prohibition of collective expulsion ensures that migration control measures uphold the principles of fairness, dignity, and equality. This integrated approach not only mitigates the risks of systemic injustice but also challenges the structural biases embedded in border and migration systems.

The European Court of Human Rights, by adopting similar interpretations under Articles 4 Protocol 4 and 14 ECHR, has the potential to enhance its protections, addressing not only procedural violations but also the broader discriminatory undercurrents in migration governance. Such advancements would represent a significant step towards ensuring that all individuals, regardless of nationality or status, are treated with fairness and respect at international borders. Turning to its sister courts and to the international level could be a helpful source for judges and litigants in collective expulsion cases.

CHAPTER 5

Conclusion and Future Reflections

This final chapter brings together the insights and analyses developed throughout the book, offering a synthesis of the findings from the preceding chapters (1). It revisits the core themes explored, from the foundational role of the prohibition of collective expulsion in protecting migrants' rights to its interpretation and application across diverse human rights regimes. By connecting these threads, this chapter not only underscores the prohibition's enduring relevance in addressing the challenges of migration but also situates it within broader discussions about global mobility, migration policies, and human rights. Building on the introduction's reflection on Hannah Arendt's concept of the "right to have rights", the past four chapter have shown how the prohibition of collective expulsion is not merely a procedural safeguard but an important mechanism for upholding due process and a path to protection at borders. In a world where migration policies are increasingly shaped by exclusionary practices, the prohibition offers a legal and moral framework to counter these trends. The past chapters took a retrospective analysis of the principle's role in human rights instruments and jurisprudence as well as a forward-looking approach to its potential to offer even more inclusive and holistic protection in expulsion and non-admission cases. By weaving together the insights of the previous chapters, this conclusion offers a lens through which to examine future cases entailing the prohibition of collective expulsion. Finally, the second part of this concluding chapter offers some final reflections on the movement of people across borders in today's globalized world, the way ahead, and the role which the prohibition of collective expulsion may play therein (2).

1 Conclusions and Core Findings

Human mobility has been a constant throughout history, driven by the quest for protection, safety, and improved opportunities. While migration can offer significant social, economic, and humanitarian benefits for both migrants and receiving states, it may also present complex challenges related to national security, political identity, and social cohesion. As migration has become increasingly politicized, public debates and legal frameworks have shifted to address the tensions between state sovereignty and

 | DOI:10.1163/9789004535077_006

the protection of migrant rights. In this context, the evolving human rights system, particularly at the regional level, has played a pivotal role in ensuring that migrants are afforded basic protections despite states' increasing and restrictive control over migration flows.

In this context, the main protagonist of this book, the prohibition of collective expulsion, emerges as a significant safeguard in this landscape, ensuring that migrants are not subjected to arbitrary or discriminatory expulsions and in upholding their fundamental rights as individuals within the broader framework of international human rights treaty law. As this book has shown, the prohibition of collective expulsion is a fundamental principle of human rights law, serving as an important safeguard for the protection of migrants and asylum seekers. This principle, deeply rooted in the notion of individual rights, requires that each foreigner's case be assessed on its own merits rather than subjecting them to arbitrary expulsion as part of a group. It transcends a mere procedural safeguard; it is a cornerstone of a legal framework that upholds migrants' and asylum seekers' rights in the face of increasingly restrictive migration policies, expulsion practices, and the extraterritorialization of migration control.

Central to the prohibition is the recognition of migrants as individuals with inherent rights, regardless of their legal status or nationality. The theoretical foundation of this right is not only visible in law but also in philosophy such as in Hannah Arendt's concept of the "right to have rights" created in the aftermath of the horrors of World War II. This concept underscores the vulnerability of stateless individuals and refugees. For Arendt, the deprivation of political recognition renders individuals invisible and exposed to grave human rights violations. The prohibition of collective expulsion directly responds to this vulnerability by ensuring that every migrant's right to remain, or to contest expulsion, is recognized and respected.

Throughout this book, this central theme is explored within the context of various international and regional human rights frameworks. On the regional level, the European Convention on Human Rights, the Inter-American Convention on Human Rights, and the African Charter on Human and Peoples' Rights, amongst others, enshrine the prohibition of collective expulsion, albeit with different nuances. These frameworks emphasize procedural guarantees, including the right to an individual assessment of each expulsion case. In doing so, they provide a broader understanding of migrants as human beings entitled to procedural guarantees and protection, not simply as faceless individuals in a group. However, despite its numerous codifications, the prohibition often remains overshadowed by other rights principles, particularly the *non-refoulement* principle.

This book aims to bring the prohibition of collective expulsion to the forefront of human rights discourse, advocating for its recognition as a relevant safeguard for migrants' rights, especially in the face of increasingly restrictive state practices.

The restrictive evolution of such practices is mirrored in the evolving jurisprudence surrounding the prohibition. The analysis of case law on the prohibition of regional and international courts, committees, and treaty bodies reveals its dynamic application in response to shifting migration patterns and state practices. Courts and human rights bodies have adapted this principle to confront contemporary challenges, ensuring its relevance in a rapidly changing global context.

A comparison of the regional codifications of the prohibition and its interpretative evolution highlights the principle's essential guarantees throughout the regional conventions. The prohibition contains procedural guarantees that must accompany any expulsion, regardless of the number of individuals involved. It is the lack of individualized assessments, not the scale of the expulsion, that defines collective expulsions and raises significant human rights concerns. In this respect, the book argues for a unified approach to these protections, stressing the importance of the procedural guarantees contained therein as well as its interconnectedness with other core guarantees such as the prohibition of discrimination, fair trial rights, and most importantly, the *non-refoulement* principle.

The latter and the prohibition of collective expulsion are intricately linked, both of which work in tandem to protect migrants from arbitrary expulsions and forced returns to dangerous situations. While these principles share a common goal, they differ in scope and application. *Non-refoulement* primarily focuses on the protection against return to persecution or torture, while the prohibition of collective expulsion ensures that expulsions are not carried out without due process, regardless of the migrant's status. Together, these principles form a minimum of a legal shield against the arbitrary treatment of migrants and underscore the need for procedural safeguards such as legal assistance, translation services, and the right to appeal.

These safeguards, explored in-depth throughout the book, are essential in ensuring that migrants are not subjected to arbitrary expulsions and that their rights are upheld in the expulsion process.

Moreover, the interplay between individual rights and collective dynamics in migration law is a key theme related to the prohibition of collective expulsion. While the prohibition is fundamentally an individual right, its application may sometimes intersect with group-based dynamics, particularly when systemic patterns of expulsions target specific nationalities or migrant groups. In this scenario, the prohibition reflects a balance between addressing systemic patterns of expulsion and upholding individual protections. While group-based expulsions often occur in response to perceived security threats or social control mechanisms, human rights law mandates that each case be evaluated individually. This ensures that the rights of vulnerable migrants are not overlooked in the face of large-scale expulsions.

In doing so, the prohibition aims to address two Interconnected levels: Individual examinations and the contextual situation of the expulsion. However, this balancing approach should be more evident in the case law of regional courts. Both group-level and individualized remedies are necessary to address systemic violations. At the same time, preserving the procedural safeguards essential for protecting individual rights remains crucial.

The book further highlights the evolving nature of the prohibition of collective expulsion, particularly in light of growing concerns over large-scale migration and security risks. States often treat large-scale migration as a security threat, leading to limitations from human rights protections. However, the global human rights framework continues to push back against such practices, advocating for a nuanced understanding of migration that balances the legitimate interests of states with the fundamental rights of migrants. This tension between state sovereignty and human rights protection remains a central challenge in the governance of migration. In this context, the prohibition of collective expulsion serves as a bridge between state sovereignty and the protection of migrant rights. While states retain the authority to control migration, the prohibition ensures that this power is not exercised in a manner that undermines basic guarantees. By requiring individualized assessments and procedural guarantees, such as access to legal assistance and the right to appeal, the prohibition acts as a safeguard against the potential abuse of state power in the realm of the movement across borders.

As we turn to the future of migration in a rapidly changing world, the prohibition of collective expulsion remains a pivotal legal principle. The increasing use of extraterritorial practices, restrictive border policies, and the growing politicization of migration raise pressing questions about the future of migrants' rights as will be shown in the following section.

2 Future Reflections on Migration in Today's World

As highlighted before, human mobility is as old as humanity itself. From the earliest migrations in search of sustenance and safety to the movement of peoples across continents to build new lives, migration has been a defining feature of human existence. It is how we survived and thrived. Yet, in today's world, particularly in the Global North, migration has become one of the most contentious issues and has arguably contributed to a rise in right-wing parties and election successes.[1]

As a consequence, states fortify borders, erect fences, and impose ever more restrictive laws and policies to control who may enter and who may not. Building walls to keep a nation's population in, as in the case of the Berlin wall, or foreigners out, as in the case of the US-Mexican border, is not a phenomenon of recent times. Critiquing their effectiveness is almost as old as their existence. Niccoló Machiavelli, a diplomat, politician, and philosopher of the Renaissance concluded in 1531 that "Fortresses do much more Harm than Good".[2]

While at the end of the 1940s, there were less than five border walls worldwide, this number consistently increased to fifteen in 1989, and almost seventy border walls in 2014.[3] The border fences between Spain and Morocco, India and Bangladesh, and Saudi Arabia and Yemen are notable contemporary examples of global fortification trends. Fortification serves as a visible symbol of power and protection, particularly in an era where states struggle to fully guarantee these attributes.[4] Border walls are widely perceived as emblems of exclusion, stability, and the preservation of a nation's perceived homogeneity, fostering a narrative of "us against them".[5] The promise of sealing off borders to exclude non-nationals has proven to be an effective political strategy, as evidenced by recent election outcomes in countries such as the United States, Poland, or Italy.

Fortification manifests in various ways, including the construction of physical barriers such as walls and fences, the deployment of high-tech security systems, military personnel, and measures like pushbacks or

---

1 On the phenomenon in Europe, see: Robinson, Kali and Roy, Diana *Europe's Migration Dilemma* Council on Foreign Relations, 31 May 2024, available at: https://www.cfr.org/article/europes-migration-dilemma. On the phenomenon in the USA, see: Cheatham, Amelia; Klobucista, Claire and Roy, Diana *The U.S. Immigration Debate* Council on Foreign Relations, 7 August 2024, available at: https://www.cfr.org/backgrounder/us-immigration-debate-0.

2 Machiavelli, Niccoló *The Discourse on The First Ten Books of Tituts Livius* Kegan Paul, Trench & Co., 1883, p. 288.

3 Vallet, Élisabeth *Borders, Fences and Walls: State of Insecurity?* (Ashgate Publishing 2014), figure 1.

4 Brown, Wendy *Walled States, Waning Sovereignty* (Zone Books 2nd edn. 2017), p. 9.

5 *Ibidem.*

pullbacks beyond state territory to prevent irregular entry. These strategies collectively reflect an escalating focus on controlling migration and reinforcing state sovereignty at borders.

This trend has been described as a response to the diminishing influence of nation-states and their waning ability to control the movement of goods, information, money, and people.[6] While fortification and extraterritorialization are often framed as strategies to adapt to an increasingly globalized world, they also reflect a deep-seated fear of losing governmental control and authority.

Issues of migration, refuge, state sovereignty, and security have become increasingly intertwined. For some policymakers, sealing off borders has emerged as the favored solution to these complex challenges, despite its contentious implications.

At the same time, research highlights the long-term ineffectiveness of border walls and increased fortification measures.[7] Scholars have demonstrated that such approaches fail to address the underlying causes of migration and often produce limited results in deterring movement.[8] Moreover, statistics from the International Organization for Migration reveal that fortification efforts come with a tragic cost, significantly increasing the death toll as people on the move are forced to take more perilous routes.[9]

As addressed, some forms of migration control violate international human rights law. Building barriers can prevent individuals from seeking asylum, contradicting the principles of refugee law. The 1951 Refugee Convention recognizes the right of asylum seekers to approach a state's border and submit a claim for protection. When border posts are inaccessible or fail to assess these claims, the object and purpose of the Convention are compromised.[10] This issue is evident at the Spanish-Moroccan border

6 Saddiki, Said *World of walls: the structure, roles and effectiveness of separation barriers* (Open Book Publisher 2017), p. 121.

7 See for example: Brown, Wendy *Walled States, Waning Sovereignty* and Jones, Reece *Borders and Walls: Do Barriers Deter Unauthorized Migration?* Migration Policy Institute, 2016, available at: https://www.migrationpolicy.org/article/borders-and-walls-do-barriers-deter-unauthorized-migration.

8 *Ibidem.*

9 International Organization for Migration *Fatal Journeys Tracking Lives Lost during Migration 2014* available at: https://publications.iom.int/system/files/pdf/fataljourneys_countingtheuncounted.pdf, p. 57.

10 Hathaway, James *Fixing the Refugee System* ESIL lecture at the Faculty of Law of the University of Amsterdam on 13 May 2016, available at: https://www.youtube.com/watch?v=e_8AL4rVedg.

fences in Ceuta and Melilla, where migrants are reportedly expelled directly to Morocco without proper evaluation, exposing them to significant risks and violating the principle of *non-refoulement*.[11] Furthermore, collective expulsions without providing an opportunity to present claims contravene the prohibition of collective expulsion. Such practices undermine the Convention's core objective of ensuring the protection and rights of refugees by denying asylum seekers the chance to have their claims properly considered.[12]

While this is not a new phenomenon, the last few decades have seen a continuous tightening of these guarantees. Following moments of profound reckoning, such as the Holocaust, the global community paused, reflected, and acted, as seen in the establishment of instruments like the 1951 Refugee Convention. Even though a child of its time, established during the Cold War era, the Convention's object and purpose "to give voice and force to rights for refugees"[13] exemplifies this. The 1951 Convention and other human rights instruments were an acknowledgment of Hannah Arendt's "right to have rights", as examined in Chapter 1, a reminder that ensuring access to basic guarantees is essential to preserving human dignity. This reflection naturally raises the question where do we stand today, and what might the future hold for migrants, asylum seekers, and refugees around the globe? We are, undeniably, at a pivotal moment.

In the United States, the reelection of Donald Trump in November 2024 has triggered forceful mass deportations of non-citizens,[14] a strategy relying heavily on neighboring countries like Mexico and Panama.[15] Such an approach exacerbates existing vulnerabilities for migrants and asylum seekers in Latin America, which have already faced pressure to implement

11 Asylum Information Data Base and European Council on Refugees and Exiles *Access to the Territories and Push Backs: Spain* available at: https://www.asylumineurope.org/reports/country/spain/access-territory-and-push-backs.

12 Feller, Erika *The Refugee Convention at 60: Still fit for its Purpose?" Protection Tools for Protection Needs* statement for Workshop on Refugees and the Refugee Convention 60 Years On: Protection and Identity, 2 May 2011, p. 4.

13 *Ibidem.*

14 Gold, Michael and Savage *Trump Confirms Plans to Use the Military to Assist in Mass Deportations* New York Times, 18 November 2024, updated 20 November 2024, available at: https://www.nytimes.com/2024/11/18/us/politics/trump-military-mass-deportation.html.

15 Alvarez, Priscilla *Trump team maps out Latin America strategy as part of mass deportation plan* CNN, 21 November 2024, available at: https://edition.cnn.com/2024/11/21/politics/donald-trump-border-politics/index.html.

stricter border controls.[16] As these nations collaborate with the US, they experience increased militarization of borders, leading to human rights violations and the criminalization of migrants.[17] Additionally, the strain on local resources resulted in a lack of adequate protection for refugees and asylum seekers, pushing many into dangerous, informal migratory routes.[18] The externalization of US-border policies also undermines regional solidarity, fracturing cooperative efforts to address migration humanely and comprehensively.

At the same time, these plans of mass deportation echo historical precedents, such as Operation Wetback[19] in the 1950s, which saw the large-scale deportation of Mexican nationals based on racial profiling.[20] Trump's approach, however, seeks to escalate the scale and severity of such actions, relying on detention camps and the abrogation of asylum to deter migrants. This represents a stark rollback of protections and a dismissal of the hard-won lessons of history.

Similarly, in Europe, the externalization of borders and pushbacks, whether at the Mediterranean or the eastern ones, reflect a broader trend of restricting access to asylum. The New Pact on Migration and Asylum, slated for implementation by 2026, envisions detention-like conditions at the EU's outer borders, raising grave concerns about its alignment with fundamental human rights standards.[21]

---

16 Riemer, Lena *Guarding the Gates: The Externalization of U.S. Migration Policies and Their Impact Across the Americas* Externalizing Asylum: A compendium of scientific knowledge, 31 July 2024, available at: https://externalizingasylum.info/guarding-the-gates/.

17 *Ibidem.*

18 *Ibidem.*

19 The name of the initiative was derived from the derogatory term "wetback", used to describe the large number of Mexican immigrants who crossed the Rio Grande to enter the United States illegally. In 1953, for instance, the US federal government apprehended approximately 886,000 individuals for illegally entering the country from Mexico. The initiative had two main goals: To reduce the influx of undocumented Mexican workers into the United States and to deter employers from hiring such workers.

20 Funderburk, Brent *Operation Wetback United States immigration law-enforcement campaign* Britannica, available at: https://www.britannica.com/topic/Operation-Wetback.

21 For a detailed assessment see: Brandl, Ulrike *Mix and Match. Detention, "De-Facto Detention" or just Restrictions of Freedom of Movement in the New Pact* EU Migration Law Blog, 14 October 2024, available at: https://eumigrationlawblog.eu/mix-and-match-detention-de-facto-detention-or-just-restrictions-of-freedom-of-movement-in-the-new-pact/.

In this context, it is important to remember that collective expulsions, restrictions on the rights of migrants and asylum seekers, and the externalization of migration controls, often underpinned by racist policies, are not confined to Global North states like the USA and the EU. These practices are also prevalent in countries such as Chile, which has continuously carried out collective expulsions in recent years,[22] the Dominican Republic, where Haitians face widespread deportations and discrimination,[23] and Tunisia, where African migrants and asylum seekers have been subjected to violent expulsions.[24] These actions violate established human rights and refugee protection standards, reflecting a broader global trend that, while not new, has intensified in recent years. This shift is accompanied by increasingly stringent measures and a pervasive anti-migration rhetoric that fuels xenophobia and undermines international legal commitments to protect the dignity and rights of those on the move.

These troubling practices raise pressing questions about the trajectory of migrants' and asylum seekers' rights, particularly at borders, where these violations often manifest most acutely. What does this mean for the future of these rights in an era marked by growing hostility and exclusion? First, the trend of restricting migration and externalizing border control appears likely to continue. States are framing migration increasingly as a security threat, a challenge to sovereignty (e.g., the "instrumentalization" of migrants), or an instrument of political leverage.[25]

This critical shift in European border policies, where migration is increasingly framed as a "crisis", a "hybrid threat", or a tool of political "instrumentalization",[26] has led to the adoption of heightened security measures, often

---

22 Doña-Reveco, Cristián *How Chile's welcome turned sour* Mixed Migration Centre, 18 April 2024, available at: https://mixedmigration.org/chiles-response-to-migration/.

23 Amnesty International *Dominican Republic: Authorities must end de facto racist migration policies* 2 April 2024, available at: https://www.amnesty.org/en/latest/news/2024/04/dominican-republic-must-stop-racist-immigration-policies/.

24 Human Rights Watch *Tunisia: African Migrants Intercepted at Sea, Expelled Apparent Policy Shift Endangers Migrants, Asylum Seekers, Children* 10 October 2023, available at: https://www.hrw.org/news/2023/10/10/tunisia-african-migrants-intercepted-sea-expelled.

25 For a detailed assessment on this development, see: Gkliati, Mariana *Let's Call It what It Is: Hybrid Threats and Instrumentalisation as the Evolution of Securitisation in Migration Management* European Papers, Vol. 8, 2023, No. 2, pp. 576 ff.

26 See, for example: Republic of Poland *A hybrid attack on Poland* 9 August 2022, available at: https://www.gov.pl/web/special-services/a-hybrid-attack-on-poland or European Union *Strategic Compass for Security and Defence* 2022, available at: https://www.eeas.europa.eu/sites/default/files/documents/strategic_compass_en3_web.pdf. p. 18 or

followed by legal adjustments justifying them,[27] that frequently come at the expense of fundamental rights, particularly at Europe's borders.[28] The ECtHR has recently become a key forum for addressing these issues, with several landmark cases pending before the Grand Chamber against Latvia, Lithuania, and Poland (*C.O.C.G. and Others v. Lithuania*[29], *H.M.M. and Others v. Latvia*[30] and *R.A. and Others v. Poland*[31]) concerning push-backs to Belarus and the alleged "instrumentalization" of migrants. These cases underscore the Court's continued relevance in clarifying the prohibition of collective expulsions under Article 4 Protocol 4 ECHR. The decisions in these and other cases in the near future will show whether the Strasbourg Court continues its more restrictive path taken since *Khlaifia* as described in this book, or cautions against a reductive, security-driven view of migration reminding states of their duty to an individualized assessment at the border in accordance with the prohibition of collective expulsion. Furthermore, as these pivotal

---

the speech of the EU Commission's President Ursula von der Leyen on 15 September 2021 where she relied on the "instrumentalization" and "hybrid war" framework on the response by Latvia, Lithuania and Poland in 2021 stressing that the EU "will continue to stand together with Lithuania, Latvia and Poland". See: European Commission *2021 State of the Union Address by President von der Leyen* Press Release, 14 September 2021, available at: https://ec.europa.eu/commission/presscorner/detail/en/SPEECH_21_4701.

27 The most prominent recent example is the European Union *Regulation 2024/1359 of the European Parliament and of the Council of 14 May 2024 addressing situations of crisis and force majeure in the field of migration and asylum and amending Regulation (EU) 2021/1147* PE/19/2024/REV/1, 14 May 2024, entry into application two years after its entry into force. For a detailed overview of the evolution of the regulation from 2020–2024, see: European Parliament *Crisis and force majeure Regulation Legislative Train Schedule* 20 October 2024, available at: https://www.europarl.europa.eu/legislative-train/theme-promoting-our-european-way-of-life/file-crisis-and-force-majeure-regulation.

28 Ineli-Ciger, Meltem *Navigating the Labyrinth of Derogations: A Critical Look at the Crisis Regulation* EU Migration Law Blog, 10 June 2024, available at: https://eumigrationlawblog.eu/navigating-the-labyrinth-of-derogations-a-critical-look-at-the-crisis-regulation/.

29 ECtHR *C.O.C.G. and Others v. Lithuania* Appl. no. 17764/22. Case details, legal summary etc., available at: https://hudoc.echr.coe.int/eng#{%22sort%22:[%22kpdate%20Descending%22],%22itemid%22:[%22002-14311%22]}.

30 ECtHR *H.M.M. and Others v. Latvia* Appl. no. 42165/21. Case details, legal summary etc., available at: https://hudoc.echr.coe.int/eng#{%22sort%22:[%22kpdate%20Descending%22],%22itemid%22:[%22002–14352%22]}.

31 ECtHR *R.A. and Others v. Poland* Appl. no. 42120/21. Case details, legal summary etc., available at: https://hudoc.echr.coe.int/fre#{%22sort%22:[%22kpdate%20Descending%22],%22appno%22:[%2242120/21%22],%22itemid%22:[%22002–14351%22]}.

cases are adjudicated, the delicate balance between national security and the rights of migrants and asylum seekers will come under further scrutiny, potentially reshaping the future of EU asylum policies and reassessing the ECtHR's role as a guardian of fundamental rights at the border. In this environment, however, rights-based protections for migrants risk being overshadowed by political expediency, public anxiety, and, often, underlying racist sentiments.

In this context, scholars, lawyers, NGOs and activists striving to extend or at least maintain the protections of migrants at the ECtHR and globally must keep these sentiments of fear and insecurity in mind, addressing them responsibly and factually without belittling their impact. By engaging with these concerns in a nuanced manner and fostering informed public dialogue, they can work to build broader societal support for the rights of migrants. Ensuring that these protections are backed by a majority of society is essential, as failing to do so risks further shrinking the space for rights advocacy. Without public buy-in, politicians driven by voter sentiment may implement increasingly restrictive policies, making the fight to preserve fundamental guarantees for migrants and asylum seekers even more challenging in the future.

At the same time, these restrictive developments in migration matters also underscore the urgent need for robust legal frameworks and judicial oversight. Courts and treaty bodies like the ECtHR, the Inter-American Court, the African Commission, or the Migrant Worker Committee remain highly relevant in upholding principles such as the prohibition of collective expulsion, ensuring that states remain accountable for protecting basic guarantees at their borders. Beyond the prohibition of collective expulsion, the case law of these courts and treaty bodies exemplifies how human rights have gained a central role in legal and political struggles to protect migrants' rights reflecting a broader trend of "humanrightization" of law, politics, and everyday practices. This trend has enabled migrants and other social actors to successfully challenge restrictive migration control policies.[32] As Bast shows, by embedding human rights principles into the discourse on migration, these processes have created a framework within which far-reaching demands for the inclusion of migrants can be articulated through recognized rules of legal argumentation.[33] However, when it comes to the ECtHR, we have also noticed a restrictive shift (see Chapters 2,

---

32 Bast, Jürgen *The Rise of Human Rights Limits to Migration Control – A European Perspective* AJIL Unbound, Vol. 118, 2024, pp. 208–213.

33 *Ibidem.*

3), which calls for observance and strategic efforts to ensure that gained standards for protection are not made null and void.

As the global challenges of migration grow more complex, including climate-induced displacement and mobility, the imperative to uphold the "right to have rights" becomes even more vital. Without collective action and renewed commitment to human rights, the erosion of migrants' protections could become the norm rather than the exception. Yet, history also shows us that moments of crisis can spark transformation. The Holocaust and World War II prompted the Refugee Convention and contributed to the creation of international human rights instruments. The question we face today is whether we can learn from the past to build a future where migration is not met with hostility, but with policies that recognize the shared humanity of all people.

This book is a call to remember and act on that responsibility. To ensure that fundamental guarantees for migrants and asylum seekers like the prohibition of collective expulsion are upheld, courts must remain steadfast in their commitment to protecting these core principles. *Non-refoulement* and the prohibition of collective expulsion are not merely procedural safeguards; they are essential protections against arbitrariness and the erosion of migrants' rights. Weakening these guarantees risks hollowing out the very foundation of human rights for migrants and asylum seekers.

This book further highlighted that fostering inter-judicial dialogue among human rights courts and treaty bodies is crucial. Courts like the ECtHR can draw valuable lessons from their counterparts in Africa and Latin America, particularly in linking the prohibition of collective expulsion with principles of non-discrimination. This approach acknowledges both the individual and collective dimensions inherent in many expulsion cases and could be reinforced through strategic litigation efforts.

On a broader societal level, combating anti-migrant sentiment requires reframing migration narratives. Public discourse must emphasize the tangible benefits of migration while addressing its challenges honestly, avoiding the pitfalls of adopting right-wing rhetoric. Migration should be recognized as part of a global justice discourse, related to decolonization, driven by factors such as war, historic economic inequality, and the impacts of climate change. Especially in the Global North, there is arguably a legal and historic duty to honor international obligations and pursue equitable solutions.[34]

34 Tendayi, Achiume E. *Migration as Decolonization* Stanford Law Review, Vol. 71, June 2019, pp. 1509–1574.

States must resist isolationist policies and focus on global solidarity by creating secure, efficient pathways for migration that avoid years of waiting in precarious conditions. This includes addressing root causes through initiatives targeting global inequality and climate justice. Migration, as an expression of human nature, demands collective action rather than unilateral border closures, reinforcing the need for cooperation and shared responsibility.[35]

Building on this analysis, it is clear that safeguarding migrants' and asylum seekers' rights requires a comprehensive and multi-faceted approach. While legal principles such as the prohibition of collective expulsion and *non-refoulement* offer crucial protections, their effectiveness depends on unwavering judicial commitment, strategic advocacy, and societal efforts to challenge discriminatory narratives.[36]

Migration policies must align with these guarantees, emphasizing global justice and solidarity over unilateral restrictions. Secure, efficient pathways and cooperative international frameworks are vital to addressing the root causes of migration, whether they stem from conflict, inequality, or climate change.

In this evolving landscape, the prohibition of collective expulsion stands as a guard of protection, adapting to the realities of contemporary migration while holding states accountable to their obligations. By continuously refining its interpretation and implementation, regional and international bodies ensure this principle remains a cornerstone of migrants' rights. As this book has shown, upholding these minimum protections is not just a legal imperative, it is a moral and historical duty.

---

35 As highlighted in the two Global Compacts on Migration and Refugees, adoption by the United Nations General Assembly on 19 December 2018.

36 Helpful academic efforts in this regard are for example, Ganty, Sarah; Ancite-Jepifánova, Aleksandra and Kochenov, Dimitry *EU Lawlessness Law at the EU-Belarusian Border: Torture and Dehumanisation Excused by 'Instrumentalisation'* Hague Journal on the Rule of Law (2024) 16, pp. 739–774, see also: Ancite-Jepifánova, Aleksandra *Migrant Instrumentalisation: Facts and Fictions Realities On the Ground at the EU-Belarus Border* 21 September 2023, available at: https://verfassungsblog.de/migrant-instrumentalisation-facts-and-fictions/.

Bibliography

Advice for Individual Rights in Europe Centre, Amnesty International, European Council on Refugees and Exiles and International Commission of Jurists *Submission for the Intervenors in ND and NT v. Spain to the ECtHR.*

African Commission on Human and Peoples' Rights *African Guiding Principles on the Human Rights of All Migrants, Refugees, and Asylum Seekers* April 2023, available at: https://www.google.com/url?sa=t&source=web&rct=j&opi=89978449&url=https://achpr.au.int/en/soft-law/african-guiding-principles-human-rights-all-migrants-refugees&ved=2ahUKEwixjJflgN2JAxWMTTABHSVjMG4QFnoECBYQAQ&usg=AOvVaw3yzA7rf8p5GyqDUYTi1O-k.

African Commission on Human and Peoples' Rights *General Comment No. 5 On the African Charter on Human and Peoples' Rights: The Right to Freedom of Movement and Residence (Article 12 (1))* October 2021, available at: https://achpr.au.int/sites/default/files/files/2021-10/generalobservationno5ontherightoffreedomonmovementandresidence.pdf.

African Commission on Human and Peoples' Rights *Principles and Guidelines on the Right to a Fair Trial and Legal Assistance in Africa* 2003.

African Commission on Human and Peoples' Rights *Resolution on missing migrants and refugees in Africa and the impact on their families* ACHPR/Res. 486 (EXT.OS/XXXIII), 28 July 2021, available at: https://achpr.au.int/en/adopted-resolutions/486-resolution-missing-migrants-and-refugees-africa-and-impact-their-fa.

African Commission on Human and Peoples' Rights *Resolution on the Implementation of the New York Declaration for Refugees and Migrants* ACHPR/Res.371(LX), 22 May 2017, available at: https://achpr.au.int/en/adopted-resolutions/371-resolution-implementation-new-york-declaration-refugees-and-mi.

African Commission on Human and Peoples' Rights *Resolution on the Respect for the Principle of Non-Refoulement of Asylum Seekers and Refugees* ACHPR/Res. 484 (EXT.OS/XXXIII), 28 July 2021, available at: https://achpr.au.int/en/adopted-resolutions/484-resolution-respect-principle-non-refoulement-asylum-seekers.

African Commission on Human and Peoples' Rights *Special Rapporteur on Refugees, Asylum Seekers, Internally Displaced Persons and Migrant in Africa* available at: https://achpr.au.int/en/mechanisms/special-rapporteur-refugees-asylum-seekers-internally-displaced-persons-and-migrant.

African Union *Migration Policy Framework for Africa and the Plan of Action (2018–2030)* 2018, available at: https://au.int/sites/default/files/documents/35956-doc-au-mpfa-executive-summary-eng.pdf.

AIRE Centre, The Dutch Refugee Council, the European Council on Refugees and Exiles and the International Commission of Jurists *S.S. and Others v. Italy*

Intervention 11 November 2019, available at: https://www.icj.org/wp-content/uploads/2019/11/ECtHR-SS_v_Italy_final-JointTPI-ICJECREAIREDCR-English-2019.pdf.

Alami, Aida *African Migrants in Morocco Tell of Abuse* New York Times, 28 November 2012, available at: https://www.nytimes.com/2012/11/29/world/middleeast/african-migrants-in-morocco-tell-of-abuse.html.

Allain, Jean *The jus cogens Nature of non-refoulement International* Journal of Refugee Law, (2001), Vol. 13, No. 4, pp. 533–558.

Allam, Wael *The Arabic charter on human rights: Main features* Arab Law Quarterly, 2014, Vol. 28, No. 1, pp. 57–63.

Alon, Amir *UN human rights experts say mass expulsion violates international law* Ynetnews, 3 March 2018, available at: https://www.ynetnews.com/articles/0,7340,L-5143004,00.html.

Alvarez, Priscilla *Trump team maps out Latin America strategy as part of mass deportation plan* CNN, 21 November 2024, available at: https://edition.cnn.com/2024/11/21/politics/donald-trump-border-politics/index.html.

Alvarez, Priscilla *Trump's Deal With Mexico Could Make Asylum Next to Impossible* The Atlantic, available at: https://www.theatlantic.com/politics/archive/2018/11/trumps-new-deal-would-make-asylum-next-impossible/576814/.

Ambrus, Mónika *The European Court of Human Rights and Standards of Proof* in: Gruszczynski/Werner *Deference in International Courts and Tribunals* (Oxford University Press 2014).

Amnesty International *Dominican Republic: Authorities must end de facto racist migration policies* 2 April 2024, available at: https://www.amnesty.org/en/latest/news/2024/04/dominican-republic-must-stop-racist-immigration-policies/.

Amnesty International *Protecting human rights: International procedures and how to use them (A Series of Amnesty International Papers): 2. The Organization of African Unity and human rights* (1991), available at: https://www.amnesty.org/en/documents/ior63/001/1991/en/.

André, Achim *Beweisführung und Beweislast im Verfahren vor dem Europäischen Gerichtshof* Kölner Schriften zum Europarecht No. 6 (Carl Heymanns Verlag KG 1966).

Arendt, Hannah *The Origins of Totalitarianism* (Schocken Books 1951).

Arendt, Hannah *The Rights of Man: What Are They?* American Labor Conference on International Affairs, Modern Review, 1949, pp. 24–37.

Arendt, Hannah *We Refugees* Menorah Journal 31, No. 1, January 1943, pp. 69–77.

Asylum Information Data Base and European Council on Refugees and Exiles *Access to the Territories and Push Backs: Spain* available at: https://www.asylumineurope.org/reports/country/spain/access-territory-and-push-backs.

Asylum Information Database *Country Report Hungary 2018 update* March 2019, available at: http://www.asylumineurope.org/sites/default/files/report-download/aida_hu_2018update.pdf.

Baerwald, Neske *The European Refugee Crisis: Crisis for Whom?* University of Oxford Border Criminologies Blog, 20 March 2018, available at: https://www.law.ox.ac.uk/research-subject-groups/centre-criminology/centreborder-criminologies/blog/2018/03/european-refugee.

Baldwin, Clive and Morel, Cynthia *Group Rights* in: Evans and Murray (eds.) *The African Charter on Human and Peoples' Rights: The System in Practice 1986–2006* (Cambridge University Press 2008).

Bast, Jürgen *The Rise of Human Rights Limits to Migration Control – A European Perspective* AJIL Unbound, Vol. 118, 2024, pp. 208–213.

Baumhof, Angelika *Die Beweislast im Verfahren vor dem Europäischen Gerichtshof* (Nomos 1996).

Bearak, Max and Cameron, Darla *Here are the 10 countries where homosexuality may be punished by death* Washington Post, 16 June 2016, available at: https://www.washingtonpost.com/news/worldviews/wp/2016/06/13/here-are-the-10-countries-where-homosexuality-may-be-punished-by-death-2/?utm_term=.a7971178d8ab.

Bekker, Gina *Mass expulsion of foreign nationals: A 'special violation of human rights' – Communication 292/2004 Institute for Human Rights and Development in Africa v Republic of Angola* African Human Rights Law Journal, Vol. 9, No. 1, 2009, pp. 262–273.

Belson, Rosemary *Central Mediterranean named most deadly route for migrants* POLITICO, 11 September 2017, available at: https://www.politico.eu/article/refugees-central-mediterranean-sea-named-most-deadly-route-for-migrants/.

Benhabib, Seyla *Exile, Statelessness and Migration: Playing Chess with History from Hannah Arendt to Isaiah Berlin* (Princeton University Press 2018).

Benhabib, Seyla *The Rights of Others: Aliens, Residents and Citizens* (Cambridge University Press 2013).

Benz, Eleanor *The Advisory Function of the Inter-American Court of Human Rights* (Nomos 2024).

Betts, Alexander and Collier, Paul *Refuge: Rethinking Refugee Policy in a Changing World* (Oxford University Press 2017).

Bilchitz, David *Poverty and Fundamental Rights: The Justification and Enforcement of Socio-Economic Rights* (Oxford University Press 2007).

Bisaz, Corsin *The Concept of Group Rights in International Law* (Brill/Nijhoff 2012).

Black Alliance for Just Immigration (BAJI), the Center for Justice and International Law (CEJIL), the Center for Immigration Law and Policy (CILP) at the UCLA School of Law, Comunidades Indígenas en Liderazgo Organizativo (CIELO),

Haitian Bridge Alliance (HBA), Migrant Works Alliance for Change (MWAC), the Promise Institute for Human Rights at the UCLA School of Law, Observatorio de Racismo en México y Centroamérica, RacismoMX, Espacio Migrante A.C, and Cameroonian Action Network *Report for the Inter-American Commission on Human Rights 186th Period of Sessions Public Hearing on the Situation of human mobility from an ethnic-racial approach* 2023, available at: https://promiseinstitute.law.ucla.edu/wp-content/uploads/2023/07/2023-Situation-of-human-mobility-from-an-ethnic-racial-approach.pdf.

Brandl, Ulrike *Mix and Match. Detention, "De-Facto Detention" or just Restrictions of Freedom of Movement in the New Pact* EU Migration Law Blog, 14 October 2024, available at: https://eumigrationlawblog.eu/mix-and-match-detention-de-facto-detention-or-just-restrictions-of-freedom-of-movement-in-the-new-pact/.

Brandl, Ulrike *Prozeßgarantien in Verfahren zur Ausweisung Fremder Art 1 EMRK/Prot 7* in: Pabel and Schmahl (eds.) *Internationaler Kommentar zur Europäischen Menschenrechtskonvention mit einschlägigen Texten und Dokumenten* (Carl Heymanns Verlag 2013).

Brandl, Ulrike *Verbot der Kollektivausweisung von Ausländern Art 4 EMRK/Prot 4 (Art 4 EMRK/Prot 4)* and *Art 1 Prot 7 (Art 1 Prot 7)* in: Pabel and Schmahl (eds.) *Internationaler Kommentar zur Europäischen Menschenrechtskonvention mit einschlägigen Texten und Dokumenten* (Carl Heymanns Verlag 2013).

Brems, Eva *The "Logics" of Procedural-Type Review by the European Court of Human Rights from Part I – Foundations and Rationales for Procedural Review by Supranational Courts Deciding Fundamental Rights Cases* in: Gerards and Brems (eds.) *Procedural Review in European Fundamental Rights Cases* (Cambridge University Press 2017), pp. 17–39.

Brown, Wendy *Walled States, Waning Sovereignty* (Zone Books 2nd edn. 2017).

Buga, Irina *Modification of Treaties by Subsequent Practice* (Oxford University Press 2018).

Camboulives, Sabrina *Luck of the draw for asylum seekers in Europe: Why the Common European Asylum System is a breach of justice and why a third phase of amendment is required* Vermont Law Review, Vol. 42, No. 393, 2017, pp. 393–425.

Cantor, David James and Barichello, Stefania Eugenia *The Inter-American human rights system: a new model for integrating refugee and complementary protection?* The International Journal of Human Rights, Vol. 17, No. 5, 2013, pp. 689–706.

Carens, Joseph *The Ethics of Immigration* (Oxford University Press 2013).

Carlier, Jean-Yves and Leboeuf, Luc *Collective expulsion or not? Individualisation of decision making in migration and asylum law* EU migration law blog, 8 January 2018, available at: http://eumigrationlawblog.eu/collective-expulsion-or-not-individualisation-of-decision-making-in-migration-and-asylum-law/.

Carlson, Scott and Gisvold, Gregory *Practical Guide to the International Covenant on Civil and Political Rights* (Transnational Publishers 2003).

Caroni, Martina *Einleitung* in: Achermann and Boillet and Caroni and Epiney and Künzli and Uebersax (eds.).

Carswell, Ken et al. *The relationship between trauma, post-migration problems and the spsychological well-being of refugees and asylum seekers* International Journal of Social Psychiatry, (2011), Vol. 57, No. 2.

Chatham House *The UK Must Not Sleepwalk into Leaving the ECHR* March 2023, https://www.chathamhouse.org/2023/03/uk-must-not-sleepwalk-leaving-echr.

Cheatham, Amelia;Klobucista, Claire and Roy, Diana *The U.S. Immigration Debate* Council on Foreign Relations, 7 August 2024, available at: https://www.cfr.org/backgrounder/us-immigration-debate-0.

Chetail, Vincent and Bauloz, Céline *Research Handbook on International Law and Migration* (Edward Elgar 2014).

Ciliberto, Giulia *Libya's Pull-Backs of Boat Migrants: Can Italy Be Held Accountable for Violations of International Law?* The Italian Law Journal (2018), Vol. 4, No. 2, pp. 489–530.

Cliffe, Jeremy *European governments in melt-down over an inoffensive migration compact* The Economist, 8 December 2018, available at: https://www.economist.com/europe/2018/12/08/european-governments-in-melt-down-over-an-inoffensive-migration-compact.

Cockburn, Harry *Dozens of refugees feared drowned in Mediterranean after waiting more than 36 hours for rescue* The Independent, 3 October 2018, available at: https://www.independent.co.uk/news/world/europe/refugees-morocco-mediterranean-drowning-deaths-walking-borders-spain-a8565196.html.

Columbia Law School Human Rights Clinic, African Refugee Development Center, Allard K. Lowenstein International Human Rights Clinic at Yale Law School, Center for Social Justice at Seton Hall University School of Law, Florida Coastal School of Law Immigrant Rights Clinic, Institute for Justice & Democracy in Haiti, Migrant and Refugee Rights Project of the Australian Human Rights Centre at the University of New South Wales School of Law, Physicians for Human Rights and Professors James Gathi, Tally Kritzman-Amir, Stephen H. Legomsky and Margaret L. Satterthwaite *Intervener brief in Hirsi Jamaa and Others v. Italy* ECtHR, 17 April 2010.

Commission of the European Union *Towards a reform of the Common European Asylum System and enhancing legal avenues to Europe* COM(2016) 197 final, 6 April 2016.

Commissioner for Human Rights of the Council of Europe *Dunja Mijatovic report following her visit to Hungary from 4 to 8 February 2019* CommDH(2019)13, 21 May 2019.

Committee on the Elimination of Racial Discrimination *General Recommendation No. 30 on the discrimination of non-citizens* CERD/C/64/Misc.11/rev.3, 2004.

Commonwealth of Independent States *official webpage* available at: http://cis.minsk.by/page.php?id=11326.

Commonwealth of Independent States *Regional Conference to Address the Problems of Refugees, Displaced Persons, Other Forms of Involuntary Displacement and Returnees in the Countries of the Commonwealth of Independent States and Relevant Neighbouring States* CISCONF/1996/5, 11 June 1996.

Coordination Francaise pour le droit d'asile, Mc Gill Centre, AIRE Centre and ECRE, *Third party Intervention in Khlaifia and Others v. Italy* ECtHR [GC] Appl. No. 16483/12, 15 December 2016.

Costello, Cathryn and Foster, Michelle *Non-refoulement as custom and jus cogens? Putting the prohibition to the test* in: Heijer and van der Wilt (eds.) *Netherlands Yearbook of International Law 2015* Vol. 46, (T.M.C. Asser Press 2016), pp. 273–327.

Council of Europe *About the Committee of Ministers* available at: https://www.coe.int/en/web/cm/about-cm.

Council of Europe and Commissioner for Human Rights *Third party intervention by the Council of Europe Commissioner for Human Rights* Applications No. 8675/15 and No. 8697/15, *N.D. v. Spain and N.T. v. Spain* 12 November 2015.

Council of Europe and European Court of Human Rights *Guide on Article 6of the European Convention on Human Rights Criminal Limb* 21 August 2019.

Council of Europe *Chart of signatures and ratification of Treaty 046 Protocol No. 4 to the Convention for the Protection of Human Rights and Fundamental Freedoms, securing certain rights and freedoms other than those already included in the Convention and in the first Protocol thereto* status as of 1 December 2019 available at: https://www.coe.int/en/web/conventions/full-list/-/conventions/treaty/046/signatures?p_auth=Ufu2Ts6m.

Council of Europe *Details of Treaty No. 117, Protocol 7 to the Convention for the Protection of Human Rights and Fundamental Freedoms* available at: https://www.coe.int/en/web/conventions/full-list/-/conventions/treaty/117.

Council of Europe *Explanatory Report on the Second to Fifth Protocols to the European Convention for Protection of Human Rights and Fundamental Freedoms, submitted by the Committee of Experts to The Committee of Ministers* H(71) 11 (1971).

Council of Europe *Explanatory Report to Protocol No. 4 to the Convention for the Protection of Human Rights and Fundamental Freedoms, securing certain rights and freedoms other than those already included in the Convention and in the first Protocol thereto* ETS No. 46, 16 September 1963.

Council of Europe *Explanatory Report to the European Convention on Establishment* 13 December 1955.

Council of Europe, Committee of Ministers *Twenty Guidelines on Forced Return* September 2005.

Dakar Meeting of Experts *Preliminary draft of the African Charter prepared during the at the end of 1979 Part II, No. 1 (a)* CAB/LEG/67/3/Rev. 1, reprinted in Human Rights Law in Africa Vol. 4 (1999), Annex.

De Boer, Tom *Closing Legal Black Holes: The Role of Extraterritorial Jurisdiction in Refugee Rights Protection* Journal of Refugee Studies, Vol. 28, 2014, pp. 118–134.

De Week, Fanny *Non-Refoulement under the European Convention on Human Rights and the UN Convention against Torture The Assessment of Individual Complaints by the European Court of Human Rights under Article 3 ECRR and the United Nations Committee against Torture under Article 3 CAT* (Brill/Nijhoff 2017).

Dembour, Marie-Bénédicte *When Humans Become Migrants Study of the European Court of Human Rights with an Inter-American Counterpoint* (Oxford University Press 2015).

Dembour, Marie-Bénédicte *Why the European Court of Human Rights is no friend to migrants* THE CONVERSATION, 21 May 2015, available at: https://theconversation.com/why-the-european-court-of-human-rights-is-no-friend-to-migrants-42129.

De Peña, Kristie *Mistaken Detainment, Racial Profiling, and Discrimination: How ICE Fails to Protect Communities* Niskanen Center, April 7, 2021, available at: https://www.niskanencenter.org/mistaken-detainment-racial-profiling-and-discrimination-how-ice-fails-to-protect-communities/.

Deumeland, Dieter *Das Verbot der Xenelasie bei Ausweisung von Ausländern in der Bundesrepublik Deutschland* AWR Bulletin, Vierteljahresschrift für Flüchtlingsfragen Vol. 22, No. 4, 1984.

Doehring, Karl *Die Rechtsnatur der Massenausweisung – unter besonderer Berücksichtigung der indirekten Ausweisung* ZaöRV, Issue 45 (1985), pp. 372–389.

Doña-Reveco, Cristián *How Chile's welcome turned sour* Mixed Migration Centre, 18 April 2024, available at: https://mixedmigration.org/chiles-response-to-migration/.

European Center for Constitutional and Human Rights *From Idomeni to Strasbourg: Refugees demand their right to have rights at the ECtHR* available at: https://www.ecchr.eu/en/case/from-idomeni-to-strasbourg-refugees-demand-their-right-to-have-rights-at-the-ecthr/.

European Commission *Communication from the Commission to the European Parliament and the Council – Towards a Reform of the Common European Asylum System and Enhancing Legal Avenues to Europe* COM(2016) 197 final, 6 April 2016.

European Commission *Fact Sheet State of the Union 2018: A fully equipped European Border and Coast Guard – Questions and Answers* 12 September 2018, available at: http://europa.eu/rapid/press-release_MEMO-18-5715_en.htm.

European Commission *Migration and Home Affairs expulsion definition* available at: https://ec.europa.eu/home-affairs/what-we-do/networks/european_migration_network/glossary_search/expulsion_en.

European Commission *Non-paper on regional disembarkation arrangements* 24 July 2018, available at: https://ec.europa.eu/home-affairs/sites/homeaffairs/files/what-we-do/policies/european-agenda-migration/20180724_non-paper-regional-disembarkation-arrangements_en.pdf?utm_source=ECRE+Newsletters&utm_campaign=846c899479-EMAIL_CAMPAIGN_2018_09_21_11_19&utm_medium=email&utm_term=0_3ec9497afd-846c899479-422312705.

European Commission *Proposal for a Directive of the European Parliament and the Council of common standards and procedures in Member States for returning illegally staying third-country nationals (recast) A contribution from the European Commission to the Leaders' meeting in Salzburg on 19–20 September 2018* COM (2018) 634 final, 12 September 2018.

European Commission *State of the Union 2018 – A strengthened and fully equipped European Border and Coast Guard* 12 September 2018.

European Commission *Support to Integrated border and migration management in Libya* adopted 27 July 2017.

European Council for Refugees and Exiles *116 expulsions in 24 hours by the new Spanish Socialist Government* 30 August 2018, available at: https://www.ecre.org/116-expulsions-in-24-hours-by-the-new-spanish-socialist-government/.

European Council for Refugees and Exiles *Spain: Rights of Asylum Seekers Deteriorating at Border with Morocco* 4 October 2019, available at: https://www.ecre.org/spain-rights-of-asylum-seekers-deteriorating-at-border-with-morocco/.

European Council on Refugees and Exiles *Hungary: Government Extends the "State of Crisis due to Mass Migration"* 13 September 2019, available at: https://www.ecre.org/hungary-government-extends-the-state-of-crisis-due-to-mass-migration/.

European Court of Human Rights Grand Chamber public hearing in case *N.D. and N.T. v. Spain*, Appl. No. 8675/15, 26 September 2018, available at: https://www.echr.coe.int/Pages/home.aspx?p=hearings&w=867515_26092018&language=en.

European Court of Human Rights *Human rights protection in the time of the pandemic: new challenges and new perspectives* Dialogue between Judges 2022, 2022, available at: https://www.echr.coe.int/documents/d/echr/dialogue_2022_eng.

European Union Agency for Fundamental Rights *Explanations relating to the Charter of Fundamental Rights* available at: https://fra.europa.eu/en/charterpedia/article/19-protection-event-removal-expulsion-or-extradition.

European Union Agency for Fundamental Rights *The situation of Roma EU citizens moving to and settling in other EU Member States* 2009, available at: http://fra.europa.eu/en/publication/2010/situation-roma-eu-citizens-moving-and-settling-other-eu-member-states.

European Union Parliament *EU migrant crisis: facts and figures* 30 June 2017, available at: http://www.europarl.europa.eu/news/en/headlines/society/20170629STO78630/eu-migrant-crisis-facts-and-figures.

Faghfouri Azar, Leina *Hannah Arendt: The Right to Have Rights* Critical Legal Thinking, 12 Jul 2019, available at: https://criticallegalthinking.com/2019/07/12/hannah-arendt-right-to-have-rights/.

Feihle, Prisca *Asylum and Immigration under the European Convention on Human Rights – an exclusive universality?* in: Aust, Helmut and Demir Gürsel, Esra *The European Court of Human Rights Current Challenges in Historical Perspective* (Edgar Elgar 2021), pp. 133–156.

Feller, Erika *The Refugee Convention at 60: Still fit for its Purpose?* Workshop statement, Workshop on Refugees and the Refugee Convention 60 Years On: Protection and Identity, Prado, 2 May 2011.

Figueira, Thomas *Xenelasia and Social Control in Classical Sparta* The Classical Quarterly, (2003), Vol. 53, No. 1, pp. 44–74.

Fink, Melanie and Gombeer, Kristof *The Aquarius incident: navigating the turbulent waters of international law* EJIL:Talk!, 14 June 2018, available at: https://www.ejiltalk.org/the-aquarius-incident-navigating-the-turbulent-waters-of-international-law/.

FitzGerald, David *Refuge beyond Reach: How Rich Democracies Repel Asylum Seekers* (Oxford University Press 2019).

Fredman, Sandra *Human Rights Transformed: Positive Rights and Positive Duties* (Oxford University Press 2008).

Fukuyama, Francis *Identity: The Demand for Dignity and the Politics of Resentment* (MacMillan Publisher 2018).

Funderburk, Brent *Operation Wetback United States immigration law-enforcement campaign* Britannica, available at: https://www.britannica.com/topic/Operation-Wetback.

Gameltoft-Hansen, Thomas *Access to Asylum International Refugee Law and the Globalisation of Migration Control* (Cambridge University Press 2013).

Gammeltoft-Hansen, Thomas and Aalberts, Tanja *Search and Rescue as a Geopolitics of International Law* in: Aalberts and Gammeltoft-Hansen *The Changing Practices of International Law* (Cambridge University Press 2018).

Gargiulo, Susanne and Guy, Jack *Denmark plans to isolate 'unwanted' migrants on remote island* CNN, 6 December 2018, available at: https://edition.cnn.com/2018/12/05/europe/denmark-immigrant-islandscliintl/index.html?utm_source=Refuge es+Deeply&utm_campaign=8daed2fe18EMAIL_CAMPAIGN_2018_12_07_12_37&utm_medium=email&utm_term=0_8b056c90e2-8daed2fe18-117928793.

Gibbons-Neff, Thomas and Cooper, Helene *Deployed Inside the United States: The Military Waits for the Migrant Caravan* New York Times, 10 November 2018, available at: https://www.nytimes.com/2018/11/10/us/deployed-inside-the-united-states-the-military-waits-for-the-migrant-caravan.html.

Gittleman, Richard *The Banjul Charter on Human and Peoples' Rights: A legal Analysis* in: Welch and Meltzer *Human Rights and Development in Africa* (State University of New York Press 1984).

Gkliati, Mariana *Let's Call It what It Is: Hybrid Threats and Instrumentalisation as the Evolution of Securitisation in Migration Management* European Papers, Vol. 8, 2023, No. 2.

Gold, Michael and Savage *Trump Confirms Plans to Use the Military to Assist in Mass Deportations* New York Times, 18 November 2024, updated 20 November 2024, available at: https://www.nytimes.com/2024/11/18/us/politics/trump-military-mass-deportation.html.

Goldenziel, Jill *Khlaifia and Others v. Italy- International Decisions* American Journal of International Law, Vol. 112, Issue 2, April 2018, pp. 274–280.

González Morales, Felipe *UN Special Rapporteur on the Rights of Migrants letter to the Representative of the USA regarding the Migrant Protection Protocols* (MPP) 7 March 2019, OL USA 4/2019.

Goodwil-Gill Guy and McAdam Jane *The Refugee in International Law* (Oxford University Press 3rd edn. 2007).

Goodwin-Gil, Guy *Expulsion in Public International Law* United Nations lecture series, video available at: http://legal.un.org/avl/ls/Goodwin-Gill_IML_video_3.html.

Goodwin-Gill, Guy *The Limits of the Power of Expulsion in Public International Law* British Yearbook of International Law, Issue 47, 1976, pp. 55–156.

Gornig, Gilbert *Menschenrechtlicher Mindeststandard* in: Schöbener (edn.) Völkerrecht (C.F. Müller 2014).

Government of Iceland *Alþing Information brochure* available at: https://www.althingi.is/pdf/Althingi2018_enska.pdf.

Grahl-Madsen, Alte *Territorial Asylum* (Oceana Publications 1980).

Grossi, Simona *Procedural Due Process* Seton Hall Circuit Review Vol. 13, No. 2 (2017), pp. 155–202.

Gruszczynski, Lukasz and Wouter, Werner *Deference in International Courts and Tribunals* (Oxford University Press 2014).

Guild, Elspeth *Art 19-Protection in the Event of Removal* in: Peers, Hervey, Kenner and Ward (eds.) *The EU Charter of Fundamental Rights A Commentary* (Hart Publishing 2014).

Gunther, Caitlin *France's Repatriation of Roma: Violation of Fundamental Freedoms?* Cornell International Law Journal, Vol. 45, 2012, pp. 205–212.

Habermas, Jürgen *The European Nation-State: On the Past and Future of Sovereignty and Citizenship* (MIT Press Cambridge 1998).

Hakiki, Hanaa, and Rodnik, Delphine *Accessing borders, accessing justice? The European Court of Human Rights' jurisprudence on pushbacks at land borders* Asyl 1/2023, pp. 3–17.

Hamacher, Werner and Mendoza-de Jesus, Ronald *On the Right to Have Rights: Human Rights; Marx and Arendt* The New Centennial Review, Vol. 14, No. 2, 2014, pp. 169–214.

Hamdan, Eman *The Principle of Non-Refoulement under the ECHR and the UN Convention against Torture and Other Cruel, Inhuman or Degrading Treatment or Punishment* (Brill/Nijhoff 2016).

Hansen, Randall *State Control: Borders, Refugees, and Citizenship* in: Fiddian-Qasmiyeh, Loescher, Long and Sigona *The Oxford Handbook of Refugee and Forced Migration Studies* (Oxford University Press 2014).

Hathaway, James *Fixing the Refugee System* ESIL lecture at the Faculty of Law of the University of Amsterdam on 13 May 2016, available at: https://www.youtube.com/watch?v=e_8AL4rVedg.

Hathaway, James *Leveraging Asylum* Texas International Law Journal, Vol. 45, No. 3, 2010, pp. 503–536.

Hathaway, Oona and Shapiro, Scott *The Internationalists: How a Radical Plan to Outlaw War Remade the World* (Simon & Schuster 2017).

Hathaway, Oona, *Why Do Countries Commit to Human Rights Treaties?* The Journal of Conflict Resolution, 2007, Vol. 51, No. 4, pp. 588–621.

Heeren, Martina and Mueller, Julia et al. *Mental health of asylum seekers: a cross-sectional study of psychiatric disorders* BMC Psychiatry, 2012, Vol. 12, No. 114, available at: https://bmcpsychiatry.biomedcentral.com/articles/10.1186/1471-244X-12-114#citeas.

Henckaerts, Jean-Marie *Mass Expulsion in Modern International Law and Practice* (Martinus Nijhoff 1995).

Herdegen, Matthias *Interpretation in International Law Max Planck Encyclopedias of International Law* (Oxford University Press 2013).

Heuman, Lars and Wahlgren, Peter *Procedural Law Court Administrations* Scandinavian Studies in Law, Vol. 51 (Stockholm Institute for Scandinavian Law 2007).

Howley, Jacob *Unlocking the Fortress: Protocol No. 11 and the Birth of Collective Expulsion Jurisprudence in the Council of Europe System* Georgetown Immigration Law Journal, 2006, Vol. 21, Issue 111, pp. 111–128.

Huijbers, Leonie *The European Court of Human Rights' Procedural Approach in the Age of Subsidiarity* Cambridge International Law Journal, Vol. 6, No. 2, December 2017, pp. 177–201.

Human Rights Watch *Abused and Expelled Ill-Treatment of Sub-Saharan African Migrants in Morocco* 10 February 2014, available at: https://www.hrw.org/report/2014/02/10/abused-and-expelled/ill-treatment-sub-saharan-african-migrants-morocco.

Human Rights Watch *EU: Shifting Rescue to Libya Risks Lives – Italy Should Direct Safe Rescues* 19 June 2017, available at: https://www.hrw.org/news/2017/06/19/eu-shifting-rescue-libya-risks-lives.

Human Rights Watch *Tunisia: African Migrants Intercepted at Sea, Expelled Apparent Policy Shift Endangers Migrants, Asylum Seekers, Children* 10 October 2023, available at: https://www.hrw.org/news/2023/10/10/tunisia-african-migrants-intercepted-sea-expelled.

Huntley, Svetlana *The CIS Human Rights Court: a possible alternative to the ECHR?* ECHR and Promotion of Human Rights in Russia, 5 October 2011, available at: http://echrrussia.blogspot.com/2011/10/cis-human-rights-court-possible.html.

Ilyer Krishna *Mass Expulsion as Violation of Human Rights* Indian Journal of International Law, Issue 13, 1974, pp. 169–175.

Inter-American Commission of Human Rights *Movilidad humana y obligaciones de protección Hacia una perspectiva subregional* OEA/Ser.L/V/II. Doc. 194, 21 July 2023.

Inter-American Commission of Human Rights *Principios interamericanos sobre los derechos humanos de todas las personas migrantes, refugiadas, apátridas y las víctimas de la trata de personas* Resolución 04/19, 7 December 2019.

Inter-American Commission of Human Rights *Report on the Situation of Human Rights of Asylum-Seekers within the Canadian Refugee Determination System* 2000, available at: https://www.cidh.org/countryrep/Canada2000en/canada.htm.

Inter-American Commission on Human Rights *List of ratifications* available at: https://www.cidh.oas.org/basicos/english/Basic4.Amer.Conv.Ratif.htm.

Inter-American Court of Human Rights *Cuadernillo de Jurisprudencia de la Corte Interamericana de Derechos Humanos No. 14: Igualdad y no-discriminación* 2019.

International Commission of Jurists *Arab Court of Human Rights: comprehensive amendments required before ratification* 8 April 2015, available at: https://www.icj.org/arab-court-of-human-rights-comprehensive-amendments-required-before-ratification-new-report/.

International Justice Resource *Center Middle East and North Africa* January 2021, available at: https://ijrcenter.org/regional/middle-east-and-north-africa/.

International Law Association *Declaration of Principles of International Law on Mass Expulsion* Report of the sixty-second Conference of the International Law Association, 1986.

International Law Commission *Draft Articles on the expulsion of aliens with commentaries* adopted by the International Law Commission at its sixty-sixth session, 2014, A/69/10, Yearbook of the International Law Commission, 2011, Vol. II, Part Two.

International Law Commission *Expulsion of Aliens Memorandum by the Secretariat* A/CN.4/565, 2006.

International Law Commission Yearbook 2004, Vol. II, Part Two, A/CN.4/SER.A/2004/Add.1.

International Organization for Migration *2024 World Migration Report* PUB2023/047/L*, (2024).

International Organization for Migration *Fatal Journeys Tracking Lives Lost during Migration 2014* (2014), available at: https://publications.iom.int/system/files/pdf/fataljourneys_countingtheuncounted.pdf.

International Organization for Migration *IOM Information Note on Access to Justice: A Migrant's Right* (2019), available at: https://migrantprotection.iom.int/en/resources/article-issuepolicy-brief-journal-blog-etc/iom-information-note-access-justice-migrants.

International Organization for Migration *INFORMATION NOTE ON THE PRINCIPLE OF NON-REFOULEMENT* (2014).

International Organization for Migration *Missing Migrants project IOM Global Migration Data Analysis Centre*, available at: https://missingmigrants.iom.int/region/mediterranean.

Italian government *Code of Conduct for NGOs undertaking activities in migrants' rescue operations at sea* proposed by the Italian government in July 2017, available at: https://www.avvenire.it/c/attualita/Documents/Codice%20ONG%20migranti%2028%20luglio%202017%20EN.pdf.

Japan Times *Myanmar to send envoys to Rohingya camps in Bangladesh to tell refugees they can go home* Japan Times Online, 2 July 2019, available at: https://www.japantimes.co.jp/news/2019/07/02/asia-pacific/social-issues-asia-pacific/myanmar-send-envoys-rohingya-camps-bangladesh-tell-refugees-can-go-home/.

Jones, Reece *Borders and Walls: Do Barriers Deter Unauthorized Migration?* Migration Policy Institute 2016, available at: https://www.migrationpolicy.org/article/borders-and-walls-do-barriers-deter-unauthorized-migration.

Joseph, Sarah and Castan, Melissa *The International Covenant on Civil and Political Rights Cases, Materials, and Commentary* (Oxford University Press 3rd edn. 2013).

Kamto, Maurice *First report on the expulsion of aliens* A/CN.4/554, ILC Report, A/60/10, (2005), chap. VIII.

Kamto, Maurice *Ninth report on the expulsion of aliens* A/CN.4/670, 25 March 2014.

Kamto, Maurice *Preliminary report on the expulsion of aliens* A/CN.4/554, 2 June 2005.

Kamto, Maurice *Second report on the expulsion of aliens* A/CN.4/573, 20 July 2006.

Kamto, Maurice *Third report on the expulsion of aliens* A/CN.4/581, 19 April 2007.

Kannyo, Edward *The Banjul Charter on Human and Peoples' Rights: Genesis and Political Background* in: Meltzer and Welch (eds.) Human Rights and Development in Africa (State University of New York Press 1984).

Kant, Immanuel *Toward Perpetual Peace: A philosophical Sketch* in: Kleingeld *Toward Perpetual Peace and Other Writings on Politics, Peace, and History* Immanuel Kant (Yale University Press 2006).

Kesby, Alison *The Right to Have Rights: Citizenship, Humanity, and International Law* (Oxford University Press 2012).

Kienzle, Isabel and Jonathan Kießling *Evidently unlawful, yet difficult to evidence: M.A. and Z.R. v. Cyprus advances Strasbourg's case law on pushbacks* Strasbourg Observer, 22 October 2024, available at: https://strasbourgobservers.com/2024/10/22/evidently-unlawful-yet-difficult-to-evidence-m-a-and-z-r-v-cyprus-advances-strasbourgs-case-law-on-pushbacks/.

Kingsley, Patrick and Bonomolo, Alessandra and Kirchgaessner, Stephanie *700 migrants feared dead in Mediterranean shipwreck* The Guardian, 19 April 2015, available at: https://www.theguardian.com/world/2015/apr/19/700-migrants-feared-dead-mediterranean-shipwreck-worst-yet.

Klabbers, Jan *International Law* (Cambridge University Press 2013).

Kohen, Marcelo *Keeping Subsequent Agreements and Practice in Their Right Limit* in: Nolte (edn.) Treaties and Subsequent Practice (Oxford University Press 2013), (*Keeping Subsequent Agreements and Practice in Their Right Limits*).

Korinek, Karl and Holoubek, Michael *Österreichisches Bundesverfassungsrecht* (Springer 2003).

Koskenniemi, Martti *From APOLOGY to UTOPIA The Structure of International Legal Argument* (Cambridge University Press reissued 2009).

Koskenniemi, Martti *The Politics of International Law* European Journal of International Law Vol. 1 (1990), pp. 4–32.

Kotzur, Markus *Migrationsbewegungen als Herausforderung für das Völkerrecht* in: Dethloff, Nolte, Reinisch (eds.) *Migrationsbewegungen Berichte der Deutschen Gesellschaft für Internationales Recht* Vol. 49 (C.F. Müller 2018).

Kowalski, Joseph *Imaginary Lines, Real Consequences: The Effect of the Militarization of the United States-Mexico Border on Indigenous Peoples* INDIAN Law Journal, Vol. 5, Issue 2 (2017), pp. 645–666.

Ku, Julian *Venezuela Formally Withdraws from American Convention on Human Rights, Blames the U.S.* OpinioJuris, 11 September 2013, available at: http://opinio

juris.org/2013/09/11/venezuela-formally-withdraws-american-convention-human-rights-blames-u-s/.

Lauterpacht, Elihu and Bethlehem, Daniel *The Scope and Content of the Principle of Non-Refoulement* in: Feller, Türk, Nicholson UNHCR *Refugee Protection in International Law: UNHCR's Global Consultations on International Protection* (Cambridge University Press 2003).

Lichuma, Caroline *In International Law We (Do Not) Trust: The Persistent Rejection of Economic and Social Rights as a Manifestation of Cynicism* in Baade, B., et al. (eds.) *Cynical International Law?* Beiträge zum ausländischen öffentlichen Recht und Völkerrecht, Vol. 296., (Springer 2021).

Lübbe, Anna *Ist der deutsche Transit österreichisches Hoheitsgebiet?* Verfassungsblog, 4 March 2016, available at: https://verfassungsblog.de/ist-der-deutsche-transit-oesterreichisches-hoheitsgebiet/.

M'Baye, Kéba *Draft African Charter on Human and Peoples' Rights (M'Baye proposal)* prepared for the Meeting of Experts in Dakar, Senegal from 28 November to 8 December 1979, CAB/LEG/67/1.

Machiavelli, Niccoló *The Discourse on The First Ten Books of Tituts Livius* (Kegan Paul, Trench & Co. 1883).

Manby, Bronwen *Civil and Political Rights in the African Charter on Human and Peoples' Rights: Articles 1–7 in*: Evans and Murray (eds.) *The African Charter on Human and Peoples' Rights The system in Practice, 1986–2006* (Cambridge University Press 2nd edn. 2008).

Manby, Bronwen *Struggles for Citizenship in Africa: Mass denationalization and expulsion* (ZED books 2009).

Mann, Itamar *Dialectic of Transnationalism: Unauthorized Migration and Human Rights, 1993–2013* Harvard International Law Journal, Vol. 54, No. 3, 2013, pp. 315–391.

Mann, Itamar *Humanity at Sea: Maritime Migration and the Foundations of International Law* (Cambridge University Press 2016).

Mapuva, Loveness *Negating the Promotion of Human Rights Through "Claw-Back" Clauses in the African Charter on Human and People's Rights* International Affairs and Global Strategy, Vol. 51, 2016, pp. 1–4.

McAdam, Jane and Durieux, Jean-Francois *Non-Refoulement through Time: The Case for a Derogation Clause to the Refugee Convention in Mass Influx Emergencies* International Journal of Refugee Law, Vol. 16, Issue 1, 2004, pp. 4–24.

McBride, Jeremy *The Case Law of the European Court of Human Rights on Evidentiary Standards in Criminal Proceedings* published as part of the European Union – Council of Europe joint project *Application of the European Convention on Human Rights and harmonisation of national legislation and judicial practice in line with European standards in Georgia.*

Messineo, Francesco *Yet another mala figura: Italy breached non-refoulement obligations by intercepting migrants' boats at sea, says ECtHR* EJIL:Talk!, 24 February 2012, available at: https://www.ejiltalk.org/yet-another-mala-figura-italy-breached-non-refoulement-obligations-by-intercepting-migrants-boats-at-sea-says-ecthr/.

Miller, David *National Responsibility and Global Justice* (Oxford University Press 2007).

Mitsilegas, Costa, Snaijer and Theodorakakou (eds.) *Elgar Encyclopedia of Crime and Criminal Justice* (Edgar Elgar 2024), pp. 102–113.

Momsen, Carsten and Willumat, Marco *Due Process and Fair Trial* in: Caeiro; Gless,

Mondelli, Juan Ignacio *La fuerza vinculante de la definición regional de la Declaración de Cartagena sobre Refugiados (1984)* (2018), available at: https://www.refworld.org.es/pdfid/5d03d0b54.pdf.

Moreno-Lax, Violeta and Lemberg-Pedersen, Martin *Border-induced displacement: The ethical and legal implications of distance-creation through externalization* Questions of International Law, Zoom-in 56 (2019) pp. 5–33.

Moreno-Lax, Violeta and Papastavridis, Efthymios *Boat Refugees and Migrants at Sea: A Comprehensive Approach Integrating Maritime Security with Human Rights* (Brill/Nijhoff 2016).

Moreno-Lax, Violeta *The "Crisification" of Migration Law: Insights from the EU External Border* in: Cope, Kevin; Burch Elias, Stella, and Goldenziel, Jill (eds.) *Oxford Handbook of Comparative Immigration Law* (Oxford University Press 1 ed.), forthcoming, pp. 1–30.

Morss, John *International Law as the Law of Collectives: Toward a Law of Peoples* (Ashgate 2013).

Murray, Rachel *Refugees and Internally Displaced Persons and Human Rights: The African System* Refugee Survey Quarterly, Vol. 24, No. 2, 2005, pp. 56–66.

Naldi, Gino *The Organization of African Unity: An Analysis of its Role* (Bloomsbury Academic 1999).

Naskou-Perraki, Paroula *The Arab Charter on Human Rights: A new start for the protection of human rights in the Arab world* Άρθρο που δημοσιεύτηκε στο Revue Hellenique de Droit International, τεύχος 1, 2009, pp. 117–136.

New York Times *Nigeria Completes the Second Expulsion of Aliens* The New York Times, 26 May 1985, available at: http://www.nytimes.com/1985/05/26/world/nigeria-completes-the-second-expulsion-of-aliens.html.

Núñez, D. Carolina *War of the Words: Aliens, Immigrants, Citizens, and the Language of Exclusion* BYU Law Review, Vol. 2013, Issue 6, Discretion & Deference: Immigrants, Citizens, and the Law, pp. 1518–1561.

Office of the High Commissioner for Human Rights *Discussion paper, Expulsion of Aliens in international human rights law* 2006.

Office of the High Commissioner for Human Rights *UN calls on Algeria to stop expelling thousands of sub-Saharan African migrants* 22 May 2018, available at: https://news.un.org/en/story/2018/05/1010392.

Olaniyan, Kolawole *Civil and Political Rights in the African Charter: Articles 8–14* in: Evans and Murray (eds.) *The African Charter on Human and Peoples' Rights: The System in Practice 1986–2006* (Cambridge University Press 2008).

Olaosebikan, Aremu and Adeyin, Thesea *Expulsion of Nigerian Immigrant Community from Ghana in 1969: Causes and Impact* Developing Country Studies, Vol. 4, No. 10, 2001, pp. 176–186.

Oppenheim, Maya *Italy's far-right government asks EU to block refugee ships from its ports* The Independent, 8 July 2018, available at: https://www.independent.co.uk/news/world/europe/italy-government-eu-block-refugee-ships-matteo-salvini-ports-a8437516.html.

Organization of American States *Conferencia Especializada Interamericana Sobre Derechos Humanos* OEA/Ser.K/XVI/1.2, 7–22 November 1969.

Organization of American States *Press release on Trinidad and Tobago's withdrawal* E-056/99ie, 26 May 1999, available at: http://www.oas.org/OASpage/press2002/en/Press99/0526991.htm.

Ortiz, Loretta *Aliens* Oxford Bibliographies, 16 August 2017.

Osterhaus, Juliane *The Arab Human Rights System* Deutsche Gesellschaft für Internationale Zusammenarbeit and Deutsches Institut für Menschenrechte, 2017.

Ouguergouz, Fatsah *The African Charter on Human and Peoples' Rights A Comprehensive Agenda for Human Dignity and Sustainable Democracy in Africa* (Kluwer Law International 2003).

Papastavridis, Efthymios *The Aquarius Incident and the Law of the Sea: Is Italy in Violation of the Relevant Rules?* EJIL:Talk!, 27 June 2018, available at: https://www.ejiltalk.org/the-aquarius-incident-and-the-law-of-the-sea-is-italy-in-violation-of-the-relevant-rules/.

Peters, Anne *The Global Compact on Migration: to sign or not to sign?* EJIL: Talk!, 21 November 2018, available at: https://www.ejiltalk.org/the-global-compact-for-migration-to-sign-or-not-to-sign/.

Peukert, Alexander and Hillgruber, Christian and Foerste, Ulrich and Putzke, Holm *Die Flüchtlingskrise kann rechtsstaatlich bewältigt werden* Frankfurter Allgemeine Zeitung, updated version of 9 February 2016, available at: https://www.faz.net/aktuell/politik/fluechtlingskrise/fluechtlingskrise-in-deutschland-rechtsstaatlich-machbar-14060376.html?printPagedArticle=true#pageIndex_2.

Pew Research Center *Immigration attitudes and the 2024 election* 6 June 2024, available at: https://www.pewresearch.org/politics/2024/06/06/immigration-attitudes-and-the-2024-election/.

Pijnenburg, Annick *From Italian Pushbacks to Libyan Pullbacks: Is Hirsi 2.0 in the Making in Strasbourg?* European Journal of Migration and Law, Vol. 20, Issue 4 (2018), pp. 396–426.

Pinto de Albuquerque, Paulo *Concurring Opinion Hirsi Jamaa and Others v. Italy* ECtHR, [GC], Appl. No. 27765/09, 23 February 2012.

Pinto de Albuquerque, Paulo *Concurring Opinion M.A. and Others v. Lithuania* ECtHR, Appl. No. 59793/17, 11 December 2018.

Pinto de Albuquerque, Paulo *Concurring Opinion Souza Ribeiro v. France* ECtHR, Appl. No. 22689/07, 13 December 2012.

Plagis, Misha; Riemer, Lena *From Context to Content of Human Rights: The Drafting History of the African Charter on Human and Peoples' Rights and the Enigma of Article 7 Journal of the History of International Law* No. 23, Issue 4, 2020, pp. 1–33.

Popelier, Patricia *The Court as Regulatory Watchdog: The Procedural Approach in the Case Law of the European Court of Human Rights* in: Popelier; Mazmanyan and Vandenbruwaene (eds.) *The Role of Courts in a Context of Multilevel Governance* (Intersentia 2013) pp. 249–267.

Pöschl, Magdalena *Artikel 4 4. ZPEMRK* in: Korine and Holoubek *Österreichisches Bundesverfassungsrecht Textsammlung und Kommentar* (Springer 2003).

Praesidium of the Convention *Draft Charter of Fundamental Rights of the European Union explanations prepared by the Praesidium*, Charte 4473/00 Convent 49.

Praesidium of the Convention *EXPLANATIONS RELATING TO THE CHARTER OF FUNDAMENTAL RIGHTS* Official Journal of the European Union C 303/02, 14 December 2007.

Raimondo, Giulia *N.D. and N.T. v Spain: A Slippery Slope for the Protection of Irregular Migrants* Border Criminologies Blog, 20 April 2020, available at: https://blogs.law.ox.ac.uk/research-subject-groups/centre-criminology/centreborder-criminologies/blog/2020/04/nd-and-nt-v-spain.

Rask Madsen, Mikael and Cebulak, Pola and Wiebusch, Micha *Backlash against international courts: explaining the forms and patterns of resistance to international courts* International Journal of Law in Context No. 14, 2018, pp. 197–220.

Rawls, John *Political Liberalism* (Columbia University Press 1993).

Rawls, John *The Principles of the Law of Peoples* (Harvard University Press 2nd edn. 2000).

Refugees Deeply *Executive Summary for December 14th* 14 December 2017, available at: https://www.newsdeeply.com/refugees/executive-summaries/2017/12/14.

Registrar of the Court *ECHR grants an interim measure in case concerning the Sea Watch 3 vessel* ECHR 043 (2019), press release, 29 January 2019.

Registrar of the Court *Rules of Court* edition of 19 September 2019.

Reservation made by Switzerland *Reservations and Declarations for Treaty No. 117– Protocol No. 7 to the Convention for the Protection of Human Rights and Fundamental Freedoms* Declarations in force as of 1 November 1988, available at: https://www.coe.int/en/web/conventions/full-list/-/conventions/treaty/117/declarations?p_auth=tOkSUeIj.

Rieger, Bernd *France, Italy ratchet up rhetoric amid migration dispute* Deutsche Welle Online, 24 January 2019, available at: https://www.dw.com/en/france-italy-ratchet-up-rhetoric-amid-migration-dispute/a-47219037.

Riemer, Lena and Scheid, Luca *Leading the Way: The IACtHR's Advisory Opinion on Human Rights and Climate Change* Verfassungsblog 18 January 2024, available at: https://verfassungsblog.de/leading-the-way/.

Riemer, Lena *Guarding the Gates: The Externalization of U.S. Migration Policies and Their Impact Across the Americas* Externalizing Asylum: A compendium of scientific knowledge, 31 July 2024, available at: https://externalizingasylum.info/guarding-the-gates/.

Riemer, Lena *How Trump's Migration Policy Erodes National and International Standards of Protection for Migrants and Asylum Seekers* EJIL: Talk!, 28 November 2018, available at: https://www.ejiltalk.org/how-trumps-migration-policy-erodes-national-and-international-standards-of-protection-for-migrants-and-asylum-seekers/.

Rietiker, Daniel *Collective Expulsion of Aliens: The European Court of Human Rights (Strasbourg) as the Island of Hope in Stormy Times* 39 Suffolk Transnational Law Review, Vol. 39, No. 3, (2016), pp. 651–682.

Robinson, Kali and Roy, Diana *Europe's Migration Dilemma* Council on Foreign Relations, 31 May 2024, available at: https://www.cfr.org/article/europes-migration-dilemma.

ROMEA *France Resumes deportation of Roma people from Romania* Czech Press Agency, article of 13 April 2010, available at: http://www.romea.cz/en/news/world/france-resumes-deportation-of-roma-peple-from-Romania.

Rubner, Nathaniel *The African Charter on Human and Peoples' Rights: Political, Intellectual and cultural origins* (provisional title). The document is on file with the author.

Saddiki, Said *World of walls: the structure, roles and effectiveness of separation barriers* (Open Book Publisher 2017).

Sardo, Alessio *Border Walls, Pushbacks, and the Prohibition of Collective Expulsions: The Case of N.D. and N.T. v. Spain* European Journal of Migration and Law, Vol. 23, 2021, pp. 308–331.

Schabas, William *European Convention on Human Rights Commentary* (Oxford University Press 2015).

Schäfer, Patrick *Art. 34* in: Karpenstein and Mayer (eds.) *EMRK Konvention zum Schutz der Menschenrechte und Grundfreiheiten Kommentar* (C. H. Beck 2nd edn. 2015).

Schmalz, Dana *Menschenrechte im Mittelmeer Der Fall S.S. und andere gg. Italien* Verfassungsblog, 27 November 2019, available at: https://verfassungsblog.de/menschenrechte-im-mittelmeer/.

Scott FitzGerald, David *Refuge Beyond Reach: How Rich Democracies Repel Asylum Seekers* (Oxford University Press 2019).

Scott, Matthew *Climate Change, Disasters, and the Refugee Convention* (Oxford University Press 2020).

Semple, Kirk *Trump Threatens to Punish Honduras Over Immigrant Caravan* New York Times, 16 October 2018, available at: https://www.nytimes.com/2018/10/16/world/americas/trump-immigrant-caravan.html.

Serghides, Georgios *Partly Dissenting Opinion Khlaifia and Others v. Italy* ECtHR, [GC], Appl. No. 16483/12, 15 December 2016.

Severance, Kristi *France's Expulsion of Roma Migrants: A Test Case for Europe* Migration Policy Institute, 21 October 2010, available at: https://www.migrationpolicy.org/article/frances-expulsion-roma-migrants-test-case-europe.

Sharpe, Marina *The Regional Law of Refugee Protection in Africa* (Oxford University Press 2018).

Sohn, Louis and Buergenthal, Thomas *The Movement of Persons Across Borders* (American Society of International Law 1992).

Song, Sarah *Immigration and Democracy* (Oxford University Press 2019).

Sorel, Jean-Marc *Article 12* in: Kamto and Collectif *La Charte africaine des droits de l'homme et des peuples et le protocole y relatif portant création de la Cour africaine des droits de l'homme: Commentaire article par article* (Emile Bruylant 2011).

Steiner, Christian and Uribe, Patricia (eds.) *Convención Americana sobre Derechos Humanos comentada* (Suprema Corte de la Nación (Mexico) and Konrad Adenauer Foundation 2014).

Stiansen, Øyvind and Voeten, Erik *Backlash and Judicial Restraint: Evidence From the European Court of Human Rights* SSRN, 2018, available at: https://papers.ssrn.com/sol3/papers.cfm?abstract_id=3166110.

Stuurman, Siep *The Invention of Humanity Equality and Cultural Difference in World History* (Harvard University Press 2017).

Suddath, Claire *Who Are Gypsies, and Why Is France Deporting Them?* TIME magazine, 26 August 2010, available at: http://content.time.com/time/world/article/0,8599,2013917,00.html.

Tendayi, Achiume E. *Migration as Decolonization* Stanford Law Review, Vol. 71, June 2019, pp. 1509–1574.

The Economist *Saudi Arabia cuts off Qatar* The Economist, 10 June 2017, available at: https://www.economist.com/news/middle-east-and-africa/21723018-kingdom-raising-tensions-its-immediate-neighbours-well-iran.

The European Council on Refugees and Exiles (ECRE), an alliance of 90 organizations in 38 countries protecting refugee rights across Europe *ECRE members express concern at annual conference: Deal after deal, Europe is outsourcing its responsibilities for refugees* 14 October 2016, available at: https://www.ecre.org/ecre-members-express-concern-at-annual-conference-deal-after-deal-europe-is-outsourcing-its-responsibilities-for-refugees/.

The Patrin Journal: Romani Culture and History *Patrin Timeline of Romani History* 1998, available at: http://www.oocities.org/patrin/timeline.htm.

Thym, Daniel *The End of Human Rights Dynamism? Judgments of the ECtHR on 'Hot Returns' and Humanitarian Visas as a Focal Point of Contemporary European Asylum Law and Policy* International Journal of Refugee Law, Vol. 32, Issue 4, December 2020, pp. 569–596.

Towfigh, Emanuel V. and Weyl, Niklas T. *Borders, Citizenship, and Global Inequality: What Barriers, Pushbacks, and Passport Controls Reveal About Our Understanding of the Equality of Humankind* German Law Journal, published online 2024, pp. 1–21.

Tretter, Hannes *Artikel 1–4 4. ZP* in: Ermacora and Nowak and Tretter *Die Europäische Menschenrechtskonvention in der Rechtsprechung der österreichischen Höchstgerichte* (Braumüller Verlag 1983).

Turack, Daniel *The African Charter on Human and Peoples' Rights: Some Preliminary Thoughts* Akron Law Review, (1984), Vol. 17, No. 3, pp. 365–381.

Uepermann-Wittzack, Robert *Ordnung und Gestaltung von Migrationsbewegungen durch Völkerrecht* in: Dethloff and Nolte and Reinisch (eds.) *Migrationsbewegungen Berichte der Deutschen Gesellschaft für Internationales Recht* Vol. 49, (C.F. Müller 2018).

Umozurike, Oji *The African Charter on Human and Peoples' Rights* (Nigerian Institute of Advanced Legal Studies 1992).

United Nations Educational, Scientific and Cultural Organization *Asylum Seeker* Social Glossary of Migration Related Terms, available at: http://www.unesco.org/new/en/social-and-human-sciences/themes/international-migration/glossary/asylum-seeker/.

United Nations General Assembly *Report of the Committee against Torture* Supplement No. 44, A/53/44, 1998.

United Nations High Commissioner for Human Rights Intervener Brief to *Hirsi Jamaa and Others v. Italy* ECtHR, filed pursuant to leave granted by the Court on 4 May 2011.

United Nations High Commissioner for Human Rights *Report Global Trends Forced Displacement in 2016*, 2017.

United Nations High Commissioner for Refugees and International Organization for Migration *Proposal for a regional cooperative arrangement ensuring predictable disembarkation and subsequent processing of persons rescued-at-sea* 27 June 2018.

United Nations High Commissioner for Refugees *Cartagena +40: Chile Declaration and Plan of Action Consolidate Regional Leadership in Refugee Protection* 13 December 2023, available at: https://www.unhcr.org/news/press-releases/carta gena
-40-chile-declaration-and-plan-action-consolidate-regional-leadership.

United Nations High Commissioner for Refugees *Mass Congolese returns from Angola could lead to a humanitarian crisis* 16 October 2018.

United Nations High Commissioner for Refugees *States Parties to the 1951 Convention relating to the Status of Refugees and the 1967 Protocol* status of current signatures and ratifications, available at: http://www.unhcr.org/en-us/protection/basic/3b73b0d63/states-parties-1951-convention-its-1967-protocol.html.

United Nations High Commissioner for Refugees *UNHCR POSITION ON RETURNS TO LIBYA* (Update II) September 2018.

United Nations Human Rights Council *Report of the Special Rapporteur on torture and other cruel, inhuman or degrading treatment or punishment. Promotion and protection of all human rights, civil, political, economic, social and cultural rights, including the right to development* A/HRC/37/5026, February 2018.

United Nations Human Rights Office of the High Commissioner *Status of Ratification International Covenant on Civil and Political Rights* Interactive Dashboard, available at: http://indicators.ohchr.org/.

United Nations Office of the High Commissioner for Human Rights *Status of Ratification International Convention on the Protection of the Rights of All Migrant Workers and Members of their Families* Interactive Dashboard, available at: http://indicators.ohchr.org/.

United Nations Office of the High Commissioner of Human Rights *Committee of Migrants Workers general information on the work of the Committee* available at: https://www.ohchr.org/EN/HRBodies/CMW/Pages/CMWIntro.aspx.

Uprimny Yepes, Rodrigo and Sánchez Duque and Luz María *Artículo 22 Derecho de Circulación y de residencia* in: Steiner and Uribe (eds.) *Convención Americana sobre Derechos Humanos comentada* (Suprema Corte de la Nación (Mexico) and Konrad Adenauer Foundation 2014).

Valetta Summit on Migration *Action Plan* 11–12 November 2015, available at: https://www.consilium.europa.eu/media/21839/action_plan_en.pdf.

Vallet, Élisabeth *Borders, Fences and Walls: State of Insecurity?* (Ashgate Publishing 2014).

Van Dijk, Pieter and Van Hoof, Fried *Theory and Practice of the European Convention on Human Rights* (Intersentia 4th edn. 2006).

Venturi, Denise *The Grand Chamber's ruling in Khlaifia and Others v Italy: one step forward, one step back?* Strasbourg Obersevers, 10 January 2017, available at: https://strasbourgobservers.com/2017/01/10/the-grand-chambers-ruling-in-khlaifia-and-others-v-italy-one-step-forward-one-step-back/#more-3466.

Viljoen, Frans *The African Charter on Human and Peoples' Rights/The Travaux Préparatoires in the light of subsequent practice* Human Rights Law Journal, Vol. 25, No. 9–12, 2004, pp. 313–326.

Villinger, Mark *Handbuch der EMRK Garantien der Zusatzprotokolle §31* (Schulthess Polygraphischer Verlag 2nd edn. 1999).

Vladisavljevic, Anja *Videos 'Prove' Croatia Forcibly Expelling Migrants, Watchdog Says* BalkanInsight, article and video 16 December 2018, available at: http://www.balkaninsight.com/en/article/bvm-proves-human-rights-violations-at-external-eu-border–12-14-2018.

Waite, Maurice and Stevenson, Angus *Concise Oxford English Dictionary* (Oxford University Press 12th edn. 2011).

Weiner, Myron *Ethics, national sovereignty and the control of immigration* International Migration Review, Vol. 30, No. 1, 1996, pp. 171–197.

Weis, Paul *The Refugee Convention, 1951: The Travaux Préparatoires analysed with a Commentary* UNHCR 1951

Winn, Patrick *Rohingya survivors face a new indignity: Banishment to a half-sunken island* PRI The World, 5 December 2018, available at: https://www.pri.org/stories/2018-12-05/rohingya-survivors-face-new-indignity-banishment-half-sunkenisland?utm_source=Refugees+Deeply&utm_campaign=8daed2fe18-EMAIL_CAMPAIGN_2018_12_07_12_37&utm_medium=email&utm_term=0_8b056c90e2-8daed2fe18-117928793.

Zirulia, Stefano *A template for protecting human rights during the 'refugee crisis'? Immigration detention and the expulsion of migrants in a recent ECtHR Grand Chamber ruling* EU Law Analysis, 5 January 2017, available at: http://eulawanalysis.blogspot.com/2017/01/a-template-for-protecting-human-rights.html.

Zölls, Anselm *The Prohibition of Collective Expulsion under Art. 4 Protocol No. 4 of the European Convention on Human Rights. Prohibition of Discriminatory and Arbitrary Expulsions* (in German), (Mohr Siebeck 2021).

Cases

African Commission on Human and Peoples' Rights

Fédération Internationale des Ligues des Droits de l'Homme and Others v. Angola AComHPR, Comm. No. 159/96, 1997

General Comment No. 3 on the African Charter on Human and Peoples' Rights The Right to Life (Article 4) AComHPR, adopted during the 57th ordinary session of the Africa Commission on Human and Peoples' Rights, 4–18 November 2015

Good v. Botswana AComHPR, Communication 313/05, (2010) 28th Activity Report, Annex Iv, 2010

Institute for Human Rights and Development in Africa (on behalf of Sierra Leonean refugees in Guinea) v. Guinea AComHPR, Comm. No. 249/02, 2004

Institute for Human Rights and Development in Africa v. Republic of Angola AComHR, Comm. No. 292/04, 2008

Malawi African Association and others v. Mauritania AComHPR, Comm. Nos. 54/91, 61/91, 164/97-196/97, 210/98, Thirteenth Activity Report 1999–2000, Annex v

Organisation Mondiale Contre la Torture and Others v. Rwanda AComHPR, 27/89-46/91-49/91-99/93, 1996

Rencontre Africaine pour la Défense des Droits de l'Homme v. Zambia AComHPR, Communication 71/92, 1996

Union Inter Africaine des Droits de l'Homme, Fédération Internationale des Ligues des Droits de l'Homme and Others v. Angola AComHPR, Comm. No. 159/96, 1997

Committee against Torture

Committee against Torture *Annex IX of the Report of the Committee against Torture* Supplement No. 44 A/53/44, 1998

Committee against Torture *Concluding observations on the fifth and sixth periodic report of Italy* (2017), CAT/C/ITA/CO/5–6, 21 November 2017

Committee against Torture *Concluding observations on the seventh periodic report of Greece* (2019), CAT/C/SR.1779, 7 August 2019

Committee against Torture *Consideration of reports submitted by States parties under article 19 of the Convention Concluding observations of the Committee against Torture* CAT/C/GRC/CO/5-6, 27 June 2012

Committee against Torture *Consideration of Reports submitted by States Parties under Article 19 of the Convention Conclusions and recommendations of the Committee against Torture: Ukraine* (2007), CAT/C/UKR/CO/5, 3 August 2007

Committee against Torture *General Comment No. 4 (2017) on the implementation of article 3 of the Convention in the context of article 22* (2018), CAT/C/GC/4, 4 September 2018

Committee on the Protection of the Rights of All Migrant Workers and Members of Their Families

Committee on the Protection of the Rights of All Migrant Workers and Members of Their Families *Concluding observations on the second periodic report of Chile* cmw/c/chl/co/2, 11 May 2021.

Committee on the Protection of the Rights of All Migrant Workers and Members of their Families *Input for the Secretary-General's Report on the Global Compact on Migration* 7 September 2017.

Committee on the Protection of the Rights of All Migrant Workers and Members of Their Families *Concluding observations on the second periodic report of Chile* Their Families *Thirty-second session (6–16 and 29–30 April 2021), General Assembly, Supplement No. 48, a/78/48.*

Committee on the Protection of the Rights of All Migrant Workers and Members of Their Families *Concluding observations on the second periodic report of Chile* Their Families *Thirty-second session (6–16 and 29–30 April 2021), General Assembly, Official Records, Seventy-sixth Session, Supplement No. 48, a/76/48.*

Committee on the Protection of the Rights of All Migrant Workers and Members of Their Families *Thirty-fifth session (19–30 September 2022) and thirty-sixth session (27 March–6 April 2023) General Assembly, Official Records, Seventy-eighth Session, Supplement No. 48, a/78/48.*

Committee on the Protection of the Rights of All Migrant Workers and Members of Their Families and Committee on the Rights of the Child *Joint general comment No. 3 On the general principles regarding the human rights of children in the context of international migration* CMW/C/GC/3, 2017

Committee on the Protection of the Rights of All Migrant Workers and Members of Their Families and Committee on the Rights of the Child *Joint general comment No. 22 On the general principles regarding the human rights of children in the context of international migration* CMW/C/GC/3, 2017

Committee on the Protection of the Rights of All Migrant Workers and Members of Their Families and Committee on the Rights of the Child *Joint general comment No. 23 On State obligations regarding the human rights of children in the context of international migration in countries of origin, transit, destination and return* CMW/C/GC/4, 2017

CMW *General Comment No. 1 on migrant domestic workers* CMW/C/GC/1, 23 February 2011.

CMW *General Comment No. 2 on the rights of migrant workers in an irregular situation and members of their families* CMW/C/GC/2, 28 August 2013

Committee on the Rights of the Child

Committee on the Rights of the Child and Committee on the Protection of the Rights of All Migrant Workers and Members of Their Families *Joint General Comment No. 3 On the general principles regarding the human rights of children in the context of international migration* CMW/C/GC/3, 2017

Committee on the Rights of the Child and Committee on the Protection of the Rights of All Migrant Workers and Members of Their Families *Joint General Comment No. 22 On the general principles regarding the human rights of children in the context of international migration* CMW/C/GC/3, 2017

Committee on the Rights of the Child and Committee on the Protection of the Rights of All Migrant Workers and Members of Their Families *Joint general comment No. 23 On State obligations regarding the human rights of children in the context of international migration in countries of origin, transit, destination and return* CMW/C/GC/4, 2017

Committee on the Rights of the Child D.D. v. Spain Communication No. 4/2016, 12 February 2019

Court of Justice of the European Union

Anklagemyndigheden v. Peter Michael Poulsen and Diva Navigation Corp. CJEU, C-286/90, 24 November 1992

Khaled Boudjlida v Préfet des Pyrénées-Atlantiques CJEU C-249/13, 11 December 2014

M.A. v Valstybės sienos apsaugos tarnyba CJEU C-72/22 PPU, *30 June* 2022.

Ministerio Fiscal (Autorité susceptible de recevoir une demande de protection internationale) CJEU, C-36/20 PPU, 25 June 2020

M.M. v Minister for Justice Equality and Law Reform and Others CJEU, C-277/11, 22 November 2012

Sophie Mukarubega v Préfet de police und Préfet de la Seine-Saint-Denis CJEU, C-166/13, 5 November 2014

European Commission of Human Rights

Alibaks and Others v. The Netherlands EComHR, Appl. No.14209/88, 16 December 1988
Becker v. Denmark, EComHR on the admissibility of Appl. No. 7011/75, 19 Yearbook European Convention on Human Rights 416, 1976
Dec. Adm. Comp. EcomHR, Appl. Nos. 3803/68, 3804/68, 4 October 1968 (unpublished); Digest of Strasbourg Case-Law relating to the European Convention on Human Rights, Vol. 5 (Carl Heymanns Verlag 1985)
K.G. v. Germany, EComHR, Appl. No. 7704/76, 11 March 1977
O. and Others v. Luxembourg, EComHR, Appl. No.7757/77, 3 March 1978
Tahiri v. Sweden EComHR, Appl. No. 25129/94, 11 January 1995
X contre la Belgique EComHR, Appl. No. 5351/72 6579/74, 18 July 1974
X v. the Federal Republic of Germany EComHR, Appl. no. 3110/67, 19 July 1968
X and Y v. Sweden EComHR on the Admissibility of Appl. No. 3803/68 and 3804/68, 4 October 1968

European Court of Human Rights

A.A. and Others v. North Macedonia ECtHR, Appl. Nos. 55798/16 and 4 others, 5 April 2022
Abdi Ahmed and Others v. Malta ECtHR, Appl. No. 43985/13, 16 September 2014
Andric v. Sweden ECtHR, Appl. No. 45917/99, 23 February 1999
Asady and Others v. Slovakia ECtHR, Appl. No. 9347/14 24 March 2020
Avşar v. Turkey ECtHR, Appl. No. 25657/94, 10 July 2001
Balde and Abel v. Spain ECtHR, Appl. No. 20351/17, 28 July 2022 (inadmissible)
Berdzenishvili and Others v. Russia ECtHR, Appl. Nos. 14594/07 and 6 others, 20 December 2016
Berisha and Haljiti v. "the former Yugoslav Republic of Macedonia" ECtHR, Appl. No. 18670/03, 10 April 2007, (inadmissible)
C.O.C.G. and Others v. Lithuania ECtHR, Appl. No. 17764/22 (pending)
Čonka v. Belgium, ECtHR, Appl. No. 51564/99, 5 February 2002
Cruz Varas v. Sweden ECtHR, Appl. No. 46/1990/237/307, 20 March 1991
D.A. and Others v. Poland ECtHR, Appl. No. 51246/17, 8 July 2021
Davydov v. Estonia ECtHR, Appl. No. 16387/03, 31 May 2005
Demir and Baykara v. Turkey ECtHR, [GC], Appl. No. 34503/97, 12 November 2008

Doumbe Nnabuchi v. Spain ECtHR, Appl. No. 19420/15, 1 June 2021
Dritsas and Others v. Italy ECtHR, Appl. No. 2344/02, 1 February 2011
Garcia Ruiz v. Spain ECtHR, [GC], Appl. No. 30544/96, 21 January 1999
Ghulami v. France ECtHR, Appl. No. 45302/05, 7 April 2009
Geleri v. Romania ECtHR Appl. No. 33118/05, 15 September 2011
Georgia v. Russia I ECtHR, [GC] (merits), Appl. No. 13255/07, 3 July 2014
Georgia v. Russia I (*Just Satisfaction*) ECtHR, Appl. No. 13255/07, 31 January 2019
Golder v. the United Kingdom ECtHR, Appl. No. 4451/70, 21 February 1975
H.K. v. Hungary ECtHR, Appl. No. 18531/17, 22 September 2022
Hirsi Jamaa and Others v. Italy ECtHR [GC] Appl. No. 27765/09, 23 February 2012
H.M.M. and Others v. Latvia ECtHR, Appl. No. 42165/21 (pending)
Hussun and Others v. Italy ECtHR, Appl. Nos. 10171/05, 10601/05, 11593/05 and 17165/05, 19 January 2010
Karner v. Austria ECtHR, Appl. No. 40016/98, 24 July 2003
Khlaifia and Others v. Italy ECtHR [Chamber] Appl. No. 16483/12, 1 September 201
Khlaifia and Others v. Italy ECtHR [GC] Appl. No. 16483/12, 15 December 2016
Klass and Others v. Germany ECtHR, Appl. No. 5029/71, 6 September 1978
J.A. and Others v. Italy ECtHR, Appl. No. 21329/18, 30 June 2023
K.P. v. Hungary ECtHR, Appl. No. 82479/17, 18 January 2024
Léger v. France ECtHR [GC], Appl. No. 19324/02, 30 March 2009
Ljativi v. Former Yugoslav Republic of Macedonia ECtHR, Appl. No. 19017/16, 17 May 2018
M.H. and Others v. Croatia (*I*) ECtHR, Appl. Nos. 15670/18 and 43115/18, 18 November 2021
M.A. and Others v. Latvia ECtHR, Appl. No. 25564/18, 29 March 2022
M.A. and Others v. Lithuania ECtHR, Appl. No. 59793/17, 11 December 2018
M.A. v. Switzerland ECtHR, Appl. No. 52589/13, 18 November 2014
M.A. and Z.R. v. Cyprus ECtHR, Appl. No. 39090/20, 8 October 2024
M.K. and Others v. Poland ECtHR, Appl. Nos 40503/17, 42902/17 and 43643/17, 23 July 2020
M.S.S. v. Belgium and Greece ECtHR, Appl. No. 30696/09, 21 January 2011
Mamatkulow and Askarov v. Turkey ECtHR [GC], Appl. Nos. 46827/99 and 46951/99, 4 February 2005
Matthews v. the United Kingdom ECtHR, Appl. No. 24833/94, 18 February 1999
Moustahi v. France ECTHR, Appl. No. 9347/14, 25 June 2020
N.D. and N.T. v. Spain ECtHR [Chamber], Appl. Nos. 8675/15 and 8697/15, 3 October 2017
N.D. and N.T. v. Spain ECtHR [GC], Appl. Nos. 8675/15 and 8697/15, 13 February 2020
Nolan and K. v. Russia ECtHR Appl. No. 2512/04, 12 February 2009

R.A. and Others v. Poland ECtHR, Appl. No. 42120/21 (pending)
Saadi v. the United Kingdom ECtHR, [GC], Appl. No. 13229/03, 29 January 2008
Sejdic and Finci v. Bosnia and Herzegovina ECtHR [GC], Appl. Nos. 27996/06 and 34836/06, 22 December 2009
Sharifi and Others v. Italy and Greece ECtHR, Appl. No. 16643/09, 21 October 2014
Shahzad v. Hungary ECtHR, Appl. No. 12625/17, 8 July 2021
Sharma v. Latvia ECtHR, Appl. No. Appl. No. 28026/05, 24 March 2016
Sherov and Others v. Poland ECtHR, Appl. Nos. 54029/17 and 3 others, 4 April 2024
Sigurdur A Sigurjònsson v. Iceland ECtHR Appl. No. 16130/90, 30 June 1993
Soering v. United Kingdom ECtHR, Appl. No. 14038/88, 7 July 1989
S.S. and Others v. Hungary ECtHR, Appl. Nos. 56417/19 and 44245/20, 12 October 2023
S.S. and Others v. Italy ECtHR, Appl. No. 21660/18, communicated to parties on 26 June 2019, (pending)
Stoica v. Romania ECtHR, Appl. No. 42722, 4 March 2008
Sultani v. France ECtHR, Appl. No. 45223/05, 2007, 26 September 2007
Takush v. Greece ECtHR, Appl. No. 2853/09, 17 January 2012
Tyrer v. the United Kingdom ECtHR, Appl. No. 5856/72, 25 April 1978
Vallianatos and Others v. Greece, ECtHR, [GC], Appl. No. 29381/09, 7 November 2013
Velikova v. Bulgaria ECtHR, Appl. No. 41488/98, 18 May 2000
W.A. and Others v. Italy ECtHR, Appl. No. 18787/17, 16 November 2023
Xhavara and Others v. Italy and Albania ECtHR, Appl. No. 39473/98, 11 January 2001
Y.F.C. and Others v. The Netherlands ECtHR, Appl. No. 21325/19, communicated to the parties on 25 June 2019, (pending)

Human Rights Committee

HRC *Concluding observations: Dominican Republic* CCPR/CO/71/DOM, 3 April 2001
HRC *Concluding observations on the sixth periodic report of the Dominican Republic* CCPR/C/DOM/CO/6, 27 November 2017
HRC *Concluding observations on the third periodic report of Greece* CCPR/C/GRC/CO/3, 7 November 2024
HRC *General Comment No. 15 on the position of aliens under the Covenant*, 11 April 1986
HRC *General comment No. 20 on Article 7 of the International Covenant on Civil and Political Rights on the Prohibition of Torture, or Other Cruel, Inhuman or Degrading Treatment or Punishment*, 10 March 1992
HRC *General Comment No. 31 on the nature of the general legal obligation imposed on State Parties to the Covenant* CCPR/C/21/Rev.1/Add.13, 26 May 2004

HRC *General Comment No. 32 on Art. 14, Right to equality before courts and tribunals and to a fair trial* CCPR/C/GC/32, 23 August 2007
HRC *General Comment No. 36 on article 6 of the International Covenant on Civil and Political Rights, on the right to life* CCPR/C/GC/36, 30 October 2018

Inter-American Commission of Human Rights

IAComHR *Annual Report of the Inter-American Commission on Human Rights 1991* OEA/Ser.L/V/II.81 Doc. 6, rev. 1, 14 February 1992
IAComHR *Benito Tide Méndez et al. (Dominican Republic) Report on the Merits No. 64/12* Case 12.271, 29 March 2012
IAComHR *Debido proceso en los procedimientos para la determinación de la condición de persona refugiada, y apátrida y el otorgamiento de protección complementaria* OEA/Ser.L/V/II., Doc. 255, 5 August 2020
IAComHR *Human Rights of Migrants, Refugees, Stateless Persons, Victims of Human Trafficking and Internally Displaced Persons: Norms and Standards of the Inter-American Human Rights System* OEA/Ser.L/V/II.Doc. 46/15, 2015
IAComHR *Informe sobre la situación de derechos humanos de familias, niños, niñas y adolescentes no acompañados refugiados y migrantes en los Estados Unidos de América* OAS/Ser.L/V/II.155, Doc. 16., 24 July 2015
IAComHR *Movilidad humana y obligaciones de protección: Hacia una pespectiva subregional* OEA/Ser.L/V/II., Doc. 194, 21 July 2023
IAComHR *Report on the Situation of Human Rights in the Dominican Republic* OEA/Ser.L/V/II.104 Doc. 49 rev. 1, October 7, 1999
IAComHR *Resolución 04/19, Principios interamericanos sobre los derechos humanos de todas las personas migrantes, refugiadas, apátridas y víctimas de la trata de personas* 7 December 2019
IAComHR *Second Progress Report of the Rapporteurship on Migrant Workers and Members of Their Families in the Hemisphere*
IAComHR *Manickavasagam Suresh v. Canada* Report on the Merits No. 8/16, Case 11.661, 13 April 2016

Inter-American Court of Human Rights

Advisory Opinion Environment and Human Rights IACourtHR, OC-23/17OF, requested by the Republic of Colombia, 15 November 2017
Advisory Opinion on family separation IACourtHR, OC-21/14,, requested by Argentina, Brasil, Paraguay and Uruguay, 19 August 2024

Case of expelled Dominicans and Haitians v. Dominican Republic Preliminary objections, merits, reparations and costs IACourtHR, Judgment of 28 August 2014. Series C No. 282, (*Expelled Dominicans and Haitians v. Dominican Republic*)

Familia Pacheco Tineo v. Bolivia IACourtHR, Serie C No. 272, 25 November 2013, (*Pacheco Tineo v. Bolivia*)

Nadege Dorzema and others v. Dominican Republic Merits, Reparations and Costs IACourtHR, Judgment of 24 October 2012. Series C, No. 251

"Other Treatie" Subject to the Consultative Jurisdiction of the Court Advisory Opinion IACourtHR, OC-1/82, requested by Peru, 24 September 1982

Ricardo Canese v. Paraguay IACourtHR, Series C No. 111, 31 August 2004

The Juridical Condition and Rights of Undocumented Migrants Advisory Opinion, IACourtHR OC-18/03, requested by Mexico, 17 September 2003

Wong Ho Wing v. Peru IACourtHR, Judgment on reparations and costs, Series C, No. 297, 26 June 2012

Wong Ho Wing v. Peru IACourtHR, Judgment on preliminary objection, merits, reparations and costs, 30 June 2015

Index of Terms

www.ingramcontent.com/pod-product-compliance
Lightning Source LLC
Chambersburg PA
CBHW051357240926
51852CB00001B/54